HISTORY
OF
BUFFALO MUSIC
&
ENTERTAINMENT

A Nostalgic Journey
into Buffalo New York's
Musical Heritage
from the 1830s
to the early 1980s

Rick Falkowski

Published by
Rick Falkowski
P.O. Box 96
Williamsville NY 14231
buffalomusichistory.com
info@buffalomusichistory.com
Facebook: History of Buffalo Music & Entertainment

History of Buffalo Music & Entertainment
ISBN number: 13-978-0692940228
            10-0692940227
1. Music – History – Buffalo
2. Social History – Music
3. Pop Culture – Buffalo, Nonfiction

Edited by: Carol Jean Swist, Tom Ryan, Marsha Falkowski
Front & Back Cover Design: Bob Ambrusko

Front Cover Photo: Color Postcard of Main Street, Buffalo, NY ca. 1960.
            Collection of The Buffalo History Museum
Back Cover Author's Photo: Marsha Falkowski

First printing: September 2017
First Edition: September 2017
Printed in the U.S.A.

INTRODUCTION

Buffalo has produced many successful national recording artists but Buffalo's musical heritage includes the songwriters, events, night clubs, theaters, radio personalities and the many musicians that made it to the fringes of national acclaim or were content just remaining in WNY to perform at our area clubs. In this book, we will reference some of the artists that performed here and the national accomplishments of Buffalo artists, but the focus will concentrate on the people, places and things that kept the people of our community entertained for the past two centuries.

When Buffalo became the western terminus of The Erie Canal in 1825, it quickly blossomed into a thriving city of industry and commerce. The citizens placed a priority on entertainment and built showplaces for theatrical and musical acts. Canal Street brought us bawdy entertainment but also developed the minstrel show. The early theaters were filled with traveling actors and orchestras, that were touring the country or were comprised of residents from Western New York.

In 1900, Buffalo was the 8th largest city in the U.S. and was en route from New York City to Chicago. During the days of vaudeville all the top entertainers made Buffalo one of their regular stops. Productions and musical groups often tested their new shows and material at area theaters and nightclubs. Buffalo earned the reputation of being a tough market. It was said that if you could make it in Buffalo, you would be successful everywhere.

The first space built in the U.S. specifically for showing motion pictures was the 72 seat Vitascope Theater located in the Ellicott Square Building on Main Street. Michael Shea operated a chain of theaters that provided both vaudeville and movies. Some of the country's first radio stations were operated in Buffalo and were innovative in the entertainment that they broadcast. Composers from Buffalo wrote many of the hit songs of the 20th century and our Symphony Orchestras and Ensembles have obtained international acclaim for classical and avant-garde performances.

Crystal Beach had the largest dancefloor in North America which drew all the most popular big bands from around the country. The big bands also performed at The Dellwood Ballroom, along with other clubs, church halls and theaters in the area.

The nightclubs and bars reopened with a vengeance at the end of Prohibition. It was as if the nightclub owners wanted to make up for the time they lost when alcohol was banned. However, some of these clubs never closed. The Jazz Triangle featured the best black touring and area musicians in floor shows at The Little Harlem, Vendome and Moon-Glo. Crowds filled the Town Casino, Glen Casino and McVans for floor shows, where all the top national acts appeared on a regular basis. Dinner clubs like The Chez Ami and in the Statler Hotel had top entertainment. There were bars in every neighborhood across the city featuring live music. During this time people from Toronto crossed over the border to shop at Buffalo stores during the day and to frequent the nightclubs in the evening.

In the 1950s the Hi-Teen Club was one of the first rock 'n' roll radio shows, broadcast from a dancehall. Buffalo's Hound Dog Lorenz was one of the first DJ's to play the original renditions of rock 'n' roll recordings on the radio and WKBW became one of the most influential radio stations on the East Coast. Area musicians created a mix of R&B, blues and rock that was called the Buffalo Sound, which influenced the style of area musicians during the 1960s and 1970s. The baby boom generation created a population surge during the 1960s. There were teen clubs, school, church and community dances in all parts of the city, suburbs and surrounding towns. Every neighborhood had their favorite teen club band and many of these bands became popular across WNY.

During the 1970s rock, progressive rock, R&B, blues, country and country rock filled the area clubs. There were lines to get into live music clubs and you could see bands performing every night of the week. Many touring Top 40 commercial rock show bands were based out of Buffalo and concerts were held at stadiums, arenas, theaters, parks and large clubs. When disco arrived the number of live music clubs may have waned but now there were lines to both live music clubs and discos. In the late 1970s clubs started featuring bands playing their own music. Good paying factory or office jobs were plentiful and frequenting clubs several times a week was affordable. Alternative forms of entertainment had not yet affected the number of revelers going to the clubs and people had not yet started moving out of the area. The drinking age in Canada was 21, so young Canadians came to Buffalo to enjoy the bands.

Suddenly things started to change. The drinking age in NYS was increased from 18 to 19 in 1982, and then on December 1, 1985 it was raised once again to 21. In 1980, Mothers Against Drunk Driving (MADD) was founded leading to stricter DUI/DWI law enforcement. Another recession in July 1981, effected businesses and more factories began closing. Pay raises failed to keep up with inflation, so the choice of entertainment included staying at home watching the new 24-hour MTV or engaging in the allure of playing video games. The baby boomers discontinued going out to clubs on a regular basis and started moving out of the WNY area. Clubs started closing or were forced to reduce the number of nights they offered live music. Live entertainment was still available but the golden days of Buffalo Music & Entertainment had waned. Due to these factors, the early 1980s was chosen as a good cut-off point for this book.

ACKNOWLEDGEMENTS

Special Thanks: There were many individuals that assisted in compiling information for this project. First, I would like to thank the following who provided data and direction for sections of the book. Raya Lee for the Pan-American Exposition and Classical Music. Nicholas Cintorino for contributions to the Theater chapter. Joey Giambra, Dick Riederer, Craig Steger for Early Jazz. Jerry Raven for Folk. Vincent Michaels for data on Moog Music & Related businesses. Kent Weber for Original Music. Phil DiRe for 1970s Jazz. Tommy Flucker, Larry Salter and Van Taylor for R&B. Ken Machelski for Polka Music. Ed Bentley and Dwane Hall for Country Music. Mark Panfil for Bluegrass.

Additional thanks are extended to the following for their valuable assistance. Without their efforts, this book may have not come to fruition. Carol Jean Swist, Tom Ryan and Marsha Falkowski for editing and Bob Ambrusko for Layout & Graphics.

I would also like to thank the following who were consulted in person, over the phone or over the internet. Alphabetized by first name.

Anthony Amigone, Bob Ambrusko, Bob Avino, Bob James, Bob Maggio, Bob Meier, Bob Paxon, Bob Skurzewski, Bob Stalder , Bob Wilczak, Bobby Lebel, Brian Dickman, Carol Jean Swist, Casey Gervase, Chuck LaChiusa, Chuck Vicario Cindy Reinhardt, Craig Cornwall, Cynthia Van Ness, Dale Anderson, Dan Bonner, Dan Gambino, Dan Macaluso, Dan Nowak, Dan Patrick, Daniel Meyers, Dave Bienik, Dave Buffamonti, Dave Constantino, David Keith, David Nathan, David Green, Debby Ash, Diane Meldrum, Dick Bauerle, Dick Riederer, Dick Terranova, Dolly Kudla, Don Eckel, Don Lorentz, Don Peters, Don Tomasulo, Doug Morgano, Ed Bentley, Ed Tice, Eileen O'Sullivan, Elmer Ploetz, Ernie Corallo, Frank Lorenz, Frank Pusateri, Frank Sansone, Frankie Scinta, Gary Calvaneso, Gary Edmonds, George Puleo, George Scott, Gerry Cannizzaro, Gordon Casper, Greg Hennessey, Hank Nevins, Howard Goldman, Jerry Meyers, Jerry Ralston, Jim Flynn, Jim Kipler, Jim Hamilton, Jim Sommer, Jim Thompson, Joe Giarrano, Joe Hesse, Joe Scinta, Joe Zappo, Joey Calato, Joey James, John Brady, John Cameron, John Culliton Mahoney, John Schmidt, John Shephard, Judy Terrose Rice, Kathy Ameno, Kathy Carr, Ken Wilczak, Kevin Townsell, Linda Lou Schriver, Marjorie Wallens, Mark Morette, Mark Panfil, Martin Victor, Mary Heneghan, Michael Campagna, Michael Gioeli, Michael Spriggs, Mike James Piccolo, Mike Kubera, Mike Kucharski, Mike Rozniak, Nancy Nathan, Nick Ameno, Nick Gugliuzza, Patsy Silver, Paul Campanella, Paul Daniel Petock, Paul Preston, Peter Haskell, Pete Holguin, Pete Millitello, Phil Dillon, Ray Wood, Rich Fustino, Rich Peters, Rich Sansone, Richard Sargent, Rick McGirr, Robbie Konikoff,, Robert Then, Ron Altbach, Ron Rocco, Rose Ann Hirsch, Sam Guarino, Sandy Dedrick, Sandy Konikoff,, Sherry Hackett, Stephanie Pietrzak, Steve Cichon, Steve Loncto, Steve Sadoff, Steven Gustafson, Steven Patrick, Steven Rosenthal, Stuart Ziff, Sue Dobmeier, Susan Slack, Tadj Symczak, Terri Skuzewski, Tom Barone, Tom Dolan, Tom Gariano, Tom Lorentz, Tom Magill, Tom Naples, Tom Ryan, Tommie Rizzo, Tommy Flucker, Tony Galla, Van Taylor, Victor Marwin, Vincert Michaels, Will Schulmeister, William Kae, William Phillips. If I missed someone, I sincerely apologize and will include you in a revised or future edition.

TABLE OF CONTENTS

1

THE BEGINNING

One of the first documented entertainment events in Buffalo history was an outdoor play *The Tragedy of Douglas*. It was presented to commemorate the end of the War of 1812 and was held at Sandytown, on March 17, 1815. Sandytown was located in the area between what is now LaSalle Park and the Erie Basin Marina, not far from Canalside.

In 1821, the first building of record to have live entertainment in Buffalo was called The Theater. It was located across the street from Buffalo's stagecoach stop, The Eagle Tavern, at Main & Court Street. The location of The Theater was in what is now Lafayette Square, where the Thursday at the Square Concerts were held until they were moved to Canalside.

In Western New York (WNY) it appears that people are going to the same places early residents frequented about 200 years ago. We will begin our journey at Canal Street chronicling many of the developments that occurred between the times of Sandytown and Canalside.

EAGLE TAVERN
Photo: Picture Book of Earlier Buffalo

CANAL STREET

The Erie Canal opened in 1825 and transformed Buffalo from a quiet village to the busy gateway to the West. The area where the Erie Canal entered Lake Erie was called the Canal Street District, where The Marine Drive Apartments and Buffalo Naval Park are now located. In addition to the warehouses and freight-forwarding businesses, this was where Erie Canal barge workers and Lake Erie sailors came to let off steam and indulge in wine, women and song. Within ten years Canal Street became a very dangerous place and was known as the infected district or The Barbary Coast of the U.S.

Beginning in the 1830s Canal Street was known for its decadence. During the 1880's it was written that 60% of the buildings on Canal Street from Erie to Commercial Street were houses of prostitution, 30% were saloons and 10% were grocery stores or other types of businesses. The towpath side of the street was even more decadent than the street side of Canal Street. A survey in 1890 listed 120 saloons, 19 free theater saloons and 75 brothels in this several-square-block area. Mixed in between these houses of ill repute were legitimate businesses and tenements, where people lived.

One of the most notorious concert saloons, or concert halls, was the Only Theater, located at the corner of Canal and Commercial Streets. Some of the other concert halls, dance halls and saloons in the Canal Street District included Joseph Hoffman's Lion Theater (Maiden & Canal), The Star, Bonney's and Alhambra. There were other concert halls on lower Main Street, lower Broadway, and the tenderloin district area of Oak Street and Michigan Avenue, but they were considered tame in relation to the Canal Street establishments.

Some accounts claim the dance halls were just a step above the brothels or just brothels in disguise. The concert halls were considered resorts of amusements where respectable people would not care to go. They were houses of music, sport and low-down vice. They offered music and dancing, or at least what passed for music and dancing, burlesque style comedy and female attendants in Mother Hubbard or revealing dresses, soliciting drinks, cigarettes and other services. In addition, there was wrestling and other athletic sports, including gouging matches – in which dim-witted contestants, with sharpened thimbles on their fingers were urged to gouge each other's eyes out.

Every night was a party on Canal Street, but the biggest nights of the year were July 4th and New Year's Eve. The saloons became so crowded on these nights that if you passed out from drinking too much, you would remain standing because the mass of the crowd would hold you up in place.

After a night on the town in the Canal Street District, many a sailor, canal worker or even local resident woke up the next morning without his money, hung over, with a black eye from a fight, bruised from a mugging or in jail for deeds they did not remember committing. Some did not wake up at all because the next morning they were found floating in the Erie Canal.

CHRISTY'S MINSTRELS

For some unknown reason, seedy areas have a history of developing new forms of entertainment, which is exactly what happened on Canal Street. In 1835, E.P. Ned Christy arrived in Buffalo, where he developed and refined the concept of the Minstrel Show, which was the forerunner to vaudeville and 20th century comedy teams.

CHRISTY'S MINSTRELS
Photo: Public Domain

Edwin Pearce (Ned) Christy was born in Philadelphia in 1815, and as a young man he was a singer with Purdy and Welch's Circus in New Orleans. He put a great deal of effort into learning the rhythms of speech and music in southern African-American culture. After leaving the South, he gained a reputation as a traveling blackface musician and comic singer.

When Christy arrived in Buffalo, he met and married Harriet Harrington, a widow who owned a Canal Street dancehall. Ned's stepson George and his friend Dick Sliter performed song, dance and comedy routines in front of the building to entice people into the tavern. Ned moved their show inside and they became the featured entertainment in the dancehall. The first shows were Ned as the ballad singer and violinist, Sliter as the jig dancer and George playing bones; a simple percussion instrument made from animal bones, similar to playing spoons. They added tambourine and banjo players and an additional violinist, performing to packed houses as the Darkey Minstrel Show.

Thomas D. Rice was the first famous blackface performer to perform his Jim Crow routine in Buffalo during 1835 at the Eagle Street Theater. Dan Emmett and the Virginia Minstrels made the minstrel show synonymous with blackface, and the Ethiopian Serenaders removed the low comedy. However, it was Christy who established the three-act template and brought respectability to the minstrel show.

As established by Christy, the actors in the minstrel show set up in a semicircle with the interlocutor (straight man, ballad singer) in the center, flanked by Tambo and Bones as the endmen or cornermen. The three-act performance started with the troupe dancing on to the stage singing and settling into their semicircle. The endmen then traded jokes and sang a variety of humorous songs. A maudlin song was added, and the first act ended with a walkaround, including dances in the form of a cakewalk. The second act was called the olio, which was more of a variety show and always included a stump speech, where the other members of the troupe made comments about the speech and the speaker always fell off his stump. The final act was the afterpiece, which was a skit set on a southern plantation, with Sambo and Mammy type characters in slapstick situations. The afterpiece would often include burlesque renditions of Shakespearean and contemporary plays.

Ned Christy was the leader of the troupe, but George Harrington was a diligent student and became the featured performer of the show. He adopted his step-fathers name and became George Christy. Once the format for their show was established, they quickly gained popularity. By 1842, they were packing the people into Harrington's Dance Hall on Canal Street. They started performing dates at the concert halls in downtown Buffalo and touring the Northeast and Midwest. In 1847, during one of these excursions later in their career, they became acquainted with Stephen Foster.

As a teenager, Stephen Foster was influenced by circus clowns and the early blackface singer Dan Rice. Rice presented shows that were of a vaudevillian style before there was vaudeville and was a contemporary of P.T. Barnum, often competing with him for a share of the same audience. In fact, it was Rice who first used the slogan, "The Greatest Show on Earth." Rice also had an influence on Samuel Clemens better known as author Mark Twain. Clemens lived in Buffalo from 1869-71, during which time he was part owner of the *Buffalo Express* newspaper. Twain referenced Rice in *The Adventures of Huckleberry Finn*. Rice's influence resulted in Foster writing minstrel style material. Foster titled his songs Ethiopian Melodies, and Christy's Minstrels were the perfect musical group to introduce his compositions.

Foster signed an agreement giving Christy's Minstrels exclusive premier rights to many of his songs, including "Oh! Susanna." The song's success gave Foster the opportunity to make songwriting his full-time profession for which he is often referred to as "America's first professional songwriter." During the time of his agreement with Christy, Foster wrote most of his best-known songs: "Camptown Races," "Old Folks at Home" also known as "Way Down Upon the Swanee River," "My Old Kentucky Home," "Nelly Was a Lady," and "Jeanie with the Light Brown Hair." In fact, "Old Folks at Home" was originally published as written by E.P. Christy. Christy paid Foster $10.00 for the song and Foster gave him permission to take credit for writing it, with the proper authorship eventually reverting to Foster.

Christy may have become popular by performing Stephen Foster's songs but he was a successful songwriter in his own right. In 1844, he wrote "Buffalo Gals Won't You Come Out Tonight." This song may have been a tribute to the women of Canal Street. "Mary Blane" was considered the most popular female captivity song in antebellum minstrelsy. The actual writer cannot be confirmed, but some musicologists credit the song to Edwin P. Christy. Although it is not known who wrote the song "Lucy Long", Billy Whitlock from the Virginia Minstrels claimed he wrote it but George Christy is credited as the person who introduced the song and made it a hit. George Christy was the premier female impersonator in minstrel shows, and in the persona of Miss Lucy, the tune "Miss Lucy Long" was his signature song. It was so popular that in the minstrel shows, the name of Lucy came to signify a promiscuous woman.

Christy's Minstrels performed their final concert in Buffalo at The American Hotel on Main Street in 1845. They moved to New York City and, with the exception of some tours, performed 25 cent nightly shows primarily at Mechanics Hall of Broadway from 1846 to 1854. During the late 1840s and early 1850s, a trip to NYC included two mandatory stops for entertainment: P.T. Barnum's Museum and a Christy's Minstrels performance. Christy was later associated with Barnum when he invested in Barnum's circus, which at that time employed Tony Pastor, who later became known as the father of vaudeville. E.P. Christy made the equivalent of millions of dollars from his performances, but Steven Foster, American's first-full time songwriter and the father of American Music, died penniless. The plight of Foster was one of the driving forces behind the early 20th century establishment of ASCAP, an organization to protect the musical copyrights of songwriters.

JENNY LIND

Jenny Lind was called The Swedish Nightingale and in the mid-19th century, she was considered the world's first music superstar. In addition to her performances, Lind was known for her charitable contributions. During a portion of 1851, she made WNY her home, and presented one of her trademark benefit concerts.

A soprano opera singer from Sweden, Jenny Lind was an inspiration for Danish author Hans Christian Andersen, who fell in love with her. When Lind rejected Andersen as a suitor, he portrayed her as The Snow Queen, with a heart of ice, in his fairy tales.

She retired from Opera at age 29, but P.T. Barnum was told of her reputation and he offered her a contract to tour America. Lind had stringent demands, but after negotiations, Barnum agreed to meet them. The contract terms probably made Lind the highest-paid performer at that time. P.T. Barnum would have to outdo himself to cover the tour expenses, but that is what Barnum thrived upon.

Barnum was so successful in promoting the tour, even before she reached American shores, that there were thousands of people waiting when Lind's boat arrived in New York in 1850. Tickets were in such demand in some cities that they were sold by auction. Due to the public enthusiasm, the American press coined the term "Lind Mania", over 100 years before another European music invasion in the 1960s called "Beatlemania." The 93-day tour netted Lind $350,000 and Barnum $500,000 (approximately $10 million and $15 million in today's currency). Lind donated most of her profits to charity, mainly the endowment for free schooling in her native Sweden.

Lind's tour covered the Eastern US, Cuba and Canada. By early 1851, Lind grew tired of

JENNY LIND
Photo: Public Domain

Barnum's relentless promotion so they amicably severed their contractual ties. She continued to tour under her own self-management. Following a concert in July 1851, at North Presbyterian Church in Buffalo, she decided to take an extended vacation in the Niagara Falls area.

In September 1851, a fire destroyed a large section of Canal Street. Keeping with her tradition, Lind organized a charity concert on October 15, 1851, at the Washington Street Baptist Church. Tickets were sold for $2.00, $3.00 and $4.00, with scalpers getting $20.00 a ticket. Sounds like the 2015 Paul McCartney concert in Buffalo. A second concert was held two days later, with these shows being Lind's return to touring in the United States, which continued until the spring of 1852.

The Buffalo area is remembered as being the temporary home of the first worldwide music superstar and, while living in WNY, Jenny Lind presented a charity concert to benefit the resident of Buffalo's notorious Canal Street.

THE FOUNDATIONS

EARLY THEATERS

Canal Street was filled with decadent entertainment, so many of Buffalo's residents never went to that district in the evening. Fearing for their safety they sought entertainment in the downtown area of Buffalo, on or near Main Street, away from the waterfront.

Following the early shows at The Theater as well as the Eagle Tavern in 1821, the first entertainment complex in WNY was called The Buffalo Museum which opened on August 6, 1829. It was operated by John McCleary in the upstairs rooms of the Exchange Building at the corner of Washington and Exchange Street. Early venues had to cater to a variety of client's interests, to attract all potential customers, and The Buffalo Museum was no exception. This building was a combination saloon, theater and exhibition hall. For an entrance fee of 25 cents, in addition to live shows you could view stuffed exotic animals, military relics and even live rattlesnakes. The employees of the Buffalo Museum opened The Seneca Street Playhouse in 1833, on Seneca between Main and Washington Streets, where they placed more of an emphasis on

EAGLE STREET THEATER aka ST. JAME'S HALL
Photo: Picture Book of Earlier Buffalo

entertainment, rather than exhibits.

In 1835, it was moved again to The Old Eagle Street Theater on the corner of Eagle and Washington, which was a fully operational theater. During the theater season, which ran from May to December, over 60 traveling actors would perform there. The cost of a theater box for the season was $100 to $150, and individual tickets to shows were 25 to 75 cents. A dollar at that time was worth about $25 in today's dollars, so admission prices were comparable to current costs. During the winter social season, when the lakes and Erie Canal were frozen, fashionable balls were held at the Eagle Street for the idle rich.

On May 11, 1852, the theater burned down after a complaint-ridden performance by the notorious diva Lola Montez (the mistress of Franz List and Mad King Ludwig). It was rumored she caused the fire, because even though she was booked to perform at the hall again the following evening, she removed her wardrobe and theater props after her performance. The night following the fire, Montez appeared at a small Washington Street theater and received much better reviews.

The theater was rebuilt and quickly reopened as the New Eagle Street Theater on September 1, 1852, with the name being changed to the St. James Theater in 1854. It burned down once again on January 9, 1862 and Peel's Minstrel Troupe lost all their instruments and wardrobe in the fire.

After this fire, it was again rebuilt and called St. James Hall, where Abraham Lincoln's body laid in state en route to his burial in Springfield, Illinois in 1865. Over 100,000 people passed through the hall to view the body of the fallen President. During the 1870s, the hall featured classical music concerts by the Buffalo Symphony Orchestra, Buffalo Singing Society, Buffalo Choral Union, operas and touring orchestras.

This location of St. James Hall was apparently prone to fires because the theater burned down again in March 1887. The 1887 fire destroyed the building and Brunnell's Museum, who had been leasing it for the past three years. After the fire, Brunnell's moved to the former Grand Central at 297-301 Michigan. The fire also burned down the neighboring Hotel Richmond, killing 15 people and severely burning dozens more. Due to the fatal fire, it was determined that the overhead telephone and telegraph wires impeded the firemen from reaching guests on the upper floors of the building. In the interest of public safety, the city of Buffalo passed an ordinance in the downtown area stating that these unsightly wires had to be placed in underground conduits.

The Hotel Richmond had been the Young Men's Association and housed the Buffalo Fine Library, in addition to rooms for the Buffalo Historical Society, Buffalo Society of Natural Sciences and other organizations. Luckily, the 25,000 volumes of books had been moved to the Buffalo Public Library on Lafayette Square. The Iroquois Hotel was built in the space of St. James Hall and the Richmond Hotel. After the Iroquois was closed and demolished, it became the present location of One M&T Plaza.

In 1835 The Buffalo Theater opened at Washington and South Division Street. It was of significance because it put on productions by traveling acting groups, which included Junius Brutus Booth and Edwin Booth, the father and older brother of John Wilkes Booth. Other theaters near the Buffalo and Eagle Street theaters in the 1840's were the Concert Hall, American Hall and Townsend Hall, all of which housed concerts, operas, poetry readings, lectures, debates and other events.

Buffalo was a city of 16,000 people in 1835 and it was growing fast. That expansion came from its location and the construction projects of Benjamin Rathbun, who started his career in Buffalo in 1819 by leasing the Eagle Tavern. The Eagle Tavern was the main stagecoach stop in Buffalo and was the building block of Rathbun's empire. During 1835 and 1836, Rathbun built 99 buildings at a cost of $500,000 including the first American Hotel. However, it was found that Rathbun financed his projects by borrowing on over $1.5 million in notes forged with the names of the most affluent Buffalonians. Rathbun was jailed, his empire collapsed and almost 2,500 people lost their jobs, with Buffalo getting a head start on the national financial panic of 1837. The American Hotel was located on Main Street between Eagle and Court Street. There was a theater in the hotel where Christy's Minstrels made their final Buffalo appearance in 1845. It burned down during a fire on March 10, 1850 and was rebuilt as the second American Hotel. Abraham Lincoln delivered a speech from the balcony of the hotel, on the way to his inauguration, and a special banquet was held in his honor at the hotel in March 1861. There was a second fire at The American Hotel in 1865, which also burned down the Eagle Tavern, located next to the hotel. After that fire, the original AM&A's department store was built on the site. That building was razed in 1960 and the Main Place Mall was built in the approximate location of the American Hotel.

The jewel of early Buffalo theaters opened October 15, 1852, on the site of the former Farmer's Hotel at 245 Main Street between Seneca and Swan Street. The Metropolitan Theater was the most elegant theater in Buffalo, decorated in velvet and lace, with ornamental wood and iron work. It had a 50-feet deep stage and seated over 2,500 people. Immediately upon its opening, it became the premier location for live entertainment in Buffalo. The name of the theater was changed to The Academy of Music in 1868, because after the assassination of Lincoln at

ACADEMY OF MUSIC
Photo: Picture Book of Earlier Buffalo

Ford's Theatre, the word theater fell out of favor with the American public. When the Academy of Music closed in 1956, it was the second-oldest continually-operating theater in the US, offering shows for over 100 years.

The prominent touring theater troupes all performed at The Metropolitan Theatre or Academy of Music when they came to Buffalo. John Wilkes Booth, the assassin of President Lincoln was listed in Buffalo newspapers as appearing in plays at The Metropolitan Theatre in 1863. All the top actors performed there including Sarah Bernhardt, Fanny Davenport, Frank Mayo and Buffalo's Chauncey Olcott. It is noteworthy that during the 1870s to 1890 the managers were listed as the Meech Brothers, who were also the managers of St. James Hall and the Saengerhalle (Main & Edward). This made the Meech Brothers the managers of the three largest entertainment facilities in Buffalo.

In 1862 The Opera House opened in The Arcade Building, which had frontage along Main and Washington Street and extended along Clinton Street. The Arcade Building was owned by the Brisbane family, and there were several other businesses in the building in addition to the Opera House. The theater featured opera and other musical events. It was the Adelphi Theatre in 1874 and became a legitimate playhouse, later known as the Adelphia Theater, Wonderland and Robinson's. The Arcade Building burned down in 1892 and was replaced by The Brisbane Building.

The Niagara Hotel was at 22-24 The Terrace between Commercial and Pearl Street. The theater in the hotel became known as The American Theatre (no association to the American Hotel). It was later operated by Thomas Carr who also ran Carr's Melodeon at 283 Main Street. Other early theaters in the Southern Main street area, included The Concert Hall (Main between Seneca & Exchange), Townsend Hall (Southwest corner of Main & Swan), McArthur's Garden (Main & Eagle), Mechanics Hall, (Seneca Street), Clinton Hall (401 Washington at Clinton), The Apollo Hall (295 Ellicott Street), the 2,000 seat Dudley Hall (119 Main), the four story American Hall (304 Main), and Goodell Hall (Delaware & Johnson Park), where they presented the Buffalo Choral Union concerts.

The German theater area was further north, predominantly at Gillig's Hall, 249 Genesee Street at Ash, and Turner's Theatre, 385 Ellicott Street near Genesee. Gillig's Hall was established in 1854 by the Turn Verein, which was a German-American social club, community center and gymnasium. The hall featured a gymnasium, theatre and restaurant, designed so the stage could be hoisted after each performance to make room for the gym. The initial performances at the hall were a variety of entertainment by a male chorus formed by Joseph Hipelius, leader of the Union Brass Band. Later in 1854, The Thalia Theatre Company, who previously put on productions at Geyers Hall on Court Street and was accompanied by Otto Schagen's Orchestra, merged with the Turn Verein at Gillig's Hall. When they performed at the hall, a dance always followed their presentation.

In 1858 the manager of Gillig's Hall suggested they purchased the building at 385 Ellicott Street, which was about to become Turner's Theater. This led to a schism with the Social Manner Turn Verein remaining at Gillig's, which was renamed the Stadt Theater, and the Turn Verein Vorwarts who moved to Turner's Theater. Turner's had a seating capacity of over 1,000, doubled as a gymnasium and had a tavern at the back of the property. Eventually when Eduard Fuerst assumed management of both theaters in 1859, the theaters worked together with Monday performances at The Stadt, Thursday performances at Turner's and sacred music concerts at both theaters on Sunday. Both facilities continued operation under various names, into the early 20th century and the Saengerbund made Turners their home until the Saengerhalle was built at Main and Edward in 1887. Other German theater and entertainment halls were Sparfelds (Genesee near Oak), Kremlin Hall (Pearl & Eagle), Harugari Hall (258 Genesee), Harmonia Hall (264 Genesee) and Roth's Hall (Michigan & Cypress), the 1853 home of Turn Verein.

A second Opera House opened on Washington Street, north of Broadway, in 1887. To differentiate it from the Opera House in the Arcade Building it was called Opera House II or the Grand Opera House. It was renamed the Lyceum Theater in the 1890s and remained popular until it was torn down to build the Lafayette Theatre. In 1882 Wahle's Opera House on Court Street was opened between Franklin & Pearl. It became the Court Street Theatre, which was later one of Michael Sheas early vaudeville houses.

One theater that was instrumental in the transition to vaudeville was the Star Theater. It was built by Emanuel Levi in 1888 and seated 1,425 people. The site of the theater was at 56 West Genesee Street at the corner of Pearl and West Mohawk, the current location of the Convention Center. It was in operation at the very beginning of vaudeville, and most of the prominent people involved with early 20th century entertainment either

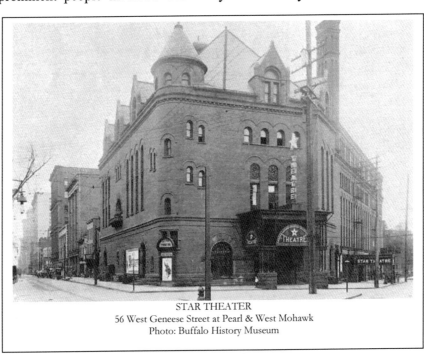

STAR THEATER
56 West Geneese Street at Pearl & West Mohawk
Photo: Buffalo History Museum

13

managed or owned the theater. In 1901, Dr. Peter C. Cornell, father of actress Katharine Cornell, gave up his medical practice to manage the theater. It initially featured various entertainment but concentrated upon legitimate theater when Cornell became manager, and during this time it was owned by Klaw & Erlanger and the Shuberts. In 1919, Cornell moved his productions across the street to The Majestic Theater at 313 Pearl Street, which was open from 1912 to 1927. When Cornell moved, Michael Shea took over management of the theater, renaming it The Criterion and began featuring movies along with vaudeville.

2

THE LATE 1800s
PAN-AMERICAN EXPOSITION
BRASS BANDS

The most popular style of music in the late 1890s was performed by brass bands which originated during the 1850s in England. There were professional military bands in England, but amateur bands were formed by companies to boost the morale of their employees. The company bands even rehearsed during regular work hours, with some of the amateur bands equal in proficiency to the professional military bands. Businesses set up competitions between their bands, and these contests became highly attended events, with enthusiasm almost equal to later day English football (soccer) matches. At times spectators at these performances resorted to physical violence between the supporters of competing bands.

A brass band, of the British tradition, had 28 members, including percussion players. With exception of the percussion, all the instruments in the British band were from the brass family: cornets, flugelhorn, tenor horns, baritone horns, tenor trombones, bass trombone, euphoniums and tubas. In other European countries and when the bands moved to the United States, they also included reed instruments such as the saxophone and the clarinet.

Brass bands started performing in the U.S. in the 1850s, but they became more prevalent during the Civil War. Each military unit had their own brass band for ceremonies which, at times, led them into battle. After the Civil War, each military armory retained and expanded upon their brass band. Ceremony and patriotism were important aspects of American culture after the Civil War, and the brass bands played a focal point in festivities. In Buffalo, the 65th Armory Band and the 74th Armory Band performed at military functions and at public events at the parks. The brass band became an important form of entertainment with most towns, organizations, theaters, touring circuses and companies forming their own unit. These ensembles presented music of patriotic nature and at times included symphonic pieces for diversity. Many Americans were first exposed to the music of classical composers through the arrangements performed by these bands.

When Frederick Law Olmsted designed the Buffalo urban park system, he included outdoor areas for music. There was a gazebo overlooking Mirror Lake in Delaware Park, music spaces in Front Park, and The Parade (later Humboldt and currently MLK Park) was conceived of as a place for military displays, including performances by marching military brass bands.

The regular performance area for brass bands were the gazebos, which were scattered across Western New York in city parks, town squares and village greens. Concerts were held at twilight or on Sunday afternoons. In WNY the most popular brass band was the 74th Armory Band, that was headquartered at the Connecticut Street Armory. They were popular for an extended period as they escorted President Lincoln to his speech at the American Hotel in 1861 and continued to perform at Crystal Beach until the early 20th century. The 74th Armory Band performed more public than military events, and membership was extended to professional musicians who were not in the military. In fact, many of the touring brass bands were professional, not military, ensembles and were led by directors such as John Philip Sousa.

When the Pan-American Exposition took place in 1901, brass bands were one of the featured forms of entertainment.

74th REGIMENT BAND – BUFFALO'S FIRST BRASS BAND
Photo: Courtesy William Kae

16

THE PAN-AMERICAN EXPOSITION

PAN-AMERICAN EXPOSITION AT NIGHT
Photo: Courtesy Raya Lee

The Pan-American Exposition (Pan Am) was held in Buffalo, New York from May 1 through November 2, 1901. Buffalo was the eighth-largest city in the country at this time and was a transportation hub for railway and water transportation. Buffalo was a center of commerce, boasting of beautiful mansions and the Olmsted-designed urban park system. Many of the elite citizens of Buffalo assisted in the planning of the Pan Am because they realized its success would enhance the reputation of the City.

The location for the Pan Am was situated next to Olmsted designed Delaware Park and could be accessed by the parkways laid out by him. It was just north of Mirror Lake, with a canal system traversing the grounds. Electricity from Niagara Falls lit the Pan Am at night, with the Electric Tower being a focal point. Admission to the fairgrounds was 25 cents (about $7 in today's currency) and 8,000,000 people visited the Exposition.

Music was an important part of the Pan Am, and the individuals responsible for planning the music were many of the same people who would shape the entertainment of Buffalo at the beginning of the 20th century. Those involved included Louis Whiting Gay, Mai Davis Smith, Marion DeForest, Charles Kuhn and educators Joseph and Carl Mishka. With this being a World's Fair, many of the top performers of the day provided the entertainment. Performing during the Expo were two orchestras, 20 professional bands and 71 organists. Victor Herbert conducted the Pittsburgh Orchestra, which was considered one of the three great permanent concert orchestras in the United States, for several weeks of performances. Buffalo Symphony conductor, John Lund directed the Pan-American Orchestra which in addition to Buffalo musicians, was made up of members from the New York and Boston Symphony, which were considered the other two great permanent orchestras.

The bands performing at the fair included John Philip Sousa and Frederick Neil Innes. Sousa composed "Invincible Eagle March" for his performance at The Pan Am. Three Buffalo bands were also featured during the Exposition, the 65th Regiment Band, 74th Regiment Band and The Scinta's Band, led by Serafino Scinta. A direct relationship could not be verified, but Buffalo's Scinta Brothers presume Serafino Scinta is probably a long-lost distant relative.

THE SCINTA'S BAND LED BY SERAFINO SCINTA
Photo: Courtesy William Kae

For larger events in the Temple of Music, like concerts by Herbert, Sousa or other special performances, there was an admission charge. The Temple of Music had a 2,200 - seat capacity. In addition to the Temple of Music, concerts were presented on five different bandstands. During the Expo, there were 1,239 concerts, each providing their own printed program. That was about seven concerts per day. In addition to the formal concerts, bands played on the gazebo bandstands strategically placed throughout the esplanade to avoid interference from any other band.

Organ concerts were also held in the Temple of Music. The Emmons Howard pipe organ, with 3,288 pipes, was one of the largest organs ever built, with an original cost of $18,000. There was an admission for some of the organ concerts, but every Sunday at 2:00 there was a free concert. After the Pan Am ended, J.N. Adam facilitated moving the organ from the Temple of Music to the Elmwood Music Hall. He insisted that these free

Sunday afternoon concerts continue for the enjoyment of all the people in Buffalo. When President McKinley was assassinated in The Temple of Music, during his reception Buffalo organist William Gomph was performing. Gomph was only 23 when he was appointed the official Expo organist, and he was playing Robert Schumann's "Traumerei" when McKinley was shot.

One of the most extraordinary features of the Pan Am was the night-time illumination of the buildings and grounds. As thousands of lights, controlled by special rheostats were gradually lit to full power, all the bands at the Pan Am were instructed by the Expo Board of Managers to play the "Star-Spangled Banner." John Philip Sousa followed orders, however when he witnessed the majesty and grandeur of the illumination, he commented in his autobiography that this was not to be experienced by a march, but rather by a hymn. The following evening, as the lights reached full capacity, he directed his band to perform "Nearer My God to Thee." His actions angered the managers who ordered Sousa return to the "Star-Spangled Banner," but the public flooded the Expo Board of Managers with requests that the hymn should accompany the final illumination. Not only was Sousa allowed to play the hymn, but all the bands performed "Nearer My God to Thee" for the remainder of the Exposition. The combination of beautiful music and the 240,000 sparkling lights was an emotional, uplifting feature of the Exposition, resulting in a long lingering memory for everyone that experienced it.

In addition to the bands and organists, there was an abundance of ethnic music performed at the Pan Am. There were musical performances by musicians from Japan, the Philippines, Hawaii, Argentina, Italy, Mexico, Africa and the Middle East throughout the midway and at cultural exhibits. Performing at the Venice in America exhibit was future opera star, Nina Morgana. Nina started singing in Buffalo when she was four years old and was only nine years old during her Pan Am performances. In 1908, Enrico Caruso heard her sing at the Iroquois Hotel during one of his scheduled concerts in Buffalo. He not only sponsored her training in Italy, but also encouraged her career with the Metropolitan Opera Company.

Band music and light classics were the featured styles of music at the Pan Am. The musical compositions by well-known composers like Scott Joplin or Stephen Foster, however were considered too popular for an Exposition. Popular music was performed at the many musical venues that existed within the city of Buffalo. In addition to the theaters, there were 52 licensed concert halls in Buffalo: 47 for music and 5 for singing.

The Pan-American Exposition, just like most World Fair's and Olympics, lost money. Inclement weather at the beginning of the event and the assassination of President McKinley resulted in lower than expected attendance and a deficit rather than a profit. However, the Exposition introduced Buffalo to the rest of the world, left a positive impression on those that visited the city, and the utility of hydroelectric power was established. Unfortunately, the only permanent structure was the New York State Building, which became the Buffalo History Museum, and now stores much of the Pan Am records. The Albright Art Gallery was not completed until several years later so the Fine Arts Pavilion housed the fabulous art exhibits. The iconic Electric Tower was demolished, but it served as the model for the Niagara Mohawk Building. It is now known as the Iskalo Electric Tower in Roosevelt Plaza. After McKinley's death, the swearing in of Theodore Roosevelt as President of the United States at the Wilcox Mansion on Delaware Avenue was one of four presidential inaugurations that did not take place in Washington DC.

PAN-AMERICAN EXPOSITION DEVELOPMENTS

Prior to the Pan-American Exposition opening in 1901, an attempt was made to clean up the city, especially the Canal Street area and Tenderloin District, bounded by Main, Tupper, Seneca and Michigan. The city leaders were worried that Canal Street and the Tenderloin District would take business away from the Pan Am beer halls.

Laws were passed that prohibited any combination of singing or instrumental music in concert halls. Singing or music was permitted, but not together. Police patrolled Canal Street and the Tenderloin District to make certain they were abiding by the new laws and to look for gambling, slot machines and prostitution. Their goal was to close the Buffalo bars or at least cut down on the number of establishments serving alcohol. The efforts were not successful; the Buffalo bars stayed open but they co-existed with the entertainment at The Pan Am.

There was no cooperation between the women working the streets and houses of ill repute in Buffalo and outsiders trying to take away some of their businesses. Legend has it that a group of ladies of the night from NYC thought there would be too much business generated from the Fair for the working women of Buffalo to handle. They boarded a train to Buffalo, but when they arrived in the Canal District they were met by a contingent of ladies from the Buffalo red-light district. The Buffalo women fought to protect their turf and numerous arrests were made. The Buffalo police gave the ladies from NYC 24 hours to get out of town. This action cleaned up the competition for the residents of the Canal Street and Tenderloin District but did not clean up the vice in Buffalo.

The police were vigilant patrolling the streets of Buffalo during the Pan Am by protecting the visitors from muggers and thieves. However, it was not the police efforts that negated the effect of Canal Street, it was a matter of time. As the Pan Am approached, Canal Street was in the process of becoming Dante Place. The railroad was replacing the Erie Canal for transportation, so there were fewer Lake Erie sailors and canal workers frequenting the bars. Buildings vacated by shipping businesses were being populated by the influx of Italian immigrants, and Canal Street started cleaning itself up due to the changes taking place, not because of government intervention.

The Raines Laws were passed on March 23, 1896, prohibiting the sale of alcohol on Sundays. Most people worked six days a week, so Sunday was the only day they could drink alcohol all day. The Lawmakers believed that if drinking could be curtailed on Sundays, people would drink less. According to the Raines Law, alcohol could only be served on Sunday at a business, if it was a licensed hotel with at least ten rooms and it served food. This backfired because taverns that otherwise would not have done so, started renting rooms above their bars. These rooms were often used for prostitution or by unmarried couples, not being operated as the anticipated type of hotel specified by the Raines Law.

The hotels that opened because of the Raines Law remained in business well beyond the days of Canal Street or the Pan Am and even flourished during Prohibition. Some have even remained open until the present day. The reason why there are these small restaurant/bars called the "blank" Hotel, is due to a 19th Century law that was passed to reduce alcohol consumption but was unsuccessful in achieving its objective.

PALACE BURLESK
Photo: Buffalo History Museum

3

THEATERS

During the late 1800s and early 1900s, the two dominant forms of entertainment were vaudeville and burlesque. They were similar but different, existing side by side, but over time moved further apart in the type of entertainment that they offered. Burlesque preceded and existed after vaudeville waned, so it will be covered both before and after the formation on vaudeville.

When Burlesque began in England it originally meant "an absurd or comically exaggerated imitation of a literary, dramatic or musical work intended to bring laughter." After it fell out of favor in England, it evolved into American Burlesque, which featured slapstick comedy, female striptease and a scantily clad female chorus line. Businesses that presented burlesque were usually in less desirable parts of the city and were often considered seedy establishments. Some theaters started as burlesque houses, evolved into vaudeville, and after the vaudeville theater closed, returned to burlesque. As time progressed, burlesque became more risqué, while vaudeville became more family oriented. It was the goal of many burlesque performers to progress to vaudeville.

Burlesque evolved from music hall and female minstrel shows, but primarily from the type of entertainment offered at Concert Saloons in the 1860s. The early theaters that featured burlesque in Buffalo were on lower Main Street, such as the Academy of Music, and surrounding theaters, or lower Broadway, like the Olympic at 10 Broadway or the original Lafayette Theater in the current location of the Rand Building. The best remembered burlesque theaters were The Palace Burlesk in Shelton Square and The Gayety at 352 Pearl.

The roots of vaudeville were a mix of medicine show, minstrel show, wild west show, freak show, American burlesque and the circus. It was initially called Variety Entertainment, offering musicians, dancers, comedians, trained animals, acrobats and more. When it removed the lewd performers typical of the saloon type shows, it became a series of unrelated acts called vaudeville. It was especially popular from the early 1880s through the early 1930s.

Tony Pastor started out as a clown, singer and ringmaster in the circus. In 1865, he was hired as the manager of a New York City Variety Entertainment Theater. The variety theater audiences were nearly all male and Pastor realized his ticket sales would double if he could draw the female audience. To attract more people and to make the entertainment more accessible to the entire family, he presented an evening of clean fun that was a distinct alternative to the bawdy shows of the time. Basically, Pastor made vaudeville more of a PG than an R rated show. He also started matinee performances aimed to draw in housewives. For his innovations, he is considered the "Father of Vaudeville."

Pastor was a performer as well as a promoter. He was often the headline performer in his presentations and he demanded top quality performances from all his acts. To introduce fresh entertainers, he traveled to Europe annually, especially England, to bring the top Music Hall performers to the U.S. He also continually auditioned and followed the progression of new acts at other theaters. This upgraded the quality of vaudeville performances at his and other theaters.

During the summer months New York City theaters usually closed, so Pastor formed a traveling vaudeville show that toured the country from April to October. These tours featured the most noteworthy, along with up and coming acts, in shows at cities across the northeast and Midwest. During the late 1800s Pastor annually came to Buffalo for usually sold out, week long engagements.

GRAND THEATER
Iconic representation of a Buffalo vaudeville theater
Photo: Public Domain

B.F. Keith and E.A. Albee also started out in the circus and, like Tony Pastor, were employed by P.T. Barnum. They became the main innovators and largest theater chain owners in vaudeville. Some historians consider Keith, not Pastor, to be the father of vaudeville because he took the next step to define vaudeville. After Pastor elevated the concept of vaudeville from the variety show, theaters had an evening performance and a matinee a few days a week. Keith and Albee came up with the concept of continuous vaudeville. The show started at 10:00 AM and repeated throughout the day until 11:00 PM, with each act performing two or three shows a day. A patron could enter the theater at any time during the day and see the entire program by staying until the acts started repeating.

Keith and Albee also took extreme measures to maintain a level of modesty in vaudeville. They wanted the entertainment to be equally inoffensive to men, women and children. The theater manager reviewed routines and the words to songs, handing out blue envelopes with suggestions to change anything they considered sacrilegious or suggestive. If the act did not adhere to these changes, they risked being fired and banned from any theaters associated with the B.F. Keith circuit. The use of the blue envelopes to identify offensive material is where the term blue (off-color) comedy came from.

The theaters that Keith and Albee operated were throughout the Eastern U.S., including Buffalo and Niagara Falls. The other major vaudeville circuits were Pantages and Orpheum. There were also some smaller circuits and independent operators, but they usually had an agreement with one of the larger circuits so they could hire quality acts at proper pricing. In 1900 the Vaudeville Managers Association (VMA) was formed by Keith-Albee and other theaters managers on the East Coast, including Buffalo's Michael Shea. In 1903 the Western Vaudeville Managers Association (WVMA) was formed by the Orpheum and other Western U.S. circuits. Together they formed the United Booking Office (UBO), which controlled over 1,500 vaudeville theaters across the country. However, they could not get along because Keith-Albee wanted to move west and the Orpheum wanted to move east. To resolve the issue and alleviate any competition, Albee secretly acquired 51% of the Orpheum Circuit, and the Keith Albee Orpheum (KAO) Theater Corp was formed.

During the early days of vaudeville, Buffalo was an important market due to its location between New York City and Chicago. Pastor, along with Keith & Albee, were associated with Buffalo. Theater pioneers, the Mark Brothers, started their operations here and were Buffalo residents. Michael Shea built a local theater empire and was involved with Keith & Albee in the formation of the VMA. The contributions by the Mark Brothers and Michael Shea, extended well beyond Western New York.

MARK BROTHERS – VITASCOPE THEATER

The name associated with theaters and vaudeville in Buffalo is Michael Shea. Locally you cannot dispute his importance and influence. However, two brothers were equally as important locally and probably had more influence nationally – Mitchel and Moe Mark. Few recognize their names or know what they accomplished. Among their achievements, they opened the world's first permanent movie theater, exclusively designed for showing motion pictures, and they were associated with the early careers of several of the major figures in the theater industry.

Mitchel and Moe Mark began their careers in the wholesale hat trade at a shop on Seneca Street, near downtown Buffalo. After a friend showed them an Edison phonograph, they made a life-altering career change. They opened The Edisonia Phonograph Parlors in 1894 at 378 Main Street, under license to Thomas Edison. In this penny arcade they exhibited the Edison phonographs, along with other amusements like the x-ray machine. The following year they installed Edison's newest invention, the Kinetoscope, an early peep-show style movie device. The Kinetoscope and Mutoscope showed moving pictures to one person at a time through a machine, while Vitascope and Cinemascope showed moving pictures through a projector which could be viewed by multiple people on a screen.

The Ellicott Square Building opened in 1896 and at that time was the largest office building in the world. The Mark Brothers decided to move Edisonia Hall to this new building. Working with a former Edison employee, Rudolph Wagner, they hired an architect and designed the first theater built specifically for showing motion pictures. The theater, located in the basement of the Ellicott Square Building, was entered through the street level entrance of Edisonia Hall, with an address of 305 Main Street.

While planning the theater, the Mark Brothers were not content to only exhibit Edison pictures, so they arranged to show the French films made by the Lumiere Brothers, who were considered the world's first filmmakers. The Mark's signed a U.S. distribution agreement with Pathe Freres to import Pathe films, which included the Lumiere titles. When they opened the Vitascope Theater, almost the entire program was Lumiere films. Their presentations may have been the premier of many Lumiere films in the United States.

The Vitascope Theatre opened on October 19, 1896 and was described as a 72-seat bijou theater, with 9 rows of luxurious orchestra seats, 8 to a row, with 4 on each side of the aisle and a floor slanted toward the screen. The theater was open from 10:30 AM to 11:30 PM, with presentations starting on the half hour throughout the day. The films featured were changed twice a week. In November of 1897, Mitchel Mark stated that during the first year of operation 200,000 visitors saw the films shown at the Vitascope Theatre. That was equal to almost half the population of metro Buffalo at the time.

Photo: Public Domain

Buffalo was on the cutting edge of the motion picture phenomenon. Shortly after the opening of the Vitascope, in November 1896 there was a Biograph at the Music Hall and in the following month the Cinematographe Theatre opened at 609 Main Street. This was north of Chippewa in the current location of the Holiday Inn Express & Suites Hotel and TGI Fridays. There are no records of how long that theater remained open but advertisements reveal they showed Lumiere films. It was never historically verified, but since the Mark Brothers were the U.S. distributors of Lumiere films, it is quite possible that they may have also been involved with the Cinematographe Theatre.

The Vitascope Theatre was in operation almost two years when the Mark brothers began running the Empire Theater at 261 Main Street, which was open from 1898 to 1900. After operating the Mutoscope concession at the Pan-American Exposition in 1901, they set their sights on New York City.

In 1903 they started the Automatic Vaudeville Company, with partners Adolph Zucker and Morris Kahn. The Crystal Hall, in Union Square, was their first location in NYC. Initially their business was similar to their Edison Phonograph Parlors, with phonographic listening devices, peep-show video and other amusements. An upstairs movie theater was added several years later. With the financial backing of Marcus Loew, Automatic Vaudeville opened similar operations in Boston, Philadelphia and Newark, building a chain of a few dozen nickelodeons and theaters. They parted ways in 1912 with Zucker later starting Paramount Pictures and a chain of movie houses, while Loew established the Loew's Theater chain and Metro Pictures, the precursor to MGM.

In 1914 The Mark Brothers opened the Strand Theatre in Manhattan. The Strand seated 2,800 people and was the first million-dollar theater palace built specifically for just showing motion pictures. Mitchel Mark made a good choice when he hired Samuel "Roxy" Rothafel to manage the theater. Rothafel later became the best-known movie showman in New York City, at the Capital and Roxy Theaters, later opening Radio City Music Hall with John D. Rockefeller Jr. and RCA chairman David Sarnoff. The success the Strand Theater resulted in the Mark Brothers opening a chain of dozens of theaters called Mark-Strand. In fact, the name Strand became synonymous with a movie theater, and in 1917 the New York State Supreme Court gave Mitchel Mark the sole right to use the name "The Strand" for a movie theater. There is a possibility they took the name Strand from The Strand, which was a street in London that was the center point for theaters and music halls during 19th century England.

The Mark Brothers may have been working on projects in other cities, but they never neglected and remained active in their hometown of Buffalo. The Empire Theater, which they opened in 1898, was later known as The People's Arcade downstairs and the Princess Theater upstairs, where they presented movies and vaudeville. The proprietors of the Peoples Arcade and the Grand Theatre, which was at this address in 1910 and 1911, was listed as Mark & Wagner or just R. Wagner (their partner Rudolph Wagner at the Vitascope). Wagner was also listed as the owner of the Little Hippodrome, next door at 263 Main Street, which opened in 1906. It was one of the first theaters to install a Wurlitzer Theater Organ, and it remained open until the early 1960s, when urban revitalization transformed Lower Main Street. They also opened the Edison Penny Arcade in the former Steve Brodie Saloon at 475 Main Street; Brodie was the daredevil that jumped off the Brooklyn Bridge and went over Niagara Falls. In 1906, they converted this saloon to a Buffalo location of the Automatic Vaudeville Company. In 1908 their former partner Rudolph Wagner reopened it as the Theatre Comique.

In 1910, they started began opening larger movie theaters in Buffalo like such as The Victoria at West Ferry at Grant Street. They also purchased, rebuilt and reopened the Academy Theater at 247 Main as a vaudeville house and opened the Family Theater, a combination vaudeville and movie theater, in the converted Buffalo Savings Bank at 441

Washington Street. In 1912 The Mark Brothers opened the 1,200 seat Strand at 355 Main Street and rebuilt the Lyric Theater a 1,500-seat vaudeville house at 449 Washington Street. Among the other theaters they built in Buffalo were, the Regent at 1365 Main Street and The Palace Theater in Shelton Square, prior to the Dewey Michael – Burlesque days.

The Mark Brothers relationship with the Lumiere Brothers films may have been one of the reasons that, in 1904, the French company Pathe opened their American Subsidiary, Pathe Company, in Buffalo. After being asked to join the Motion Picture Patents Company (MPPC), Pathe utilized the MPPC to distribute their French films and their Fort Lee, New Jersey films, including the *Perils of Pauline* productions. Pathe opened their film exchange or distribution center in Buffalo, and soon other film companies followed their lead. Prior to 1920, the area of Pearl, Franklin, Church and Swan Streets had film exchange offices for about 20 other distributors like Universal, United, Paramount, 20th Century Fox, MGM and Warner Brothers. Buffalo remained the distribution center for films to an area encompassing Syracuse to Cleveland, and Erie, Pennsylvania to Toronto, Ontario through the early 1960s.

Mitchel Mark, the older brother who initiated most of their business ventures, died at his home on Richmond Avenue in Buffalo in 1918 at age 50. His younger brother, Moe Mark, carried on their businesses and sold most their theaters to the Stanley Theater chain in 1926. Stanley Theaters later merged with Warner Brothers, to whom Moe sold the rest of the theaters in 1929. When he passed away in 1932, Moe was on the Warner Brothers board of directors. If Mitchel Mark had not died at an early age, who knows what else he and his brother would have accomplished.

MICHAEL SHEA

Michael Shea is acknowledged as the father of theater and vaudeville in Buffalo. Mitchel Mark was his contemporary and possibly accomplished more on a national scale. However, it was Shea who branded his theaters with his name and so it is the Shea name that is remembered.

Growing up in South Buffalo's First Ward, at age 15 Michael Shea left school to work as a laborer on the docks and later as an ironworker. In 1884, when he was 25, he opened a saloon at 535 Elk Street. Still living at his parents' 244 Katherine Street home, he was saving his money to implement his ideas for entertaining the residents of Buffalo. He had big plans.

In 1892 Shea put his ideas in motion when he opened Shea's Music Hall at 11 Clinton Street, in the Arcade building. It was located next to Robinson's Musee Theater, in the hall that had been the Opera House I. Music Halls were popular with the working class in England for decades but this was one of the first to open in the U.S. To provide an authentic music hall experience Shea hired performers from England and France for week long engagements. The Music Hall differed from the theater because patrons were seated at tables, could drink alcohol beverages and smoke tobacco while watching the show. This venture abruptly ended when the Arcade Building was destroyed by a fire on December 14, 1893. After the Arcade burned down, Robinson moved his Musee Theater to the Court Street Theater. The Brisbane Building was constructed on the site of the former Arcade Building.

Michael Shea remained in business after the fire, by opening the Shea's Tivoli on Washington Street. This business was diagonally across the street from the former Arcade Building and next door to and south of the Lafayette Hotel. The Tivoli was similar to Shea's Music Hall, as the word Tivoli was the name brand for Music Halls throughout the British Empire. The entertainment offered was of music hall style and anticipated the advent of vaudeville because he also booked singers, actors, acrobats, jugglers, magicians, trained animals and novelty acts.

In 1895 there were articles in the Buffalo newspapers that Shea was planning to open Shea's Music Hall on the site of the former John Seifert Saloon on Washington Street near East Huron. The plans were made but that hall never opened.

SHEA'S MUSIC HALL IN THE ARCADE BUILDING
Photo: Picture Book of Earlier Buffalo

SHEA'S GARDEN THEATRE
Photo: Buffalo History Museum

His next venture was Shea's Garden Theater on Pearl Street at Niagara. This was in the former Casino Skating Rink and Casino Palm Garden. When Shea moved into this location in 1898, it featured a ten-piece orchestra directed by Henry Marcus and it was his first theater totally committed to vaudeville entertainment. To improve the reputation of the theater and comply with the national vaudeville movement, he banned smoking and the drinking of alcohol beverages in the building.

Being an early vaudeville theater, many memorable events happened or were reputed to have happened at the Garden Theater. Buffalo native Charmian performed the first striptease act in Buffalo and one of the first in the country by throwing her jacket and garter into the audience during her trapeze act. According to legend, when Will Rogers first appeared at The Garden he only did stunts with his lasso, rope act. After watching Rogers' show, Michael Shea suggested that adding a little monologue would enhance his act. Eddie Cantor played one of his first dates at the Garden. Mae West and her sister had an act combining dancing and acrobatics, W.C. Fields did comedy juggling with cigar boxes and George M. Cohan, as a child, performed with his parents and sister as the Four Cohans. When Shea moved out of the Garden Theater in 1905, it became a burlesque house run by William Graham.

In 1905 Shea moved into the Court Street Theater and renamed it Shea's Vaudeville House on Court Street. This was a larger and more elaborate theater so he needed access to more entertainers. In 1900 Michael Shea's brother suggested to Keith and Albee that they form an association to assist with booking vaudeville acts, similar to The Syndicate that was established by Klaw & Erlanger for legitimate theater. This resulted in the

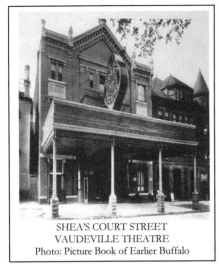

SHEA'S COURT STREET
VAUDEVILLE THEATRE
Photo: Picture Book of Earlier Buffalo

formation of the Vaudeville Managers Association (VMA). In 1906 this was expanded to the United Booking Office (UBO) which controlled the booking of vaudeville acts, initially across the Northeast and eventually across the country. The UBO benefited both the theaters' managers (access to more performers and the break-up of packaged tours) and the performers (access to more theaters and better routing between engagements). This organization also benefited Michael Shea because he now had access to all the top vaudeville acts in the country and could bring them to perform at his Buffalo theater.

1914 was a significant year for Michael Shea, because he opened the Hippodrome Theaters in both Buffalo and Toronto. The site of the Buffalo Hippodrome had an interesting history. It was the location of the initial home of Buffalo's first mayor Ebenezer Johnson, which after it burned down was replaced by the North Presbyterian Church, the first venue where Jenny Lind performed in Buffalo. The church was demolished and the property was sold to E.B. Keith, who after he did not build a theater on the site, sold it to Michael Shea. The Hippodrome's address was 580 Main Street, south of Chippewa, and it held over 2800 people with approximately 100 employees. It was built to show silent pictures and to accompany the movies they had a 26-member orchestra, which was called the Hipp Symphony Orchestra. The music directors at The Hippodrome were Harry Wallace and Al Greenberg. It was the director who had a contract with the theater. The musicians were hired and employed by the music director, not the theater. In 1922 the theater added a Wurlitzer organ and they also featured the Forova Dancers in conjunction with the movies. Special vaudeville programs were sometimes scheduled at The Hippodrome, but they were accompanied by movies. Above the theater was the Hippodrome Billiard Hall and next to it were several business locations, including the first office of Buffalo Optical. The name of the theater was changed to the Center Theater in 1951 and its location is now the approximate site of Fountain Plaza.

The Toronto Hippodrome was the largest vaudeville theater ever built in Canada. It seated 3,200 people and was located on Bay Street. This was not the first theater Shea operated in Toronto. Shea previously opened Shea's Victoria in 1910, which was built to replace an earlier small Sheas Theater on Younge Street. The Victoria was built for vaudeville and legitimate theater, but it also showed movies. Both locations were later operated by the Canadian Famous Players chain of motion picture theaters.

The Wurlitzer organs from both the Buffalo and Toronto theaters have histories worth recording. The Buffalo organ is now in the Colonial Theatre in Phoenixville, PA. This is the theater that is featured in the classic Science Fiction movie, *The Blob*. The Toronto organ was moved to the Maple Leaf Gardens and was the organ used for Toronto Maple Leaf hockey games. When the Maple Leaf Gardens was remodeled in 1963, the organ was put in storage until it was relocated to the great hall at Casa Loma in 1970. Both organs remain in use and are considered two of the best restored Wurlitzer Theater organs. The two Wurlitzer Theater organs that still exist in the WNY area are the organs at Shea's Buffalo and The Riviera Theatre in North Tonawanda.

Michael Shea felt all neighborhoods should have a theater of first magnitude. It was Shea's belief that a theater should capture the imagination of the movie goer and with a grandiose detailed setting, lift him to a place where he would feel his dreams were coming to life on the silver screen. That is what he accomplished with the opening of the North Park Theatre on Hertel Avenue in North Buffalo.

Upon its opening in 1920 the *Buffalo Evening Times* proclaimed the North Park as "Buffalo's finest neighborhood theatre", with its décor rivaling "in beauty and appointment that of any opera house in America". It was designed by Buffalo architect Harry Spann and included six murals that were created by Pan Am painter Raphael Beck. Above the marquee was an Arts Nouveau stained glass window. The theater became the cornerstone of the North Buffalo business district and was the first of the neighborhood theaters that were opened by Shea. Other neighborhood theaters included the Seneca, Elmwood, Bailey and Kensington. Shea's Seneca, which opened in 1930, was his largest regional theater, seating over 2,000 people and was also designed by Harry Spann.

In 1926 Michael Shea opened his flagship Shea's Buffalo at 646 Main Street. It was designed by Chicago architects C.W. and George L. Rapp to resemble the opulent baroque opera houses of Europe from the

16th and 17th century. The interior was designed by Louis Comfort Tiffany, the furnishings were supplied by Chicago's Marshall Field Company and included immense Czechoslovakian crystal chandeliers. The original budget was one million dollars, but no expenses were spared so the building costs escalated to almost two million dollars. To provide a basis for the magnitude of this cost, during the mid-1920s a new house cost $3,000 and a Model A Ford cost $1,000. The theater originally seated over 4,000 people and was designed for movies and live performances. Due to the size, elegance and prestige of the theater, all the biggest name acts performed at Shea's Buffalo when they came to Buffalo.

Shea's theaters flourished until the Great Depression began after the stock market crash in October 1929. It was estimated that during the depression Michael Shea was losing approximately one million dollars a year. However, Shea refused to lay off any of his employees. This was a verification of his devotion to his employees and to providing entertainment for WNY.

Michael Shea retired in 1930 and passed away in 1934, at 75 years old. After Shea's death V.R. McFaul owned and operated several dozen Sheas Theaters in the metro Buffalo area, until his death in 1955. McFaul was Shea's protégé, who at first personally ran the company and later formed a corporation to manage the operations, with the stockholders being McFaul, Loew's and Paramount Theaters.

LEGACY OF MICHAEL SHEA

The legacy of Michael Shea lives on today, not just from what he accomplished during his career, but due to future developments at some of his properties.

SHEAS SENECA was his largest regional theater and during the mid-1960s the side seats were removed, so teens could dance to bands performing before, between or after the movies. Eventually all the seats were removed and on September 27, 1968 the psychedelic rock club Psycus opened. This was one of the largest concert clubs in Western New York, with a capacity of over a thousand people and featuring national touring recording groups, along with Buffalo area bands. Buffalo's Robert Then coordinated the light show from the former private box balcony to the right of the stage. This presentation was equal to the San Francisco acid-rock light shows. The lobby was decorated in a black light accented Alice in Wonderland theme and the ballroom was filled by throbbing strobe lights and liquid bubble light shows projected on the walls, ceiling and stage. Psycus never obtained a liquor license and was only open a little over a year.

In the area above the commercial space facing Seneca Street, was The Sky Room bar, restaurant and banquet rooms. The theater entrance had been on the right side of the building and this entrance was on the left side, with an address of 2186 Seneca Street. In 1981, it opened as Rooftops and was later known as The Salty Dog and Country Club Skyroom. This club held over 1,000 people and was one of the main concert clubs during the early to mid-1980s. Performing at the club were touring acts like Inxs, Bon Jovi, Stevie Ray Vaughan and REM, along with metal shows by groups like Metallica and Wasp. The club had live music six nights a week and was always crowded. After the bar closed for the night, it became quite popular to stop at the Mighty Taco, located several doors away on Seneca Street.

The stores in the commercial area of the Seneca included an F.W. Woolworths, W.T. Grants, Endicott Johnson Shoes, along with other retail and service businesses. The theater auditorium was torn down, but the entrance lobby, the downstairs commercial space and upstairs former concert club space remain. In late 2016, it was announced that a development is planned at the property, to include apartments, a private function space, live theater and a restaurant.

THE CENTURY THEATER at 511 Main Street was owned by concert promoters Harvey & Corky in the 1970s. All the major touring bands, performed at The Century Theater. The balcony used to sway when everyone started stamping their feet to get the bands to play an encore. Harvey Weinstein from Harvey & Corky followed Michael Shea into the movie business. In 1979, years before they closed the concert promotion company, he and his brother Bob founded Miramax Films. After selling Miramax to Disney, they are now the owners of The Weinstein Company.

THE GREAT LAKES THEATRE at 612 Main Street was built in 1927 by Loews and Fox in the days when the major movie companies were building their own theaters across the country. Initially they presented movies and vaudeville at the Great Lakes which seated 3,300 people. When Shea's purchased it in 1931, that resulted in his company owning all the major theaters in the Main Street theater district and in downtown

Buffalo, except the Lafayette. Paramount was a partner in the 1931 purchase of the property but it was not until 1949 that the name was changed to The Paramount Theater. It was next door to the popular MacDoel's Restaurant at Main & West Chippewa. When the Paramount closed in 1965 the building became the nine story Nemmer Furniture Store. In 1996 the structure of the building was steel reinforced and four additional floors were added. It became City Centre Condos, the first upscale high rise condo complex in downtown Buffalo.

THE NORTH PARK THEATER fell into disrepair until it was purchased by attorney Thomas Eoanneau and restaurant owner Mike Christiano. The restoration was done by the same company that restored Sheas Buffalo, and the marquee was rebuilt to the original 1940s blueprints by the same company that originally designed and installed it, Flexlume Signs. The North Park is again, as Michael Shea envisioned, the cornerstone of the Hertel Avenue Business District.

THE RIVIERA THEATER on Webster Street in North Tonawanda was built by the Yellon family. It was designed by architects Leon H. Lempart & Sons, who drew the plans patterned after the Italian Renaissance style. It was originally called the Twin Cities Rivera and seated 1,140 people. When it opened, the theater initially featured movies, along with vaudeville and musical acts. The Mighty Wurlitzer Organ, which is a central fixture and still in operation at the theater, was installed for the grand opening on December 30, 1926 and during the first decade of operation featured organists Fred Meyer, Al Bollington, Dusty Rhodes, Jack Ward and Art Welgier.

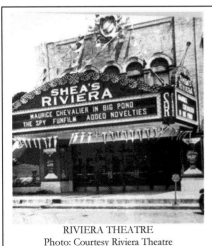

RIVIERA THEATRE
Photo: Courtesy Riviera Theatre

During the Depression, the theater was acquired by Shea, with the name being changed to the New Rivera and eventually to Shea's Riviera. It was operated by Shea's until the mid-1960s, when it became part of the Dipson chain. Afterwards, the Riviera had several different owners and all were concerned about the preservation of the Wurlitzer organ. Instrumental in protecting and upkeeping the organ from the

1940s through the early 1970s were Carlton and Harry Finch, along with organ technician William Hatzenbuher. The fate of the Wurlitzer at the theater was so important that in 1988 the Niagara Frontier Organ Society purchased the theater. They are now known as the Riviera Theatre and Organ Preservation Society (RTOPS) and they are still the current owners of the theater. The theater was placed on the Register of Historic Landmarks by the U.S. Department of the Interior on April 22, 1980.

The Riviera has been continually upgraded. An important improvement was the purchase of the former Genesee Theatre chandelier in 1974. This chandelier measures 10 feet in diameter, 14 feet high, contains 15,000 French crystals and has three circuits of 35 bulbs each, and was installed in the main theater dome. At the same time in 1974, they purchased the chandelier from the original Park Lane Restaurant for installation in the Riviera's outer lobby. The volunteers of the RTOPS, a not-for-profit corporation, spent thousands of hours restoring and upkeeping the theatre. They have been successful in obtaining grants to refurbish the marquee and to expand, along with upgrading, the facilities. The Riviera Theatre is currently utilized for organ concerts, special movies and concerts by touring rock, country and oldies acts. It is the cornerstone of the North Tonawanda Webster Street business district.

THE BELLEVUE THEATER at 1711 Main Street in Niagara Falls was built for vaudeville and movies in 1921, and was initially operated by B.F. Keith's RKO Company. In 1928 Sheas-Publix Theater Corp. signed a lease to run The Bellevue. It was the first location where Shea used RCA equipment for 100% talking movies. In the early 1960s it was purchased by the Strand Cataract Theater Corp. This is the same company that operated the Cataract & Strand Theaters on Falls Street near 1st Street. That theater was in the approximate location of where the Old Falls Street concerts and events are currently held. The Main Street theater was renamed the Rapids Theatre and continued in operation until the Main Street commercial area of Niagara Falls stagnated economically in the early 1970s, causing several businesses to close.

In 1974 the theater reopened as the Late Show discotheque, which was the largest concert style nightclub in the Niagara Falls area for over 20 years. Starting in 1995, the building went through several owners and business names until it was purchased by John Hutchins and again named The Rapids Theatre. These owners obtained several grants and the facility is again a concert and special events facility. An interesting feature of the venue is it is equipped with removable tables and chairs. This allows it to be configured for chairs, table seating or standing room, depending upon the event.

Along with several other former Michael Shea properties, The Rapids Theatre is reputed for its paranormal activity. Some people believe Michael Shea's spirit, or that of other departed souls, make their presence known at his former theaters. The Syfy channel *Ghost Hunters* did an episode at The Rapids Theater and put on a presentation at The Riviera. Personally, the author of this book, believes he had an encounter with Michael Shea's spirit backstage at Psycus in the former Seneca Theatre in early 1969.

SHEA'S BUFFALO fell into disrepair during the decline of Downtown Buffalo during the 1960s and 1970s. At that time, the building was owned by Leon Lawrence Sidell, and since 1948 it had been leased by Loew's Theater Corporation. When it became apparent that the theatre would default to the city of Buffalo for back taxes owed by Sidell, Loew's was planning to vacate the building and strip it of its contents, including the chandeliers, furniture, organ and projection equipment.

A community group called the "Friends of the Buffalo Theater," led by Curt Mangel, was formed to save the theater. In conjunction with the City of Buffalo they filed a legal counter claim that the items Loew's wanted to remove were part of the building and not included in the lease. The court ruled in favor of the City and Friends. Under the supervision of City Comptroller George O'Connell, the "Friends of the Buffalo Theater" were given the operating privileges of the building. They began the massive restoration of the theater with the assistance of government grants and a performance series. At the grand reopening in 1976, the featured performers were Cab Calloway, who performed at Shea's Buffalo during its opening week in 1926, and George Burns, who performed there in the 1940s.

The property is now operated by the Shea's O'Connell Preservation Guild Ltd., and they expanded the backstage and stage facilities. This has allowed them to accommodate the larger, high profile, touring theater productions. The Wurlitzer Organ was restored in cooperation with the American Theatre Organ Society. Now known as Shea's Performing Arts Center, it is the anchor of the Buffalo Theatre District and its Curtain Up! celebration every fall. It is befitting that the name of Michael Shea is still associated with theater in Buffalo.

LAFAYETTE THEATRE

On February 27, 1922, The Lafayette Square Theatre opened as a vaudeville and first run movie theater. It was designed by Leon H. Lampert, Jr. who was also the architect for several other Buffalo theaters: The Allendale, Center, Strand on Main Street, Hollywood in Gowanda, Riviera in North Tonawanda, Rapids in Niagara Falls and Palace in Lockport. The Lafayette was owned by A.C. Hayman, who also owned the Cataract Theater in Niagara Falls, which featured vaudeville, opera and elaborate shows.

The Lafayette was the only downtown theater that was not operated by Shea's and it was the only major theater that was not directly in the theater district on Main St. It was built in the space formerly occupied by the Lyric Theater and Opera House II, which had an address of 447 Washington Street. The auditorium portion of the Lafayette was built in their previous location. Since the lobby entrance faced Lafayette Square, the address of the theater was listed as 4 Broadway.

LAFAYETTE THEATRE
Photo: Buffalo History Museum

The Lafayette was designed so it could present off Broadway plays. The backstage area had three floors of dressing rooms, backstage production facilities comparable to New York City theaters, the largest stage in Western New York and the auditorium seated 4,200 people. The orchestra pit could accommodate a symphony orchestra, which was directed by Professor Ralph Schwartz. Their Hope-Jones Wurlitzer Theatre Organ was played by the most famous theater organist of the day, C. Sharpe Minor. The interior was patterned after European opera theatre designs, to obtain the best possible acoustics. The heating and ventilation system for the Lafayette Theatre and Office Building was so efficient, that a tunnel was built under Washington Street, and it was utilized to heat and ventilate the air at the Olympic Theater and businesses in that building.

In March 1927, The Lafayette premiered Al Jolson in *The Jazz Singer* because they were the only theater in WNY equipped for talking pictures. For this premiere The Lafayette installed Vitaphone sound. In May 1928, *Tenderloin,* starring Dolores Costello, premiered at The Lafayette. This was the first film in which the actors spoke their lines. Sound was only heard during musical numbers in *The Jazz Singer*, with exception of Jolson's introduction, "You ain't heard nothing yet."

In 1943 The Basil Theaters purchased the Lafayette Theater and office building. They continued offering first run movies and productions at the theater and the occupancy of the office building was rented to full capacity. As the downtown theater district started to decline, they sold the theater and office building to Benderson Development. The theater portion of the building was torn down in 1962, to create parking for the office building, and in 1972 the entire office building was demolished. The site of The Lafayette Theater and office building is now a parking lot, across the street from the Downtown Public Library.

OTHER THEATER OPERATORS

Many of the theaters in WNY changed hands, with different chains operating them at different times. The operators included: Sheas (Paramount-Publix), Buffalo Pictures (Paramount), New Buffalo Amusements (Loew's), Dipson Circuit, Schine Theaters, Basil Theaters and some companies that owned only a couple theaters.

BASIL THEATERS

Basil Theaters began when the Basil Brothers; Nick, Gus, Bill and Tom, expanded their confectionary stores to include a movie theater. In 1923, they opened the Clinton Strand Theater at 1800 Clinton Street in the Kaisertown section of East Buffalo. That was followed by the Linden at 943 Jefferson and Central Park at the corner of Main and Fillmore. In 1927, they purchased the existing Oriole Theatre at 1600 Genesee Street and replaced it with the Genesee Theatre. At that time, the Genesee was the fifth largest theater in WNY and the largest that was not located in downtown Buffalo. When it opened, in addition to movies, accompanied by a theater organ, they had an orchestra and presented live vaudeville. Basil Theaters moved their corporate offices to the second floor of the Genesee Theatre. By 1934 Basil had 14 theaters in WNY.

The Basil Theater chain and Dipson Theaters started working together on some projects. In 1938, they formed Dipson-Basil Theatre Enterprises. Their first joint project was the Franklin and Ridge Theatres in Lackawanna and in 1939 they took over The Century Theater, originally the Loew's State, when Shea's Publix did not renew their lease. That theater was managed by William Dipson and in addition to movies they featured live shows from big band to The Three Stooges. In 1940 Dipson purchased seven Basil Theaters.

In 1943 the opportunity of purchasing The Lafayette Theater from A.C. Hayman presented itself. With this acquisition, Basil moved their corporate offices from the Genesee to the seventh floor of the Lafayette Theater ten story office complex. At the Lafayette, they presented many live events and off-Broadway plays. They also worked on cross promotions with The Town Casino. Acts at the Town Casino would appear at the Lafayette to introduce movies and invite patrons to the nightclub after the movie. Many of the major acts performing at Lafayette Theatre productions or shows at The Town Casino would stay at the seventh floor penthouse suites, which the Basils maintained at the Lafayette Theater office tower.

The Lafayette became the Basils' showcase theater, but they still presented events at The Genesee. With over 2,000 seats, the Basils' showcased rock 'n' roll movies at the Genesee in the 1950s. Under the management of John Basil, who wrote the unpublished "True Theatre

History During the 20th Century," dancing was permitted in the back of the show. The theater was also the center for many Variety Club events but when movie attendance started to decline in the early to mid-50s, the Genesee Theatre became the largest and one of the first theaters to bring Adult Movies to Buffalo. The Basils leased the Varsity Theatre on Bailey to Fred Keller, who changed the name to The Circle Art, where he promoted what was called art films or foreign movies.

The Lafayette Theater was sold in 1962, along with most of their other properties. Many of their remaining theaters were purchased by Dipson Theaters in the late 1960s. Basil was successful in selling all 25 of their WNY properties before their company ceased operations.

DIPSON AND OTHER THEATERS

Nikitas Dipson first entered the theater business in 1926 when he purchased The Palace Theatre (now the Reg Lenna Center for the Arts) in Jamestown, New York. It opened in 1923 and featured high class vaudeville and short films. He operated the theater on the same format until he leased it in 1930 to Warner Brothers theaters but Dipson retained ownership of the property. Dipson had started his business in Batavia during the 1920s and originally concentrated on theaters in the outlying towns of WNY. In 1939, he incorporated his business and moved into the Buffalo market, working independently by taking over some of the leases Sheas did not renew and formed a company with Basil Theaters to operate other theaters. Dipson eventually purchased most of the Basil properties and became the largest locally based movie theater chain in WNY. They owned or operated movie and drive-in theaters in New York, Pennsylvania, Ohio and West Virginia. Dipson still has several properties in WNY and their headquarters is located on Evans Road in Williamsville, NY.

Dewey Michaels is remembered as the owner of the Palace Burlesk Theater in Shelton Square, but his family also owned other theaters. The Plaza Theatre on William and Monroe opened in 1915 and was one of several black vaudeville theaters in Buffalo. It held 1,000 people, and it was said that Sammy Davis, Jr. performed there when he was five years old. Other than theaters on Main Street, it was one of the last vaudeville theaters in Buffalo. Hound Dog Lorenz held early rock 'n' roll shows at

The Palace trying to make it Buffalo's version of the Apollo Theater in NYC. The Palace closed in 1964.

In addition to the downtown, neighborhood and matinee theaters operating in the city of Buffalo, there were regional theaters, which were considered someplace between a downtown and neighborhood theater, in the suburbs and towns of WNY. When the Palace Theater in Hamburg opened, it had a ten-piece orchestra to provide the music during the movies. Other regional theaters were the Depew on Main Street in Depew, the Aurora in East Aurora, the Palace in Lockport, Diana in Medina, Joylan in Springville and the Hollywood in Gowanda, the Riviera in North Tonawanda and the Star Theater on Young Street in Tonawanda, overlooking the Erie Canal.

DRIVE- IN THEATERS

Drive-in theaters were a dominant form of entertainment from the 1940s through the 1980s. During their peak, there were over 4,000 in the U.S., but less than one tenth of them remain. In 1941 the first drive-ins were opened in WNY. They were the Buffalo Drive-In on Harlem Road in Cheektowaga and the Niagara Drive-In on Niagara Falls Boulevard near the Youngman Expressway. Other suburban Buffalo drive-ins included the Aero (Union Road across from the current location of The Galleria Mall), Broadway (on Broadway near Harlem), Delaware (Tonawanda at Delaware and the Youngman Expressway), The I-290 (replaced and became the new name of the Delaware), Park Drive-In (Orchard Park Road in West Seneca), Sheridan (Ensminger Road in Tonawanda), the Star (Lake Road in Blasdell), Twin (Walden and Dick Road in Cheektowaga), and Wehrle (Wehrle and the Transit in Lancaster).

In the outlying areas, the drive-in theaters were the Boulevard in Wheatfield, the Falls Auto Vue in the town of Niagara, the Delevan on Route 16 in Delevan, the Grandview in Evans, the Lockport in Gasport, the Nite-Way in Pendleton, the Skyway in Athol Springs, the Starlite in the town of Niagara, the Sunset in Middleport and the Transit in Lockport.

One of the main reasons the drive-in theaters were closed was due to them being built on prime land in the suburbs, businesses like large department stores, home improvement stores and even medical centers wanted the land for their projects. With the decline in patrons, the drive-in owner could make a larger profit by leasing or selling the land to a developer, than by continuing to operate them as drive-in theaters.

LEGITIMATE THEATRE

In addition to the vaudeville halls, burlesque houses and movie theaters, there were theaters that presented what was called legitimate theatre – plays and musicals. Theatrical productions were nothing new to Buffalo because they were presented at early theaters like the Old Eagle Theater (St. James Hall), Buffalo Theater and Metropolitan Theater (Academy of Music). Around the turn of the century the Star Theater and other theaters produced plays. However, it was in the 20th century that off-Broadway style productions started being staged in Buffalo at the Teck Theater, Erlanger and Lafayette Theater.

Located at the corner of Main and Edward, The Buffalo Music Hall, erected for the German Young Men's Christian Association was remodeled by Jacob Schoelkoph into the Teck Theater in 1900. The first production was a play by actress Lillian Russell on September 10, 1900, with a sold-out show attended by 2,000 people. It was produced by the Shubert Stock Company, who would later lease the theater in 1908. In 1912, Buffalo author Marian de Forest's dramatization of Louisa May Alcott's "Little Women" premiered at the Teck Theatre. When the Dockstaders Minstrels performed there an unknown member of the troupe brought the house down with his performance. That singer's name was Al Jolson.

When the Shuberts leased the Teck, they often used it for rehearsals and as a showcase theater for their new touring plays and musicals. Following the Shuberts lead, other production companies, including musical groups also tested their new shows in Buffalo. That was because Buffalo had the

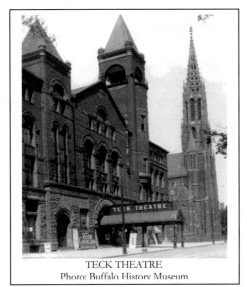

TECK THEATRE
Photo: Buffalo History Museum

reputation of being a tough market. It was said that if you could make it in Buffalo, you could make it anywhere.

The Shuberts continued presenting plays and musicals at The Teck Theater until 1933. It was closed for several years until it reopened as the Teck movie theater in 1945. When Pearl Street was extended to Main Street in the 1980s, to allow traffic from The Kensington Expressway (Route 33) to be directed downtown, the rear of the building was demolished. The remainder of the theater was demolished in 1992, and the lot has been vacant since that time.

The Erlanger Theater was built in 1927 by Ellsworth Statler across the street from his Statler Hotel on Delaware Avenue. The facility was built for legitimate theater but presented some acts that could be considered vaudeville. It was leased to Abraham Lincoln Erlanger, after whom the theater was named. Erlanger, along with his partner, Marc Klaw, formed the Theatrical Syndicate in 1896. This organization gave them almost monopolistic control of the bookings at legitimate and vaudeville theaters in the country. Over the next 16 years they set the rates and controlled who would be hired at over 700 houses. They could make or break any entertainer and their shameless greed made them countless enemies.

ERLANGER THEATRE
Photo: Buffalo History Museum

One of the biggest adversaries to Erlanger & Klaw were the Shubert brothers, Lee, Jacob and Sam Shubert. The Shuberts, who are considered responsible for establishing the Broadway theater district in New York City broke the Theatrical Syndicates monopoly by establishing the Shubert Organization. During the 1920s The Shuberts owned, operated or managed over 1,000 theaters and by the 1940s they controlled over half of the theaters on Broadway.

After Erlanger filed bankruptcy, the Shuberts took over management of The Erlanger Theater in Buffalo. Although the Erlanger's acoustics were inferior to The Teck - there was an acoustically dead spot in the center of the theater - the Shuberts continued booking the top touring theatrical productions at The Erlanger until the property was transferred to the Dipson Theater chain in 1941. The Erlanger was then operated as the 120 Building by the Kavinoky Family and discontinued as a theater in 1956. After that it functioned as commercial space, providing the offices for Lawley Insurance. In 2007 building was razed for the construction of The Federal Courthouse.

Katharine Cornell's acting career earned her the nickname of "The First Lady of the Theater," a title she shared with her friend and contemporary, Helen Hayes. Cornell was born in Germany in 1893, where her father was studying medicine at the University of Berlin. Upon returning to Buffalo, the family moved into a home at 174 Mariner Street, in the Allentown district of Buffalo. Katharine acted in school plays and observed family productions in her grandfather's attic theater in his home at 484 Delaware Avenue. She also performed at the Buffalo Studio Club parlor theater located at 508 Franklin Street and attended the University of Buffalo. In 1915, following the death of her mother, Cornell moved to New York City where she joined the Jessie Bonstelle's theater company, which divided its summer performances between Detroit and Buffalo. After achieving fame on Broadway in New York City, Cornell never returned to live in the "Queen City" but she would bring her productions to her hometown of Buffalo on a regular basis. Many of these productions were presented at The Erlanger Theater.

THE STUDIO ARENA had its beginnings in 1920 when Frederick Kitson Cowley formed the Buffalo Players, a community theater group. Their first production was at The Allendale Theater in 1923. The Buffalo Players included members of Knox, Schoellkoph and several other prominent Buffalo families. In 1927 Jane Keeler assumed leadership of The Buffalo Players, along with artistic director Sheldon V. Kiele and president Lars Potter. The Buffalo Players changed their name to The Studio School of Theatre and moved into a second-floor lodge meeting hall at Elmwood and Anderson. They later relocated to the Gayety Theatre and in 1934 moved to the second-floor concert hall of the Teck Theater. The Studio Theater School was incorporated with the playhouse as an educational institution in 1936, under the New York State Board of Regents. In 1937 the organization purchased the former Universalist Church at 305 Lafayette, which was home to The Studio Theatre School until the early 1960s.

Under the leadership of Neal DuBrock the Studio Theatre School evolved into a professional Equity Theater. In 1965 the former Town Casino Nightclub at 681 Main Street was transformed into The Studio Arena Theatre, a not-for-profit professional regional theater. They moved across the street to the former Palace Burlesque Theater at 710 Main Street in 1978. When they moved, their former home in the Town Casino became the UB Theater and Dance Department, UB Pfeiffer Theatre.

The Studio Arena filed for bankruptcy in 2011 and neighboring Shea's Performing Arts Center assumed ownership renaming it Shea's 710 Main Theatre. During the history of The Studio Arena, it produced many notable plays and world premieres, including works by Edward Albee, A.R. Gurney and Lanford Wilson. In 1970, Buffalo West Side native and Cathedral School, Canisius High School, Buffalo State graduate Tom Fontana staged his first play at Studio Arena, before moving on to a successful career in television with shows like *St. Elsewhere*, *Oz* and more. During the 1960s – 1980s, new actors, including Kathy Bates, Glenn Close, Olympia Dukakis, John Goodman, Jon Voight, Christopher Walken and Buffalo native Christine Baranski, made early career appearances at Studio Arena.

THE SHAW FESTIVAL is held in Niagara-on-the-Lake in Ontario. The Buffalo connection is that the University at Buffalo professor and philanthropist Calvin Rand, assisted Ontario attorney and playwright Brian Dohety in starting the festival. Their first production was in 1962 at the Court House Theatre. The opening of their new Festival Theater in 1973 was attended by Queen Elizabeth. This festival of George Bernard Shaw plays is the second largest repertory theater company in North America.

BUFFALO THEATER COLLECTIVE was started by Neal Radice when he began presenting plays in 1980. When Greyhound built its new bus terminal, the city of Buffalo purchased the old Greyhound terminal on Main Street in the theater district for use as a police station. The police were not using the entire terminal, which was a set for the 1979 movie *Hide in Plain Sight*, so Radice leased space from the city to open Alleyways Theater. In 2000, when the city built a new downtown police station, Radice purchased the property and now presents plays in the entire 33,000 square foot building.

HALLWALLS was founded in 1974 as a contemporary art, interdisciplinary facility for visual artists, musicians, writers, filmmakers, video and performance artists. The founders, included Diane Bertolo,

Charles Clough, Nancy Dwyer, Robert Longo, Cindy Sherman and Michael Zwack, who carved out a performance space in a former ice house on Essex Street on Buffalo's West Side. Their mission has been to bring the newest and most challenging work in the contemporary arts to the community in an eclectic programming mix. Due to attacks on artists' free speech, Hallwalls has taken a role of being a fearless advocate for artistic freedom and innovation. In 2006, they moved its exhibition galleries and performance facilities to Ani DiFranco's Babeville in the former Asbury Delaware Methodist Church on Delaware and Tupper.

IRISH CLASSICAL THEATER. In 1985 brothers Vincent and Chris O'Neill, originally from Dublin, were performing a play in the dining room of a Buffalo hotel. Former Dubliners Josephine Hogan and Dr. James Warde assisted the O'Neill brothers in forming the Irish Classical Theater. They performed on rented stages until they established a permanent home at the Calumet Arts Café on Chippewa. In 1999, they moved into the St. Andrew's Theatre on Main Street, across from Sheas.

SHAKESPEARE IN THE PARK was founded in 1976 by Saul Elkin as part of the University of Buffalo theater department. It is held in Delaware Park on a Tudor style stage, which is at the base of a hill that serves as a natural amphitheater. Seating consists of blankets and lawn chairs. The production takes place during June, July and August on Tuesdays through Sundays and draws an audience of over 40,000 spectators each summer. It is one of the largest free Shakespeare festivals in the country. In 1991, Shakespeare in the Park became an independent non-profit organization, with actors seasonally hired during an annual open audition process. A small troupe of professional actors are employed year-round for presentations and workshops on Shakespeare at area high schools.

THEATER OF YOUTH (TOY) was formed in 1972 by Rosalind Cramer and Toni Smith Wilson at Daemen College. They relocated to the Center Theatre and Franklin Street Theatre before purchasing the Allendale Theatre in 1986. After a 13 year, $3.5 million renovation project, the Allendale Theater was saved and reopened in 1999. The objective of TOY is to stimulate the imagination, nurture the creative spirit and enhance the education of young people by engaging them in relevant, child centered and professionally produced live theater programs. Employing over 60 actors and craftsmen, each season over 30,000 children attend TOY performances.

COLLEGES. In addition to The Theater of Youth, which originated at Daemen College, Western New York colleges have made contributions to the theater in Buffalo. The Katharine Cornell Theatre, named after the Buffalo stage actress, opened on the University of Buffalo Amherst Campus in 1974. It is used for the university's acting and dance classes, in addition to being the venue for student produced plays. UB theater graduates include Maury Chaykin (character actor in over 150 films), Shep Gordon (manager of Blondie and Alice Cooper), Ted Kryczko (VP of Walt Disney Records and two-time Grammy winner) and Rob Liederman (Buffalo comic and director).

At Buffalo State College, Rockwell Hall has been the flagship building of the campus and its performing arts center since the building opened in 1931. The Performing Arts Center was refurbished and reopened in 1987, only to see another $1.2 million upgrade in 2005. The Louis P. Ciminelli Recital Hall is also located on the third floor of Rockwell Hall in the former Burchfield Penney Art Center, which in 2008 moved to a new building that was built on the Buffalo State campus.

In 1908 D'Youville College opened its theater known as the Auditorium. It was closed in 1972 and during the 1970s a professional theater company called Stage Center presented productions in the Porter View Room at the campus. By 1979 there were sufficient funds to restore the theater, which reopened as The Kavinoky Theater in 1980. Under the direction of David Lamb, this is a paid professional actor's theater and over the past 37 years they have produced over 200 shows. Since its inception, The Kavinoky has had an influence on live Buffalo theater. There are currently over thirty production companies in Western New York and many of the actors and artistic directors began their careers at The Kavinoky.

The Buffalo Theatre District Association was founded in 1979 to promote the neighborhood known as the Theatre District. Its members are the businesses in this downtown Main Street area and in 1981 they started Curtain Up! the annual September event that begins the theater season. Participating theaters have been extended beyond just the vicinity of the theater district and Curtain Up! now marks the beginning of the theater season for all community and professional theaters in WNY.

END OF AN ERA

DECLINE OF VAUDEVILLE & BURLESQUE & MOVIE THEATERS

The decline of vaudeville began during the Depression. Due to high unemployment levels the public did not have the money to attend vaudeville shows. Many people chose to stay home and listen to the radio. With fewer people attending vaudeville shows, the theaters could no longer afford to pay the top acts, resulting in these performers moving to Hollywood to appear in the movies.

The Jazz Singer was released in 1927 and it was the first full length motion picture synchronized with sound. The movie was set in a beer garden and a vaudeville theater, with six songs sung by Al Jolson and songs by other performers in the movie. Many vaudeville performers were tired of the constant travel and two or three shows a day in the theaters. They could now perform their act once in a movie and get a big payday. However, this meant a successful routine that took time to develop and was performed repeatedly at vaudeville theaters for years, could be shown once in a movie and be seen by everyone during the run of a film. The big-name performers no longer needed to tour all year but some of the lesser known performers were burnt out after just one performance of their act in a movie.

The end of big time vaudeville occurred when the Keith Albee Orpheum Theater Corp (KAO) was purchased by Joseph Kennedy and his associates. The 700 KAO theaters were converted to RCA movie theaters. Vaudeville continued at smaller theaters, without the big-name attractions, but it lost the luster it had during its heyday. Some small-scale vaudeville theaters remained in Buffalo and those that survived were closed when television lured the remaining well-known acts to the small screen in the late '40s and early '50s.

With the decline of vaudeville, some of the performers moved back to burlesque theaters and burlesque style floor shows at night clubs in Western New York. Burlesque comedians like Red Foxx or Joe E. Ross were a major draw to theaters and night club shows but over time the importance of the comedian diminished. The most successful artists moved to TV variety shows or sitcoms, and the burlesque show was dominated by striptease acts. During the 1950s and 1960s, in addition to the Palace Theater, burlesque floor shows were still an attraction in Buffalo at nightclubs like Frank's Casa Nova, Federal Gardens, The Billboard Lounge, Stage Door and Old Barn in East Aurora. Public opinion began to turn against striptease shows, and by the 1970s very few burlesque floor show clubs remained. Their decline was attributed to regular nudity in motion pictures and nudity at gentlemen's clubs featuring topless dancers. Recently there has been a resurgence of burlesque shows, emphasizing the elaborate costuming, implied striptease and comedy, rather than the actual striptease aspect of the entertainment.

DECLINE OF DOWNTOWN MOVIE THEATERS

In the Buffalo area, there existed what was called a standard distribution system for motion pictures. A successful movie would initially be shown for about three weeks at the first run theaters, which were the downtown Buffalo and Niagara Falls theaters. They would then be shown for about a week at the perimeter theaters like the Star in Tonawanda, Palace in Lockport & Hamburg, Riviera in North Tonawanda and Aurora Theaters. That would be followed by a week at the large neighborhood theaters like the Kensington, North Park, Elmwood and Bailey. The following week they would be shown at the medium neighborhood theaters like the Victoria. Colvin, Apollo, Niagara, Riverside and Granada. After that run was completed the movies went to the smaller neighborhood theaters like the Lovejoy, Strand, Seneca, Capitol, Rivoli, Broadway, Genesee and the remaining nickelodeon or matinee theaters. Some of the movie houses could change position in the sequence in which they received the films. If a movie did not do well at the first run theaters, it progressed more quickly through the distribution cycle.

This standard distribution system remained until about 1962, when the James Bond movie *Dr. No* premiered at the Colvin Theater. Drive-In theaters started gaining in popularity and they started receiving movies sooner. First run movies began premiering at a few neighborhood, regional and drive-in theaters. When the downtown theaters lost their distribution prominence, The Lafayette closed in 1962, followed by the Paramount in 1964. Due to the advent of shopping plazas, with free parking, fewer people were shopping downtown, and with roving groups of teenagers in the downtown area, it was perceived to be an unsafe place to go after dark. The downtown theaters became too expensive to operate, and in 1965 General Cinemas opened their first Cinema 1 & 2 in the Boulevard Mall. Due to the preponderance of multiplex theaters opening in the suburbs, the downtown theaters and most of the neighborhood theaters closed. The construction of the Buffalo subway further contributed to the demise of any theaters that remained in the downtown theater district.

Currently there are few movie theaters from the glory days of motion pictures still open in WNY. The only remaining downtown theater that presents movies or live theater productions is Sheas Performing Arts Center. Close to downtown on Allen Street, The Allendale is home to the TOY theater. Other remaining theaters include The Riviera in North Tonawanda, North Park on Hertel, Palace in Hamburg, New Angola in Angola, Joylan in Springville, Hollywood in Gowanda and the Palace in Lockport. The only remaining drive in theater in the immediate Buffalo area is The Transit Drive-In in Lockport, while the Sunset Drive-In is still open in Middleport and, south of East Aurora the Delevan Drive-In is still in operation on Route 16 near Lime Lake.

The suburban multiplex theaters have been upgraded to reclining seating and state of the art sound. The IMAX and 3D movie screens make you feel like you are inside the movie. However, movie theaters no longer have that nostalgic feeling of excitement that you experienced when going to a movie premier or matinee, while enjoying reasonably priced candy, soda and buttered popcorn. It is no surprise that Michael Shea's ghost has been reported at some of his former theaters. Possibility his spirit is looking for the nostalgic good old days of theater, which can never be totally recaptured.

4

AMUSEMENT PARKS

CRYSTAL BEACH

Baby Boomers will remember Crystal Beach as the amusement park that you drove to in your parents' car or arrived by bus on neighborhood community days. It was riding the Comet, spending an hour in The Magic Carpet fun house, eating cotton candy, playing skee-ball in the arcade, sitting on the beach or staying at one of the many summer cottages. If you are not a baby boomer you probably heard your parents or grandparents talking about Crystal Beach or you remember going there when you were young, before it closed in 1989.

For prior generations, to get to Crystal Beach they took the one hour ride on *The Canadiana* from the foot of Commercial Street in downtown Buffalo. Crystal Beach had many amusement park rides, including the legendary wooden roller coaster the Cyclone, which preceded the Comet. However, the main attraction was the Crystal Ballroom, which opened in 1925. This ballroom had the largest dance floor on the continent and it was where the most popular Swing Era Big Bands from both the United States and Canada performed. Touring bands were featured at The Crystal Ballroom but most of the bands or orchestras came from the Buffalo or Southern Ontario area.

CRYSTAL BEACH BALLROOM WITH THE CYCLONE ROLLER COASTER
Photo Courtesy William Kae

The first recorded dance at Crystal Beach was in 1891. Originally there was a dance hall called The Crystal Beach Dance Pavilion in the area where the Giant Coaster was later located. When the Crystal Ballroom was built for the 1925 season, the dance pavilion became a roller rink. Through the 1925 season there was also a vaudeville theater on the Crystal Beach midway called The Crystal Theatre which also presented plays. The first advertised theatrical production was held during the summer of 1894.

One of the first bands featured at Crystal Beach Amusement Park was the 74th Regimental Band. They were also considered the premier entertainment at WNY gazebos and parks starting in the 1890s. During 1898, the 74th Regimental Band provided afternoon and evening concerts every Thursday and Sunday. The concert series was so successful that they performed at the park on a regular basis for almost 20 years. They expanded their concert schedule and also performed on the Crystal Beach Line steamers. The director of the 74th Regiment was Justus C. Miller, who was also the leader of The Miller Brass Band. The orchestra expanded to 35 members, with both military and civilian members from both bands, and was called Miller's 74th Regimental Band. Their final performance at Crystal Beach was in 1916.

One of the members of the 74th was xylophonist and drummer Fred Asmus. In 1918 he began performing with the Lake Erie Excursion Company Orchestra on the company's steamers the *Canadiana* and *Americana*, and at the original dance hall located near the grove. There was also a band called The Crystal Beach Brass Band, but starting in 1922, The Crystal Beach Orchestra became the house band at the park. Asmus was the director of this 17-member orchestra and a smaller five-piece version that performed on the steamers. They performed at Crystal Beach through the 1924 season. Asmus was also a soloist with orchestras at Buffalo movie theaters and wrote several songs that were published by H.C. Weasner & Company, a music publishing company that was based in Buffalo.

Harold Arlen's band The Southbound Shuffles played on the *Canadiana* during the summer of 1923. The entire band earned $80.00 per week, plus meals, for performing on the daily cruises from Buffalo to Crystal Beach. They also performed at the Hotel Royal

HAROLD ARLEN
Photo: Courtesy William Kae

Casino at Bay Beach, which was a short walk from the Crystal Beach Pier. The band changed its name to the Buffalo Yankee Six, with the members being Joe Rosen (drums), Ray Walter (trumpet), Stan Meyers (sax), Warren Bullock (sax), Ralph LaGuardia (guitar) and Hyman Arluck (piano/vocals); Harold Arlens's original name. They expanded to an eleven-piece orchestra and became the house band at Crystal Beach during the summers of 1924 and 1925, having the distinction of being the last house band at the old Dance Pavilion and the first band to perform at the new Crystal Ballroom. Arlen relocated to NYC, but his band renamed themselves the Southbound Shufflers and returned without Arlen as the Crystal Ballroom house band for the summer of 1926.

The Crystal Beach Ballroom which opened on May 1, 1925, was an architectural wonder, as the entire structure was supported by steel girders, without using any support beams. The dance floor measuring 165 by 230 feet, providing almost 38,000 square feet of space, with room for 1,500 couples. Between the break wall and the dance hall a promenade was built with benches where the dancers could go outside to take a break. The wall facing the promenade was comprised of sliding doors, which could be opened to let in the cool breeze coming off the lake. On either ends of the hall was a balcony, where spectators could watch the dancers below or just relax and listen to the music. Originally the bandstand was located in the center of the building. It was an octagonally shaped stage and had eight wooden deflectors to disperse the music throughout the hall. Later the bandstand was moved to the south end of the hall, complete with a new amplification system.

In 1925, The Cliff Keyser Orchestra started playing on the steamers and at the Ballroom. Two members of this group were Sal Rizzo and Angie Maggio. Sal was later the president of the Buffalo Musicians Union and his son Tommie Rizzo later became a regular performer on the *Canadiana* and at the Ballroom. Starting in 1927, Angie Maggio's Crystal Beach Orchestra was appearing at the park. They were regulars at Crystal Beach through 1936 and during the off season the band performed at events and ballrooms in Buffalo. The members of the band included: Angie Maggio, Joseph Scotch, Angelo Siracuse, Thomas Sicurella, Louis Quitt, John Elliott, Joseph Puglisi and Clayton Spooner.

Harold Austin began his 20-year association with Crystal Beach in 1935. Crystal Beach Amusement Park owner George Hall Sr. was impressed with Austin's operation of the Dellwood Ballroom in Buffalo.

Hall hired Austin to manage the entertainment at both the Crystal Ballroom and on the *Canadiana*. In addition to performing with his band at The Ballroom, he brought in all the top big bands like: Stan Kenton, Woody Herman, the Dorsey Brothers, Glenn Miller, Gene Krupa, Artie Shaw and Lionel Hampton. In 1938 the Harold Austin Orchestra included Harold Austin, Leonard Sciolino, Bobby Nicholson, Arnold Tenglund, Pat Vastola, Edward Heim, Gus Farrell, Tiny Schwartz, Bill Jors, Cliff Sawson, John McFadden, Phil Todd and Ralph Westfield.

In the 1940s the "Stand-in Band Rule" law was passed in Canada. Even though Crystal Beach had always employed both U.S. and Canadian bands, this regulation required that if a U.S. band was hired to play at a Canadian club, a Canadian band of the same size had to be hired and paid local union scale to perform an equal amount of time at the club. This resulted in non-stop entertainment at the Crystal Beach Ballroom where a United States and Canadian Big Band would alternate sets.

BALLROOM DANCERS
Photo: Courtesy William Kae

There were two different policies for admitting people to the Crystal Ballroom. The "Social Plan" was a pay one price admission charge, with no restrictions to the dance floor. This plan was applied when well-known orchestras performed. The "Park Plan" was the regular admission policy to the Ballroom. With this plan, no admission charge was required to enter the Ballroom but a couple had to pay ten cents a dance and ushers, with a rope, herded people off of the dance floor after each song. With a 1,500-couple capacity and the bands playing 20 songs an hour (three minutes a song), this generated $12,000 during a four-hour dance; quite a lot of money during the 1920-1950s.

The most popular Canadian bands that performed at Crystal Beach were the Bert Niosi Orchestra, Maynard Ferguson Band and Benny Louis Band. Bert Niosi started playing at Crystal Beach with his 16 piece orchestra in 1935 and continued regular appearances through the 1950s. His performances at The Palais Royale dance hall at Sunnyside Amusement Park in Toronto, where Niosi's Orchestra was the house band from 1932 to 1950, were broadcast on the radio by the Canadian

Broadcasting Company. Niosi was also the music director for three Canadian television shows from 1965–1979: *Four for the Road, Cross Canada Hit Parade* and *The Tommy Hunter Show*. These radio and television performances, along with his dance hall performances, earned Niosi the title of "Canada's King of Swing".

While still a teenager, Maynard Ferguson led the house band at Crystal Beach during the summers of 1946 and 1947. Ferguson then moved to the U.S., toured with different big bands and recorded 46 soundtracks for Paramount Pictures. His band returned for a concert on Memorial Day in 1959 and in 1976 he released the hit single "Gonna Fly Now" from the movie *Rocky*. In 1985 his band was hired for a concert by "Friends of the Canadiana" to raise funds to save the steamer. Before that 1985 show he was quoted, in promotional material, as recalling the "Park Plan" policy of ten cents per dance that was in effect when he played at Crystal Beach 40 years earlier. "They didn't want me playing no long tunes, you know, because it was a dime a dance, and then they would rope the people off the dance floor."

Benny Louis was born in Niagara Falls, Ontario and he was the leader of the house band at Crystal Beach during the 1949, 1950 and 1951 seasons. He was known to audiences across Canada from his CBC nationally broadcast radio shows *Live from Casa Loma* in Toronto.

The big band era at Crystal Beach continued through the mid-50s and music at the Crystal Ballroom was discontinued with the 1967 season. In 1974 there was a fire that almost required the Ballroom to be demolished, but they were able to repair any structural damage. However, about one half of the dance floor was severely warped beyond repair from the water damage.

For detailed information on Crystal Beach and the people who performed there, see the following two books: *Crystal Beach Live*, by William D Kae. *Crystal Beach – The Good Old Days*, by Erno Rossi.

POLKA BANDS AT CRYSTAL BEACH

When big band swing concerts and ballroom dancing started to decline in the late 1950s, the Crystal Beach Ballroom began offering polka band concerts. Polka music was becoming popular in the late fifties and many of the cottages at Crystal Beach were owned by people of Polish heritage from the East Side of Buffalo, Kaisertown, Riverside, North Tonawanda and Cheektowaga/Depew area. Buffalo television aired some local polka dance party shows. The hiring of polka bands extending the life of live entertainment at the ballroom for another decade.

Starting in 1951, Frank Wojnarowski and his polka orchestra performed at Crystal Beach for eleven seasons. Hailing from Fairport Connecticut, Frank was one of the first band leaders to introduce polka music to ballrooms. He presented these shows at Crystal Beach, ballrooms throughout New England and areas of the Midwest like Detroit and Milwaukee. When WGR Television Channel 2 wanted to produce a local polka music show, they contacted Wojnarowski because of his popularity at Crystal Beach. The *Pic-A-Polka* show began airing in 1960 and at that time in Buffalo it had higher ratings than *The Ed Sullivan Show*.

Joe Macielag only spoke Polish until he entered grammar school. As a young boy, he learned Polish folk songs from his father, who emigrated from Poland, so Joe became proficient in Polish language enunciation. This resulted in Macielag becoming one of the most authentic Polish vocalists in Buffalo Polka music. His band the Melody Bells first performed at Crystal Beach in 1957 and returned on a regular basis through 1964. The Melody Bells started appearing on Frank Wojnarowski's *Pic-A-Polka* TV show and in 1960 they became the Pic-A-Polka Orchestra. Eventually Channel 2 realized Macielag was doing most of the work on the TV show, so they made him the host and featured vocalist. When the TV show ended in 1966, they retained the name of the Pic-A-Polka Orchestra. The members of the orchestra were Joe Macielag, Len Kubera, Ed Zasowskim Len Arent, Dan Arent, Dan Kuminski, Dick Sadowski, Jack Gburek and Edwin Chmielewski, who was the owner of Chimes Music Store in Cheektowaga NY.

Walt Jaworski was a Buffalo accordion player who performed at Crystal Beach during the 1962 and 1964 seasons. His polka band backed up Frankie Yankovic on the Channel 7 *Polka Time* television show in 1962. Frankie, who resided in Cleveland, was called "America's Polka King" because he was the first artist to win a Grammy Award in the Polka category. Walt Jaworski and his Orchestra released several singles on RCA Records. He and the Eddie Olinski Orchestra released an album together on the DALA Record Label, owned by Gene Wisniewki.

The Eddie Olinski Orchestra performed at Polka Town on Cayuga Road in Cheektowaga for five years during the 1950s. The venue was

EDDIE OLINSKI ORCHESTRA
Front row Carl Suhr, Eddie Olinski, Henry Winkowsk back row Larry Struzik, Bob Radominski,
Wally Pigeon, John Kuzma, Matt Kantor, Al Carlin   Photo: Courtesy William Kae

always crowded and the band used it as a home base to obtain dates outside of the Buffalo area. It was at here where they met Walt Ostanek, who had a polka orchestra that performed at Crystal Beach for three seasons. The members of the Eddie Olinski Orchestra were Eddie Olinski, Carl Suhr, Henry Winkowski, Larry Struzik, Bob Randominski, John Kuzma, Al Carlin, Matt Kantor and Wally Pigeon. They released two albums on DALA Records. When not performing with his orchestra, Eddie Olinski contributed to WNY entertainment by being an employee of Stoney Point Distributors (Ballantine, Utica Club and Heineken beers) for 22 years and Try-It Distributors for 21 years. Wally Pigeon was the owner of U-Crest Music in Cheektowaga. The Eddie Olinski Orchestra was the last band to perform at the Crystal Beach Ballroom during the summer of 1967, which was the last year of music at the park, until the music revival in the 1980s.

Many other amusement parks started booking rock bands during the 1960s and 1970s. Crystal Beach management decided against booking rock bands because at some other parks they attracted disruptive and rowdy crowds. These audiences were often under the influence of alcohol and/or drugs, resulting in violence that had to be defused by the police. Crystal Beach was a family-oriented park and they wanted to maintain their reputation. During 1960s and 1970s Crystal Beach still had a relative amusement park monopoly in WNY and had the patronage of hundreds of company and neighborhood association picnics. Keeping these customers and catering to the many cottage owners resulted in not allowing rock bands, so the owners decided to turn the ballroom into a roller rink.

Crystal Beach returned to featuring live music in 1984. Following a 1974 fire at the ballroom, they had to refurbish the dance floor of the ballroom and build a new stage. The new dance hall lacked the art deco stylings of the old stage, and the dance floor was half its original size. The other part of the dance hall was the area damaged by the fire. It became a lounge with a carpeted floor and seating for the dancers to enjoy beverages and snacks.

The first band to appear at the new dance hall was Buffalo Swing. This was the band featured in the movie *The Natural*, which was filmed in Buffalo and released in 1984. The band was originally the six piece New Dixie Minstrels, but Robert Redford requested they add seven more members so they could perform swing music as a big band. The group was led by Bill Champion and included pianist Dr. Joe Baudo. From 1984 to 1987, Buffalo Swing performed 14 times at the new Crystal Beach Dance Hall. In memory of the heyday of Crystal Beach and early big band ballroom dances, Buffalo Swing released an album *10 Cents a Dance* in 1983.

From 1984 until the park closed in 1989, the Crystal Beach Dance Hall presented concerts by big bands, along with local and touring groups, that performed polka, country and, at long last, rock music.

The location of the park is now named the Crystal Beach Tennis & Yacht Club. All that remains from the original park is the ruins of the pier, but the memories of Crystal Beach Park, *The Canadiana*, the rides and the ballroom bands, for many will never fade away.

CRYSTAL BEACH BOAT

Crystal Beach Park began in the 1880s, originating as a Chautauqua which was an entertainment and culture movement, with speakers, teachers, preachers and musicians. The original and most famous Chautauqua was The Chautauqua Institute on Lake Chautauqua near Jamestown, New York. The concerts, talks and religious services at Crystal Beach gave way to other amusements and in 1890 The Crystal Beach Company was formed by John Evangelist Rebstock and associates. That company acquired more of the beach property, developed the park and built a pier. This was prior to the time of the automobile so you only could get to Crystal Beach by either train or by boat. The quickest and easiest way was the short cruise across the water. The first ship was the *Dove* in 1896 and the last of that era was the *State of New York* in 1907. During this period a total of 17 different ships, either leased or owned by the park, sailed this route. It was necessary to concurrently utilize several ships to accommodate the increasing crowds. The Lake Erie Excursion Company was formed to operate the park and Fred Kirby was hired to build larger boats for the company. The first ship Kirby constructed was the *Americana*, which was launched in 1908 and sailed through 1928.

The second ship that Kirby built was the *Canadiana*. This ship became known as The Crystal Beach Boat to the generations of Buffalo

THE CANADIANA
Photo: Courtesy William Kae

residents that sailed to Crystal Beach Amusement Park from 1910 – 1956. It was built by Buffalo Dry Dock Company at 191 Ganson Street and was the last passenger vessel to be built in Buffalo at the end of the Great Lakes maritime era.

When the Buffalo and Crystal Beach Corp., headed by George Hall, Sr. purchased the park in 1924 the sale included the land, midway attractions, the *Americana*, the *Canadiana* and the docks in both Buffalo and Crystal Beach. It was George Hall Sr. who was responsible for building the Crystal Beach Ballroom and Cyclone Roller Coaster.

The *Canadiana* was an elegant ship with three decks of stately Victorian architecture. The salons were done in rich mahogany, with beveled mirrors, brass railings and lighting fixtures. The grand stairways had sweeping banisters and stately newels. The walls were accented by stained glass windows, with gilded plaster Neptune heads between them. The ceilings were embellished with three-dimensional plaster formations of grape vines and rose clusters enhancing ovals of mahogany molding, which framed still life and hand painted scenes. The *Canadiana* had the largest dance floor of any passenger steamer that ever sailed on the Great Lakes. During Prohibition, drinking alcoholic beverages was allowed only when the ship left the Buffalo Harbor. Slot machines were also legal while on international waters but they had to be covered when the boat docked.

Due to the volume of passengers going to and from Crystal Beach from 1910 to 1928, both the *Americana* and the *Canadiana* sailed back and forth across the lake. Since it was a one-hour voyage, one of the ships left Buffalo and Crystal Beach every hour, carrying up to 3,500 passengers on each crossing. When the Peace Bridge opened in 1927 many people started to travel to Crystal Beach by car. Due to the diminished transport demand, the *Americana* was sold in 1929.

Many bands performed on the trip including songwriter Harold Arlen's Southbound Shufflers during the summer of 1923. The orchestra most associated with the ship was the Harold Austin Orchestra which started performing on the *Canadiana* in 1935. In addition to playing on the ship during the trip to Crystal Beach, every Sunday the Harold Austin Orchestra was featured during a three-hour moonlight cruise that left Buffalo at 8:15. There was also an afternoon three-hour dance cruise. These Sunday cruises started because of the Canadian Blue Laws. On Sundays, no dancing was allowed and alcohol could not be sold in Canada, so the Crystal Ballroom was closed. Cruises on the ship that had allowed Americans to drink during Prohibition now allowed Canadians to drink on Sundays.

Tommie Rizzo was the son of Sal Rizzo, who had performed with the Cliff Keyser Orchestra on the steamers and at the Crystal Ballroom in 1925. In 1943 Rizzo auditioned for the Harold Austin Orchestra and since many Buffalo musicians had been drafted during WWII, at 17 years old he

HAROLD AUSTIN ORCHESTRA ON DOCK
Front Row: Leonard Sciolino, Bobby Nicholson, Harold Austin, Arnold Tenglund, Pat Vastola Back Row: Edward Heim, Gus Farrell, Tiny Schwartz, Bill Jors, Cliff Dawson, John McFadden, Phil Todd, Ralph Westfield
Photo: Courtesy Jeanne Klaus-Austin from the collection of William Kae

secured the position as bass player and vocalist on the *Canadiana* and at the Crystal Ballroom. That position did not last long because later that year, Tommie was also drafted. When Rizzo was discharged from the service, he got his job back with the Harold Austin Orchestra. Tommie recalled that six days a week the orchestra would play on the 8:00 PM *Canadiana* cruise from Buffalo to Crystal Beach. When the boat docked at the Crystal Beach pier the band members rushed through Canadian Customs, ran through the park carrying their instruments, so they could be on time for their performance at the Ballroom. After they finished their second set at the Ballroom, the musicians reversed their dash through the park to get back to the Crystal Beach boat. They had to make certain they were on board for the 11:45 cruise back to Buffalo as they were scheduled to perform on the cruise, which was also the last transportation of the day returning to Buffalo.

During Memorial Day weekend in 1956 there were several fights between black and white youths at Crystal Beach Amusement Park. On May 30, 1956, several confrontations broke out during an afternoon cruise to Crystal Beach. These altercations continued at the park when nine youths (five black and four white) were arrested by the Ontario police. During the day there were numerous fights on the midway and at least ten people required medical attention at the first aid station. On the 9:15 trip back to Buffalo over 1,000 people were on the ship and soon after the *Canadiana* departed the Crystal Beach docks, fights erupted. Youth gangs roved the ship, with people being shoved to the deck and beaten by groups of attackers. Fireworks were tossed at passengers, causing powder burns and knives were brandished. The ship security could not control the fighting because as soon as they stopped one altercation another started. A number of passengers took refuge in the downstairs dining room which the guards were able to secure. Families were segregated by worried crew members in the roped-off areas. When police met the *Canadiana* upon its return to Buffalo around 11:00 PM, they arrested three people, six went to the hospital and many others suffered cuts and bruises.

F.L. Hall, the general manager of Crystal Beach said it was the first time an incident of this kind had happened in the history of the park, and management would take steps to assure that this never happened again. The press called it a race riot, while others considered it simply as gang fights between black and white youths. Regardless, the fights at the park and on the ship resulted in negative publicity and not a good way to start off the summer of 1956. After this incident, attendance on the *Canadiana* diminished and never recovered. It was the final year for the Crystal Beach Boat service to the park. The last voyage was on Labor Day weekend, at the end of that season. Harold Austin, the long-time band leader played "Taps" as the final song, on the last approach to the Buffalo dock.

The *Canadiana* was sold to a Cleveland company at the end of the 1956 season. After the ship was involved in an accident in 1958, it deteriorated until it sank at its berth in Cleveland during 1982. A non-profit group, the Friends of the Canadiana was formed in 1983 to attempt to save the ship and return it to service. They brought it back to Buffalo in 1984, where it was stripped down for restoration and towed for drydocking in Port Colborne, Ontario. Throughout the 1990s fund raising and applications for grants continued but the group, now called The S.S. Canadiana Preservation Society, Inc., was unsuccessful in its restoration efforts. The *Canadiana* was cut up for scrap in 2005. The ship's engine was salvaged and returned to Buffalo, along with much of the wooden superstructure, including the pilot house. Some of the salvaged wood has been manufactured into various memorabilia. If the *Canadiana* could have been restored to sailing condition or at least floated as a preserved docked museum/restaurant, it would have been a perfect addition at Canalside.

A former ferry-cruise boat was purchased from Circle Line and placed in service to Crystal Beach for the 1988 and 1989 seasons. The ship was renamed the *Americana*, but it was smaller version of the original ship, carrying only 578 passengers. After Crystal Beach closed at the end of the 1989 season, the *Americana* was used for lake cruises, until the owners, Ramsey Tick's Lake Erie Boat Cruise Corporation filed for bankruptcy.

Currently there are cruises offered by the *Miss Buffalo, Spirit of Buffalo* schooner, *moondanceCat* a 65- passenger catamaran, Buffalo River Tours and Grand Lady Cruises, but it would be historic if the *Canadiana* was still part of that fleet.

OTHER AMUSEMENT PARKS

OLCOTT BEACH

There was Crystal Beach in Canada, but for people who wanted to stay in the United States, on the American side of Lake Ontario there was Olcott Beach. In fact, the earliest record of an amusement park in Western New York was an advertisement for an Olcott picnic grove and man-powered carousel in the *Buffalo Courier Times* in 1853. With its Rialto and Dreamland (aka Luna Park) Amusement Parks, it was like Crystal Beach, but on a smaller scale. During its heyday, around the turn of the century, about 100,000 people a year came to Olcott on the IRC Railroad & Trolley (who owned and opened The Rialto Park in 1902), which connected to Lockport, the Tonawanda's, Niagara Falls and Buffalo. There were also piers where lake steamers docked, bringing passengers from Toronto, Hamilton, Rochester and other locations on Lake Ontario.

The Olcott Beach Hotel had a 14,000 square foot ballroom. Luna Park had the Dreamland Ballroom, where vaudeville shows were presented, and the Rustic Theater concert venue was near the current location of Krull Park. Top entertainers performed at the ballrooms and theater. In 1899, a crowd over 20,000 spectators came to the Rustic Theater to hear a speech by Teddy Roosevelt during Pioneer Days.

With the advent of cars in the 1920s, the need for hotels was negated because people could drive back home. Then the Depression hit in the 1930s. The hotel burned down in 1936 and Pioneer Days ended with the advent of World War II in 1941. During the 1940s the New Rialto and Olcott Amusement Park opened in Olcott. Neither park achieved the popularity of the Olcott parks of the early 20th century and both closed in the 1980s. Today there is just a small park called Olcott Beach Carousel Park, with kiddie rides and some arcade games. They restored the carousel roundhouse from Olcott Beach Amusement Park, and during the summer concerts are held on the bandstand in Krull Park.

ERIE BEACH PARK

Erie Beach Park was located across the Niagara River from the Buffalo harbor, on the Lake Erie side of Fort Erie Ontario, ten miles closer to Buffalo than Crystal Beach Amusement Park.

The park opened in 1885 and was originally known as Snake Hill Grove, catering to Canadians but also advertised to Americans in Buffalo. Starting in 1887, you reached the park by taking the ferry to Fort Erie and boarding the Fort Erie Ferry Terminal Railway to the Grove. The railway was affectionately known as the Sandfly Express. If you are familiar with the summer evening insect population of this area, you can understand how it got that name.

Based upon the success of the midway at the Pan Am in Buffalo, the owners changed the name of the park to Lake Erie Grove and decided to add amusement attractions, starting with a carousel model called Flying Ponies from the Armitage-Herschell Company in North Tonawanda. They added the Lighthouse Slide, The Scenic Railway (a figure eight roller coaster), the 65 room Erie Beach Hotel and a 4,000-foot beach promenade. Frank Bardol purchased the property in 1910 and changed the name to Erie Beach Park, so he could compete with Crystal Beach. He added the world's largest swimming pool (the ruins can still be seen at Waverly Beach), many additional rides, a 3,500 capacity stadium for major acts and a three story casino, which included a bath house, bowling alley, restaurant and ballroom. Canada's most famous big band, Guy Lombardo and the Royal Canadians, were contracted to perform at the park in 1924. Direct ferry service was established from Buffalo to the park, and on weekends up to 20,000 people would visit this park.

Erie Beach Park closed at the end of the 1930 season. The property, as well as its assets, was purchased by the owners of Crystal Beach Amusement Park, to prevent future competition from any amusement park being built at the Lake Erie Park location.

FAIRYLAND was located at the corner of Ferry and Jefferson. It opened after the Pan-American Exposition closed and took the names of many of its attractions directly from those on the Pan Am midway. They charged a five-cent admission in the afternoon and ten cents in the evening. In addition to approximately 30 attractions, they had sacred music concerts on Sundays, Wild West shows and a circus in the stadium, a free vaudeville theater, and dancing at the White Horse Tavern. Since Ferry and Jefferson is the back portion of the parcel of land at Ferry and Main, it is possible that Fairyland was the back portion of Athletic Park or the entrance was extended to Main Street and the name was changed.

ATHLETIC PARK - LUNA PARK – CARNIVAL COURT. When the Pan-American Exposition closed, the residents of Buffalo wanted a full-time park offering entertainment and the midway rides that were offered during the Pan Am. To fill this void on May 25, 1904, the five acre Athletic Park opened at the corner of Main and Ferry Street. They advertised 30 attractions and concessions, including a figure eight roller coaster, a vaudeville hall with two performances a day, a 200-foot long dance hall, military band concerts and circus acts. For the 1907 season they added land north of the park, extending down Main Street toward Delevan, and changed its name to Luna Park. Luna Park expanded the dance pavilion and added more attractions, concerts and vaudeville acts. But on May 30, 1909, a fire broke out in the skating rink and spread through most of the park, destroying almost everything except the grandstands. For the summer of 1910, all ten acres of the park were rebuilt with new attractions, featuring an octagonal dancing pavilion and the new name Carnival Court. The park remained open until 1:00 A.M. and electricity filled the midway with light. However, even though it was the largest amusement park in the Buffalo city limits, it could not sufficiently expand to compete with the lakeside resorts like Crystal Beach or Olcott Beach, and it closed in 1918.

GLEN PARK was located next to Glen Falls in the village of Williamsville. Some rides were operating since 1933, including the carousel that was purchased from Erie Beach Park when it closed. The park was probably the most popular kiddie park in the area, with nine acres of rides, games, novelty stands, food stands and a petting zoo. It included The Glen Park Casino, which was the summer home for top name entertainers that appeared in downtown Buffalo at the Town Casino and was also owned by Harry Altman. On September 23, 1968, a fire destroyed the casino, which had been renamed The Inferno, and another fire in 1973 destroyed many of the remaining buildings. When the park closed, its popular petting zoo animals were donated to The Buffalo Zoo, and the Town of Amherst and the village of Williamsville created the current scenic park, which is often used for wedding party photo shoots.

FANTASY ISLAND
Photo: Courtesy Rose Ann Hirsch

FANTASY ISLAND which was originally opened by Lawrence A. Grant in 1961, has gone through several transformations and is still in operation today. They initially wanted to name the park Fantasy Land but had to change the name because it conflicted with some copyrighted areas of Disneyland. At first, there were attractions with storybook characters, but they quickly found their niche with a Wild West show, complete with bank robberies, shootouts, cowboys falling off roofs and can-can dancers in the Golden Nugget Saloon. Various live music performances were also an important part of the entertainment offered at the park. During the 1960s the park had primarily kiddie rides and shows, including lion tamer Tarzan Zerbini, but in the 1970s it made an effort to attract an older audience. Fantasy Island was expanded to 85 acres, and added adult rides such as the Wildcat Roller Coaster and Devils Hole, where the floor would drop down, when the barrel began to spin, and the riders were held against the wall by centrifugal force. Fun? WOW!!!

DARIEN LAKE

Freezer Queen Food's founder Paul Snyder purchased 164 acres of land with seven small lakes on Route 77 near Corfu as a family getaway. Around 1955 he developed a sandy beach on the large lake, and after building a snack bar, opened the property to the public as a picnic park with swimming. In 1964 he added 23 campsites to accommodate tents and trailers and opened a small restaurant. A Cornell University study recommended developing the property into a large camping facility, so Snyder increased the park's size to 1,000 acres and started to add attractions.

By the late 1970s the main attractions were the campgrounds, where you could rent trailers by the weekend or entire season, lakes, pools and most of all, the Rainbow Mountain waterslides. Another focal point was the clubhouse called The Pub. It had a snack bar, bar, arcade games and performances by area polka, country, oldies and commercial rock bands. The management began to concentrate on live entertainment and mechanical rides, which continue to remain the main attractions.

Based upon the success of Rainbow Mountain, in 1979 the first mechanical rides arrived at the park. With the 1981 season Darien Lake changed to a pay one price admission charge to enjoy the rides, waterslides and entertainment at the Jubilee Theater. The Lakeside Theater, an outdoor 8,500 seat concert venue, was developed for major acts and 25 acres of land was paved for parking spaces for the daytime theme-park visitors. Campground visitors entered on the opposite side of the park.

In 1982, The Viper Roller Coaster was added and in 1983 The Giant Wheel, which was the largest Ferris wheel in North America. Paul Snyder had spent $75 million developing Darien Lake and in 1982 he sold half of his interest in the property to the national amusement park company Funtime, Inc. They purchased the total park in 1985, ending local ownership in Darien Lake. Over the next 30 years ownership has changed and the park has continued to expand. It is now one of the premier roller coaster parks in the country and the 20,000 seat Performing Arts Center presents concerts featuring many top recording acts.

OTHER SMALL AMUSEMENT PARKS

Lalle's Casino was in Angola on the Lake and opened as a dance pavilion in the 1920s. It was one of the summertime homes for big band swing music. They expanded upon the music by continually adding amusement rides and booths through the 1940s and 1950s.

Elmwood Beach on Grand Island was open from 1894 to 1910. It was a beach and picnic grove with some amusements and novelties opened by the White Line lake steamer company as a destination for its passengers. They referred to it as The Island Paradise of Buffalo and it was operated by Harvey Ferren, the owner of the Court Street Theatre. Even prior to Prohibition, it was an alcohol-free park, which made it popular with church groups. To get to the park you took a steamer from the foot of Ferry Street. The area of the park is now part of Beaver Island State Park.

Another Grand Island Park was Edgewater Park on East River Road. It opened in 1886, and the visitors arriving by steamship enjoyed dancing, boating, bathing and mechanical rides. Since most of the customers arrived by ship, the opening of the Grand Island bridges in 1935 had a negative effect on the park and by 1940 all the rides were sold. The Edgewater Park Hotel remained a popular rock music club during the 1960s and into the early 1970s. It closed when a large portion of the hotel collapsed during a storm in April 1974.

There was also the Sheenwater Park, which opened in 1878 on West River and Love Road in Grand Island. It featured a carousel, train, a figure eight roller coaster and concessions. It closed during the Depression. Eagle Park, located on East River, closed after the collapse of its pier in 1912, resulting in the death of 37 people.

There was a park called Lein's Park on Union Road, just south of Cazenovia Creek, near the current location of Southgate Plaza. It was open from about 1895 to 1913 and had a bear's pit, bowling alley and dance hall.

Bellevue Park was a 30-acre park on Como Park Blvd, along Cayuga Creek. The park was open around the turn of the century and it was the last stop on the trolley line from Buffalo. The Bellevue Hotel was part of this sprawling complex.

Another Cheektowaga park was Liberty Park on the corner of William and Union. It featured kiddie rides, a dance hall and bingo hall. The park extended along the bank of Cayuga Creek.

Woodlawn Beach Park was advertised as the "American Resort for Americans" and tried to compete with Crystal Beach. It opened in 1892 and was serviced by a steamer that made four trips daily from Buffalo Harbor. They built several attractions and in 1894 began promoting that the park was now illuminated by electricity. By the 1920s you could get to the park by a seven-minute trolley ride from Buffalo. It was only a short trip to experience their roller coaster and other amusements. The park closed when Bethlehem Steel purchased part of the property for a slag dump.

Kiddleland parks were opened by shopping centers like the Thruway Plaza at Walden & Harlem and stores like Twin Fair at Walden & Dick Road. The owners believed that if the parents brought their children for the kiddie rides, they might shop at their stores. Fun and Games Park was opened next to the Twin Fair and the I-290 Drive In on Young Street in Tonawanda. When Glen Park closed, Fun and Games Park purchased most of their kiddie rides, and during the 1970s they annually added more adult rides, along with carnival games. A rock music nightclub called Mother Tuckers, which later changed its name to He & She's, was also in this complex. This park closed in 1980 when Twin Fair began an expansion of the plaza to add more retail stores.

The days of these amusement parks lived on at church lawn fetes and firemen's picnics. These community events brought kiddie rides, carnival games and live entertainment, usually polka bands, to towns and parks during the 1950s-1980s. Some even continue today. Department stores extended the draw of kiddie rides in their parking lot by often having a ride in the front lobby or just outside the front door, where parents were persuaded by their pleading child to insert a coin so the child could have a ride.

For more detailed information on area amusement parks, see the book titled Western New York Amusement Parks by Rose Ann Hirsch, which is available through the Arcadia Publishing Company Images of America series.

5

NIGHTCLUB & EARLY JAZZ ERA

Orchestras and bands have been performing in area restaurants, hotels and theaters since the days when Buffalo was still a village. Starting in the 20th century, the style of music being performed at places of public assembly was American popular music, most of which originated with the music publishers and songwriters of Tin Pan Alley in New York City (NYC). Some musicologists contend this style of music started in the 1930s when the phonograph supplanted sheet music, while others felt it started with vaudeville. The music was first performed at shows in NYC like George Whites Scandals or Ziegfeld Follies, at places like the Cotton Club or in productions at Broadway theaters. It was performed by big bands and smaller combos and played by both the popular music groups and jazz bands. This music which has been referred to as The American Songbook remained popular until Tin Pan Alley was replaced by The Brill Building and the rise of rock music in the later '50s and early '60s. This chapter will cover the ballrooms, nightclubs and bars, along with the orchestras, bands and musicians that performed popular music and jazz from the 1920s through the early 1960s.

Big Bands and orchestras playing swing music performed in the Buffalo area at theaters, amusement park dancehalls, area nightclubs and large neighborhood halls. The theaters and amusement park dancehalls were covered in previous chapters. Some of the neighborhood halls included The Aud. at Elmwood and Utica, Union Hall at Broadway and Fillmore, St. John Kanty's Lyceum, St. Ange's and St. Peter & Paul Hall, but the most prominent venue for big band swing bands was The Dellwood Ballroom at Main and Utica.

THE DELLWOOD BALLROOM

In the early 1920s Harold Arlen performed at The Dellwood Ballroom with his Yankee Six Orchestra.

However, the Dellwood Ballroom became the destination for big band dances when Harold Austin started leasing the venue in 1926. From Fredonia, NY, his actual name was Clyde Harold Foute, but he adopted his mother's maiden of Austin because he thought it sounded better for the name of an orchestra. Before he was a teenager, he was playing trumpet in the house band at the Fredonia Movie Theater and while in high school he started playing with bands at area nightclubs and community events. In 1922, Austin moved to Buffalo to continue his education by studying business at Bryant & Stratton. Harold often attended classes wearing a tuxedo because when the school day ended, he had to rush to a performance at a nightclub or theater. After graduating from Bryant & Stratton and while attending the Eastman School of Music, he formed the Harold Austin Orchestra when he was 22. That band traveled the Midwest and Canada.

After leasing the Dellwood Ballroom, his orchestra performed there six nights a week, attracting some of the top musicians in the area to join his group. In 1931 the members included: Ollie Mathewson, Harold Austin, Pat Vastola, Vincent Impellitter, Hilton Shofner, Clem Hoth, Lou Hurst, Ford Leary, John Sedola, Edward Heim, Jack Fisher, Cliff Dawson, Jesse Ralph and William Nassal. Many of these musicians went on to successful careers in Buffalo and with national touring orchestras

In 1935, Austin was hired as the manager of the entertainment at The Crystal Beach Ballroom and onboard the *Canadiana*. Austin hired all the top touring big bands to perform during the summer at Crystal Beach and during the rest of the year at The Dellwood Ballroom. Austin was not the type of leader that stood in front, directing the band. He was seated in the trumpet section and led the band as a member of the orchestra. When he had to devote more time to the business affairs of his operations, he hired musicians like Bobby Nicholson or Tommie Rizzo to lead the group.

During WWII, there were two dances every night at The Dellwood. The first dance was from 9:00-1:00 and the second was from 1:00-4:00, for people that worked the second shift at the war factories. Both dances would be crowded. WEBR radio would broadcast from the Dellwood every night and DJ Ed Little would conduct interviews with recording artists like Andy Williams, Pat Boone or Tony Bennett between their performances. The Hi-Teen Club dances were held at The Dellwood on Saturday afternoons and were also broadcast live on WEBR, with DJ Bob Wells. These dances had an average attendance of 2,000 people.

The Dellwood Ballroom was located at the corner of Main and Utica. It was on the second floor of the building, above several retail businesses. To enter the ballroom, you had to walk up two flights of steep stairs. When you reached the top of the steps, you were greeted by two very big bouncers. If you were under the influence of alcohol, looked like a trouble maker, or if you were not dressed properly, you were turned away at the door. The Dellwood Ballroom had a reputation as a safe place to dance and see top big band orchestras. The management worked hard to maintain that reputation and it remained a respectable place that people were never afraid to frequent. Music was always the main attraction of the Dellwood Ballroom because it never had a liquor license. The snack bar at the front of the building served soft drinks (soda) and food.

Austin retained his position as the main provider of big band music in WNY by starting the Over 29 Club at The Dellwood in 1960. This was not an actual club, it was the name of the big band dances. These dances were moved to the Brounshidle Post in Kenmore in 1976. During the Blizzard of '77 the water pipes burst in the space occupied by The Dellwood, causing substantial damage to the building. The building was demolished and a Family Dollar is now at the corner of Main & Utica.

THE HAROLD AUSTIN ORCHESTRA ON STAGE AT THE DELLWOOD BALLROOM
Photo from the collection of William Kae Courtesy Jeanne Klaus-Austin

CHEZ AMI SUPPER CLUB

The Chez Ami at 311 Delaware Avenue was opened in 1934 by Philip Amigone. Prior to being remodeled into a nightclub, in 1929, the property was a movie theater called The Little. In 1930 it became The Hollywood, which was run by the Basil Theater chain and was the only movie theater on Delaware Avenue.

Among its distinctions, the Chez Ami was one of the premier nightclubs in Buffalo, was one of the first supper clubs in the country and had the first revolving bar in the U.S. Their advertising slogan was "Dance to America's Finest Orchestras." The interior was designed by C. Theodore Macheras who used art-deco elements of mirrors, neon, indirect lighting and plush carpeting to achieve what was as that time considered a modern entertainment experience.

CHEZ AMI FLOOR SHOW WITH ORCHESTRA
Photo: Courtesy Anthony Amigone

Many of the headline acts were booked out of New York City and they arrived complete with elaborate costuming and props. The house band consisted of area musicians and was led by Pat Geraci, who was a performer at the nightclub for almost the entire time that the Chez Ami was open. Harpist Tony Geonetti played dinner music at the nightclub from when it opened in 1934 until it discontinued serving dinners.

After a fire in 1941, the nightclub was again remodeled, further enhancing the art deco ambience, enlarging the dancefloor, expanding the balcony seating and updating the revolving bar. In addition to operating The Chez Ami, Philip Amigone established the restaurant/lounge at Buffalo Memorial Auditorium and Kleinhans Music Hall. From 1930-1945, Al Amigone operated Café Continental at 212 Franklin Street. At that time, the Continental was a dinner club without entertainment; it became the original music Continental Lounge in the 1980s. Cousin Daniel Amigone was in a different line of business. In 1926, he started Amigone Funeral Homes. However, Daniel was also the early owner of The Stage Door at 414 Pearl Street, where The Three Sons performed early in their career. When Daniel sold the business in 1952, the new owners changed to burlesque style entertainment at The Stage Door.

After entertainment tastes changed in the 1960s, Philip Amigone put the Chez Ami through another transformation. The live entertainment was replaced by recorded music, and much of the dining area became an expanded dance floor, making The Chez Ami Buffalo's first discotheque. After Amigone's death, the business was sold to other owners, who did not achieve the previous success of the nightclub. It was torn down in 1971.

As a tribute to the memory of the Chez Ami, the restaurant at the Curtis Hotel is named The Chez Ami Restaurant, complete with its signature revolving bar.

TOWN CASINO

The Town Barn was a dance hall and beer hall at 681 Main Street. After it burned down, Harry Altman and Harry Wallens built the Town Casino, which opened in 1945. The Town Casino was billed as the largest nightclub between NYC and Chicago. They booked many of the same acts that played at the Copacabana in NYC, and WEBR had a permanent radio booth in the nightclub to broadcast live shows and interviews with the entertainers. Harry Altman also owned the Glen Casino in Williamsville, where the touring recording acts performed during the summer months.

The Town Casino Nightclub featured elaborate productions, complete with decorative sets, costumed show girls, a house band, big name entertainers and MC Lenny Paige. Some of the acts included: Sammy Davis Jr., Milton Berle, Jack E Leonard, Danny Thomas, Mae

TOWN CASINO SHOW
Photo: Courtesy Marjorie Wallens

West, Julius La Rosa, Dorothy Dandridge, Johnny Ray and Perry Como. They also featured top jazz artists: Dizzy Gillespie, Charlie Parker, Carmen McRae, Duke Ellington, Nat King Cole, George Shearing, Denzil Best, John Coltrane, Pearl Bailey, Errol Garner, Les Paul, Louie Armstrong, Dinah Washington and Miles Davis.

TOWN CASINO BAND WITH CARMEN MIRANDA
Top Row: Morri Youngman, Pat Scime, Gino Bono, Carmen Miranda, Miranda's music
director, Vince Impellitter, Nelson Provenzano
Bottom Row: Jack Fisher, Carl Saxon, August Brucklier, Jack D'Amico
Photo: Courtesy Dick Riederer

The Town Casino house band was led by piano player Moe Balsom. The members of the final house band included Dick Riederer (trumpet), George Holt (trumpet), Ange Callea (trombone), Morri Youngman (sax) Joe Digati (bass) and Pete Suggs (drums). Other musicians that were prior members of the house band included: Vince Impellitter (trumpet), Jesse Ralph (trombone) and Tony Costantini (trumpet). When touring recording artists performed at The Town Casino, the band was often augmented with additional musicians per the performers requirements. After McVans discontinued floor shows, their MC Tony Oddi joined Town Casino MC Lenny Paige as co-MC at Town Casino, working together on skits and introducing the floor shows. The Town Casino had three floor shows a night at 7:30, 10:30 and 1:30, dinner was served from 5:30 to 9:00 and there was dancing between the shows.

There was a second stage in the bar area, where smaller groups like Tommie Rizzo's Tic Toc Timers, Eli Konikoff's band or The Vibratos performed. Piano player Larry Pirrone alternated sets with the front room band and was accompanied by various female vocalists. The front lounge and back showroom were separated with sufficient sound proofing, that allowed both rooms to simultaneously have music.

The house band from the Town Casino was also the house band at the Glen Park Casino. With the Town Casino open from October to May and the Glen Casino was open from May to October, the house band musicians had year-round employment. The final night of entertainment at the Town Casino was New Year's Eve 1964. When the Town Casino closed, The Glen Casino focused more on area entertainment and became the rock nightclub The Inferno.

After the Town Casino, the building at 681 Main Street became the home of the Studio Arena Theater. When the Studio Arena Theater moved across the street to the former Palace Burlesque Theater, the former Town Casino property became UB's Pfeiffer Theater, the Sphere Entertainment Complex and in 2005 it returned to its former glory as The Town Ballroom, which again featured touring recording acts.

STATLER HOTEL

In 1923 The Statler Hotel was opened by Ellsworth Statler at Niagara Square on the site of the former home of Millard Fillmore (the 13th president of the US). After he left the presidency in 1853, Fillmore lived at this address from 1858 until 1874. During that time, he helped establish many Buffalo cultural institutions, including the University of Buffalo, Buffalo Historical Society, Buffalo Medical Center, the Albright Knox Art Gallery, The Buffalo Club, Buffalo Public Schools, Buffalo Science Museum and the Buffalo SPCA.

When the hotel opened, it was called the Hotel Statler and it was the grandest hotel in Buffalo. It replaced a previous Hotel Statler at the corner of Washington & Swan Street, which was renamed The Hotel Buffalo. The Statler Hotel boasted many firsts or innovations in the nationwide hotel industry. They were: a private bathroom with a bathtub in each of the 450 rooms, hot and cold water in each bathroom, a wall light switch, a closet light, an electric lamp on a desk and a radio.

Entertainment and dining were important aspects of The Statler Hotel. There were three rooms with regular entertainment; The Rendezvous Room, Terrace Room and The Golden Ballroom. Other lounges were available for private parties and special events. The

Rendezvous Room was a supper club that had two orchestras performing for continuous entertainment. After the Elmwood Music Hall closed, The Golden Ballroom was the home for special concerts. The Ballroom also hosted many of the large society events, and the BPO even presented some concerts there in the 1930s. The Statler was later known as a center for live jazz entertainment, especially when William Hassett owned the property.

MCVANS

The history of McVans precedes prohibition. Since it was located on Niagara Street at the foot of Hertel Avenue, on the Niagara River it was "rumored" that smugglers used the basement of McVans as the distribution point for Canadian whiskey, that was brought across the river. Lillian McVan and her family were the owners of the nightclub, and they were known for their top-quality floor shows, coordinated by MC Tony Oddi. Some of the performers that worked at McVans included Jack Benny, Gypsy Rose Lee, Nat King Cole and Sammy Davis Jr. There were three floorshows every night at 9:00, 12:00 and 2:30. The last show of the night often did not start until 3:00 and McVans had the reputation as the late-night home for entertainment in Buffalo. Their advertising publicized McVans as "Buffalo's Busiest Night Club".

There was originally an upstairs supper club at McVans, but only the downstairs nightclub area was utilized in later years. In 1963 the former mayor of Buffalo Steven Pankow purchased the business and started the transition from floor shows to rock music. More on that incarnation of the club, along with owner Joe Terrose, in the chapter on the 1970s.

In addition to these large night clubs, there were several supper clubs that offered entertainment prior to WWII. These included: Dan Montgomery's, Murphy's Omega, Leonardo's, Alhambra, Polish Village, King Arthur's, The Calumet, The Park Lane and The Peter Stuyvesant Room.

The Peter Stuyvesant Room, in The Stuyvesant Hotel on Elmwood, was built by Darwin Martin, the property owner for whom Frank Lloyd Wright designed the historic "Prairie School" era house on Jewett Parkway. During a six-month engagement at the club, guitarist Herb Ellis formed the Soft Winds Trio, which was patterned after the Nat King Cole

Trio (Nat played early in his career at The Anchor Bar). A then unknown Oscar Peterson often came to see Ellis at the Stuyvesant on Saturday nights because the Canadian Blue Laws required Ontario bars to close at 11:00 PM on Saturday. A musical collaboration began and in 1953, Ellis became a member of the Oscar Peterson Trio. In addition to the ambience of the club and great music, the cocktail lounge of the Peter Stuyvesant Room was known for its elaborate glass dance floor.

On the corner of Main and East Utica, across the street from The Dellwood Ballroom, was the Hotel Markeen. It was a luxury apartment style hotel, of the same concept as The Hotel Lenox on North Street. Originally built in 1896, a three-story dining room addition designed by Stanford White, was added in 1900 for the Pan-American Exposition. Wealthy families rented suites at The Markeen, making it their full-time residence. The dining room was the center of West Side social activity. It hosted wedding receptions and was utilized by many clubs and organizations, with the dining room being called The Ionian Music Club. Early in his career, Bing Crosby sang at The Markeen. The building was torn down in 1966 and the property is now a Metrorail station.

THE JAZZ TRIANGLE

Just east of Main Street in downtown Buffalo was an area known as The Jazz Triangle, which included three of the top Black Nightclubs in WNY. They were Ann Montgomery's Little Harlem at 496 Michigan, Club Moonglow at 460 Michigan and The Vendome at 175 Clinton Street. These clubs featured floor shows, chorus girls and nationally renowned jazz entertainers.

ANN MONTGOMERY'S LITTLE HARLEM

The Little Harlem was one of WNY's premier nightclubs and its name will always be associated with Ann Montgomery, who ran the club for 68 years and who was one of the first female African-American business leaders in Buffalo.

The club started as an ice cream parlor in 1910, became a billiard hall in 1922, a supper club in 1929 and a cabaret in 1934. Everyone was welcome at The Little Harlem: black and white, gay and straight, politician and call girl. Everything and anything happened at The Little Harlem, evidenced by the history of it being raided several times during prohibition for the suspicion of selling alcohol and its risqué entertainment.

Many black entertainers got their start or refined their skills at The Little Harlem. Entertainers like Lena Horn, Della Reese, Sarah Vaughan, Billie Holiday, Count Basie and Louis Armstrong performed at the club and countless Buffalo musicians had to the opportunity to work with these performers or at floor shows at the club. It was a large nightclub with a seating capacity of 350 and a dance floor. To give you an idea of the caliber of the entertainment at The Little Harlem, it was compared to the Grand Terrace in Chicago and the Cotton Club in New York City.

ANN MONTGOMERY'S LITTLE HARLEM NIGHTCLUB
Photo: Buffalo History Museum

The business was originally started by Dan Montgomery and his wife Ann. In addition to the Little Harlem, they were also listed as the owners of Dan Montgomery's Hotel at 158 Exchange Street; and in 1930 they acquired the Montgomery Hotel at 342 Curtiss Street near the Buffalo Central Terminal railroad station. In addition to these properties, Ann's sister Mamie Ellis operated the Gallant Fox jazz club in the Jazz Triangle area. Dan and Ann Montgomery divorced in 1938, with Ann marrying Paul Woodson (a Tuskegee airman and descendant of President Thomas Jefferson and Ann Hemings) in the early 1940s. It appears that after the divorce Dan retained the hotels and Ann kept the Little Harlem. After their marriage, Paul assisted in managing the Little Harlem with Ann, retaining ownership for several years after her death, before selling the property to Judge Wilbur Trammell

Jazz violinist LeRoy "Stuff" Smith was initially hired to play during radio broadcasts and sing with the band at The Little Harlem in 1930. He became the band leader at the Little Harlem until Lil Armstrong arrived in Buffalo. Lil Armstrong was the wife of trumpeter Louis Armstrong and she helped establish him as a solo artist. When she moved to Buffalo in 1933, she took over leadership of the twelve-piece band at the Little Harlem. Stuff Smith remained in the employment of the Montgomery family because he was the manager of the Montgomery Hotel on Curtiss Street from 1935-37. The MC at the Little Harlem around this time was Pearl Bailey, years before she became a Tony and Emmy award, winning vocalist and actress. Stuff Smith later performed with Duke Ellington's Band, was considered the first electric violinist and was one of the 57 notable jazz musicians in the famous *Esquire Magazine* "A Great Day in Harlem" photo. That photo taken in 1958 is considered the greatest picture ever taken of the musicians from the jazz era. Two other members of Buffalo Musicians Local #533 were included in that photo: Bill Crump and JC Higginbotham.

Several musicians attributed their experience performing at The Little Harlem as important in launching their careers, including Jimmie Lunceford and singer Jean Eldridge. Lunceford led the group at The Little Harlem in 1931 and said it was at the club that he developed his two-beat style that launched the Swing Era. Vocalist Jean Eldridge was discovered by Duke Ellington while performing at the Little Harlem in 1938. She joined Ellington's band and had a successful performing and recording career with Ellington and other orchestras.

CLUB MOONGLO

Club Moonglo which was located at 460 Michigan at the corner of William was open from 1936 to 1961. It was known for its sepia floors shows, complete with chorus girls and a jazz orchestra. When national jazz artists were staying in Buffalo, they often became members of the Moonglo house band.

During the 1930s to 1950s, members of touring black orchestras were not permitted to stay at the major downtown Buffalo hotels. These musicians would often stay at Dan Montgomery's Hotel on Exchange Street. That hotel was not far from Club Moonglo, so the musicians would come to see the floorshow at the club and often sit in with the house band.

Elvin Shepherd returned to Buffalo in 1947, after working for several years with the Lucky Millinder Band, which was the house band at The Savoy in NYC. He was still a trumpet player and when he was with Millinder, at one time the trumpet section consisted of Shepherd, Dizzy Gillespie and Miles Davis. Shepherd took a job with the Pete Suggs Band, the house band at The Moonglo. Around this time the MC at the club was Chicago native and future internationally-known jazz singer Joe Williams, who worked at the Moonglo for about a year. In 1951, Shepherd injured his right hand in an accident at work. It was difficult for him to play trumpet with his left hand and due to the popularity of sax players, he borrowed the sax of future Judge Wilbur Trammell. Trammell claimed he was not using his sax that often because he was too busy in law school. Shepherd then toured as a sax player with various jazz orchestras and became a teacher and mentor to aspiring Buffalo sax players, with one of his students being Grover Washington Jr.

When performing at the Moonglo, C.Q. Price initially turned down an offer from the Count Basie Band so he could continue playing sax at the club. After WWII Price eventually joined Basie's band and became their arranger. Cozy Cole came to the Moonglo and offered Dodo Greene a position with his group. She turned it down to remain singing at the club but later went to NYC, where she joined Cab Calloway on Broadway. Buffalo bass player Irving "Bo Peep" Greene played in the house band at the Moonglo for several years and accompanied Della Reese, who was performing at Club Moonglo early in her career.

HOTEL VENDOME

Was located at 175 Clinton Street, not far from Michigan Avenue. It was in operation from 1938 to 1962 and there are allusions in articles about the Vendome that it was the largest nightclub in Buffalo and may have been the largest nightclub between NYC and Chicago. For some reasons, information about the Vendome was not listed in the newspapers and its promotional material did not survive. All that is know for certain is that Jonah Jones and Jimmie Lunceford's Orchestra performed there.

Just like all the large clubs in the Jazz Triangle area, The Vendome was frequented by both black and white audiences but the entertainment was by black performers. The early shows at these nightclubs were attended by mainly white audiences, and the late show was usually an almost all-black clientele. This was not a written policy, but it was what usually occurred.

TENDERLOIN DISTRICT

The area of Oak, Elm and Michigan, between William, Clinton and Eagle was known as the Tenderloin District. This was the red-light district east of Main Street. The red-light district west of Main Street was Canal Street, which was given the name of the Infected District. Areas of ill repute usually breed new forms of music. The Infected District gave us the minstrel shows of Christy's Minstrels, and the Tenderloin District was the center of the black jazz scene, which included the clubs of the Jazz Triangle and many other live music venues. The City of Buffalo passed laws to close the concert saloons of the Canal Street Infected District because they were considered a front for prostitution. This was extended to the Tenderloin District's soda or soft drink bars and private homes that illegally served alcohol, along with having other services for sale in the upstairs rooms. The Mayor of Buffalo, Frank Schwab, went undercover and confirmed the illicit activity of the Tenderloin District. To resolve the issues, funds were obtained to extend William Street to Broadway. This cleared the worst part of the district which was Vine Street and Vine Alley, streets that no longer exist. But this extension also resulted in the demolition of two historic buildings, Bethel AME Church and the Vine Alley Colored School, which were an integral part of the early Buffalo Black Community. At one time, William Street was second to Main Street in commercial importance. The extension of William to Broadway contributed to the decline of the William Street commercial district and it resulted in the loss of many smaller musical venues.

EARLY JAZZ PROMOTERS

Beginning in the 1920s, promoters brought the top touring black orchestras and musicians to Buffalo for regular performances. In addition to the clubs in the Jazz Triangle, these artists would perform at The Paradise Ballroom, Bluebird, Weiss Hall, Broadway Aud, Frontier Elks Hall, Elmwood Music Hall, Semper Fidelis and Memorial Auditorium. The promoters were initially Jack & Madelyn Thompson in the 1920s, followed by Art Nelson, who was the main promoter through the late 1940s. Later promoters included Ed Malone, Sylvester Turpin, Guy Jackson and Fred Perry. There were also dances in the 1930s at The Memorial Center Urban League on Friday Nights. These dances often featured Guy Jackson and his WPA Orchestra. Dodo Greene was a guest vocalist at some of these dances, performing with her husband musician Jimmy Greene.

JIMMIE LUNCEFORD

Jimmie Lunceford was born in Mississippi, raised in Oklahoma City and went to high school in Denver, Colorado, where he studied music under the father of band leader Paul Whiteman (who blended symphonic music and jazz – earning him the title of the King of Jazz). After recording his first album on RCA in the late 1920s, Lunceford made Buffalo his home base from 1930 to 1933. It was in Buffalo that he developed his distinctive style, which was to influence big band swing that was called the "Lunceford Two Beat." He originated the show aspect of big bands, which other acts copied, like his trumpet section throwing their instruments in the air and catching them on the beat. It was said that his band rivaled on record and exceed in person the orchestras of his contemporaries like Duke Ellington, Benny Goodman and Count Basie.

Lunceford was relentless in rehearsing his band, to the extent that complaints were filed against him at the Buffalo Musicians Union. Some even believe sanctions filed against him by the Buffalo Union led to Lunceford leaving Buffalo, which resulted in his moving to the national stage at NYC's Cotton Club in 1934. His orchestra remained a highly-produced and extensively-rehearsed show, complete with costumes, skits and obvious jabs at mainstream white orchestras like Paul Whiteman (his high school teacher's father) and Guy Lombardo. The reputation Lunceford established in Buffalo may have contributed to his demise, as the cause of his death at 45 was officially listed as a heart attack but was most likely the result of racially-motivated food poisoning.

THE COLORED MUSICIANS CLUB

To perform at the theaters or nightclubs in downtown Buffalo, musicians needed to join the Musicians Union. However, in the early 20th century black musicians were not allowed to join the white Musicians Union. Black musicians formed their own union in 1917, Local #533 of the AFM, while the white musicians were members of Local #43.

The Colored Musicians Club was at 145 Broadway at the corner of Michigan, in the Jazz Triangle. The Union offices were in the downstairs portion of the building, while upstairs was a rehearsal hall, restaurant and bar. When a traveling black band arrived in Buffalo, the band leader or his representative had to report to the union office. He was required to advise where the band would be performing, the length of the engagement, the names of the individual musicians, and to verify each musician's union membership.

When the musicians returned to the union local office to pay their travel dues, they often went upstairs for reasonably priced food and beverages. These traveling musicians sat in with the band performing at the club. Local musicians came to the club after performing their club dates and jam sessions would often last until dawn. These jam sessions became so popular, that people stood in line to get into the club.

COLORED MUSICIANS CLUB JAM SESSIONS
Dizzy Gillespie with Buffalo's Elvin Shepherd, Wilbur Trammell
Photo: Courtesy John Shepherd

Segregation was the reason that there were two separate Musicians Unions. However, the Colored Musicians Club set the standard for integration in Buffalo. It was one of the first places where white and black musicians performed together. It was also one of the first places where many white jazz musicians were exposed to and had the opportunity to play authentic black jazz. Today the membership of the Colored Musicians Club is fairly-well split between black and white members.

When the Civil Rights Acts mandated that the separate unions be merged, there was resistance from the black Local #533. They were a profitable organization, offered lifetime membership after 25 years and a $1,000 insurance policy. They also wanted to protect the existence of the Colored Musicians Club. Prior to the merger, in the 1940s, the Colored Musicians Club became a separate entity owned by the club members. It had no affiliation with the Union, other than renting it office space. This protected the club from being transferred in the union merger and is one of the reasons that The Colored Musicians Club is still in existence today.

The former union offices in the downstairs area of The Colored Musicians club is now a museum and the clubrooms upstairs continue to hold big band rehearsals on weeknights. The Colored Musicians Club celebrated its 100th Anniversary with a gala dinner at The Lafayette Hotel on April 15, 2017

MUSICIANS - EARLY JAZZ PERIOD

Since the early 20th century Buffalo was known for its talented musicians. Many area musicians from the big band or later jazz club era were hired by touring national bands, returning to Buffalo later in their career. The accomplishments of several of these artists are covered in other sections and information on others follow.

THE BERNIE SANDLER ORCHESTRA evolved from the Bennett High School Dance Band in the late 1930s. They were previously known as the Club Royal Orchestra and played at Buffalo night clubs like the Colvin Gables in Tonawanda and Glen Casino in Williamsville. The orchestra toured the Northeast and Midwest in 1941 and 1942, including six weeks at the Arcadia Ballroom in NYC. When some of the members were drafted during WWII, the group disbanded.

The Orchestra from 1938 through 1942 included: Bernie Sandler (vocalist), Eleanor Powers (vocalist), Ettore Porreca and Dick Maurer (trumpet); Vince Ryan, Abe Paul, Al Pellegrino and Norm Easton (tenor sax and clarinet); Nelson Provenzano, Paul Cecala, Jack Keith and Bill Benz (alto sax and clarinet); Al Fisher and Jim Chambos (trombone); Bob Stevens (guitar), Bobby Weiser (piano), Bobby Goodman and Jack Saruth (drums) and Bernie Goodman (bass).

SAM NOTO. During the 1950s, trumpet player Sam Noto recorded and toured with Stan Kenton. He returned to Buffalo in 1960 and released a live recording of "Spanish Boots", which became a popular regional jazz single. It was recorded at Big Mothers Club near UB with Don Menza (sax), Larry Covelli (sax), Nick Molfese (bass) and Clarence Becton (drums). Noto operated The Renaissance on Pearl Street during 1965 and 1966, as a coffee house that did not have a liquor license. That allowed it to remain open and have music from 3:00 – 6:00 AM, after all the other bars shut down for the night. The Renaissance became a popular gathering place for musicians of all musical styles, who came to the club after completing their performances. After closing The Renaissance Sam Noto went on the road and toured with many national jazz artists including Charlie Parker, Count Basie, Dizzy Gillespie, Buddy Rich, Red Rodney, Don Menza, Joe Romano, Louis Bellson, Frank Rossolino and Mel Lewis. During the 1970s he released solo albums on Xanadu Records. The Buffalo Jazz Collective celebrated Sam Noto's 87th Birthday on April 9, 2017, with a concert at The Buffalo History Museum.

TOMMIE RIZZO started playing with the Crystal Beach Band during WWII while he was still a teen. After being discharged from the Army, he resumed his position as bass player and vocalist with The Harold Austin Orchestra on the *Canadiana*, at the Crystal Beach Ballroom and The Dellwood Ballroom. Tommie was also a member of the WBEN Radio studio orchestra, which led to two early Channel 4 television shows – *Club Canandaigua* and *One Chorus Only*. In 1949, he formed the Tic Toc Timers with Russ Messina (accordion), Vince Brundo (guitar) and Dick Fadale (drums and vibes). They performed at The Anchor Bar, Peter Stuyvesant Room, Fosters Supper Club and Toronto's Town Tavern. They were also the intermission band at The Town Casino. When regular Town Casino MC Lenny Paige had a day off, Tommie often filled in as the MC for the floor shows. In 1953, Rizzo started working with the Harry Stern Orchestra, one of the premier society bands in WNY through the mid-

1960s. When Tommie was 55 years old, he decided to go to law school. He began by enrolling at a law school in Florida and he graduated from the UB School of Law in 1983. Rizzo is still a practicing attorney, sharing offices with another musician who became an attorney – Stuart Shapiro.

TONY MILITELLO moved to Buffalo from Sicily at age 12 and was a professional classical and jazz guitarist from the 1930s through the 1960s. He was a featured soloist at concerts with the BPO, was in the orchestra at Sheas Buffalo Theatre and traveled with the Horace Heidt show. Tony also performed at Hotel Buffalo and Victor Hugo's in addition to giving guitar and banjo lessons at his 7th Street home on the West Side. A musician until the end, Militello died of a heart attack while playing a show at the Whirlpool Restaurant in Niagara Falls on July 27, 1962.

RAY CHAMBERLAIN started his career as a trombone player in the First Army Band, where he was stationed at Governor's Island near Manhattan during the Korean War. While in the Army, he decided to concentrate on guitar, practicing five hours a night in the barracks. After he was discharged, Chamberlain moved to LA to further his guitar studies and work at jazz clubs. He developed a unique guitar style where he covered horn lines and parts. Returning to Buffalo in 1953, Ray played at Buffalo clubs like The Royal Arms, Fosters, Bafo's, the Copa and Anchor Bar. He became a member of the Pete Argiro Quartet, that left Buffalo for dates in Florida and eventually Las Vegas. That led Ray back to LA where he performed and toured with Frances Faye and Jack Costanza (Mr. Bongo), along with several big band jazz groups including the Stan Kenton Orchestra. Chamberlain left the national touring jazz scene and returned to Buffalo in 1957, where over the next 30 years worked in the computer departments at UB and Buffalo State College. In 1970, he lost feeling in two fingers on his left hand, resulting in his having to quit playing guitar and switching to bass. Starting in 1975, Chamberlain was a fixture with big band jazz groups in the Buffalo area, performing until just prior to his death at 87 in April 2017.

JOEY GIAMBRA is a Buffalo trumpet player, vocalist, actor, writer and former Buffalo police detective. He recalled that it was quite interesting playing at the area clubs in the 1950s to early 1960s. Due to the large mob presence in the city, there were unwritten rules that had to be followed. On Friday evening a mob member would come in to the club with his girlfriend and you would play them their favorite song. That same mob member would return on Saturday with his wife and you would play them their favorite song. He might then return on Sunday with his family and you would play their favorite song. You never wanted to make the mistake of playing the wrong favorite song. Giambra started playing trumpet in area nightclubs when he was still in his teens and has been performing jazz standards for six decades. As a police detective, he was directly involved in the investigations upon which the movie *Hide in Plain Sight* was based; and as a writer/actor, he consulted on the filming of the movie in Buffalo. Giambra is currently writing a biography of Sam Noto, working on a play, editing a movie and recording an album of 15 jazz standards.

ELI KONIKOFF began his career by playing trombone in big band groups, but starting in the 1950s Konikoff focused on Dixieland. He formed the Yankee Six, who worked six nights a week at the Town Casino, and were regular performer at society dates, country clubs, festivals, concerts and night club until 1973. Eli later worked with the Morgan Street Stompers and Sentimental Journey. His wife Frances sometimes performed as the piano player in Konikoff's band, and their children followed them into the music industry. Their son Eli Jr. was with Spyro Gyra, Ross played with Buddy Rich, daughter Randi did studio session vocals, while Barbara sang in choruses and groups. Music was Eli's passion. He played New Year's Eve 1995 at The Buffalo Yacht Club, passing away eight days later at age 80.

THE BAR-ROOM BUZZARDS were formed in 1966 by Jim Koteras (cornet) and Paul Preston (clarinet), who previously worked with Eli Konikoff. Early members of the band included Dan McCue on guitar and Dick Brownell on bass. The quartet's career began by playing for three years at The Speakeasy Restaurant in Niagara Falls, followed by four years on The Showboat, which was docked at the foot of Hertel Avenue. For 26 years they were with the Mark Russell Comedy Specials on Channel 17, making many on-camera appearances. Starting in 1975, The Bar-Room Buzzards began a 28-year association with Miss Buffalo Cruise Lines. The Bar-Room Buzzards have

BAR ROOM BUZZARDS
Dan McCue, Jim Koteras
Dick Brownell, Paul Preston
Photo: Courtesy Paul Preston

released three albums and two CDs of Dixieland and jazz material. They have appeared at jazz festivals across the country and continue to perform at summer outdoor concerts in several area town parks.

THE SADATES were Dick Fadale's quartet that played during the later '50s and early '60s at Fosters Supper Club. The bass player was Wally Schuman, who is the father of Tom Schuman, keyboardist with Spyro Gyra. Bob Poloncarz played bass clarinet and flute, with Julie West on vocals and percussion. After ending their engagement at Fosters, Fadale and Schuman worked as a duo at other clubs, while Bob and Julie got married and continued working together in different groups.

GEORGE FEUSI. Buffalo sports teams always had music as a regular part of their events. In the early 20th century there was an organization called Buffalo Sports Boosters, which was limited to 50 members. Membership was passed on from father to son or at least usually kept in the family. This group supported all the sports teams playing in the Buffalo area. George Feusi was a member of the group, and he put together an eight-piece band that performed at baseball games, football games and other type of sports-related event presented at The Aud. During early AHL Bison's hockey games, the band would set up next to the player's entrance and perform songs before, during and inbetween periods of the game. Feusi's contacts through the Buffalo Sports Boosters helped him obtain the contracts to perform for the Ice Capades and other Aud events.

JOE RICCO programmed jazz at WHLD, WEBR, WWOL, WGR and WUFO during the 1950s and the 1960s. As a promoter, he broke the color barrier at local venues in 1949 by presenting integrated bands and brought the Newport Jazz Festival to Buffalo for during the 1960s. An indication of his influence on the jazz world is he had three records recorded in his honor: "Jump for Joe" by Stan Kenton, "Port of Rico" by Count Basie and "Buffalo Joe" by Louis Bellson. He also owned a nightclub called Joe Rico's Milestones

Other musicians from time period include: Pianist Joe Guercio became the music director for Elvis Presley's Orchestra...Drummer Mel Sokoloff changed his name to Mel Lewis and worked with Stan Kenton...Angelo Lorenzo played trumpet with Artie Shaw and The Lucky Strike Hit Parade Orchestra...Ange Callea played trombone with Tommy Dorsey and Artie Shaw...Hank D'Amico played clarinet with Bob Crosby, Red Norvo and the CBS Orchestra...Don Paladino played trumpet with Les Brown and Stan Kenton...Tony Terran played trumpet with Horace

92

Heidt and Desi Arnez...Don Menza played sax with Maynard Ferguson and Buddy Rich...John Sedola played sax with Isham Jones...Wade Legge played piano for Dizzy Gillespie...Frankie Dunlap was the drummer with Thelonious Monk...Louis Mucci played trumpet with Miles Davis ...Charlie Parlato played trumpet with Lawrence Welk.

SMALLER CLUBS

Across the city of Buffalo, during the 1920s through the early 1960s, there were live music clubs in just about every neighborhood. If you were to visit these small neighborhood taverns today, you would often find a small stage, with an upright piano, and a dance floor in the back room. There are no records of every bar, tavern or nightclub that had live entertainment and since there were so many, it would almost be impossible to compile that list. Following is information on *some* of the places, *some* of the musicians who performed there and special events that occurred at these establishments.

Beginning with the Jazz Triangle, on the west and through the Lower East Side, were the black clubs that featured jazz, R&B and blues. These clubs included: Rhythm Club (392 Michigan), Savoy (416 Michigan), 5 & 10 (Clinton & Michigan), Havana Casino (143 Goodell), Golden Gloves Lounge (479 Genesee), The Kitty Kat (97 Genesee), Brogans (183 Seneca), Ryan's (140 Seneca), Horseshoe Bar (214 William), Mandy's (278 William), Apex (311 William), Zanzibar where Billie Holiday performed (525 William), Paradise (375 Jefferson), Silver Grill (Maston & East Ferry), Bon Ton (182 East Ferry), The Revilot (257 E Ferry) and Pine Grill (1447 Jefferson), home of the club for which the Pine Grill Reunion is held at MLK Park.

The downtown area was home to almost all of the movie theaters but on the streets on or just off Main Street were many live music clubs, including: Jan's (621 Main Street), Bafo's (724 Main Street), Copa Casino (952 Main), where they featured national jazz acts on a regular basis, Anchor Bar (1047 Main), where they relocated after their previous location became part of the Memorial Auditorium site, Fosters (Delaware & Huron), Flamingo Room (Delaware next to the Hotel Richford), Versailles Lounge (Delaware next to Hotel Touraine), Colony Club (Delaware & Virginia), Jazz Center (634 Washington), a jazz coffee house run by promoter Frank St. George, Onyx Club (Main & Goodell), Les Simons' (East Ferry), Caparella's (North Fillmore near East Ferry), Hotel Worth (200 Main), Red Garter Room run by Joe Rico (in Hotel Buffalo), Johnny's Ellicott Grill (395 Ellicott), Gayety (Washington), Ciro's at (75 W Chippewa), one of the few live music clubs on the then notorious Chippewa Street red-light district, Royal Arms at 19 West Utica (next to the Dellwood Ballroom which featured touring jazz and blues acts), Prince Edward Hotel (490 Pearl) and The Renaissance (Pearl & West Tupper) run by Sam Noto and Lou Marinaccio in 1966, which was one of the last clubs from what is being considered the early jazz era.

The West Side had the Tivoli Gardens (in the Hooks on Dante Place), Royal Garden (Busti & Georgia), Banny's (Niagara), Andy's (on Lower Terrace); where in 1939 Frank Sinatra came to sing after performing shows at Sheas with Harry James, Joe Sacco's Rex Grill & The Playbar (West Ferry), 50/50 (Massachusetts Street), Frank's Lounge (Busti & Hudson) and Dan Dee's (Niagara & Pennsylvania).

In the Riverside and Black Rock area, the main club was McVans but music was also featured at Orchid Lounge, Sauerweins and Everglades (on Hertel). South Buffalo was separated from the rest of the city by railroad lines and factories. Many of the South Buffalo and Lackawanna clubs were predominently frequented by people from that area.

The Far East Side included the Polish music clubs such as The Polish Village, Warsaw Grill and Broadway Grill on Broadway, along with Chopin Singing Society on Kosciusko Street and Lawida's Gay Way. The Evening Star featured popular music and the early country music bar, Club Romway was on Broadway. In Kaisertown Ray's Lounge, along with a few other bars on Clinton Street had live music. During the 1930s to 1950s not many clubs with live music were operating in Cheektowaga and West Seneca. Most of the clubs in that suburban area started music during the later 1960s.

FLOOR SHOWS

Predominately located in the city there were nightclubs that had floorshows, featuring singers, comedians, ventriloquists and dancers. Most of these floor shows featured exotic dancers, which were on the line of a burlesque show but some were more subdued, like the early variety shows.

The most famous burlesque shows in Buffalo were at the Palace Burlesk theater in Shelton Square. Many musicians played in the pit orchestra claiming the pay was good, but it was a lot of work. Sam Noto recalled that when he played at the Palace in the late 1940s he received $155 a week. However, he had to play 29 shows a week, four a day Sunday through Friday and five shows on Saturday.

At Frank's Casa Nova, Fred Raiser was the piano player at the floor shows for 27 years from 1947 to 1974. He played there for six nights a week and performed three shows a night, so over the 27 years, Raiser logged 25,272 shows at the club.

Other clubs that had floor shows included Federal Garden's (1237 Genesee), Chin's Pagoda (621 Main), Stork Club (161 Seneca), Brogan's (183 Seneca), Café Aloha (East Ferry & Masten), Bon Ton (637 Ridge in Lackawanna), Coconut Grove (432 Connecticut), Club Rainbow (241 Court), Havana Casino (Elm & Goodell), Old Barn (East Aurora), Chandu's (781 William), Billboard (Swan & Ellicott) and Shell's Lounge (Broadway).

SOCIETY BANDS

These bands or orchestras played commercial renditions of popular songs at parties attended by the upper-class members of Buffalo society. The Dave Cheskin Orchestra, Harry Stern Orchestra and Irving Shire Orchestra were three of the society bands that performed at the elite functions. These events were held at the exclusive private clubs like The Buffalo Club, 20th Century Club, Montefiore Club, Saturn Club, Buffalo Athletic Club or the Westwood, Buffalo and Park Country Clubs, and at the mansions on Delaware Avenue, Middlesex or Central Park area, and during the summer at the mansions along Lake Erie, on Old Lake Shore Road.

THE ROYAL ARMS & ROUNDTABLE RESTAURANT

The Royal Arms was opened by Max Margulis in 1956. It was at 19 West Utica Street, around the corner from the Dellwood Ballroom. The

Dellwood featured big bands while the Royal Arms presented smaller jazz and blues combos, with the entertainment playing on a stage that was behind the bar. Top national acts like Miles Davis, Aretha Franklin, Mel Torme and Jimmy Smith performed at the club. One afternoon an ambitious young businessman that was visiting Buffalo stopped at the club. His name was George Steinbrenner, who was working for his family's Great Lakes shipping company, Kinsman Marine Transit Company. George, who played piano in bands while in college, struck up a friendship with Max Margulis and insurance executive Jimmy Naples. In 1965, Margulis, Naples and Steinbrenner opened the Roundtable Restaurant at 153 Delaware Avenue, in the former location of The Chateau in downtown Buffalo.

The Roundtable became one of the premier restaurants in Buffalo, frequented by politicians and local sports celebrities like OJ Simpson and Jack Kemp. Steinbrenner also had an interest in sports. He was a graduate assistant to football coach Woody Hayes, when Ohio State was the 1954 undefeated national champion and won the 1955 Rose Bowl. Steinbrenner earned a Master's Degree in Physical Education from Ohio State. He was also an assistant under head coach Lou Saban, at Northwestern University. In 1960, Steinbrenner purchased the Cleveland Piper's, of the professional American Basketball League, generating his desire to own professional sports teams. It was at The Roundtable Restaurant, in 1973, that George Steinbrenner announced he purchased the New York Yankees. When The Roundtable closed in 1978, Steinbrenner placed Margulis in charge of all food and beverages at Yankee Stadium.

SONGWRITERS

The Buffalo area developed several successful songwriters that penned songs of all musical styles. Beginning with writers that started out in minstrel shows through writers of current songs, Buffalo writers have contributed many popular songs, covering all time periods.

E.P. CHRISTY is known as the founder of Christy's Minstrels, but he was also a writer or presumed writer of minstrel songs. In 1844, he wrote "Buffalo Gals Won't You Come Out Tonight" and is considered by some musicologists to be the writer of "Mary Blane," It is not known who wrote the song "Lucy Long" but E.P. Christy's step-son George Christy is credited for introducing and possibly writing it. E.P. Christy was listed as the writer of some Steven Foster's songs, but he had paid Foster for the rights to the songs and the writer credit was eventually corrected.

CHAUNCEY OLCOTT was born in Buffalo in 1858 and started out by working in minstrel shows. After studying singing in London during the 1890s, he was mentored by actress Lillian Russell. Olcott is best known for his songs "My Wild Irish Rose" and "When Irish Eyes Are Smiling." The movie *My Wild Irish Rose* was a fictionalized bio-pic of Chauncey Olcott's life, tracing the rise of an Irish-American tenor to stardom at the end of the 19th and start of the 20th century. The movie was nominated for an Academy Award in 1948.

RAY HENDERSON was born in Buffalo in 1896, started his career as an accompanist for vaudeville song and dance acts. After moving to NYC, he became a popular composer in Tin Pan Alley. His most popular songs were written in the 1920s and included "Bye Bye Blackbird" and "Five Foot Two, Eyes of Blue". He was responsible for writing several editions of George White's Scandals and the most successful Ziegfeld Follies. The 1956 movie *The Best Things in Life Are Free*, was a dramatization of Henderson's life and his collaboration with songwriting partners Lew Brown and Buddy De Sylva, with whom he also owned a publishing company.

JACK YELLON was raised in Buffalo and worked as a reporter for *The Buffalo Courier* before becoming a full-time songwriter. His song "Happy Days Are Here Again" was the theme song for Franklin D Roosevelt's 1932 presidential campaign and was associated with the Democratic Party throughout the 20th century. He also wrote the Tin Pan Alley classic "Ain't She Sweet", which was even recorded by The Beatles. During his career, he wrote over 200 songs, owned a successful music publishing company and collaborated with vaudeville star Sophie Tucker, writing many of her songs including "My Yiddishe Momme." Yellon was one of the earliest members of ASCAP and served on the ASCAP Board of Directors for two decades, working to protect the rights of songwriters. He retired to his Morton Corners Road home in Concorde (Springville) where he passed away in 1991 at the age of 98.

RAY EVANS was born in Salamanca NY. He played clarinet in his high school band and attended the University of Pennsylvania's Wharton School, where he was a member of the college dance orchestra. During school vacations, the orchestra performed on international cruises, and

Evans started a song-writing partnership with fellow student Jay Livingston. When they graduated in 1936, they moved to NYC and eventually Hollywood, working as a song-writing team. They have the distinction of winning three Academy Awards for "Buttons and Bows" in 1948, "Mona Lisa" in 1950 and "Que Sera Sera" in 1956. In addition to these Oscar-winning songs, they wrote other popular songs including "Dear Heart" and the Christmas classic "Silver Bells." Evans and Livingston later wrote for television, composing several series theme songs including *Bonanza* and *Mr. Ed*. During Evans career, he wrote over 700 songs for screen, stage and television. In his honor, the movie theater in Salamanca was renamed the Ray Evans Seneca Theater.

HAROLD ARLEN is one of the most successful songwriters of the 20th century, publishing over 400 songs during his career. He was born Hyman Arluck in 1905 and was the son of a Jewish cantor who directed the choir at the Pine Street synagogue. A talented vocalist and pianist, his father wanted him to follow in his footsteps. To his parent's dismay, at 15 he started playing professionally at movie houses, with vaudeville troupes and in the Buffalo red-light district with the Snappy Trio, a group that included Hymie Sandler (drums) and Ted Myers (violin). This was a successful trio for these three teens, as Arlen purchased one of the first Model T Ford's in his lower East Side neighborhood. Arlen also performed in Buffalo with the Southbound Shufflers, which included his brother Julius Arluck on sax, Yankee Six (a popular collegiate dance circuit band) and the Yankee Ten Orchestra, who changed their name to The

HAROLD ARLEN WITH HIS BAND ON THE CRYSTAL BEACH BOAT
Photo: Courtesy William Kae

Buffalodians when they started playing outside of the Buffalo area. When he was 18, The Southbound Shufflers were playing on the Crystal Beach Boat, earning $80.00 per week for the entire band, plus meals. The Yankee Ten Orchestra has the distinction of being the last house band at the old Crystal Beach Ballroom and the first band to perform at the new Crystal Beach Ballroom. By the time Harold Arluck was 20, his reputation for modern jazz-inspired arrangements and bluesy rhythm numbers was earning him $75.00 to $100.00 a week, a very respectable salary in 1925.

When Arlen was performing with The Buffalodians at Geyer's Ballroom in the Teck Theater, he met dancer Ray Bolger, who was appearing there in a play. Bolger became a life-long friend, his roommate when Arlen moved to NYC and the actor that played the scarecrow in the *Wizard of Oz*. The Buffalodians performed in Cleveland and Pittsburgh before securing an engagement at Gallagher's Monte Carlo in NYC. Ray Bolger was also performing at this nightclub and Harold decided to remain in NYC and share an apartment with Bolger. It was in NYC in 1926 that he changed his name to Harold Arlen, combining his parents last names of Arluck and Orlin. He found work as pianist/vocalist in bands, rehearsal pianist for plays, accompanist for vaudeville performers and piano player for Ethel Merman. In 1930, Arlen, with lyricist Ted Koehler, composed his first hit song "Get Happy," which began as a variation of the pick-up music he played to summon the dancers during play rehearsal.

The Cotton Club was the place to be in Harlem to hear the music of Cab Calloway and Duke Ellington, watch top celebrity talent and enjoy the beverages that were banned by Prohibition. Starting in 1930, Arlen and Koehler began writing two shows a year for The Cotton Club, a position they continued for the next four years. During this time, they composed many hit songs including "I've Got the World on a String" and "Minnie the Moocher's Wedding Day." While at a Cotton Club party, they composed the song "Stormy Weather." Arlen also started writing with other lyricists for Earl Carroll's Vanities and Broadway plays.

Arlen moved to Hollywood, where in 1939 he and Yip Harburg were commissioned to write the music for the movie *The Wizard of Oz*. The soundtrack yielded several successful songs, including "Over the Rainbow". The movie starred Arlen's former roommate Ray Bolger and launched the career of Judy Garland. "Over the Rainbow" not only won an Oscar for best song of the year, the RIAA (Recording Industry Association of America) and NEA (National Endowment for the Arts) awarded it the

20th Century's #1 song. Arlen was one of the most prolific songwriters of the 20th Century and a major contributor to the Great American Songbook.

ADOLPH DEUTSCH was born in England, but by his late teens he was living in Buffalo, playing accompaniment to silent movies. This experience gave him a background in musically interpreting the moods and ambience of a movie scene. He translated this knowledge into writing music and orchestrations for Broadway plays and Hollywood movies. Deutsch won three Academy Awards for Best Original Score for the movies *Oklahoma, Seven Brides for Seven Brothers* and *Annie Get Your Gun.*

DAVID SHIRE is the son of Buffalo band leader and piano teacher Irving Shire. After graduating from Yale, he moved to NYC where he wrote for stage, film and television. He won a Best Song Academy Award in 1979 for "It Goes Like It Goes" from the movie *Norma Rae*. Shire has also received Grammy, Tony and Emmy nominations. His scores include *The Conversation* and *Saturday Night Fever*. For several years, Shire was the accompanist for Barbara Streisand, who recorded five of his compositions. In addition to writing for many other artists, his song "With You I'm Born Again" was an international hit for Billy Preston and Syreeta in 1980.

Many Buffalo musicians have written songs that they or their bands have recorded. There were several other songwriters associated with Buffalo who have written material which was recorded by other artists. Eric Andersen has written songs recorded by Johnny Cash, Bob Dylan, Judy Collins, Linda Ronstadt and the Grateful Dead. Jackson C. Frank had his songs covered by many artists including Simon & Garfunkel. Peter Case played in Hamburg, NY area groups as a teen, and songs he wrote for The Nerves and Plimsouls have been recorded by other artists including Blondie. Michael Spriggs songs have been covered by country artists like Tammy Wynette, Louise Mandrell and Kenny Rogers. Willie Nile, Phil Dillon, Nick Distefano, Michael Campagna and Debby Ash also wrote songs that were successful recordings for other artists. Joan Baez lived in Clarence Center for several years as a child. The home she lived in was two blocks away from the crash site of Flight 3407. Joan was in grammar school while living in Clarence Center and took piano lessons, but was not yet a performer. Her songwriting and recording accomplishments culminated in her being inducted into the Rock & Roll Hall of Fame in 2017.

6

EARLY RADIO & TELEVISION STATIONS IN BUFFALO

WGR RADIO

WGR was the first radio station to begin broadcasting in the Buffalo market on May 22, 1922. (WWT was the first radio station granted a license in Buffalo on March 25, 1922 but it intermittently broadcast and went off the air on October 2, 1922.) WGR was started by FTTC – Federal Telephone & Telegraph Company, which was manufacturing fully assembled radio sets. Since there were not any broadcast radio stations in the Buffalo area, residents that purchased radios had to pick up stations from other cities. To fill that void, FTTC applied for a commercial radio license from the Dept. of Commerce. Having a local radio station would also help them sell more radios. One of the major investors in FTTC was George Rand, from the Remington Rand Company and president of Marine Trust Company. Ironically the station call letters were WGR – W George Rand, which stood for World's Greatest Radio.

The broadcasts on the first day of WGR Radio were an address and prayer from Canisius College President Reverend Ahern, a discussion on Buffalo business growth by the head of the Chamber of Commerce and a discussion by Dr. Roswell Park on the advantages of a college education. The first day of broadcasting also included a concert by the Yankee Six Orchestra, led by Hyman Arluck; who later changed his name and became one of American's greatest songwriters – Harold Arlen.

The station was in the FTTC factory at 1738 Elmwood Avenue, but interference from the manufacturing necessitated a move. In 1923, WGR relocated to the newly opened Statler Hotel in downtown Buffalo. The move provided the station with access to live orchestra performances from the Golden Ballroom, with microphone wiring carrying the signal to WGR's 18th floor studio. The station also hired The Dave Cheskin Orchestra as the in-house radio station band.

WGR RADIO STUDIO BAND – THE DAVE CHESKIN ORCHESTRA
Photo: Courtesy Buffalo Musicians Union

All the major radio stations had in-studio orchestras and radio network programs were almost exclusively broadcast live. In fact, the national networks prohibited the airing of recorded programs until the late 1940s because of, what they considered, the inferior sound quality of phonographic discs. Local stations were free to use recordings and often made substantial use of prerecorded syndicated programs distributed on transcription discs. A transcription disc was officially called an electrical transcription and was recorded specifically for radio rebroadcast. It differed from the commercially distributed records of the 1930s and 1940s time period because they were 16" in diameter and recorded at 33 1/3 rpm (revolutions per minute) rather than being 12" in diameter and recorded at 78 rpm. In 1947, the national radio stations started using magnetic tape recordings which achieved higher fidelity, at high speeds, than the electrical transcription discs. Remember the commercial "Is it live or is it Memorex?"

During the early days of WGR Radio, in 1932 a 15-year-old Robert Emil Schmidt played piano and sang with The Hi-Hatters. This three-piece vocal group included Foster Brooks, who later became famous playing a drunk on *The Dean Martin Show*. Robert Emil Schmidt later changed his name to Buffalo Bob Smith, who was a DJ on WGR in 1942 and later created *The Howdy Doody Show*.

After 90 years of continuous broadcasting, WGR 55AM is still on the air, functioning as an all sports talk radio station and acquiring the rights to broadcast the Buffalo Bills and Buffalo Sabres games.

WEBR RADIO

The second radio station in Buffalo was WEBR, signing on in 1925. It was originally located in the back room of Howell Electric Company on Franklin and Niagara before moving into its long-time home at 23 North Street. After receiving the call letters of WEBR from the FCC it developed the slogan We Extend Buffalo's Regards. The station has the distinction of being owned by the two major newspapers in Buffalo, *The Buffalo Evening News* in 1936 and *Buffalo Courier-Express* in 1942.

The program director at WEBR in the late 1920s was Fran Striker, who was born in Buffalo and attended Lafayette High School and UB. Fran wrote scripts for radio shows, and one of his western adventures had a hero by the name of *The Lone Ranger*. The first episodes of *The Lone Ranger* were broadcast on WEBR with Buffalo actor John L. Barrett in the Lone Ranger role, later made famous by actor George Seaton. Striker was very prolific, writing over 156 Lone Ranger scripts a year, along with the comic strips for this and his other series. In addition to The Lone Ranger, Striker also created the Green Arrow and Sgt. Preston of the Yukon characters. These radio programs became syndicated while Striker was working for WXYZ in Detroit, but he had permanently moved back to Buffalo before he died in an automobile accident in Elma, NY in 1962.

In 1931 WEBR had 27 staffers and a studio orchestra conducted by Joe Armbruster. The station was known for its elaborate radio productions, some having as much as three weeks rehearsal before being broadcast. During the 1940s and 1950s the broadcast roster included Jack Eno, Ed Tucholka, Cy Buckley, Bernie Sandler and Al Meltzer.

WEBR became known for remote broadcasts of concerts from The Dellwood Ballroom, Bob Wells hosting the Hi-Teen Club at The Dellwood Ballroom, Ed Little hosting shows at The Town Casino and Ed Tucholka broadcasting from Polish Village. These remote broadcasts led to jazz programming with Carroll Hardy's *Jazz Central* and jazz legend Joe Rico.

WNY Public Broadcasting purchased WEBR in 1975 and it became the country's first public all-news station. In 1978, WEBR was named the nation's top-rated public radio station. Although officially known as an "all-news station" WEBR continued its tradition of jazz programming after 8:00 PM with Al Wallack's *Jazz in the Nighttime*. The show featured live performances from the Tralfamadore Café, Blue Note and Statler Hotel. Wallack was joined on the air by jazz DJ's Pres Freeland, Jim Santella, George Beck, Bill Besecker and John Warick. In 2013, WEBR, which had become WNED-AM, moved its programming to WBFO-88.7 FM. The 970AM frequency was sold to the WDCX Radio Group in Rochester NY, a Christian radio network that has been broadcasting for over 50 years.

WBEN RADIO

WBEN went on the air in 1930, but the history of the station goes back to the 1920s. It was originally known as WMAK and was launched in Lockport, NY in 1922, eventually moving to North Tonawanda. The station was owned by Buffalo Broadcasting, who also owned WGR and WKBW. When federal regulators began investigating the concentration of media ownership in the nation's largest radio markets, Buffalo Broadcasting decided to shut down WMAK, along with WKEN, a small local station in Kenmore.

    The Buffalo Evening News was granted a radio license as WBEN – We're the Buffalo Evening News, and purchased the decommissioned transmitting studio on Shawnee Road in NT. The station built the two-tower transmitter facility on Grand Island, which is still in use and the studio was moved to the Statler Hotel in 1930, so it would have access to the live orchestras. WBEN remained at The Statler Hotel until 1960, when it moved

WBEN ORCHESTRA
Top Row: Ed Radel, Tom Sist,
2nd Row: Bob Armstrong, Andy Dengos, Pat Vastola, Dan Brittain, Unknown
3rd Row: Unknown, Bill Wullen, Stan Zureck John McFadden, Jack Prolejko, Dick Fisher, Charlie Wullen
Photo: Courtesy Buffalo Musicians Union

to their new facilities at 2077 Elmwood Avenue, originally built for the radio and television operations by the NBC Network.

Prior to WWII, Jack Paar was an announcer at WBEN. He was drafted and chose not to return to Buffalo after the war. Jack Paar's replacement in 1943 was Clint Buehlman, who was hired, along with Buffalo Bob Smith, from competing station WGR. Buehlman remained at WBEN until 1977 and has been referred to as the King of Buffalo Broadcasting.

The music director of the WBEN in-house orchestra was Bob Armstrong, who led the orchestra when Jack Paar was at the station. When Jack Paar's *Tonight Show* was on TV from 1957 to 1962, Armstrong was the music director. After leaving the *Tonight Show*, Armstrong was a musical arranger for RCA Records and was nominated for two Grammy Awards. In 1994 Armstrong died of suspicious causes, at The Buffalo Veterans Hospital, after being attacked twice by another patient.

WBEN also started the first FM radio station in Buffalo, and in 1948 started the first Buffalo TV station – WBEN TV. Many of the initial programs on the television station were local music shows. When the television station premiered, the director of the in-studio radio band was Max Miller. Miller was also the BPO concertmaster and performed jazz at The Anchor Bar. He was the band leader on one of the first WBEN-TV shows called *Club Canandaigua*. It aired on Thursday nights at 7:30 and featured Miller along with Vince Brundo, Russ Messina, vocalist Joan Nichols and Tommie Rizzo, who was the band leader at the Dellwood Ballroom.

Another WBEN TV show called *One Chorus Only* featured Bobby Nicholson, who was the in-studio band leader at WKBW Radio. That shows aired Saturday nights at 10:00 PM and included Tommie Rizzo, Vince Brundo and vocalist Harry Schad, who was known as the bashful baritone and was on several WBEN radio programs. Nicholson later became the music director for the *Howdy Doody Show* with Buffalo Bob Smith. Nicholson was also the voice of Corny Cobb and played Clarabell for two years, after Bob Keeshan left the *Howdy Doody Show* to start the *Captain Kangaroo* children's television show. After leaving Howdy Doody, Nicholson was the director of the NBC Symphony for ten years. He also led the Tonight Show Band, when Skitch Henderson was not available, and founded the Westchester Philharmonic and the Florida Symphonic Pop Orchestra.

WKBW RADIO

WKBW was started by the Rev. Clinton Churchill in 1926. The call letters stood for <u>W</u>ell <u>K</u>nown <u>B</u>ible <u>W</u>itness. In 1928 WGR and WKBW formed Buffalo Broadcasting Corp, which also included WMAK (later WBEN) and WKEN (a local Kenmore, NY station). When the government started investigating the concentration of radio station ownership, Buffalo Broadcasting closed WMAK and WKEN. Then in 1942, when the FCC limited ownership to only one station in each market, Churchill took back ownership of WKBW. It was in the 1940s that it signed on with the NBC Blue network, which later became ABC.

The original transmitter site for WKBW radio was at 1430 Main Street in Buffalo. At that time it was a 5,000-watt station, being the first area station to raise its broadcast power to that level. In March 1941, WKBW opened a new transmitter plant south of the town of Hamburg, NY and increased its signal to 50,000 watts. With this power, its night time signal could be received all along the East Coast of the U.S.

In 1951 the owner of WKBW, Rev. Churchill, opened a new home for the radio station in what he called Radio City at the 1430 Main Street address. This replaced their previous studio in the Victor Building in Downtown Buffalo. The new site was the first radio station studio built specifically for broadcasting. The station at this time was a full service network affiliate station, primarily broadcasting network programming and offering local news. When not offering network programs, WKBW broadcast a wide variety of ethnic and country western music, and it became a pioneer in early rock 'n' roll and R&B programming.

The next stations to begin broadcasting in the Buffalo market were WBNY, founded by Roy Alberson in 1934, and WWOL, which was started by Leon Wyszatycki in 1947. More information on these stations and the rock transition of WKBW, is in the section on 1950s and early 1960s radio.

BUFFALO TELEVISION STATIONS

When television started it was the major radio networks that started the major television networks. The Buffalo radio stations that had the major network affiliations were WBEN, WGR and WKBW. Therefore, it was only a matter of time until these three stations became the first television stations in the Buffalo market.

WBEN TV

The first station that went on the air in Buffalo was WBEN-TV, in 1948 and it has been the CBS affiliate since 1949. It was the second television station to start broadcasting in upstate New York and at that time there were only 25 television station in the U.S. However, the beginning of television in Buffalo started well before the initial sign on date.

The Buffalo Evening News applied for permission from the FCC to build a television station in Buffalo in 1945. The other daily local paper, *The Courier Express*, had applied for a license a year earlier, but dropped their request. Bob Thompson of WBEN radio was instrumental in convincing the Butler family, who owned the News and WBEN radio, to move forward with this novel communications innovation. When permission for the station was granted, Fred Keller and three other employees were hired to gather information from experimental television stations around the country. Keller became the first Program Director assembling a team of seasoned radio professionals and WWII veterans to build a transmitter, control room and studio.

On May 13, 1948 WBEN telecast the consecration of Rev. Lauriston Scaife, the Episcopal Bishop of WNY, and started regular daily broadcasting the next night. The programming on the first day included ventriloquist Jimmy Nelson and wrestling from Memorial Auditorium. During early news broadcasts, the announcers just read the latest edition of the Buffalo Evening News, that was delivered to the television studio on the 18th floor of the Statler Hotel. The original announcing staff at WBEN was Ed Dinsmore, Ward Fenton, Jack Oglivie and Harry Webb.

Program director Fred Keller and Ray Wander wrote the first dramatic series that was shown on US television. The show was called *The Clue* and

DAYLIGHTERS – 1949 TV Show
Bassie Wilkinson, Reggie Willis,
Kenny Strother, Eddie Inge
Photo: Courtesy WIVB-TV

featured WBEN radio/TV columnist Jim Tranter as Private Eye Steve Malice. It started in 1948 and remained on the air for 5 years, every Tuesday at 7:30. Another early TV show featured veteran vaudeville dancers Mildred and Bill Miller. Their program, *Meet the Millers*, which offered a mix of cooking tips and humorous personality interviews, premiered in 1950 and remained on the air for 20 years.

Other early shows on WBEN TV included: wrestling from Memorial Auditorium in 1949 hosted by Chuck Healey and Ralph Hubble, *Beat the Champ* in 1957 hosted by Chuck Healy, *Uncle Jerry Club* in 1955 hosted by Jerry Brick, *Popeye's Playhouse* in 1952 hosted by Mike Mearian, and *Fun to Learn*, along with *Your Museum of Science* in 1952 which were hosted by Virgil Booth and Museum Curator Ellsworth Jaeger.

A VISIT TO SANTA CLAUS in 1954
Christmastime tradition 1948-1973
Photo: Courtesy WIVB-TV

The show that all baby boomers looked forward to every year was *A Visit to Santa Claus* which premiered in 1948. That show began broadcasting on the day after Thanksgiving every year with Ed Dinsmore as Santa, Johnny Eisenberg as Forgetful the Elf, Gene Block as Grumbles the Elf and Warren Jacober as Freezy the Polar Bear. The show received up to 50,000 letters a year to and remained on the air until 1973.

Changes were taking place behind the scenes at Channel 4. In 1952, WBEN moved their transmitter from the roof of the Statler Hotel to a hilltop in Colden, NY. This allowed them to reach TV sets across WNY and into Southern Ontario. In 1960, the television station and radio stations moved into new facilities at 2077 Elmwood Avenue. These facilities had been built by NBC for their locally owned and operated UHF station WBUF-TV (Channel 17) which went off the air in 1958.

When *Buffalo Evening News* owner Katherine Butler passed away in 1977 without any heirs, the Buffalo News, WBEN AM & FM radio and WBEN TV were put up for sale. The new owners changed the name of the station to WIVB TV, with the IV representing the Roman Numeral 4, and adopted the slogan We're For (IV) Buffalo. They also changed the name of their news broadcast from *First Team News* to *News 4 Buffalo*. The station followed the electronic news national transition from film to video tape in 1978 and in the 1980s it was the first to implement satellite reception.

The on-air staff that people are familiar with started in 1979. After Carol Crissey moved to Buffalo, she married and changed her name to Carol Jason. Jacquie Walker moved from Rochester to host the noon news but soon co-anchored the 5:00 and 11:00 News with Rich Newberg. Meteorologist Don Paul joined the staff in the early 1980s and was soon joined by Mike Cejka. This news team was joined by sports director, Van Miller, who was also known as the voice of the Buffalo Bills.

WGR TV

WGR-TV went on the air August 14, 1954 as the area NBC affiliate, broadcasting as VHS Channel 2. The beginning of the station dated back to 1948 when WGR Radio and The Niagara Gazette both filed applications with the FCC for a television station. However, the FCC put a freeze on new television station applications until 1952. At that time WGR and The Niagara Gazette refiled their applications. Two other parties also filed applications, Victor Television – an investment group led by the owner of Victor Furniture Store, and Niagara Frontier Amusement – a group of prominent WNY businessmen. During the negotiations, WGR Radio was sold to the other three groups, who successful obtained the license under the name of WGR Corporation.

The station was initially located at 184 Barton Street in Buffalo, sharing the studio with UHF outlet, WBUF-TV – Channel 17. From 1956 to 1958 they were an ABC affiliate because NBC decided to switch their affiliation to UHF on Channel 17. All television sets could not receive UHF signals, so that switch was not successful and NBC returned to Channel 2 to stay in 1958.

The first television show broadcast from the Channel 2 studios on Barton Street, a former rug-cleaning facility, was

WGRZ STAFF 1980s
Barry Lillis, Ed Kilgore,
Ann Urbanato, Rich Kellman,
Susan Banks
Photo: Courtesy WGRZ-TV

the Mr. Wizard Show. That was followed later in the day by a dedicatory program hosted by George Goodyear (spokesman for the investment group) and WGR radio personality Billy Keaton. They introduced the views of the station, their personnel, the programs and future plans. The NBC line-up provided entertainment by Bob Hope, Milton Berle, Sid Caesar, Ernie Kovacs and former Buffalo DJ, Buffalo Bob Smiths's *Howdy Doody Show.* Personalities from WGR radio provided local programming like Helen Neville hosting *Two for Breakfast* and Mary Lawton playing musical games, along with remembering audience member's birthdays on *The Mother Goose Show.* The spacious Barton Street facilities were also the home of wrestling matches with Ilio DiPaolo and the first *Variety Club Telethon* in 1962. It was even transformed to resemble the Statler Rendezvous Room for a musical dance show featuring the Dave Cheskin Orchestra. Other music shows on the studio were *The Pic-A-Polka Show, Hit & Miss* Dance Show with Tommy Shannon, *TV Dance Party* with Pat Fagan and a weekly country music show hosted by Ramblin' Lou.

PIC-A-POLKA SHOW
Photo: Courtesy WGRZ-TV

The transmitter towers for Channel 2 were located on top of the Lafayette Hotel, with back-up towers on Elmwood Avenue. In the 1960s, they moved the transmitter site to South Wales, New York. WGR Corp. purchased other radio and television stations across the country and changed their name to Transcontinent Broadcasting, becoming Taft Broadcasting in 1964. In 1972, Channel 2 moved from Barton Street to their new facilities at 259 Delaware Avenue. The broadcast team in the late 1970s was Barry Lillis, Ed Kilgore, Sheila Murphy, and Rich Kellman. When Taft sold the television station, they sold the radio station to a different group, which retained the radio station name as WGR. The TV station had to change their name to WGRZ, choosing that name because the Z looked like a 2. In the mid-80s the newscast was Ed Kilgore, Fred Debrine, John Chandik and Susan Banks. It was not until the early '90s that Mary Alice Demler and Kevin O'Connell joined the station.

WKBW TV

The Buffalo Courier Express newspaper wanted a television station in Buffalo so they could better compete with *The Buffalo Evening News*. They put in a bid for the last remaining VHS allocation (Channel 7 license), but the FCC chose Dr. Clinton Churchill, who was the owner of the 50,000-watt WKBW radio 1520 AM. The original home of the TV station was next to the radio station at 1420 Main Street, between Utica and Ferry. They moved to 7 Broadcast Plaza, near the waterfront, in 1978.

On November 30, 1958, the person that signed on the station was Rick Azar, with the words "Ladies and Gentlemen, WKBW TV Channel 7 is on the air!" Channel 7 was originally licensed to be an independent station. However, shortly before they went on the air, WBUF the UHF Channel 17 NBC affiliate went off the air. This allowed Channel 2 to resume their NBC affiliation. When Channel 2 relinquished their ABC affiliation, Channel 7 became the ABC affiliate, giving them the programming provided by the ABC network.

In addition to the ABC affiliate programming, local productions were an important part of the station. In 1962 *Rocketship 7*, with Dave Thomas and Promo the Robot (played by John Banaszak from Johnny & Jimmy), was the weekday morning children's program. The show remained on the air until Dave Thomas relocated to a television station in Philadelphia in 1978. Tom Joel's *Commander Tom Show* was on weekday afternoons starting in 1965. It was a mix of cartoons and Commander Tom interacting with the puppets Dustmop, Matty the Mod and Cecily Fripple, with her evil sister puppet Cecile. The show was on weekdays until 1978 and weekends until 1991. *Dialing for Dollars* started in 1964 with hosts Liz Dribben and Nolan Johannes, along with the music duo of Johnny & Jimmy. That show evolved into *AM Buffalo,* which is still on the air and often features musical guests.

DIALING FOR DOLLARS
Jimmy Grazanowski & Johnny Banaszak
Nolan Johannes, Dave Thomas
Photo: Courtesy WKBW-TV

The late-night newscast began with "Its 11:00 o'clock. Do you know where your children are?" This was how the trio of newsman Irv Weinstein, sportscaster Rick Azar and weatherman Tom Jolls introduced themselves every week night. They were on the air together from 1964 to 1989, becoming the longest- running news team in the history of television, presenting the early and late newscasts together for 24 years.

As the ABC affiliate, WKBW broadcast *American Bandstand* every afternoon just after everyone got home from school. WKBW also had a local dance show called *Buffalo Bandstand*, which was the local franchising of *American Bandstand*. It was hosted by Rick Azar, who once filled in for Dick Clark on the national show. Buffalo Bandstand was later hosted by WKBW radio DJ Tommy Shannon. In addition to the rock 'n' roll music shows, Channel 7 presented a Polka TV show hosted by Frankie Yankovic in 1962 and later by The New Yorkers. Channel 7 is also the home of the annual Variety Club Telethon, which raises money for Buffalo Children's Hospital and is hosted by area entertainers like Clint Holmes, The Scinta Brothers and Terry Buchwald, in addition to featuring many other WNY performers.

As the local ABC affiliate, Channel 7 has the broadcast rights to Dick Clarks New Year's Eve telecast from Times Square in NYC. This is combined with WKBW broadcasting the Buffalo Ball Drop from the Electric Tower in Roosevelt Square. The Buffalo New Year's Eve celebration is the second largest ball drop in the country, with over 40,000 people coming in person and most of WNY watching on TV, music by a Buffalo band and fireworks from the Electric Tower to bring in the new year.

UHF CHANNELS IN BUFFALO

Buffalo was initially served by only one VHF station – WBEN Channel 4. In 1948 the FCC put a freeze on the issuance of new VHF television licenses so the government could formulate a master plan for television in the U.S. The freeze was supposed to last for about six months but due to the Korean War, the freeze lasted four years. During this time, there were only 108 VHF television stations on the air and over 700 new applications on hold.

In the Buffalo market, the allocated VHF (Very High Frequency) channels ended up being 2, 4 and 7, with the VHF signal being broadcast on channels 2 – 13. To receive any channels above 13 you needed a UHF (Ultra High Frequency) converter, with UHF being broadcast on channels 14-83. Since all homes did not have converters, only the VHF channels had 100% market saturation, so their channels were more valuable. A UHF channel was more of a risk, but it was easier and less costly to obtain a UHF license.

In 1952, to break the one-station monopoly of WBEN, Buffalo businessmen applied for and received two UHF licenses. One license went to Buffalo-Niagara Television Corp for Channel 59 and the other was to Sherwin Grossman and Gary Cohen for Channel 17. Both stations started construction in 1953, with Channel 17 building their WBUF studio at 184 Barton Street. The station went on the air in August 1953, becoming the second station in Buffalo. Three months later they increased their signal twelve-fold, allowing the UHF signal to be received on an indoor, rather than an outdoor antenna. However, they soon encountered competition from the second VHF license that was granted in the Buffalo market, WGR Channel 2, located in the same building at 184 Barton Street. WGR was granted the NBC franchise for the Buffalo market. WBUF Channel 17 knew they were in trouble, they put the station up for sale.

In the 1950s, according to FCC regulations, networks could only own five VHF stations in the U.S. but they could add two UHF stations. NBC was at the five station VHF limit, so they decided to conduct a market research test in the Buffalo market by operating a UHF station. In 1955, they bought WBUF Channel 17 and utilizing the best available technology, built a two-million-dollar studio and transmitter tower at 2077 Elmwood Avenue. In 1956, they transferred the NBC affiliation from

Channel 2 to WBUF, but with the sometime inferior UHF converters, some viewers in the eastern portion of WNY tuned to WROC channel 5 in Rochester for better picture reception of the NBC broadcasts. NBC launched an aggressive marketing campaign to increase the number of UHF converters installed in the Buffalo market. However, by the end of 1956, they only reached 53% of the available TV sets in WNY and the station had more expenses than revenue.

In 1957 the third and final VHF license was granted in Buffalo to WKBW TV Channel 7, which was planning to operate as an independent station. Even the deep pockets of the national NBC television network, the station could no longer sustain the losses being experienced with the WBUF UHF channel 17 experiment. In September 1958, NBC pulled the plug on WBUF, shut down the station and put the broadcast facilities up for sale. Channel 2 got back the NBC franchise and when Channel 7 went on the air in November 1958 they acquired the ABC franchise.

The failure of NBC Buffalo experiment gave UHF a bad name in the broadcasting industry and with the viewing public. UHF was put on the back burner by commercial stations until federal legislation could make it more feasible. To add insult to injury, in 1960 the two-million-dollar facility that NBC built at 2077 Elmwood Ave was purchased at a much-reduced price by Channel 4, the local CBS affiliate.

Channel 17 was off the air for several months, and in March 1959 it reemerged as WNED TV – Public Broadcasting. It was New York State's first noncommercial television station. They eventually obtained sole possession of the 184 Barton Street studio they had shared with Channel 2. In October 1993, WNED moved to their state-of-the-art facilities in Horizons Plaza at 140 Lower Terrace near the Buffalo waterfront. WNED-TV continues to be ranked among the most watched U.S. public television stations. From 1975 to 2004, Buffalo-born political satirist Mark Russell telecast at least four annual PBS specials live from the WNED studios. Other public broadcasting programs were produced at their state of the art studios.

Channel 59 WBES which was also granted a UHF license in 1952, and raced with Channel 17 to become the second television station to begin broadcasting in Buffalo. Channel 59 located their offices in the Lafayette Hotel and planned to use the hotel ballroom as their studio. They built a tower on top of the Lafayette Hotel but programming and construction delays allowed Channel 17 to begin telecasting six weeks prior to the

Channel 59 premier on September 29, 1953. Poor advertising sales resulted in WBES turning their license back into the FCC after less than three months on the air. Their tower on top of the hotel became the new transmitter tower for Channel 2.

It was not until after the FCC "All Channel Act" that UHF channels became a viable alternative to VHS. With the passage of that legislation, UHF channels could be received on all TV that were sold effective in 1964, a UHF converter was only needed on pre-1964 television sets. The first commercial UHF channel in WNY was WUTV channel 29. It was founded by Stan Jasinski, who was a popular Polish broadcaster and also the owner of WMMJ 1300 AM. To assist in funding Channel 29, Jasinski sold WMMJ in 1970 to Ramblin Lou Schriver, who renamed it WXRL-classic country radio. Channel 29 is now the WNY Fox affiliate. During the 1980s, two UHF channels began broadcasting, Channel 49 WNYO and Channel 23 WNEQ. Reception for these stations was no longer an issue because of government "must carry" regulations for cable television providers. These regulations stipulated that cable provider's systems must carry locally-licensed broadcast network and independent television stations. Channel 49 became affiliated with Channel 29 and shares their 699 Hertel Avenue studios. Channel 23 was originally affiliated with Channel 17 but it was determined that Buffalo was not large enough for two public television stations. It was sold to Channel 4, under the original commercial license held by the original Channel 17 WBUF. Channel 23 now shares the 2077 Elmwood Avenue studios with Channel 4. In 1997 the last station started in WNY, WNGS channel 67, was launched. This station became WBBZ, invoked the must-carry rules and lobbied Time Warner to assign them the coveted channel 5, which had been the location of analog HBO before the digital transition on June 12, 2009. WBBZ is owned by local television veterans and emphasizes local programming.

7

CLASSICAL MUSIC

One of the first significant Buffalo classical music concerts was in November 1869 when the Theodore Thomas Orchestra performed at St James Hall. This Orchestra had 80 members and was one of the greatest touring orchestras of the 19th Century. Their objective was to introduce the European master to new listeners and inspire audiences to develop their own professional orchestras in the cities where they performed. Thomas achieved his goal in Buffalo, because within a few weeks of this performance, a Buffalo orchestra conducted by William Grosscurth presented a concert at St. James Hall.

THE BUFFALO ORCHESTRA ASSOCIATION 1891
Photo: Courtesy BPO Archives

In 1887, the Buffalo Orchestra Association was formed under the direction of John Lund. The funding of the expenses for the orchestra was provided by Frederick Lautz, who was the owner of The Lautz Soap Company. This 53-member ensemble was also known as the Buffalo Symphony Orchestra and they performed until 1898, when Lautz was no longer able to make up the Orchestra's deficit from the shortfalls of ticket sales and advertising.

The Buffalo Chromatic Club was formed in 1898 and they assisted in starting the Community School of Music, which still exists on Elmwood Avenue. In 1922 they sponsored the first concert by the newly formed

BUFFALO SYMPHONY ORCHESTRA 1924 – 1925 SEASON
Photo: Courtesy BPO Archives

Buffalo Symphony Orchestra. This 70-piece orchestra was conducted by Arnold Cornelissen and consisted of all local musicians, who also performed at movie houses and vaudeville theaters in WNY. The orchestra operated under The Buffalo Plan, which stipulated that the orchestra and all soloists consist only of local musicians. It was formulated by concert presenters Mai Davis Smith and Marian de Forest. The local only plan was a great idea to promote Buffalo area musicians but it proved to be impractical. This plan impeded the formation of a permanent symphonic orchestra because the orchestra could only include area residents.

Many European immigrants, especially from Germany, Italy and Poland settled in Buffalo and brought their instruments with them. There were sufficient musicians to form ensembles, but finding musicians to fill all the positions of a professional orchestra proved difficult in the 19th century. The new immigrants also arrived with their passion for singing, and it was easier to assemble choirs. The most significant vocal ensembles were the German men's choirs Buffalo Orpheus and the Schwaebischer Saegerbund and Polish community choir, the Moniuszki Singing Society. The Chopin Singing Society was formed in 1899. At their club house and rehearsal facility on Kosciuski Street, the Dyngus Day Parties were started in Buffalo.

The Buffalo Symphony Orchestra re-emerged in 1932 as a 75-member professional level orchestra with maestro John Ingram. In addition to conducting the orchestra, Ingram conducted several theater orchestras, including Sheas Buffalo. The musicians were grateful for their theater work but felt their technique for classical repertoire was wanting. This ensemble performed under a variety of names including the Buffalo Civic Orchestra, Buffalo Community Orchestra and the Buffalo Philharmonic Orchestra. As the BPO, they were designated as the official orchestra for

Buffalo's 1932 centennial celebration. However, the orchestra was not incorporated as the present day organization until 1935.

During the 19th Century, symphonic performances took place at The Opera House I (in the Arcade Building), Grand Opera House (on Washington Street), St James Hall, Adelphi Theatre, Star Theatre, American Hall, Townsend Hall, McArthur's Garden, The Music Hall, Teck Theater and The Academy of Music. Before the Elmwood Music Hall became the home for orchestra performances, the Buffalo Broadway Auditorium hosted many events.

The Broadway Auditorium at 201 Broadway was built in 1858, and during the Civil War it served as the armory for the 65th and 74th Regiments. It was a National Guard armory from 1884 to 1907 and in 1910 was remodeled into an auditorium and arena. In this building promoters presented boxing matches, circuses, conventions, dances, concerts and sporting events. Joe Lewis and Jack Dempsey both boxed at the arena, in 1931 the Buffalo Majors of the American Hockey Association played games there and the Six Nations indoor box lacrosse team (with star Harry Smith – aka Jay Silverheels, Tonto on the Lone Ranger TV Show) played their games there. The arena also hosted a Woodrow Wilson political rally, along with concerts by Enrico Caruso, Ella Fitzgerald and Cab Calloway. This building stopped functioning as an arena when Buffalo Memorial Auditorium opened in 1940. During WWII the building reverted back to being an armory. The Buffalo Department of Public Works took over the building in 1948, and it became known as the Broadway Barn, the home to Buffalo's sanitation trucks, snow plows and the garage for highway salt storage. Currently, the public works department may be building a new facility, so the future of the building that once housed the Broadway Auditorium, Buffalo's premier site for indoor assembly from 1910 to 1940, is unknown.

The Elmwood Music Hall at 400 Virginia Street at the corner of Elmwood was designed by Bethene & Bethune, the architectural firm that also designed the Lafayette Hotel. Louise Blanchard Bethune of that company earned the title of the nation's first female architect. The building was originally designed as the 74th Armory. When the 74th Infantry moved to the Connecticut Street Armory in 1899, the city of Buffalo acquired the property and turned it in to a concert hall named Convention Hall. After the Broadway Auditorium opened, there was confusion between the two

ELMWOOD MUSIC HALL
Photo: Courtesy BPO Archives

facilities, so in 1912 it was officially renamed The Elmwood Music Hall, but often just referred to as The Music Hall.

When the Pan American Exposition closed, the organ from The Temple of Music was supposed to be installed at St Louis RC Church. However, the organ was too big for the space at the church, so J.N. Adams presented the organ to the city and it was installed in the Elmwood Music Hall. Organ recitals were the first musical presentations at the hall, followed by Charity Balls and other social events. Eventually it became the home of the Buffalo Symphony Orchestra during the 1920s, and on November 7, 1935, the Buffalo Philharmonic Orchestra presented its first concert at Elmwood Music Hall. However, the building was designed as an armory, so folding chairs had to be set up for the concerts. Also, the hall did not have the acoustics or sound proofing of a concert hall. Concert attendees could often hear the outside traffic and trolley cars during performances.

Buffalo needed a music hall, and in the early 1930s renowned Buffalo architect E.B. Green submitted a neoclassical design for a music hall as an addition to the Buffalo Museum of Science in Humboldt Park. This building would have been an all-inclusive music complex with several concert halls, entertainment centers and education facilities, but it was never built.

The need for a new music hall escalated after The Elmwood Music Hall was condemned. Nelson Eddy performed the final recital there on February 25, 1938. The building was torn down after that event, and BPO concerts for the 1938/9 and 1939/40 seasons were temporarily held at the Buffalo Consistory, now Canisius High School. Concerts were also held outside of the city of Buffalo in Niagara Falls and Akron.

Funding for Kleinhans Music Hall came from the estate of Edward and Mary Seaton Kleinhans, who owned Kleinhans Clothing Store. They died within three months of each other in 1934 and bequeathed $710,000 to the Community Foundation for the construction of a music hall. The depression organization Public Works Administration (WPA) contributed an additional grant of $600,000. A building location was selected on the site of the Truman Avery mansion on The Circle at Richmond and Porter Avenues. Architects Eliel and Eero Saarinen submitted a futuristic exterior design based on the shape of a violin. No expense was spared with the interior design, resulting in Kleinhans being considered one of the foremost acoustically designed concerts halls in the country. At 2,839 seats, reduced to about 2,400 seats after recent renovations, it is also one of the nation's largest concert halls. The BPO performed the first concert at Kleinhans on October 12, 1940. Buffalo finally had a world class, permanent concert hall.

BUFFALO PHILHARMONIC ORCHESTRA

The Buffalo Symphony Orchestra was presenting concerts at The Elmwood Music Hall, and despite the economic climate of the depression, Buffalo yearned for its own full-time professional symphony orchestra. Some community leaders recognized that President Franklin D. Roosevelt's public works programs created to assist in alleviating unemployment during the depression, could transition this fledging orchestra into a fully-contracted professional organization.

Established in 1934, the Emergency Relief Bureau (ERB) was designed to support theater projects, and the theaters needed music. Buffalo applied for and received funding through the Theater Workshop Department for a Buffalo ERB Orchestra led by Lajos Shuk. The Works Project Administration (WPA) was founded in 1935, and in addition to providing funding for buildings like War Memorial Auditorium, The Buffalo Zoo and Kleinhans, it provided support for Federal Art, Writers and Theatre Projects. In Buffalo, there were 104 musicians assigned to six different units that ranged from popular dance to classical recitals. Programs were presented at hospitals, schools and community centers, along with concerts at the Elmwood Music Hall, Statler Golden Ballroom and Albright-Art Gallery. In August 1935, WPA funding, with support from WPA administrator and former Cleveland Symphony Orchestra maestro Nikolai Sokoloff, was secured for the Buffalo orchestra. Under the

BUFFALO PHILHARMONIC ORCHESTRA 1938
Photo: Courtesy BPO Archives

direction of Lajos Shuk, the first BPO concert was presented on November 7, 1935, and the BPO Society was incorporated in spring 1936.

The Federal Music Project was funded by the WPA, and for the 1936/7 season they brought Franco Autori to Buffalo. During that season, Lajos Shuk held the title of music director, while Autori functioned as resident guest conductor. The WPA funds that Autori brought with him, allowed additional members to be hired for the BPO and the 36/37 season to expand to 21 concerts. Autori was appointed music director for the 37/38 season, and a fund-raising campaign was organized by BPO Society, headed by president Florence Wendt, known as Mrs. Edgar F. Wendt. The fund raising was successful because when the WPA Federal Music Project funding expired with the 38/39 season, the BPO was able to expand its programming for the 39/40 season. During this time, the Young People's and Pops concerts were inaugurated by the orchestra.

In addition to Mrs. Edgar F. Wendt, three important members of the BPO Society were Samuel Capen, Cameron Baird and Frederick Slee. For their contributions, they are considered the founders of the BPO, and they were also responsible for starting the Music Department at UB. Capen was the chancellor of UB from 1922–1950 and he hired Baird, who was responsible for setting up the music department. Working with them, providing a fellowship for visiting composers and funding the Budapest String Quartet was Slee. For these contributions, buildings and locations at UB are named after Capen, Baird and Slee.

When Zorah B. Berry moved to Buffalo from Detroit in 1922, she became involved with classical music. She and her husband had been involved with the Philharmonic Concert Company based in Detroit. After her husband's death, she took over management and assumed ownership of the Buffalo branch of the organization. In 1926, she launched Zorah Berry Presents at the Buffalo Consistory (now Canisius High School) Auditorium. Events she presented individually and in collaboration with the BPO brought an endless stream of star-studded symphonic, opera and ballet performances and artists to Buffalo. In 1957, the Zorah Berry Concert Series merged with the BPO, and she was named BPO Concert Manager, responsible for handling ticket sales and artistic programming. Her 40-year career with symphonic presentations continued until 1962.

The Buffalo Philharmonic Orchestra has had many prominent music directors including Lajos Shuk, Franco Autori, William Steinberg, Josef Krips, Lukas Foss, Michael Tilson Thomas, Julius Rudel, Semyon Bychkov, Maximiano Valdes and JoAnne Falletta. During the 1990s, Doc Severinsen, of the Johnny Carson Tonight Show Band was the pops conductor and was followed by Marvin Hamlisch. Several guest conductors were Leonard Bernstein, Arthur Fiedler, Igor Stravinsky, Ralph Vaughan Williams, Sir Neville Mariner and Henry Mancini. During the regular concert season, the BPO presents classical concerts, pops concerts, educational youth concerts and family concerts at Kleinhans Music Hall. During the summer, the orchestra performs at parks and outdoor venues across WNY. For detailed information on the BPO see the book *Buffalo Philharmonic Orchestra – The BPO Celebrates the First 75 Years* by Raya Lee and Edward Yadzinski. Also see the Buffalo Philharmonic Orchestra web site bpo.org.

Dr. Joseph Wincenc was the Assistant Concertmaster of the BPO for its first concert at Kleinhans in 1940. As he explained in a newspaper interview, in 1940 each philharmonic musician was paid $18.00 per week, the first chair musician got $21.00 and the assistant concertmaster received a salary of $25.00 per week. Wincenc has been instrumental in promoting classical music in WNY by forming the Amherst Symphony Orchestra in 1946, the Orchard Park Symphony Orchestra in 1950 and the Clarence Outdoor Concerts in 1959. He was also responsible for starting the Buffalo State College Music Department and became the BPO associate conductor, concertmaster and first violinist. His daughter Carol Wincenc is an internationally-known classical flutist.

During the 1960s, Buffalo earned the distinction of being a center for avant-garde presentations. Two of the people leading this movement were Seymour Knox at the Albright-Knox Art Gallery and Lukas Foss with the BPO. The first Buffalo Festival of the Arts was held from February 27 to March 13, 1965, sponsored by the Albright-Knox Art Gallery in cooperation with the BPO, Buffalo State College, UB, the Erie County Public Library and the NYS Council on the Arts. The steering committee of the festival included Lukas Foss, Allen Sapp, Seymour

Knox, businessman Max Clarkson and Gordon M. Smith, the art gallery director. Seymour Knox decided to subsidize most of the funding through his foundation rather than seek national foundation support. The two-week festival drew an attendance of 186,640 people. The Second Buffalo Festival of the Arts Today was a 16-day presentation of art, theater, film, music, dance and writing, in March of 1968. It was a slightly smaller presentation but still drew well over 100,000 people.

June in Buffalo contemporary music festivals began in 1975. The initial festivals were started by Morton Feldman and sponsored by UB and its Center of the Creative and Performing Arts, which was later called the Creative Associates and Center for 21st Century Music. These organizations continue the June in Buffalo festival, Slee Sinfonietta Chamber Orchestra concert series and the Guest Artist Series of performances, lecture presentations and workshops. For detailed information on the Buffalo Festival of the Arts and June in Buffalo see Rene Levine Packer's book *The Life of Sounds: Evenings for New Music in Buffalo.*

OPERA, CHAMBER MUSIC & MORE

Opera was performed at many of the early theaters and also at churches in Buffalo, with WNY having a long history of offering cultured entertainment. Three of the area theaters that were originally dedicated to opera performances included The Opera House in the Arcade Building, The Opera House II on Washington north of Broadway and Wahles Opera House on Court Street. Other dedicated opera houses were the Lockport

LANCASTER OPERA HOUSE
Downtown Lancaster 1908
Photo: Courtesy Lancaster Historical Society

Opera House (opened in 1871), Lancaster Opera House (opened in 1897) and Fredonia Opera House (opened in 1891). There was also an opera house, diagonally across the street from the Riviera Theater in North Tonawanda, located on the second floor of the building that now is Crazy Jakes Restaurant.

Buffalo audiences supported and welcomed opera after the performances of Jenny Lind in 1851. A few years later, Adelina Patti, who became one of the highest-paid opera performers, presented several concerts in Buffalo when she was still an adolescent. After the Civil War, opera companies from Europe often performed in Buffalo, including Italian Tenor Pasquale Brignoli. Hardware store owner Hobart Weed was a supporter of opera in Buffalo, and in 1918 both Victor Herbert and John Lund composed music for a tribute to Weed, performed by John Lund's Orchestra and the Philharmonic Chorus. Gary Burgess organized the professional Buffalo Lyric Opera, which merged with the WNY Opera Theater to form the Greater Buffalo Opera Company in 1988. Burgess was also the founder of the opera program at SUNY Buffalo. Buffalo Opera Unlimited has been presenting opera in Buffalo since 1985.

Ballet has also had a presence in Buffalo going back to the early theaters. The Buffalo Ballet Theater was founded by Barry Leon in the 1960s, and the Buffalo Inner City Ballet was established in 1972 by Karl Singletary. Ballet is taught at many dance studios across the WNY area.

The Buffalo Chamber Music Society was founded in 1924 and is one of the oldest chamber series in the U.S. Its first concert was held on March 12, 1924, at the Hotel Statler Ballroom. These concerts continued until 1940, when they were moved to the Mary Seaton Room of Kleinhans Music Hall. Marian de Forest, also the founder of Zonta International, was one of the individuals responsible for forming the society and later assisting in the formation of the BPO. In 1931, The Buffalo Chamber Music Society presented the first Buffalo concert by the Budapest Quartet, who were supported by Cameron Baird of the UB Music Department. The society celebrated its 90th anniversary in 2014.

ARS Nova Musicians is a chamber music orchestra directed by Marylouise Nanna. Since the 1980s it has been presenting the Viva Vivaldi Festival at the First Presbyterian Church on Symphony Circle. Their television concerts from Canisius College were nominated for a Peabody Award and were broadcast nationwide on PBS-TV.

The Buffalo Schola Cantorum was established by Jessamine E. Long in 1937, with the first rehearsals being held at her home. It later became the Buffalo Philharmonic Chorus. Long led the chorus until 1945, was then succeeded by Cameron Baird, and later followed by Thomas Swan, who had a 22-year tenure. The Philharmonic Chorus is an independent symphonic chorus, with a roster of approximately 110 singers that presents self-sponsored concerts and is the primary choral partner of the BPO.

QRS Great Performers series was started in Buffalo by Ramsi Tick, who was the manager of the BPO from 1956-1964. The series brought performers like Vladimir Horowitz, Arthur Rubenstein, Andres Segovia, Beverly Sills and Isaac Stern to Buffalo. In 1966, Tick purchased the QRS Piano Rolls Company from New York City and relocated it to Buffalo. He sold the company to Richard Dolan in 1989, with Bob Berkman later becoming president of the firm. QRS remains the only piano roll manufacturer in the country and they still make 12 to 15,000 piano rolls a year at their 1026 Niagara Street factory. They updated their product line, to include state of the art computer based technology, and changed the company name to QRS Music Technologies.

The Buffalo Museum of Science had their own orchestra that presented Twilight Music Hour concerts. It began in 1936 with the the Symphony Training Orchestra of the Museum. This became a self-supporting organization that offered students, amateurs and semi-professionals the opportunity to read and study orchestral music. In 1938 it presented a 61-member orchestra at concerts.

The Cheektowaga Symphony Orchestra was founded in 1960 to provide the residents of Cheektowaga and surrounding communities the opportunity to play in a symphony orchestra, to offer an enriching cultural experience for each member of the community, and to encourage appreciation of a wide repertoire of music. The Orchestra provides programs in all four school districts in Cheektowaga: Cheektowaga-Sloan, Cheektowaga Central, Cleveland Hill and Maryvale. Their programs range from classical to popular music and have been presented in the Cheektowaga community at the Polish-American Arts Festival, Flag Day celebrations, the Cultural Center and Cultural Weekend. Robert Mols was the conductor from 1961-1971, followed by Frank Collura (1971-3) Manuel Alvarez (1973-5), Marylouise Nanna (1976-1991) and John Landis (1991-2015).

The American Legion Band of the Tonawandas was formed in 1929 and at full strength has 90 members. Many members of this all-volunteer band are instrumental music educators, graduates or students of university music programs. The band performs up to 30 concerts annually, has won numerous National American Legion Band titles and traveled internationally.

The Amherst Saxophone Quartet (ASQ) was a chamber music ensemble that performed locally, nationally and internationally for almost three decades. They were formed in 1978 as the Modern Yadz Quartet, in honor of their mentor Edward Yadzinski, a member of the BPO and saxophone professor at UB. The founding members were Sal Andolina (soprano sax), Michael Nascimben (alto sax), Steven Rosenthal (tenor sax) and Harry Fackelman (baritone sax). Rosenthal and Fackelman remained active with the quartet during its tenure, Russ Carere had been

AMHERST SAXOPHONE
QUARTET
Photo: Courtesy Steven Rosenthal
Photo Credit: Mary Fote

associated with the ASQ since 1982 and became a member in 1990, while Susan Fancher joined in 1998. They released numerous albums and performed across the U.S. from Maine to Hawaii, and in Japan and the Caribbean. In addition to many radio and television appearances (including *The Tonight Show*), they had multiple appearances at Carnegie Hall, Kennedy Center, Lincoln Center, and the Chautauqua Institute. The ASQ commissioned national composers to write works for them, with these pieces becoming part of the ASQ's regular repertory. The quartet also presented educational workshops at schools and received numerous awards for their accomplishments.

8

1950s ROCK 'N' ROLL

The Hi-Teen Club dances at The Dellwood Ballroom could be considered the transition point between Big Band Music and 1950s music in Buffalo, especially for the teen audience. WEBR started these dances in January 1946 at the USO Club, which was located on Niagara Square. They moved to several locations, including Kleinhans Music Hall, The Elks Ballroom and Eagles Club, until finding a permanent home at the Dellwood Ballroom.

The shows were hosted by WEBR disc jockey Bob Wells and were held on Saturday afternoons from 2:00 to 5:00, with over one thousand teens showing up every week. In addition to providing music for the kids, the Hi-Teen club was a structured environment which offered wholesome entertainment and socially acceptable experiences. The Hi-Teen Club involved teens in fund-raising and community activities such as clothing drives, food drives and a variety of charitable ventures. Boys had to wear a tie to be admitted to the Dellwood Ballroom and if someone showed up without one, a rack of ties were available at the entrance. Teens were encouraged to join the Hi-Teen Club and membership peaked at 22,000 during the early 1950s.

When the Hi-Teen club began, big band was the most popular style of music and the singers were the stars. Recording artists like Perry Como, Pat Boone and Tony Bennett would appear at the Dellwood Ballroom to promote their records. The success of the program was verified by *Billboard Magazine*, who rated the Hi-Teen Club the third most popular record show in America. When musical tastes started to change to rock ' n' roll, artists like Frankie Avalon, Fabian and Jerry Lee Lewis came to perform at The Dellwood Ballroom. This transition resulted in the dancing switching from big band swing to the jitterbug, the bop, hand-jive, the stroll or the twist.

Buffalo became a launching pad for hits and an appearance at the Hi-Teen club could be a booster for recording artists. The popularity of The Hi-Teen Club was evidenced when Ted Horn, from WFIL TV in Philadelphia, came to Buffalo to observe the airing of The Hi-Teen Club. Horn was impressed with the concept of the show and when he returned to Philadelphia he started a television show called *The Ted Horn Bandstand*. Horn left the show in controversy and he was replaced by a young Dick Clark, who was working at the radio station affiliated with WFIL. When Dick Clark became the host, the name of the show was changed to *American Bandstand* and it became a network television program, broadcast every afternoon on ABC.

The basics of *American Bandstand* came from the Hi-Teen Club and the Buffalo's ABC affiliate WKBW had a show called *Buffalo Bandstand*, in addition to broadcasting *American Bandstand*. The host was Rick Azar, who at one time was a fill-in host for Dick Clark on the nationally syndicated show. Channel 7 also had a television show called *Hit N Miss*, which was hosted by Tommy Shannon and Channel 2 had a show called *TV Dance Party*, hosted by Pat Fagan, which featured national and local bands and was telecast on Saturday from their Barton Street studio.

Rock 'n' roll music was becoming the dominant form of music for the growing teen population in WNY and soon there were bands playing at area schools, churches and community centers. Radio was important during the late 1950s and early 1960s, with the radio station DJs working with these bands to bring rock 'n' roll music to the teen generation.

ERSEL HICKEY

After an Everly Brothers concert, Ersel Hickey met Phil Everly and told him he wanted to be a singer. Everly replied "Well, you got to have a song." So Ersel went home and wrote "Bluebirds Over the Mountain," which was the first song by a Buffalo rock 'n' roll artist to reach the national charts. In 1958, it peaked at #74 on the Billboard charts and was later covered by The Beach Boys. Ersel's version of the song at one minute 24 seconds in length, was the shortest Top 100 hit in history.

Self-promotion was one of the keys to Ersel's success. Next door and upstairs to Jan's, a popular music club at 621 Main Street, was Gene Laverne's "Studio of the Stars". This was a photography studio that specialized in photos for burlesque dancers, where his sister had her promotion photos taken. Wearing his trademark look: a black tie, white shirt, reddish/orange jacket with yellow lining and rust colored pants with stitching down the sides, he had his promo photo taken at the studio. Even though the photo was in black and white, it became one of the most iconic photos of rock 'n' roll and was considered to best exemplify the look and attitude of 1950s performers. It was used as the opening page photo of *Rolling Stone* magazines *1976 Illustrated History of Rock & Roll*.

Wearing his trademark outfit, he went to the Town Casino and because of how Hickey looked, the manager put him on stage during a Sam Cooke show. The crowd loved him. The next day he was put on the bill at the Glen Casino, where Cab Calloway was headlining; once again he was a success. Photographer Gene Laverne suggested that Ersel should sign a management contract with Mike Corda, a Buffalo bass player. Corda liked the song "Bluebirds Over the Mountain," so he paid for and played on a demo of the song, recorded at National Studio in NYC. While Ersel was making personal appearances in Buffalo, Corda was in NYC plugging the song. Epic Records released the demo as a single and signed Ersel to a contract. The next thing Ersel knew, he was appearing on *American Bandstand* and touring across the country.

Ersel Hickey was not a one hit wonder. He wrote songs recorded by other artists, including "Don't Let the Rain Come Down" which was a top-10 single by The Serendipity Singers in 1964. He was inducted into the Rockabilly Hall of Fame and continued recording and making personal appearances until just prior to his death at age 70 in 2004.

TUNE ROCKERS

The Tune Rockers had the distinction of being the first rock 'n' roll band from Buffalo to hit the charts. In 1958, their song "Green Mosquito" was on the Billboard charts for ten weeks and peaked at #44. The band members were Gene Strong (lead guitar), Fred Patton (guitar), Tim Nolan (bass) and Mickey Vanderslip (drums). Ed Bentley (guitar) was also an early member of the band and Johnny Capello (sax) later joined the group.

THE TUNE ROCKERS
Gene Strong, Ed Bentley, Fred Patton
Tim Nolan, Paul Barclay
Photo: Courtesy: Ed Bentley

The band members were from the Eggertsville area and they started playing dances at St Leo's in Eggertsville. After DJ Dick Lawrence from WBNY became their manager, they began performing at record hops with Lucky Pierre at Commodore Hall, Washington Hall, Union Hall, and Morgans Point in Canada. After the release of their record, they appeared on *American Bandstand*, Dick Clark's *Saturday Night Beechnut Show* and embarked on a national tour.

The Tune Rockers were also one of the first bands to play their own instruments at dances and record hops. Previously, most music groups pantomimed the songs and vocal groups lip-synced to the records that were being played. After the Tune Rockers broke up in 1959, Gene Strong remained active in the area music industry as a guitar teacher and steel guitar player in various country bands.

THE ROCKIN REBELS

The Rebels were formed in 1957 by 14-year-old twin brothers, Jimmy Kipler (guitar) and Mickey Kipler (sax). The other original members of the band were Paul Balon (rhythm guitar) and Tom Gorman (drums).

The Kiplers played some of their first jobs at South Buffalo bars such as The City Line Hotel, Bonners, Mr. Lucky, The Phone Booth and Russo's Trophy Room. The band was not paid by these bars so they passed the hat for donations. Since none of the members were old enough to drive Tom Gorman would place his drums in a wagon and wheel them to the club. Amplifiers were much smaller and not as heavy in the 1950s, so the guitarists could just carry them to the job.

The band was hired to play a record hop at Baker Victory High School where radio personality Tommy Shannon was spinning the records. Shannon was impressed with the band and invited them to come to Buffalo Recording Studio, at 291 Delaware Avenue, where he wanted them to record an instrumental version of "Short Shorts." While waiting for producer Tony Sperry to set the instrument levels, Jim Kipler began playing the chords to Tommy Shannon's radio show theme song. Mickey joined in and began playing the melody on sax. The song "Wild Weekend" was born. Phil Todaro became their manager and the song was released on Marlee Records, a record label started by Tom Shannon and Phil Todaro, of Shan -Todd Productions. It sold 12,000 copies locally and The

ROCKIN REBELS
Top: Tom Gorman
Jimmy Kipler, Paul Balon, Mickey Kipler
Photo: Courtesy Jim Kipler

Rebels, changed their name to The Buffalo Rebels and eventually to The Rockin Rebels.

With the exposure of "Wild Weekend" being played on WKBW radio, The Rockin Rebels started performing at record hops with Tom Shannon in Ontario, the Southern Tier of New York and in Northern Pennsylvania, and in 1960, they appeared on *American Bandstand*. The Rockin Rebels were strictly an instrumental band, but they played dates backing up other vocalists. Their popularity due to being played on WKBW Radio and the exposure on *American Bandstand* secured them appearances in Philadelphia and Baltimore. In these cities during 1961-1962, they were the back-up instrumental band for performers like Roy Orbison, The Everly Brothers, Freddie Cannon and Del Shannon.

Swan Records, which was associated with Dick Clark, picked up the song and released it in 1963, with it reaching #8 on the national charts. "Wild Weekend" sold over one million copies, but due to disputes with Shan-Todd Productions, the Kiplers refused to continue as the Rockin Rebels. They were paid well for their appearances but did not receive additional record royalties when "Wild Weekend" became a million selling record. Since Tom Shannon and Phil Todaro owned the name The Rockin Rebels, they hired other bands such as The Jesters and Hot Toddy's to record and perform as the group.

After they stopped performing as The Rockin Rebels, The Kipler Brothers started playing at area clubs during the 1960s, performing at The Ivanhoe on Forest, Colony Lounge and Everglades on Hertel, and Ciro's on Chippewa. When they were playing at Ciro's, Emil Lewandowski, who later changed his name to Cory Wells, would often sit in as a guest vocalist. After performing at a Bobby Sox & Blue Jeans concert at The Aud., Dionne Warwick came to Ciro's and sat in with the band. Jim Kipler became a staff guitarist at Melody Fair and Studio Arena, also performing with The Ice Capades and BPO. He went to LA and through Buffalo guitarist Tommy Tedesco's connections, was hired for some of the Wrecking Crew recording sessions. Jim returned to Buffalo and after enlisting in the Army, became a recruiter for the Western New York area, a posting from which he continued long enough to retire with a military pension. He and his brother were members of the Coincidentals during the late 1970s and early 1980s, performing at The Executive, Jacobis and Cousins Three. Jim is now the business agent for Local #92 of the Musicians Union and still performs dates in WNY.

JESTERS – ROCK-ITTS

The Jesters were hired to play at Jan's Candy Cane Lounge at 621 Main Street for two weeks in 1962. However, that two-week engagement ended up lasting over a year. The bands members at that time included Peter Haskell (bass), Eddy "Hoagland" Jay (sax), Tony DiMaria (drums), Junie Schenck (vocals/guitar) and Lee "Markish" Carroll (guitar). The band was intertwined with The Rock-Itts, who were originally formed by Bill Lehman in 1958 who released three singles. When Bill was with the group they were also known as Billy Lehman and the Penn-Men. After he left the band, he became the manager of a later version which included Billy Quad, Johnny "Holiday" Capello, Stan "Pembleton" Robbins, Dave Rosean and Peter Haskell. An example of how they were intertwined, a later version of the Rock-Itts included Junie Schenck, Tony DiMaria and Lee Carroll. A 1959 single "First Sign of Love" released by Billy Lehman & The Penn-Men, featured Junie Schenck on vocals, with Art Roberts of WKBW Radio providing the voice over narration. Bass player Mousie Gage (bass) and Billy Quad were the vocalist on other releases. Collectively they released over ten singles, including some 45's under The Rockin Rebels name. Johnny Capello was later the sax player with The Tune Rockers and as a vocalist he released a single with The Graduates. Junie Schenck remained a popular performer in the Jamestown area and in 1963 purchased the Bemus Inn, which he operated as The Surf Club for the next 42 years.

During the 1950s and early 1960s, there was another group called The Rock-Its, spelled with one "t" rather than two. The members of this band were not related in any way to The Rock-Itts and included: Dick Johns (guitar), Larry "Blascak" Blaze (sax), Bob "Stoblinski" Stobi (piano) and Lou Teddy (drums). They played at The Mon Inn and Club 78. When they decided to add Bobby DeSoto as a vocalist, the club owners did not want to pay extra for someone who just sang. Bobby passed the hat after singing a few songs with the band and started making more money than all the band members combined. DeSoto later worked with several other groups like the Castells and sang with the Jerry Lee 12-piece Band at The Dellwood Ballroom. As a solo artist, DeSoto had a charting single "Don't Talk, Just Kiss" b/w "The Cheater".

DAWN BREAKERS – JACK BLANCHARD & MISTY MORGAN

Jack Blanchard and Misty Morgan both started performing in Buffalo but never met until they were playing at different nightclubs in the Hollywood, Florida area. In the early 1950s Jack could be seen playing piano at The Anchor Bar, Chez Ami or at The Park Lane. Don Fronczak had won a competition with a vocal group while he was in the military and decided to form a band when he returned home. He recruited Blanchard as a vocalist, guitarist and pianist. The Dawn Breakers went through several member changes but the nucleus of the four-piece vocal group was Jack Blanchard, Don Fronczak, Jim Warren and Harry Madrid, who was replaced by Buddy Lee Baker. The group performed at McVans, The Glen Casino, and clubs throughout Canada, Erie, PA and Detroit. They recorded several songs, with most recordings at Howell Studios, that primarily recorded radio commercials direct to acetate disc. In 1956, they released a single "Boy with the Be Bop Glasses" on Coral Records. During their career, they did not release any 'hits', but Jack's experience with the band allowed him to concentrate on and progress with his song writing. After the group disbanded, Blanchard moved to Florida.

Maryanne Donahue started playing piano with small combos while she was still a student at Tonawanda High School. Even though she did not read music, she had the ability to play and recall almost every song after she heard it. After graduation, she played in groups and as an accompanist at jazz clubs across New York State. Maryanne was offered the solo piano position at The Town Casino, but moved to Cincinnati, Ohio, where she performed at Doris Day's parents bar, eventually moving to Florida.

After Jack and Maryanne met in Florida, they played together in a band, worked as a duo and recorded many of Jack's original songs on several different Blanchard owned labels. They were married in 1967, between dates while their group was touring the East Coast and mid-west. To be more natural, they decided to change their show from formal attire to a more casual style of dress. Maryanne Donahue also changed her name to Misty Morgan and they began performing to full houses in Key West and in the Miami area. Another series of record releases followed. Mercury Records took notice and signed them to a contract.

The Blanchards moved to Nashville and while in the recording studio, near the end of the session, Jack wrote a novelty song called "Tennessee Bird Walk" in only 20 minutes. It soared to the top of the country charts, was nominated for a Grammy Award and in 1970 Jack Blanchard and Misty Morgan won *Billboard* magazine's Country Duet of the Year award. During their 50-year career, they have traveled the country, released dozens of recordings, appeared on various television shows and logged 119 weeks at the top end of the country charts.

THE DEL-TONES

Grover Cleveland High School students Frank Aguglia, David Conti, Mike Gioeli and Anthony Grisanti, enjoyed singing and formed a vocal group in 1958. They were regulars on Buffalo's *TV Dance Party* and at the Hi-Teen Dance Show at the Dellwood Ballroom. One of the regular dancers at their

DEL-TONES
Frank Aguglia and Michael Gioeli
with Bobby Rydell in center
Photo: Courtesy Michael Gioeli

shows was Michael DiFiglia, who moved to New York City and became a Tony Award winning theater director, producer, dancer and choreographer. DiFiglia changed his last name to Bennett, the high school from which he graduated in Buffalo. Michael Bennett's credentials include being the creator of *A Chorus Line,* the longest running show in Broadway history. Just like DiFiglia, The Del-Tones also went to NYC to audition with Capital Records, but they were not offered a contract.

In 1960 Frank Aguglia and Michael Gioeli, acquired a manager, wrote their own songs, started their own record label, Count Records, and even had their own Fan Club. They traveled across New York State and Pennsylvania, performing at record hops with DJs Lucky Pierre and Tommy Shannon. The band that backed them up on recordings was The Premiers, with members Tommy Calandra and Carl LaMacchia. However, they did not travel with the band because at the record hops the Del-Tones lip-synced to their records. The only time they sang live was at their appearances at the Town Casino, Glen Casino or Three Rivers Inn in Syracuse. The Del-Tones were the opening act, at area shows, for '50s recording artists like Frankie Avalon, Bobby Rydell, Connie Francis, Jerry Vale and Paul Anka, who was only 16 when they opened for him at the Dellwood Ballroom, where he was promoting his first record release.

The Del-Tones did not become a successful '50s recording act, but they did get to perform during the 1950s and early 1960s when almost every church and community hall in Buffalo had dances. Frank Aguglia later changed his stage name to Frankie Nestro and he released records with The Fascinates and The Belvederes. Nestro was later a DJ and the entertainment director on *Royal Caribbean Cruise Lines* for many years.

THE PLAYBOYS – GRADUATES

The Playboys were formed as a 1950s-style vocal group in 1956 by members primarily from Lafayette High School and Hutch Tech. The original members were Jack Scorsone, Ronald Page, Bruce Hammond, Raymond Baunler, Harold Rogers and Anthony Mancuso. They were initially called The Rays but when they got to NYC to record, they heard a song on the radio by another group with the same name, so they needed to quickly come up with a new one. There was a *Playboy* magazine in the hotel room and the name change was made – they became The Playboys. From this recording session, in 1957 on Mercury Records they released "Why Do I Love You, Why Do I Care" b/w "Don't Do Me Wrong", both written and sung by Jack Scorsone.

The Playboys changed their name once more and since some of the members were in the process of graduating from high school, they now became The Graduates. Harold Rogers and Anthony Mancuso left the band and Johnny Capello joined as lead singer. Capello had previously played sax for The Jesters and Tune Rockers. They released "Ballad of a Girl & Boy" on Shan-Todd Records which received airplay across the country, reaching #74 on the charts. This resulted in some good paying dates, with the band once getting paid $1,500 for a show in Rochester.

FONVILLE & HERNANDEZ

Bobby Fonville and Ralph Hernandez were songwriters that tried creating in Buffalo what Barry Gordy did in Detroit with Motown. They started writing together in 1950 and formed an eight-piece all girl group named The Dezville Singers to perform the songs they wrote. The group rehearsed at the YMCA on Michigan Avenue. Fonville & Hernandez also became associated with The Vibraharps, with their guitarist Donnie Elbert assisting them with arrangements for their songs. In 1955 the other members of The Vibraharps were Danny Cannon, Donald Simmons. Douglas Gibson and Charles Hargo. Donnie Elbert went on to a career as a successful soul, R&B singer in the U.S. and England. He was known for his strong falsetto voice and his remake of "Where Did Our Love Go" which reached the Top 10 on the R&B charts in 1972.

Fonville & Hernandez became associated with Ted Powell who was producing recording sessions for Beech Records. He was interested in recording both groups and asked that they come to NYC to record. The Dezville Singers recording session did not go well but The Vibraharps recorded a single that received airplay in Buffalo and other markets. In 1958 the writers placed their song "Thumb Thumb" as the B side of the Frankie Lymon single "Footsteps", which sold well in Europe. When reviewing the songwriter's royalty statement, they found an unknown person received 1/3 or the royalties for the song. It was required to add that person as a writer or Lymon would not have included "Thumb Thumb" as the B side. With the success of that song they formed a publishing company HER-FON Music and later started their own record label DAB Records.

Songs written by Fonville & Hernandez were recorded by The Four Dates, the back-up singers for Frankie Avalon and Fabian. Vocalist Hargo, from the Vibraharps, released the single "Over & Over" which sold 16,000 copies in Buffalo. Their songs were also recorded by The Fendermen, The Derby's, Elsie Strong, Jimmy Raye, Ronnie Elbert and Niagara Falls singer Monroe Chapman. Popular Buffalo vocalist Neil Darrow released the single "Asphalt Jungle."

Chess Records was interested in a song for one of their artists and in 1963 Fonville went to Detroit. When he was in Detroit, Motown Records offered him a position with the company but Fonville turned it down because he felt Motown was a similar organization to what he and Hernandez were trying to accomplish in Buffalo. In a conversation with Bob Skurzewski for his book *No Stoppin' this Boppin'*, Fonville admitted that going with Motown would have enhanced his career and there had been second thoughts about taking the offer.

QUARTERNOTES

Tony Sperry and the Quarternotes were one of the first rock 'n' roll bands in Buffalo. Tony was a classically trained piano player but he was also proficient at playing boogie-woogie. The Quarternotes had a real advantage over other early bands because Tony's father owned Sperry's Quarter Note Lounge at the corner of Michigan and Cherry where he let the band perform. Over the years there were many musicians who were members of the group, including vocalist Neil Darrow and saxophonist Sam Scamacca. The Quarternotes signed a seven-record contract with Imperial Records but stopped recording with the label because they wanted to play rock, not commercial songs. Later they released several rock 'n' roll records with one of their best remembered rock recordings being "Record Hop Blues". In later years, The Quarternotes became more of a supper club band and Sperry, with his wife, played for 14 years at the Big Apple on French Road in Cheektowaga and for seven years at the Orchard Downs in Orchard Park.

RHYTHM ROCKERS

The Rhythm Rockers were formed by Wade Curtis a/k/a Ted Russell. Curtis was confined to a wheelchair and had a special guitar made that he could play backwards, sort of like a steel lap guitar. Pro-wrestler Dixie Dee a/k/a Richard Derwald was a singer and bass player, who also had a band called the Rhythm Rockers. In 1959, they released the song "Brang", with Curtis as the vocalist, and Nick Salamone on sax. In 1961, they released "Voodoo Mama" with Dixie Dee as the lead vocalist. That song was recorded on a Sunday and was receiving airplay on WKBW the following Thursday. Wade Curtis left Buffalo in 1961 and moved to Nashville, where he worked as a song writer and promoter. In the 1970s, he became a professional wrestling manager, appearing in and around the ring in his motorized wheel chair. Richard Derwald is now known as Mr. Fitness and is the coordinator of the Erie County Senior Fitness Program. His son Richie Derwald, who was his former wrestling tag team partner, is an entertainer and producer of Viva Niagara Productions.

NINO TEMPO & APRIL STEVENS

Nino Tempo was born in Niagara Falls and at the age of four won a talent contest. When he was seven years old, Benny Goodman was performing at Sheas Buffalo and Nino approached the stage. He tugged at Goodman's jacket and told him his grandfather offered him ten dollars if he sang a song with the band. Goodman let him sing "Rosetta." The audience loved it and Goodman had Nino come back during the remaining six nights of his Buffalo performance.

Nino's family moved to California, ending his early appearances in Buffalo. In California, Nino played tenor sax with The Maynard Ferguson Band for six years and became a session musician and saxophonist with the Wrecking Crew, who did studio work for numerous '50s and '60s recording acts. His sister Carol LoTempio, adopted the name of April Stevens and began a successful singing and recording career in the 1950s. Later in the 1950s Nino and April started working as a duo and in 1959 released a song Nino wrote called "Teach Me Tiger" which reached #86 on the Top 100. In 1963, they recorded a remake of the 1930s hit song "Deep Purple". It reached #1 on the charts and earned them a Grammy Award for the Best Rock 'n' Roll Recording of the year.

TOMMY TEDESCO

Tommy Tedesco is considered the most recorded guitarist in music history. Originally from Niagara Falls, he played dates in the Buffalo clubs before moving to LA. Once he arrived in California, Tedesco became a member of the Wrecking Crew; the group of musicians that was the recording studio band on many early '60s popular music and rock music sessions. He was part of Phil Spector's Wall of Sound, played on recording sessions for many California rock bands, as well as being the guitarist on Elvis Presley and Frank Sinatra recording. It was Tedesco who played the guitar solos on many of the early Beach Boys surf songs. He also played the guitar on television theme songs like Bonanza, The Twilight Zone and Batman, and appeared as an on-camera band member in many comedy and game shows. In addition to television, Tedesco performed on many film soundtracks and was the guitarist in Roxy version of The Rocky Horror Show. Tedesco passed away in 1997. His son Denny Tedesco produced a documentary on The Wrecking Crew in 2008, which was released in 2015 after clearances were finally obtained for the music.

ADDITIONAL PERFORMERS AND GROUPS

Joanie Sommers was born in Buffalo, NY as Joan Drost. In 1951, at age 10, she won a talent contest by singing "Your Cheating Heart" on a Buffalo television show. When Joanie was 14 years old, her family moved to California, where she sang in high school and college. In 1959, she recorded "Kookie's Love Song" with Edd Byrnes ("Kookie" from the *77 Sunset Strip* TV series) and in 1962 she released the hit single "Johnny Get Angry". Sommers was billed as "The Voice of the Sixties" and referred to as "The Pepsi Girl", from singing the early 1960s Pepsi commercial "For Those Who Think Young".

Vic Dana left Buffalo to find success as a tap dancer in LA. When tap dancing declined as a popular form of entertainment, Dana became the live performance vocalist for The Fleetwoods, when their lead singer was in the U.S. Navy. In 1965 Dana released the hit single "Red Roses for a Blue Lady".

WBEN newsman John Zach was known as John Zachwieja when he was a teen growing up during the 1950s in the Kaisertown area of South Buffalo. He formed a band called John Zach & the Furies that played high school dances. At one of these dances he met WBNY DJ Danny Neaverth who encouraged him to study broadcasting. After college, in 1961 he secured a job with WKBW where he remained until the news department closed in 1988. John Zach & the Furies did not get a record contract, but the band paved the way for nearly six decades of radio time for John Zach.

Chic & the Diplomats was Chic Cicero (sax), who later played with The Vibratos. Other members included Denny Fox (drums) and Joe Madison (organ). They were regular performers at the Ivanhoe and often played opposite The Jesters at the Candy Cane Lounge, which featured two stages.

The Rhythm Teens were a band from the late 1950s from Niagara Falls that played at the Dellwood Ballroom Hi- Teen Shows. The members were Fran Lally (piano), Claus Leyden (guitar), Daryl Miller (guitar), Teddy Denler (sax) and Bob Evacheck (drums).

The Hot Shots were a group that featured songs by The Everly Brothers. Members were Jerry Ralston (vocals), Ed Bentley (vocals/guitar), Larry Cole (lead Guitar) and Loren Hartman (upright bass). They played WKBW Record Hops with Danny Neaverth and Rod Roddy at many different area fire halls, school gyms and community centers.

EARLY ROCK 'N' ROLL RADIO IN BUFFALO

HOUND DOG LORENZ

George "Hound Dog" Lorenz started in radio at WXRA and WBNY in Buffalo but since they would not let him play what he wanted he left for WJJL in Niagara Falls in 1948. He hosted the morning show and being a big fan of Hank Williams, played a lot of his country music. Lorenz also began playing rhythm & blues and rock 'n' roll records, when they started to be released. In 1951, George Lorenz started being called the Hound Dog. This nickname derived from the 1940s expression "doggin' around." He would go on the air and say, "Here I am to dog around for another hour." The Hound Dog was born.

From 1953 to 1955 Lorenz was also on the air in Cleveland, Ohio, where Alan Freed was already a popular radio personality. Freed had been using the name the Hound Dog, but when Lorenz arrived in Cleveland, Freed changed his nickname to the Moondog. With Freed and Lorenz both being on the radio in Cleveland, it became considered the birthplace of rock 'n' roll music. That is one of the reasons why the Rock N Roll Hall of Fame was built in Cleveland.

When Freed left Cleveland and moved to WINS in NYC, Lorenz moved back to Buffalo and took over the night time air waves at WKBW in Buffalo. The Hound broadcast his nightly show from 7:00–10:00 p.m. from the front window of the Zanzibar Club on William Street. What differentiated Lorenz from other DJ's is he played the original black version of the song, not the watered down white cover, which many record labels at that time were releasing. His music affected the '50s generation and he inspired musicians in WNY to perform rhythm and blues oriented rock 'n' roll music, which became identified as The Buffalo Sound. With the 50,000 watts of WKBW radio, he was heard across the entire U.S. East Coast, building a reputation for himself and promoting rock 'n' roll music. Like Freed, who promoted rock 'n' roll shows in NYC and on the East Coast, Lorenz promoted rock shows in Buffalo and upstate New York. Many of these

Photo: Courtesy Frank Lorenz

shows were at the Plaza Theatre, which was on William Street near Monroe Street, not far from the Zanzibar. He concentrated on black acts but presented integrated rock shows and was the first person to bring Elvis Presley to Buffalo in 1957. Unlike Freed, Lorenz was never implicated in the payola scandals.

Lorenz had the top-rated radio program in Buffalo while he was on WKBW. When WKBW switched to the Top 30 format in 1958, Lorenz did not to go along with this restricted playlist. He would not be able to pick his own songs and talk about the artists, so he resigned from the station. WKBW General Manager, Al Anscombe assisted Lorenz in obtaining a position at WINE in Williamsville. This was a smaller station but it would allow Lorenz to select his own material and have time to syndicate his programs.

Hound Dog Lorenz recorded his syndicated radio shows in a studio on Delaware Avenue near West Chippewa. The programs Lorenz created were some of the first syndicated radio shows and they were aired at stations in the US and overseas. When Lorenz song played a song on the show, it was immediately included on the best sellers list. The Hound would often travel to a station that was going to carry his syndicated show and be live on the air at the station for a week. When the syndicated shows started, many listeners did not realize they were listening to shows on tape.

In 1962 George Lorenz headed a group of investors that applied for the last FM frequency in the Buffalo Market – 93.7 FM. At that time, FM stations primarily broadcast classical music but The Hound had the idea to put a rhythm and blues music station on the FM dial. Many in the industry thought the concept would never work, but not only was it successful, over time most of the music programming moved from the AM to FM format and Lorenz was one of the first to start that transition. WBLK became known as "The House that The Hound Built" and he continued his mission of showcasing black talent. On May 29, 1972 George "Hound Dog" Lorenz died of a heart attack. He was only 52, but during his short lifetime he introduced his listeners to the rhythm and blues aspect of rock 'n' roll and helped transform the radio industry with his contributions to FM broadcasting and syndicated programming.

WWOL

In 1947 Leon Wyszatycki started WWOL (1120 AM) in Lackawanna, NY. He was assisted in building the station and transmitter site by Stan Jasinski, who was the first Program Director and later the founder of Channel 29. In 1954, they signed on their FM counterpart WWOL-FM, which is now 104.1 WHTT-FM.

Fred Klestine was the morning DJ on WWOL in the 1950s, Stan Jasinski broadcast his early Polish programs and Ramblin' Lou started playing country music at the station. The station relocated to Shelton Square in downtown Buffalo and was one of the first stations to play rock 'n' roll music.

There was a scene in the *Buddy Holly Story* where a DJ in Buffalo locked himself in the studio and played the same Buddy Holly song over and over again. That is not *exactly* what happened but the scene may have been a combination of two occurrences at WWOL. In 1954 Lucky Pierre played the song "Sh-Boom", non-stop alternating versions by The Crew Cuts, The Chords and other renditions. This continued for most of his air shift. The big event was on July 3,1955 when WWOL disc jockey, Tom Clay a/k/a Guy King climbed out of the studio window onto a billboard in Shelton Square. He played Bill Haley's "Rock Around the Clock" non-stop, asking listeners to come downtown and honk their horns in support for him to continue playing the song. He caused a traffic jam and was arrested, but not fired by the radio station. In fact, Clay was not even reprimanded because it was a great PR stunt.

WBNY

WBNY was started by Roy Albertson Sr. in 1934 and was the fifth radio station to sign on in Buffalo. Like most early radio stations, WBNY featured live programming with a mix of ethnic, classical, big band and news, with an emphasis on editorials, mainly political in nature. The station was licensed by the FCC for 24-hour broadcasting but Mr. Albertson felt being on the air from 6:00 a.m. to midnight was sufficient.

The station was doing well but when founder Roy Albertson, Sr. suffered medical problems his son, Roy Albertson, Jr., took it over and moved it in a new direction. Dick Lawrence was hired as Program Director and in 1957, using the Top 40 format, WBNY 1400 AM became the first consistent rock 'n' roll station in Buffalo. The other stations that played rock 'n' roll featured it during a specific radio personality's show and broadcast other styles of music on other shows. This change made WBNY the first station that played rock 'n' roll all day on all shifts. Broadcasting from their studio at 485 Main Street, at the corner of Mohawk, some of the early DJ's included Lucky Pierre and Danny Neaverth. Air personalities that later joined the station were Joey Reynolds and Fred Klestine.

Dick Lawrence was hired away from the station by WKBW in 1958. WBNY retained their rock 'n' roll format after he departed and provided competition to the WKBW Top 30 format. It was said that when he was employed by WKBW, Dick Lawrence would always have two radios, one tuned to WKBW and the other to WBNY, so he could monitor what each station doing. In 1979 the Albertson's sold the station but it retained its rock 'n' roll format. They maintained a strong presence in the market, with Lucky Pierre being a popular air personality and promoter of record hops. During 1960 Casey Kasem was at WBNY for about three months. This was years before he started *American Top 40* which was syndicated to over 500 radio stations.

WINE

WINE was located at 1080 AM and their FM side WILY was at 103.3 FM. WINE was a rock 'n' roll station previously called WXRA, which was on Niagara Falls Blvd. in Tonawanda. It was moved to 13 South Cayuga

Street just off Main Street in Williamsville, where the station was located when Hound Dog Lorenz was on WINE from 1958 to 1960. When Gordon McLendon bought the station in 1960 he changed WINE from a rock 'n' roll station to WYSL "Whistle" easy listening "beautiful music" from 1961 to 1965. Due to its position on the dial, 1080 AM was a dawn to dusk station, but McLendon wanted a 24-house station and the FCC rules stipulated a company could only own one AM station in a market. He sold the 1080 AM position to Dynamic Broadcasting in Pittsburg, which wanted to start a station directed toward the Buffalo black audience. That station became WUFO, with Hound Dog Lorenz being one of the initial air-personalities on the station. McLendon then purchased WBNY, which was at 1400 AM. WYSL took over the 1400 AM dial position, WBNY disappeared and 103.3 became WYSL FM.

WBNY FM – the other WBNY

The WBNY AM name disappeared in 1961, when Gordon McLendon retired it. The sister station of WBNY 1400 AM was WBNY 96.1 FM, which changed its name to WJYE in 1979. In 1982 at Buffalo State College on Elmwood Avenue another WBNY FM was born. This station had nothing in common with the other two previous WBNY stations. Program Manager Tom Connolly was instrumental in getting FCC approval and funding from student government to start the radio station. WBNY 91.3 FM always featured local Buffalo bands and the policy was that regardless of a show's format, at least one song by a Buffalo band had to be played every hour. Alumni of WBNY FM included 107.7 music host Tina Peel, former MTV-VH1 Network president Tom Calderone, former Channel 4 News anchor Mylous Hairston, WGR Sports Director Howard Simon and Buffalo Mayor Byron Brown.

WKBW

WKBW was very successful as a block programming radio station. This type of format had different types of shows at different times and it was the style of the show that drew its specific audience. One of their most successful shows was Stan Jasinski's *Polka Beehive*, where he announced the show in Polish. However, their most successful show was the R&B Rock of Hound Dog Lorenz every night at 7:00. It was the top-rated radio program in Buffalo and with WKBW's 50,000-watt signal, it was popular across most the East Coast of the U.S.

In 1957 WBNY changed their format to Top 40 Radio, playing rock and roll 24 hours a day, not just in any particular time slot. Their ratings soared and it was the radio station's format, not only a specific program block, that was attracting the audience. WKBW Station Manager Al Ansombe took notice of the ratings that WBNY was obtaining. To replicate WBNY's success he did not just try to copy it, he hired WBNY's Program Director Dick Lawrence to work at WKBW. Lawrence started at the station six months before they changed the WKBW format from block programming to rock music.

The date chosen to make the change was July 4, 1958 calling the new format Future Sonic Radio – Top 30 (the top 10 songs on the charts and the 20 up and coming songs). With six months of planning invested in the change, the debut of the new format was a huge promotional event. There was a free concert at the Central Park Plaza with The Four Dates and Fabian coming in from Philadelphia, the Pony Tails from Cleveland and Faron Young from Nashville. Local Buffalo bands were represented with the Tune Rockers playing on the roof of one of the stores in the plaza. The new DJ's were introduced at the event and prizes were given out to everyone attending. Despite a big rainstorm, a couple thousand people were at Central Park Plaza for the event.

The new air personalities were hired from various cities across the county. There was one constant trait of each of the DJ's, each one was rated #1 in their former market and each had a reputation for ingenious broadcasting techniques. The announcers were Perry Allen from Denver, Russ Syracuse from Syracuse, Art Roberts from Akron, Ohio and Dick Biondi from Youngstown, Ohio (who had the distinction of having to take over the Hound Dog Lorenz time slot). Only one announcer was retained from the previous WKBW format and that was over-night DJ Jack Kelly. In addition to the new music format and new staff, the new WKBW featured a lot of contests and community involvement. The station news department of Jim Fagan, Irv Weinstein, and John Zach offered "*Pulse Beat News*", with two segments every hour, and WKBW was the first station to have traffic reports in conjunction with State and local police.

When WBNY discontinued their rock format in 1961 and even before the change, Danny Neaverth, Joey Reynolds, and Fred Klestine moved over to KB. There were many other popular DJ's at KB including Tom Shannon, Sandy Beach, Tom Donahue, Jack Armstrong, Steve Mitchell, Bob Diamond, Hank Nevins, Stan Roberts and Rod Roddy, who was later the voice of *The Price is Right*.

THE BEATLES CONCERT IN BUFFALO THAT NEVER HAPPENED

With their 50,000-watt signal WKBW could be heard at night by people from New England to Florida. A song played on WKBW received exposure throughout the Eastern U.S. This influence was realized by the management of The Beatles and they approached WKBW about a concert in Buffalo the day after their scheduled Ed Sullivan Show premier. That concert would have been on Monday, February 10, 1964. The promoters, Danny Neaverth and Joey Reynolds, turned down the offer because they were not certain a large crowd would come to The Aud. on a cold Monday night in February to see what at that time was a relatively unknown band in the U.S. When they were offered the show, Beatlemania had not yet started and no one could anticipate the impact The Beatles would have with their Ed Sullivan TV Show appearance. But – the Beatles asking price for the concert was only $3,500. The Beatles first concert ended up being on Tuesday, February 11, in Washington, DC and Buffalo missed out on hosting what is one of the most important dates in U.S. rock music history. This was a miss for Buffalo just as big, if not bigger, than Scott Norwood's "wide right" in Super Bowl XXV.

WAR OF THE WORLDS IN BUFFALO

On October 31, 1968 WKBW Program Director Jefferson Kaye presented an updated presentation of the 1938 Orson Wells *War of the Worlds* radio broadcast. It substituted WNY locations in the broadcast, with the oil refinery near Grand Island being blown up by the Martian spaceships. For several weeks WKBW advertised that this dramatization was going to be broadcast and at the beginning of the show, Danny Neaverth read a statement and warning about the fictitious nature of the show. However, the broadcast fooled many people including some local police departments and the Canadian military, which was dispatched to the Peace Bridge. In addition to Jeff Kaye and Danny Neaverth, some of the other participants in the radio broadcast were Sandy Beach, Henry Brock, Jim Fagan and Irv Weinstein. Although it was recreated three more times, the program never had the impact of the 1968 broadcast. That 1968 version is considered one of the classic events of radio.

WKBW remained on top of the radio ratings and with their 50,000-Watt signal blanketing the East Coast, the record companies would give them preferential treatment. The station would often receive advance copies of new releases. It was a promotion that benefited both the record company and the radio station. Promos would be aired stating that a new song by one of the top groups would be played at a certain time. People would listen to the station and other radio stations would also tune in to hear the new song, with many people anxiously waiting with their cassette tape player to record the song. So that everyone knew where the song was being played, at the beginning of the song and several times during the middle of it, the announcement "WKBW Exclusive" interrupted the record. Another radio station could not play the song because of the embedded WKBW promo and people playing the song for their friends were also playing a promotion for WKBW. Buffalo bands would wait to tape the song so they could learn it before other groups. It was observed that some Buffalo bands would say "WKBW Exclusive" in the appropriate places, as a joke when playing a new song that was not yet available in the record stores.

WYSL

After WBNY went off the air in 1961, WKBW had a virtual monopoly in the rock music market. WGR tried to compete with KB, but soon went back to their former programming. The station that replaced WBNY at 1400AM was WYSL, with their easy listening format. Gordon McLendon was the owner of the station when it discontinued the rock 'n' roll of WBNY and in 1965 he put the rock back into WYSL to challenge WKBW. Using a format of catchy jingles, teenage announcers and an experienced news department, WYSL was only a 1,000-Watt station but they kept the 50,000-Watt WKBW on their toes. The competition probably made each station excel. Some of the DJ's that started at WYSL, who moved on to other stations in Buffalo, were George Hamburger, Jerry Reo, Kevin

O'Connell and Roger Christian. The station eventually moved their programming over to WYSL 103.3 FM and became the progressive rock station WPHD in 1970. In 1978, WYSL morning host Harv Moore, teamed up with WYSL veteran Bob Taylor, to form the WPHD FM morning team of Taylor & Moore, who were on the air through the 1980s.

WNIA

Another memorable '60s radio station was WNIA 1230AM. The station and transmitter was in a ranch house at 2900 Genesee Street, just east of Harlem Road in Cheektowaga. It went on the air in 1956 and was owned by Gordon P. Brown, with station manager Mary Lounsbury. WNIA was a low budget station and money was always an issue because the owner placed more emphasis on playing music than obtaining advertising revenue. The announcers all worked under the assigned names of Tommy Thomas in the morning, Jerry Jack in the afternoon, Mike Melody at night and Mac McGuire on weekends. When someone new took over a time slot, the voice changed but the name remained the same. Many area DJ's got their start as Tommy Thomas, Jerry Jack or Mike Melody, with some air personalities assuming multiple identities. Some DJ's are proud to admit to, at one time, having assumed these names. The station was very supportive to the community by playing records from local Buffalo bands and had a loyal following, especially for the nightly All Request Hour. This show let you call in to dedicate a song to your boyfriend or girlfriend or just to say hello to someone. The station signed off every night at 12:30 (the same time as their dial location) with the song "Midnight Mood" followed by "The Star-Spangled Banner". WNIA went off the air in 1979 and was replaced at 1230 AM by WECK. The current Niagara University WNIA 89.1 FM is no relation to the WNIA of the '50s, '60s and '70s.

RECORD HOPS

During the late 1950s and early 1960s Disc Jockeys (DJs) started presenting record hops at schools, church halls and fire halls. The record hops provided the opportunity for radio personalities to promote their shows. It also allowed the DJs to create a bond with their listeners by appearing in-person, not just being heard over the airwaves. Record hops also evolved into a money-making opportunity for the disc jockeys. They collected the money from the door and they often asked the bands to perform in return for the promotion and exposure that they would receive from event advertising and performing at the show.

Dick Lawrence was the program director at WBNY and he was involved in a multitude of additional projects. He owned an artist management company, music publishing company and was affiliated with a PR company in Beverly Hills. Lawrence was also the manager of The Tune Rockers and paid for the recording of their singles "Green Mosquito" and "No Stoppin' This Boppin'."

Lawrence encouraged the disc jockeys who worked for him to become involved with record hops and area bands. Lucky Pierre worked for Lawrence at WBNY and he became one of the most popular disc jockeys at record hops and personal appearances. Danny Neaverth was another in-demand deejay at the record hops. Some disc jockeys took their involvement a step further like Tommy Shannon, who with Phil Todaro, started his own record company. Shannon can be credited for producing a million selling record when his radio theme song was recorded as "Wild Weekend" by the Rockin Rebels, a band name to which he owned the rights. Other disc jockeys released records, like Danny Neaverth and Joey Reynolds who released the regionally successful "Rats in my Room." Several disc jockeys were members of bands and The Cosmic Cowboy Shane "Brother Shane" Gibson formed a group with himself as the lead singer.

The term Sock Hop evolved from the dances that were held in school gyms. The high school gym teachers and coaches did not want people scuffing up their well varnished floors. To protect the floors, the students had to remove their shoes before entering the gym. Everyone danced in their socks, so the sock hop was born.

Record hops were significant because they provided entertainment for the earliest members of the baby boom generation and brought the music directly to them. The record hops evolved into the dances at high schools, community centers, fire halls and veteran's posts. They also resulted in the development of a new place for entertainment in the 1960s – the Teen Club.

Everyone associates the 1950s with the advent of rock 'n' roll but another style of music was also gaining popularity at that time – folk music. In Buffalo, there was a vibrant folk and acoustic music scene that produced local and nationally prominent performers.

EARLY FOLK SCENE & ACOUSTIC MUSIC

The very beginning of the folk scene was in the 1940s during the days of the Woody Guthrie and The Weavers, which included Pete Seeger. In Buffalo, there were not any clubs featuring folk music, so early performers like Tony DeCorse would go into restaurants and play for tips.

During the mid '50s, the first actual folk style club in Buffalo was called Coffee Encore on Franklin near West Tupper. It was a stereotype coffee house, with a very Greenwich Village atmosphere and featured music by acoustic artists. The coffee house was owned by Dominic Trapani and Sam Farrell (Fiorella), and the club became very popular with the arts community. Joel Lippes purchased the business in 1971 and operated it for over 40 years. He changed the name to Rue Franklin West and designed it as a European style coffee house. The club featured live music by performers like Ros Magorian, John Brady and Joe Head. Expanding upon the traditional coffee house, they obtained a beer and wine license and served food on weekends. In 1980, he remodeled and changed the Rue Franklin to the foremost upscale French restaurant in WNY.

In 1956 The Limelight Gallery at 49 Edward Street near Franklin was opened by several people, including Jim Baritot, Joe McCann and Tyler Dunn. They sold it to Lee Bluestein in 1959. It was also a Greenwich Village style coffee house and was frequented by employees of nearby Roswell Park Hospital and students who studied at the Grosvenor Library. The library was across the street at the southeast corner of Edward and Tupper and included the Cyclorama Building as part of its complex. Lee hired Jerry Raven (Revzin) and Don Hackett to perform there in 1959.

While performing at The Limelight, Raven and Hackett entered a talent contest at WGR TV Channel 2, where the prize was a two-week engagement at The Town Casino. After they won the contest and were given the award envelope they discovered that the prize sheet page inside was blank. It was explained to them that to perform at the Town Casino they had to be members of the Musicians Union, so the prize was only valid if they became union members. Jerry and Don passed their union auditions and their two-week Town Casino engagement was extended to several weeks. During their engagement, they performed the early show at the Town Casino and walked over to The Limelight to play the rest of the night.

In 1960 Jerry Raven and Don Hackett purchased the Limelight, and acoustic folk music was further highlighted as the main attraction at the coffee house. Jerry performed every night and they worked as a duo on weekends. On Sunday night's they started the first open mic in the WNY area. The attraction of playing at The Limelight and Jerry's previous musical contacts brought many promising and already known performers to the club for the open mic and regular performances.

In the late 1950s Raven lived in Woodstock where he played many dates and became friends with Peter Yarrow. After Yarrow formed Peter, Paul and Mary, they often came to The Limelight whenever they played a concert in Buffalo. Before he joined The Chad Mitchell Trio, singer Joe Frazier was a staff performer at Melody Fair in North Tonawanda for a summer and got to know Jerry Raven. After a Chad Mitchell Trio concert at Kleinhans, members of the trio came to The Limelight with their stage accompanist Roger McGuinn (years prior to him forming The Byrds). They performed at the club until dawn.

Jerry Raven recalled some of the people that performed at The Limelight, some of whom may have played their first public performance at the Sunday Open Mic. Prior to Williamsville native Eric Andersen leaving Buffalo to attend Hobert College in Geneva, New York, he performed at the club on a regular basis. Andersen's career has spanned over 50 years. During his career he has recorded over 25 albums and his compositions have been covered by numerous recording artists. When German native John Kay lived in Buffalo, one of the only clubs he sang at was The Limelight. After moving to California, he formed the band Steppenwolf. One of Jackson C. Frank's first public performances was at the Limelight. Jackson, who was

JERRY RAVEN
Photo: Courtesy Jerry Raven

one of the students injured in the tragic Cleveland Hill High School fire in Cheektowaga, later moved to England, where he was at the center of the English folk scene and recorded an album produced by Paul Simon.

While living in Williamsville, John Boylan sang at the club. Boylan moved to California and, as Linda Ronstadt's manager, he helped put together her back-up group, which became The Eagles. Boylan later produced many groups including The Charlie Daniels Band, Commander Cody and Boston, winning a Grammy Award for his work. He also won a Grammy for the 1999 "Elmopalooza" children's album, based on the television series. Terrance Boylan, John's brother, also sang at The Limelight. While at Bard College, Terrance and John put together a group that played at The Night Owl Café in Greenwich Village. Together they recorded an album "Appletree Theatre" on Verve Records and Terrance released two albums on Asylum Records.

Judy Roderick's family was related to Frederick Law Olmsted and had family property in Sardinia called Camp Olmsted. When staying there during the summer she would always come to perform at The Limelight. She later signed with Vanguard Records, was produced by John Hammond Jr. and performed at the 1964 Newport Folk Festival. Terry Knight, later the producer of Grand Funk Railroad, also performed at the open mic sessions. Future King Harvest keyboardist Ron Altbach played at The Limelight in 1964 as the bass player in the folk group, The American Singers, with twin brothers and guitarists, Frank & John Jelinak. Performing at the club is what got Ed Taublieb, owner of The String Shoppe, interested in starting a guitar repair company. Many area performers like Tom Naples, Jim Vozga, Charlie Castalli and Madeline Davis also started out by singing at The Limelight.

During the summer in the early 1960s, Jerry Raven produced folk concerts at area movie theaters in the Buffalo area. He realized business was slow at theaters on Mondays nights and some were not even open. The concerts would bring in additional business and promote folk music. It was quite successful. Jerry used the money from the admission to pay the artists, and the theaters made money from the concession sales. In 1961 Jerry Raven & Don Hackett had a WBEN-AM Radio Show *Don't Sing Love Songs* on Tuesday and Thursday evenings. In 1962 and 1963, Jerry Raven appeared on *I'll Sing You a Song,* which was one the last black & white television shows on Channel 17. In addition to The Rue Franklin and Limelight, other early folk music clubs were The Golden Boar on Pearl &

Tupper, La Critique on Franklin Street, Mac Mahoney's Greensleeves on Elmwood near Brinks, Lower Level at 587 Potomac near Elmwood, Bell Book & Candle in Southern Ontario and in the early '70s Greenfield's Restaurant, a vegetarian co-op style restaurant on Greenfield near Main. The open mic concept started at The Limelight was duplicated at many other clubs. One of the most successful and longest running was hosted by Michael Meldrum at Nietzsche's on Allen Street. In addition to the open mic nights, Meldrum's Buffalo Songwriters Project helped develop the

ANI DiFRANCO & MICHAEL MELDRUM EARLY IN ANI'S CAREER
Photo: Courtesy Estate Michael Meldrum

talents of many area singer-songwriters. Meldrum was a Buffalo recording artist, as well as Ani DiFranco's teacher and mentor, with Ani crediting Meldrum for launching her career. DiFranco performed much of her career as a solo artist. She is considered a cross-over folk rock, alternative rock artist, with songs sensitive to social issues. She has released over 20 albums on her own label, Righteous Babe Records, was managed by Buffalo News writer Dale Anderson, and financed the multimillion dollar preservation of the Ashbury Delaware Methodist Church, on Delaware and Tupper, into Babesville, a multi-use performance and arts facility.

After the Limelight closed, for seven years in the mid '70s, Jerry Raven worked six nights a week at The Park Lane Restaurant as a strolling minstrel performer, dressed in a renaissance style outfit, singing English, Irish and contemporary folk songs. He also formed a folk trio called The Hemi Demi Semi Quavers, which musically means a 64th note, with Don Hackett and Sherry Hackett.

HEMI DEMI SEMI QUAVERS
Jerry Raven, Sherry Hackett, Don Hackett
Photo: Courtesy Jerry Raven

This trio performed at Buffalo and Toronto folk clubs. With Steve Moscov and Stuart Shapiro, in 1974 Jerry formed the Hill Brothers to give performances of American Folk, Erie Canal and Renaissance Music at area schools. Other musicians that were associated with the Hill Brothers include Judd Sunshine, Chick Oletto, Don Hackett, Mark Panfil, Doug Yeomans, Dave Ruch and Sue Rozler. The Hill Brothers are now led by Judd Sunshine and they still present over 100 school concerts every year.

In 1970 David Keith Nehrboss and Bob Bakert formed the acoustic duo Gold. By 1971 Bob Frauenhein joined the band, with Bob Bakert leaving to perform as a solo act and releasing two albums. During most of 1971 they played every Wednesday, Friday and Saturday at The Inn Between on Forest Avenue, and in 1972 they moved to LA. There David and Bob reunited with former Buffalo musician and now LA producer, John Boylan, who they knew from The Limelight. Gold performed in LA and through Boylan's contacts received a lot of record label interest but decided to return to the Buffalo area. An executive from A&M Records saw Gold perform while they were living in Woodstock, signing them to a five-year record contract. This was one of the first major label contracts signed by a Buffalo band. Gold released one album and two singles on A&M Records in 1974. Due to medical reasons Bob Frauenhein left the duo and in 1975 David Nehrboss became David Keith, joining the then folk-rock band Sky, which featured vocalist/keyboardist Sherry Hackett whom he had met at The Limelight.

Founded in 1978, PeopleArt was an existing Arts organization on Elmwood Avenue when Mike Meldrum and Bob Stalder added music to the program. When they moved to Lexington near Ashland, Bob along with Stephanie Brooks and Dave Goodard, ran the organization. They currently present original and traditional acoustic music in a 1960s style coffee house atmosphere in the basement of Unity Church on Delaware Avenue. Over the past four decades these acoustic performances have featured many musicians including Ani DiFranco, Michael Meldrum, Nan Hoffman, Tim Baldwin, Katie Miller, Kathy Moriarty, City Fiddle, Dave Ruch, Tom Stahl, Tom Naples, Jim Yeomans, Tom Callahan, Silhouette, The Jazzabels, Cathy Carfagna & David Meinzer, Joanne Fahey & Tom Fenton, Kilissa Cissoko, Dee Adams, Jo Ann Vacarro, Marie Lyons, Clarke McAllister and Katie Kestel.

Buffalo Friends of Folk Music was formed in 1981 by a group of folk music enthusiasts including Ros Magorian, Nan & Keith Hoffman,

Judy Zygmunt, Bob Stalder and Stephani Brooks. The BFFM continues to present regular concerts to promote acoustic music in the Buffalo area, currently holding their events at The Meeting House on Main Street in Williamsville.

During the '70s, there were still coffee house atmosphere venues, but as time progressed acoustic music became more light-rock oriented and performed at a variety of area restaurants and bars. In the early '70s, when bands were not appearing at the club, acoustic groups performed at The Bona Vista on Hertel Avenue and were featured every Monday night. Ash & Campagna (Debby Ash & Michael Campagna) and Dillon & Brady (Phil Dillon & John Brady) performed there acoustically or with a backing band. Another regular performer was Polla Milligan. In addition to the Bona Vista, some of the other clubs featuring acoustic performances were JP Bullfeathers (where Mike Meldrum & Danny Gambino hosted an open mic), Granny Goodness (the former Aliotta's), Binky Browns, Mr. Goodbar, Currans, The Central Park Grill (CPG) and the original Tralfamadore at Main and Fillmore.

Later in the '70s and during the '80s some of the popular acoustic acts included The Thirds (Charlie O'Neil, Joe Head & Jim Brucato), Ray & Jeff (Ray Wood & Jeff Munzert, who later formed Two Hills), George Doran (also a later member of Two Hills but primarily a solo artist), Roger Kowerko, Milligan & Milligan (Polla & Randy Milligan), Joe Wagner, Dooleys (Paul Swisher, Greg Opalinski & Glen Colton), Just Us (Dave Milo & Mike Kustreba), Lombardo & Wahl (Ron Lombardo & Norn Wahl), Filbert & Volkman (Carl Filbert & Bob Volkman), Kurzdorfer & Cady (Jim Kurzdorfer & Kim Cady), Pat Shea, Tim Wright, Korki, Kathy Moriarty, Michel Weber, Ani DiFranco, Jazzabels (Cathy Carfagna & Killissa McGoldrick) and Lombardo & Ramsey (10,000 Maniacs founder John Lombardo & later 10,000 Maniacs vocalist/violinist Mary Ramsey). These acoustic acts performed at Bourbon Street, Scotch & Sirloin, Rosies, Café Casablanca, Nietzsche's, Ground Round Restaurants and weeknights in area Top 40 and rock clubs. In the current day, open mics remain a popular entertainment, featuring both original and cover artists.

THE FREE DESIGN

The Free Design was a band of brothers and sisters from the Dedrick family in Delevan, NY, south of East Aurora. The initial band consisted of Chris, Sandy and Bruce. They were joined by their younger sister, Ellen on their second album and their cousin Jeff accompanied them on guitar at performances. The Dedricks grew up in a musical household. Their father, Art Dedrick, was a trombonist and musical arranger for big bands, including Vaughn Monroe and Red Norvo, and was an arranger for staff orchestras at Buffalo radio stations WBEN and WGR. Later he became a music teacher in the Delevan-Machias school district and one of the founders of Kendor Music, the nation's foremost publisher of high school level arrangements of popular music and musical charts for school orchestras.

In 1966 Chris Dedrick enrolled at the Manhattan School of Music, where his uncle Rusty, a former touring big band jazz trumpet player, was an instructor. His sister Chris and brother Bruce were already in New York and they started performing at the Greenwich Village folk clubs, playing Peter, Paul & Mary style material, in combination with their original songs.

THE FREE DESIGN
Bruce, Sandy, Jeff, Ellen & Chris Dedrick
Photo: Courtesy Sandy Dedrick

The group signed with Enoch Light's Project 3 Records in 1967 because the label offered them the artistic freedom to pursue what would become their trademark style of complex harmonies, jazz-like chord progressions and off-beat time signatures, all products of Chris's classical training. From 1967 to 1972 The Free Design released seven albums, with the single "Kites are Fun" peaking at #33 on the *Billboard Magazine* Adult Contemporary Charts. The Free Design occasionally performed in the

WNY area, and was one of the featured recording groups at the 1968 WKBW Fun-A-Fair, along with The Union Gap and Roy Orbison. Additional Buffalo area dates were with the Buffalo Philharmonic Orchestra or school orchestras at Kleinhans Music Hall and high school auditoriums.

Their music has been labeled as sunshine pop, with prominent vocal harmonies, lush orchestrations featuring New York's top studio musicians and seemingly simple lyrics about kites, bubbles or dolphins, that often revealed more serious issues on closer listening. Being a family band, they are reminiscent of their contemporaries such as the Beach Boys, Carpenters and The Cowsills, together influencing the popular TV family band The Partridge Family. Three of the members moved to the Toronto, Ontario area where Chris became a television music producer, arranger and composer. He was nominated for 16 Gemini Awards, the Canadian equivalent of the Emmy Awards, winning a total of four for shows such as *The Great Polar Adventure, Road to Avonlea, Shipwreck on the Skeleton Coast* and *Million Dollar Babies.* Sandy Dedrick was a music teacher at high schools in Western New York and later taught at Ontario, Canada, schools. Bruce Dedrick was a music teacher and band leader on Long Island. Starting in 1976 Chris, Sandy and Ellen and younger sister Stefanie were the core members of The Star-Scape Singers, a Toronto based classical vocal ensemble that toured internationally through the 1980s and 1990s.

WILLIE NILE

Bobby Noonan grew up in the Cleveland Hill area of Cheektowaga in a house filled with music. His grandfather had been an orchestra leader and vaudeville piano player in Buffalo. In the late 1970s, he changed his name to Willie Nile and moved to New York, where he got involved with the Greenwich Village and CBGB's scene. Considered a folk, alternative, rock performer, he was the opening act on The Who's 1980 summer tour. Nile dropped out of music during the early to mid-1980s, reappearing at a Olso, Norway concert by Buffalo native Eric Andersen. After that concert, Columbia Records signed him to a recording contract. Willie Nile has released over ten albums and is still touring, again performing concerts in the Buffalo area.

9

1960s BUFFALO SOUND

The music that Hound Dog Lorenz played on the radio influenced many musicians in the Buffalo area. It introduced them to the original black recordings of blues and R&B songs, not the watered-down remakes that were recorded by white groups. These musicians, who were predominantly born in the mid-1940s, sought out this style of music at black clubs on the East Side and in downtown Buffalo.

Like all other major cities in the late '50s, Buffalo was very segregated. In fact, it was reported that Buffalo even had a KKK chapter on the second floor of an office building on West Chippewa Street. The black neighborhood of Buffalo was east of Main Street to Jefferson Avenue. There were many live music clubs in these neighborhoods, and aspiring white musicians gravitated to these clubs to learn how to play what was originally called race music and eventually became rock 'n' roll.

The music scene was becoming integrated, while the city of Buffalo remained segregated. Black and white musicians got together at clubs like Johnny's Ellicott Grill, The Pine Grill, Lucky Clover, Zanzibar, The Savoy, Governor's Inn, Revilot, Royal Arms, Bon Ton, Shandus, Polly Juniors, and Shalamar. The white musicians were influenced by James Peterson, Count Rabbit, Matt Nickson, Elmmore "Spoon" Weatherspoon, Joe Madison, Lonnie Smith, Ronnie Foster and more. The music that evolved was a unique R&B rock style, which became identified as The Buffalo Sound.

STAN & THE RAVENS

The Buffalo sound gradually evolved with early bands at clubs like Jan's and Bafo's on Main Street, but the first band to become identified with it was Stan & the Ravens. Stan Szelest started the band in 1958; but at 17, he left town in 1960 to perform with Ronnie Hawkins and the Hawks, based out of Toronto. That group included Levon Helm, Rick Danko and Robbie Robertson, who later became Bob Dylan's back-up musicians and The Band. They added piano player Richard Manuel and organist Garth Hudson after Szelest left the group.

When Szelest returned to Buffalo in 1962, he brought Rebel Payne with him from the Hawks and added Buffalo drummer Sandy Konikoff and guitarist Chuck McCormick to reform Stan & the Ravens. Stan and Chuck had previously worked together at clubs in Quebec in an R&B group that included Buffalo drummer Denny Fox. Peter Haskell soon replaced Payne on bass. For club dates Stan liked to use an upright piano. Many clubs had a piano but if they did not, he would have to move one there. Szelest took a piano out of one club and decided to move it to the next place where he would be playing. After he got the piano out of the bar, they began pushing it down the street until they realized the other club was a couple miles away. Eventually, with the assistance of a truck, the upright arrived. This may be one of the reasons Stan switched to an electric piano.

Sandy Konikoff was told about guitarist Ernie Corallo by Tom Calandra. After he heard Ernie practicing guitar in his attic, playing along with BB King records, he knew Ernie would be a good fit in Stan & the Ravens. Sandy came to Art Kubera's Music Store, where Ernie Corallo was teaching guitar. He told Ernie about Stan's band and asked him to come to the Hideaway to hear them. Ernie went to the club and was hired as the new guitarist, replacing Chuck McCormick. This almost did not happen because just before leaving for the Hideaway, Ernie got a call from a girlfriend, who asked him if he could drive her to the airport to pick up her brother who was coming home on leave from the Air Force. Ernie said he would not be able to help her out because he was just about to leave his house to see a friend's band that night. Later that evening, both Ernie's friend and her brother were killed in the car crash, when their automobile was hit by a train, after they left the airport. Ernie was fortunate that he chose to go to The Hideaway, not to the airport, that night.

Lu Lu Bells on Humboldt and Best and The Hideway on East Delavan, across from the Chevy Plant, were the steady bars for Stan & the Ravens. The band played on a low stage right in the front window of the Hideaway. They got the reputation of being the loudest band in Buffalo but since the room was usually jam packed with people, their bodies help absorb the sound. The only complaint was from the club owner, Helen

STAN & THE RAVENS AT LULU BELLS
Stan Szelest, Chuck McCormick
Peter Haskell, Sandy Konikoff
Photo: Courtesy Peter Haskell

Morton, who claimed she could not hear people placing their drink orders at the bar. She also believed the volume at which the band played broke the thermopane picture window behind the stage.

Peter Haskell left the band and for a short period of time was replaced by Frank Mahaney. Bass player Tommy Calandra was known to the members of Stan and the Ravens because the first band he played in included Ernie Corallo. Sandy often went to see Calandra play in the band Tommy & the Continentals. At this time, Tommy was playing with The Premiers, who had recorded a couple songs and were playing record hops with WKBW DJ's. The Premiers were considered one of the more successful bands in the Buffalo area. But after Tommy came to see Stan & the Ravens perform at The Hideway, he was impressed by the line of people waiting to get in and the band's R&B sound. So, Calandra joined the group and six-night-a-week performances followed at The Hideaway.

Stan previously left Stan & the Ravens to perform with Ronnie Hawkins and other acts, and now Hawkins decided to turn the tables on Szelest. He came to Buffalo and asked Sandy Konikoff and Ernie Corallo to join the Hawks. Ernie turned him down, but Sandy accepted the offer and left for Toronto that night. Taking his place was Gary Mallaber, who previously played in a band with Ernie and was a member of another popular area group, The Vibratos.

After joining Stan & the Ravens, Mallaber soon got himself in trouble. One day he decided to set up his drums on the roof of The Hideaway to practice. A crowd gathered to listen to him playing drums, until calls from the neighborhood resulted in Helen, the owner of the Hideway, demanding that he stop. Due to the complaints, she asked Stan to fire Gary from the band. Stan refused and told Helen that Mallaber should not be fired, his rehearsal probably resulted in more people wanting to come see the band at the club.

After the initial version of Stan & the Ravens broke up, Stan recorded with Garland Jeffrey's Grinderswitch and other artists like King Biscuit Boy, David Wilcox, Roy Buchanan and Lonnie Mack. He also toured with many acts including Lonnie Mack, The Bill Black Combo (Elvis Presley's original bass player) and Jackson Browne. Stan continued to return to Buffalo between recording sessions and tours, always putting together solid bands. In 1984, he performed with Levon Helm in the Woodstock All-Stars, and after Richard Manuel's death, Szelest again became a member of The Band. In 1991, while recording at The Band's Woodstock, New York studio, Stan Szelest died of a heart attack.

RISING SONS – RAVEN

The musical careers of the members of Stan & the Ravens and The Rising Sons kept crossing paths and it was only a matter of time until they would eventually work together.

Some background on the member's early bands and their relationships were, Tony Galla began singing with his parents in a family band that appeared on Ted Mack's *Original Amateur Hour*. His first group was The Flares with drummer Fred Mayer, who was later in The Rising Sons. Before he joined The Vibratos, Gary Mallaber was in The Shadows with Ernie Corallo. Tommy Calandra played with Ernie Corallo in The Royal Flames. These groups preceded them playing together in Stan & the Ravens. Jim Calire's first band was The Rockets, before he formed a R&B trio at Casa Savoy with guitarist Matt Nickson.

As the 1960s progressed, The Rising Sons were formed with Galla (vocals and bass), Mayer (drums), John Weitz (guitar) and Mike Bell (keyboards). When Bell left, he was replaced by Jim Calire (keyboards and sax). With the assistance of deejay Joey Reynolds, this group recorded the single "In Love" which charted nationally and was one of the last releases on Swan Records.

At this time, the members of Stan & the Ravens were Stan Szelest (keyboards and vocals), Ernie Corallo (guitar), Tom Calandra (bass) and Gary Mallaber (drums). Stan & the Ravens had just recorded "The Farmers Daughter" and "Howlin' for my Darling" with producer Dave Lucas in NYC. Due to a dispute on writing credits for "Farmers Daughter" there was growing animosity in the band. Since Stan was often leaving the band to perform with Ronnie Hawkins or other artists, Tom and Gary proposed having Galla and Calire join the band. Stan was against it.

A rehearsal at Calandra's Poultry Street studio with Calandra, Calire, Weitz, Galla and Mallaber jelled. They recorded "There's Nothing Going For Us" b/w "I'm Feeling Down" as the new version of the Rising Sons. Unfortunately, drummer Fred Mayer from the Rising Sons and guitarist Ernie Corallo were the odd men out. However, there were occasions when Weitz could not play some dates and Corallo filled in with the band. When they found out there was another Rising Sons in NYC, they became Raven, a direct tribute to their mentor Stan Szelest.

The band was booked into the original Inferno at Glen Park and a legal dilemma was uniquely solved. John Weitz was not yet 18 years old so he could not play in the bar. In order to perform the date, Weitz played guitar in his car parked outside of the club, with a monitor speaker to hear the music and a 200' long guitar chord to connect to his amplifier on stage. Tony Galla recalled another occasion that occurred at The Ivanhoe on Forest. Weitz was playing guitar in the basement, with a chord going through the ceiling to the stage. Unfortunately, he had a microphone that he took with him to the bathroom and a flushing toilet was heard through the PA system. The owner heard the sound, found Weitz in the basement and kicked him out of the club because he was not yet the legal drinking age of 18.

In addition to these clubs, the band played locally at The Hideaway, Mug, Aliottas, Gilligans and Royal Arms. They drew off their experience and the collective Buffalo music conscience, perfecting their "Buffalo Sound" and added a unique twist with Weitz playing his jazz/blues stylings through a Fender Twin Reverb and Leslie speaker. Critics could not specifically label the band as they were a trailblazing jazz/blues/rock band and more.

The persistence of their manager, Marty Angelo, got Raven booked into the NYC club, Steve Paul's The Scene. Everyone who was anyone came to see the band perform. Jimi Hendrix jammed with them and Janis Joplin was a big fan, even trying to hire keyboardist Jimmy Calire. Calire turned her down and recommended Niagara Falls keyboardist Richard Kermode, who became a member of Joplin's band. George Harrison was quoted in the book on the Beatles *The Longest Cocktail Party* that "The Raven is one of the best American bands I've ever heard". He even tried signing them to Apple Records. Rumor has it that it was Hendrix who influenced Raven to sign with Columbia.

Raven's first album on Columbia Records sold about 100,000

RAVEN
John Weitz, Tom Calandra, Jim Calire
Tony Galla, Gary Mallaber
Photo: Courtesy Tony Galla

copies, they played the Fillmore East, opened one of Led Zeppelin's first U.S. dates at The Boston Tea Party and toured England. Their second album was recorded but not released by Columbia; only a single "Children at Our Feet" was pressed. Raven self-released an LP "Live at the Inferno" but the recording did not properly capture their signature live sound. In 1970, after two years of touring, they returned to Buffalo to play a homecoming concert at Kleinhans Music Hall and disbanded shortly afterward.

The band Raven was gone but the members individually found success in the music industry. Most members eventually moved to California except Tom Calandra who stayed in Buffalo. Through his BCMK (Buffalo College of Musical Knowledge) recording studio on Hobmoor Avenue and later on Delaware near Hertel, he recorded many of the Buffalo area original bands, releasing some on BCMK Records. He also wrote radio jingles, like "Danny Moves Your Fanny in the Morning" and the Buffalo Sabres song, "We're Gonna Win That Cup".

Tony Galla moved to LA where he recorded several blues, big band and Italian music albums, and toured to support these albums. He worked as an actor on various TV shows and is the in-demand vocalist/band leader for celebrity weddings and exclusive special events in the LA area.

John Weitz released a jazz fusion album by the JR Weitz Band, produced by Billy Cobham. John and the band relocated to California where they performed on the West Coast. He worked for Digidesign, developing electronics for guitarists, created audio recording techniques and received several patents for his inventions. His brother Paul Weitz is currently a popular LA area jazz guitarist.

Jim Calire was the arranger, music director and session musician on various productions and was a member of the band America. His son Mario is the drummer with Bob Dylan's son Jacob's band, The Wallflowers.

Mallaber is one of the most sought-after session drummers in rock music. He recorded with Van Morrison, Bruce Springsteen, Eddie Money, Bob Seger and numerous others. Gary was the drummer with the Steve Miller Band for over 10 years and played on eleven Steve Miller albums and seven of his hit singles. Mallaber has over 70 gold or platinum albums to his credit and has recorded or toured with three different bands that were inducted into the Rock and Roll Hall of Fame in Cleveland.

The band Raven and all the members of the group have been inducted into the Buffalo Music Hall of Fame. An interesting event happened at Tony Galla's induction in 1998. Someone stole Galla's induction statue from the Tralf. Later that night a musician that was at the show just happened to stop at a local bar and someone had the statue with him. Noticing that the person with the plaque was not Tony Galla, he took it from him and mailed it to Tony in LA. The thief has never been identified.

The last date all the member played together was a reunion concert at The Tralf in 1993. Tommy Calandra and John Weitz have passed away, but the three surviving members annually return to Buffalo for a reunion show at The Sportsman's Tavern, being joined by various Buffalo musicians including Bobby Militello.

VIBRATOS

The original Vibratos were formed in the late '50s by Dick Terranova, Joe Ferrara, Vic Caputy and Jim Morrow. Like many of the initial rock 'n' roll bands in Buffalo, they were an instrumental band consisting of three guitarists and a drummer; vocalists and bass players came later. This band played early Tom Shannon record hops and added vocalist Kenny Dee (DiPerro) when they began playing the Lucky Pierre record hops. The Vibratos played at the Hi-Teen dances at the Dellwood Ballroom on Saturday afternoons and Dellwood combination big band/rock 'n' roll dances on Sunday nights. At the Sunday night Dellwood dances, they alternated weeks with The Royal Knights, Bobby DeSoto and The Rockin Rebels.

Although not yet 18 years old, the legal drinking age at that time, The Vibratos began playing at bars in a round-about way. A band had an audition at a club called The Rose Room, which Dick Terranova thinks was on Chippewa, and they asked Dick and Kenny Dee to go to the audition with them. After the band got the job their drummer quit, so Joe Ferrara joined the band. Then Dick's brother Jack Terranova joined the group as a second vocalist. When the trumpet player who went to the audition quit, all the members of the band at The Rose Room were from the Vibratos.

Still under age, The Vibratos were hired at The Mansion House, across the street from the WKBW studios on Main Street. The club soon afterwards changed its name to The Peppermint Lounge. During the time, they were performing at the club, Mike Lustan (guitar) and Joe Rogowski (drums) joined the group.

When The Vibratos were appearing at Shells Lounge on Broadway, organist Al Fiorelo joined the group. One night a singer named Emil Lewandowski, who was home on leave from the Air Force, sat in with the band. He made a strong impression on the group and joined the band after he was discharged from the service, becoming the vocalist and bass player when Kenny Dee departed. It was this version of The Vibratos that succeeded Stan & the Ravens at the Sunday afternoon Glen Park Casino teen dances, which drew a couple thousand people every week. The Rising Sons opened for The Vibratos at some of the Sunday dances, exemplifying how everyone in the early Buffalo music scene was intertwined.

In 1963, two groups called The Vibratos were performing every Friday and Saturday in WNY. Emil, Dick and Joe were playing as a trio in the lounge at The Town Casino, while Jack, Mike and Al were joined by drummer Gary Mallaber and sax player Chic Cicero at The Play Bar on Grant and West Ferry.

THE VIBRATOS AT TOWN CASINO
Al Fiorelo, Jack Terranova, Dick Terranova
Chic Cicero, Gary Mallaber
Photo: Courtesy Dick Terranova

At this time Lewandowski and Lustan decided to leave the band and formed a new group called The Enemys. After they played a few dates at Lu Lu Bells as The Vibratos, they moved to Los Angeles. There they became the house band at LA's Whiskey A Go Go, and Emil Lewandowski changed his name to Cory Wells. In 1967, Cory formed Three Dog Night, one of the most successful bands of the late '60s and early '70s. The band had twelve gold albums, 21 consecutive Top 40 hits and seven million selling singles. Cory performed with Three Dog Night until the fall of 2015, just prior to when he passed away at his home in Dunkirk, NY.

The Vibratos continued with Dick, Jack, Al, Chic and Gary as the Town Casino house band for several years. This version of the band was also the house band for the Joey Reynolds WKBW TV show, opened many concerts at Melody Fair and released the single "Stubborn Kind of Fella".

Later incarnations of the band featured many prominent area musicians including: Paul Herman, Al Rizzuto, Buddy Brundo, Brad Grey, Jimmy Wozniak, the Kipler Brothers and many more. They worked the popular late '60s/early '70s clubs like: The Three Coins, Russo's in South Buffalo, Andante on Hertel – formerly The Everglades, The Scene, Brighton Acres and McVans.

After the Vibratos disbanded in 1974, Dick formed Alive & Well with Raven's Tony Galla (vocals/bass) and Jim Calire (keyboards/sax), along with Paul Lieberson (drums) and vocalist Janice Mitchell (who was later a Ray Charles Raelette, touring worldwide for five years). They played all the top clubs, predominantly The Executive and Gabriel's Gate. After a year, Alive and Well broke up, with Dick Terranova and Tony

Galla performing as a duo. During the mid-1970s, Jack Terranova also had a duo with organist Paul Herman. When the Terranova brothers received a request for a larger band to perform at a wedding or special event, the two duos combined and were augmented by some of the many musicians that worked with the Vibratos over the years.

By the late 1970s, many of the musicians involved with The Vibratos had moved to California and some, including Dick Terranova, still live there. The later achievements of several members of The Vibratos where discussed in other sections, with info on Buddy Brundo and Chick Cicero following. When Buddy Brundo was in WNY he ran a recording studio above his parent's music store in Niagara Falls. In 1976 he purchased Conway Recording Studios in LA and developed it into one of the premier recording studios in the country. Chick Cicero, left his music career in Buffalo behind and became one of the most influential proponents of ceremonial magic, is president of The Hermetic Order of the Golden Dawn and is the author of several books.

ASH & CAMPAGNA

Debby Ash and Michael Campagna worked at the Bona Vista in the early 1970s, playing steady Monday and Tuesdays, along with many weekends, for almost four years. Even on weeknights, there were often lines to get in the club. Monday was more of an acoustic night, which they shared with Polla Milligan and a different guest opening performer every week. The focus of the night was original music. Jeremy Wall usually joined them on piano. Tuesdays were an electric night, at times bordering on the avant-garde new music movement of Morton Feldman at UB. A revolving list of musicians joined Debby and Michael on Tuesdays including: Jimmy Calire, Steve Sadoff, Tom Walsh, John Weitz, Steve Nathan, Gary Brox, Jeremy Wall and Jay Beckenstein. On weekends, Ash & Campagna usually began the night backed up by members of their Tuesday band, but performing a mix of originals and R&B or blues covers. Later in the night, they were often joined by Elmo "Spoon" Weatherspoon and other members of The Houserockers. Ash & Campagna and the Lost Buffalo's Band also played other clubs in WNY, and shows at UB, Buff State and Delaware Park events.

Campagna started playing in his teens and took classical guitar lessons from Oswald Rantucci. He practiced in an early teen basement band with future Parkside guitarist Joe LaCoco and played bass in his first band at 16 with JP & the Blues Messengers at The Colony Lounge on Hertel. While still a teen Michael played with Jesse James and the Outlaws blues band, which was James Peterson's (Lucky Peterson's father) house band at The Governors Inn. When blues guitarist Freddy King played the Governors Inn, he needed a bass player and upon James Peterson's suggestion, Campagna filled in on bass for the one week engagement. Michael was later the guitarist for Cisum Revival with Steve Nathan, Joe Scinta and Larry Rizutto. His musical training included mentoring from jazz piano player Joe Azarello and Livingston Gearhart, who was his piano professor at the UB School of Music.

Ash & Campagna initially met at a Bennett High School talent show, when Debby was a sophomore auditioning for the event and Michael was a senior who was coordinating the show. Michael was so impressed by Debby's natural blues-based talent that he offered to play guitar for her performance. They reunited two years later, during a Cisum Revival show at Aliotta's, which led to their dating, marriage, formation of a duo, group and songwriting partnership. Since Ash was a theater major at UB and performed with the Buffalo Theater Workshop, they integrated a theatrical aspect into their musical act.

The Bona Vista was Ash & Campagna's musical home and it

ASH & CAMPAGNA AT THE BONA VISTA
Tom Walsh, Jeremy Wall, Gary Brox, Jay Beckenstein, Debby Ash, Steve Sadoff, Michael Campagna
Photo: Courtesy Debby Ash

171

provided some memorable shows. One night Joe Cocker came to the club after a concert and Michael asked him to sing. Cocker had been drinking heavily after his concert, almost knocked over the PA speakers when he got on stage and Michael had to hold him up. But when he started singing it was like the alcohol left his system and he brought the house down for almost an entire set. Another night Bonnie Raitt and Jackson Brown came to the club. Raitt did not want to leave the stage and afterwards told Michael and Debby that their original songs were great and they should move to LA. In 1975 Ash & Campagna followed Raitt's advice and moved to California.

In California, Ash & Campagna wrote songs that were recorded by Chaka Khan, Maxine Nightingale and Jennifer Holliday. In 1977, they recorded at Niagara Falls native Buddy Brundo's Conway Records, in 1984 recorded *Opus #1* with Gary Mallaber and released "Baba Bollo" in 1985. Campagna also toured and recorded with the industrial group Psychic TV and funk rock group The Average Johnsons. He has written songs with Gary Mallaber for the Dan Patrick radio and TV show. Michael is currently the Creative Director of the South Pasadena Music Center and Conservatory. Debby is the president of Campashe Music, which controls the publishing of the Ash & Campagna catalogue. She performs in the LA area with her blues R&B, soul group. In addition, she is a youth advocate and founder/director of the New Generations youth program for at-risk teens at the Pasadena Playhouse. Debby is currently combining her advocacy and music talents in writing the original Urban Opera Musical *Red Sneakers*.

COLD SOUP – FLASH

Cold Soup was formed as an evolution of the teen band Nobody's Children. Dan Gambino was continually upgrading the band and with his cousin Mike Gambino sharing the vocals, they formed Cold Soup with James Ralston (guitar), Larry Swist (bass), John Wade Jr (keyboards) and Richie Pidanick (drums). They performed early blues rock and covered Eric Clapton, early Chicago, songs by the Buffalo band Raven and their own compositions.

In 1969 and early 1970 Cold Soup regularly performed at Aliotta's, opening shows for BB King and Dr. John, and performed at other area clubs and some special outdoor shows at Griffis Park, opening for Joe Cocker. Their original songs were well received by the listeners so

Ralston, Pidanick and Swist decided to form a new band performing all original material, with Dan Gambino leaving to join the Ugly Brothers.

Ralston, Pidanick and Swist formed Flash, initially managed by Joe Aliotta. They added Phil Dillon on lead vocals/acoustic guitar and Julliard graduate Dean Mooney on organ/piano. The band members wrote

FLASH AT ALIOTTA'S
Dean Mooney, James Ralston, Phil Dillon
Richie Pidanick, Larry Swist
Photo: Courtesy Phil Dillon

songs and rehearsed until Flash had a full night of original material. Their premier was on November 4, 1970, when they played to a full house of 300 people at Aliotta's. Flash also played regular dates at UB's Fillmore Room and even without a record release, it was only a matter of time until regular followers of the band knew every word to the Dillon/Ralston originals.

Flash had assistance from Marty Angelo (Raven's manager), Gene Jacobs & Mike Lustan (who were associated with Cory Wells band – The Enemys), and Jerry Meyers and Rich Sargent in reaching their recording goals. They recorded an album at PCI Studios in Rochester and a single at Jerry Meyers Act One studio, but nothing was released.

After performing at other area clubs and touring with NRBQ, Brownsville Station and The Charles (John Valby's band), they showcased in Los Angeles. After two months of LA showcases without obtaining a record contract, all the members except Mooney returned to Buffalo. They worked in the recording studio for another two years, but did not perform another club date.

However, all members were individually successful in the music industry. The band and the four members that returned to Buffalo have all been inducted into the Buffalo Music Hall of Fame. For 30 years Ralston was the guitarist and band leader for Tina Turner. Dillon moved to Nashville where he became a successful studio musician, engineer, producer, song writer and performer. Swist became an audio engineer, where he worked on nine records that reached #1 on the Billboard charts, earning him five gold records and two platinum records. He recorded

WNY area artists, Spyro Gyra, Chuck Mangione, Talas and Gamalon. Swist also owned a company that designed the acoustics for recording studios, including a line of recording studio monitor speakers. Pidanick toured with several national acts and became a vice president with the music store chain – Guitar Center.

POSSE

The original version of Posse recorded at Columbia Records in NYC and were almost offered a recording contract with the label. That group performed songs written by vocalist/guitarist Doug Kenny, and included Richard Calandra (drums), Val Masencala (keyboards) and Joe Giarrano (bass).

After not obtaining a recording contact, they returned to Buffalo in 1971 and Richard and Joe put together the version of Posse that most remember with Billy McEwen (vocals), Doug Morgano (guitar), Jim Ehinger (keyboards) and Ron Davis (keyboards). This double-keyboard band is recalled for their five-night-a-week summer engagements at Bill Millers in Angola. Giarrano left the band to work with The Houserockers and was replaced by bassist Andy Rapillo. After Richie Calandra was in a serious car accident and could no longer perform with the band, drummer Pete Holguin joined the group.

Prior to becoming a member of Posse, vocalist Billy McEwen, sang with The Embers Blues Band at South Buffalo and Angola area clubs during the 1960s. After Posse broke up, he formed several groups with a revolving nucleus of well-known area musicians. In 1975, he formed The Billy Bright Band with Billy McEwen (vocals, harmonica), Doug Yeomans (guitar), Jimmy Beishline (piano), Chris Haug (bass) and Ron Zelewski (drums), who was later replaced by Pete Holguin. The Billy Bright Band was booked by Pelican Productions out of Rochester, which was the agency that booked dates for Duke Jupiter, the band that released the single "I'll Drink to You", with their album produced by Al Cooper from Blood Sweat & Tears. The agency booked both bands at many of the same clubs and college dates across the state, resulting in many lucrative dates. The Billy Bright Band often played at The Bona Vista and opened for many national concerts at The Belle Starr. The group disbanded in 1978.

In 1980 *The Blues Brothers* movie, along with John Belushi and Dan Aykroyd's skits on *Saturday Night Live*, created an interest in high energy blues and soul music. To capitalize on this revival, the band The Buffalo Blues Brothers was formed. Like the Blues Brothers, the band featured two lead vocalists, Billy McEwen and Jon Rose, with Jay Dzina (guitar), Nick Veltri (bass), Clay Stahka (keyboards), Pete Pecora (sax), Nick Salamone (sax) and Pete Holguin (drums). They recorded a live album in 1981 at The Warehouse in Rochester and later changed their name to The Buffalo Blues Band.

The first Buffalo Blues Band broke up in 1982 but returned as The Soul Invaders with members Billy McEwen (vocals), Doug Morgano (guitar), Jay Dzina (guitar), Nick Veltri (bass), Pete Holguin (drums) and Jeff Hackworth (sax). That group eventually changed their name to The Billy McEwen Band and had several member changes, but the core of the band continued working together for the next 30 years.

SPOON & THE HOUSEROCKERS

THE HOUSEROCKERS AT THE BELLE STARR
Jim Claire, Phil DiRe, Sandy Konikoff, Jay Beckenstein
Joe Giarrano, Ernie Corallo
Photo: Courtesy Phil DiRe

Elmore "Spoon" Witherspoon's playing influenced many young white R&B musicians, who would come to see him perform at inner city bars, where he worked with other trendsetting players like Count Rabbit and Joe Madison. The music Hound Dog Lorenz played on the radio that introduced these musicians to R&B, but it was live shows by Stan Szelest and Spoon that motivated the musicians to perform the music.

In the early 1970s, former Stan & the Ravens guitarist Ernie Corallo got a Sunday afternoon job a at bar called Sundays on Elmwood Avenue.

He formed a group with Joe Giarrano (bass) and Brad Grey (drums). They decided to ask Spoon to join them and named the band The Houserockers. There were no formal rehearsals for their first job, the four musicians showed up and just started playing. It was raw energy, drawing off Spoon's soulful vocals and unique guitar stylings.

The Sunday afternoon crowds started to grow and so did the band. Jay Beckenstein joined on sax, bringing fellow horn players Phil DiRe and Joe Ford with him. There were alternating and sometimes multiple keyboardists with Jim Calire, Jimmy Ehinger and Steve Nathan playing with the group. When Sandy Konikoff joined them, there were times when they had double drummers. Ralph Parker also started playing guitar with the band, giving them two guitarists.

The Houserockers were almost like two bands in one. Spoon had a second shift factory job, so often the first two sets featured material by Barbara St. Clair and the second two sets featured material by Spoon. Another version of the group had Ash & Campagna covering the vocals in the first sets at The Bona Vista and Spoon playing the later sets. Their regular clubs were Sundays, Brinks and Caseys on Elmwood, One Eyed Cat on Bryant, Bona Vista on Hertel and Belle Starr in Colden.

The Houserockers were a very successful and profitable band but most of the musicians went on to other projects and many moved out of the Buffalo area. A later version of The Houserockers included Spoon, Phil Youakim, Ron Davis, Carl Gottman and Bob Dominiak. Unfortunately, Spoon passed away at an early age in 1975, but he influenced a generation of musicians and helped set the foundation for the Buffalo Sound.

ERNIE CORALLO

When Stan & the Ravens and The Rising Sons merged to form Raven, the musician that appeared to be left out was guitarist Ernie Corallo. Ernie had a hand in bringing the members of Raven together and before leaving Buffalo for a successful career as a studio musician, he helped bring a number of other musicians together in The Houserockers.

When he was young Ernie lived down the street from the Channel 2 studios at 184 Barton Street. He would watch a Saturday morning music show on channel 2, and if he liked the band he would ride down to the studio on his bike. That is how he met Ronnie Hawkins when he was 15. Several years later Ernie played guitar in Hawkins band.

Ernie was influenced by his father who was a drummer, performing under the name of Sam Corey in 1930s and 1940s dance bands. Ernie started out on trumpet, taking lessons from Sam Scamacca. When rock 'n' roll came out he wanted to play guitar, so his father took him to guitarist Tony Militello. That led to lessons from Andy Roma at John Sedola's Music Store, with Ernie later teaching guitar at Kubera's and Kenmore Music.

Ernie worked with many musicians in the early R&B scene, including Count Rabbit. He played in bands with Tommy Calandra and Gary Mallaber, that preceded their involvement with Stan & the Ravens, a band for which Ernie was the primary guitarist during most of the late 1960s. After Stan & the Ravens, he recorded with John Cale, on the first solo album Cale recorded after leaving the Velvet Underground. Ernie also played with Garland Jeffreys on the Grinderswitch LP in 1970.

Corallo returned to Buffalo and formed The Houserockers, a band that included many of the musicians associated with what is called The Buffalo Sound. In 1973, he moved to California where he worked as a studio musician. He was a long-term member of the Paul Williams Band, earning a Platinum album for the *Muppets Movie* soundtrack. Ernie also recorded with The Average White Band and Ned Doheny.

BARBARA ST. CLAIR & THE PIN-KOOSHINS featured the vocals of Barbara St. Clair (Barbara Spivey), who was given the moniker of "Buffalo's Queen of Soul." Prior to forming this band, while still in her teens, Barbara was in a four-piece vocal band called Sessions, performing at the Lucky Clover, Town Casino, Glen Casino and at record hops with Lucky Pierre. In addition to Barbara, the members of The Pin-Kooshins were John Culliton Mahoney (guitar), Ron Zalewski (drums), Bill Phillips (bass) and Jake Jakubowski (organ), with Jake later replaced by keyboardist Ronnie Davis and Carmen Castiglione taking over on bass. During the 1960s and early 1970s, they were

BARBARA ST CLAIR & THE PIN-KOOSHINS
Ron Zalewski, Jake Jakubowski, John Culliton Mahoney,
Barbara St. Clair, Carmen Castiglione
Photo: Courtesy John Culliton Mahoney

regular performers at The Inferno, The Colony Lounge and The Mug and they recorded for Mercury Records. Barbara later formed, Barbara St. Clair and The Shadows, with Paul Campanella and long-term member Carol Jean Swist. As a tribute to Barbara, who passed away in 2013, Chris Haug continues the Shadows with Terrie George, who replaced DeeAnn DiMeo Tompkins as the female vocalist. Bill Phillips was later a member of The Group, a Niagara Falls based band that recorded on Atlantic Records, and toured with The Coasters and other national groups. John Culliton Mahoney released several albums and was also a member of the 1980s group Sundance with Jay Dzina, Jerry Bass, Bob Ambrusko and Tom Bucur.

BLUE OX was formed in early 1970s. When the band was recording at Cross Eyed Bear in Clarence Center, keyboardist Ron Davis was working at the studio. They talked Ron into joining Blue Ox and not moving to Suffern, NY with Sypro Grya's Cross-Eyed-Bear production team. The band members were Willie Schoellkopf, Charlie O'Neil, Phil Yocam, Morris Lewis and Ron Davis. Joe Frontera and Pete Holguin played drums in the group at different times. They were regular performers at The Belle Starr, Bruce Jarvis' Outside Inn, Spectrum and Poor House. The band broke up after they relocated to Phoenix Arizona. Ron Davis later began playing Zydeco accordion and performs with his band LeeRon Zydeco & The Hot Tamales, at New Orleans and Cajun style events.

ARGYLE STREET BAND. Not all Buffalo bands got together and started playing in WNY. The Argyle Street Band was formed in LA by Buffalo area musicians who were living on the West Coast. The name of the group came from the street in LA where the band started rehearsing. Willie Schoellkopf (guitar) and Ron Davis (keyboards) moved to California after Blue Ox broke up in Phoenix Arizona. In California they joined forces with Tom Walsh (drums), who had been working with Jim Calire in America; Steve Sadoff (bass), who was playing with Ash & Campagna; and Doug Morgano (guitar), who was in LA after working with Martha & the Vandellas. Argyle Street played dates in the LA area, where Sandy Konikoff (drums) also worked some dates with them. Walsh and Konikoff decided to remain on the West Coast but the rest of the members decided to move back to WNY. When they returned to Buffalo, drummers Pete Holguin and then Jerry Bass worked with The Argyle Street Band at area clubs from 1978 to 1980. The band recently has been performing annual reunion shows at The Sportsman's Tavern.

STAN & THE DOGS. After several years of touring, Stan Szelest again returned to Buffalo and put together a band called Stan & the Dogs. This group played area clubs from 1973 to 1975. In addition to Stan, the band included, Steve Nathan, Eric Ferguson, Ralph Parker and Pete Holguin. Stan and the Dogs auditioned with the management of Martha Reeves from The Vandellas and were offered the position as her back up band. All the band members did not want to travel, so they turned down the offer but gave them the names of Doug Morgano and Jim Ehinger, who secured the jobs as guitarist and keyboardist for Martha's group. Doug and Jim played a two-month European tour with Martha and Doug remained with the band for two years, eventually becoming the musical director.

LONNIE SMITH is known as a jazz organist; however, he was one of the musicians that had an influence on the Buffalo Sound. Lonnie started performing in vocal ensembles and one of his first bands in the 1950s was called the Teen Kings, with sax player Grover Washington, Jr. His first instrument was trumpet, but with the encouragement of Art Kubera, owner of Kubera's Music Store, he was given the opportunity to learn to play organ; and it was from Kubera's that he obtained his first Hammond B3.

Smith's initial bookings were at The Pine Grill, where he garnered the attention of national jazz artists and aspiring musicians from Buffalo who came to experience and learn from his Hammond Organ artistry. His Hammond style and sound is one of the basics of what is called The Buffalo Sound. In 1966, Lonnie left Buffalo to work with George Benson and became part of the stable at Blue Note Records. In 1969 *Downbeat Magazine* named Lonnie Top Organist of the year and from 2003-2014 he was awarded Organist/Keyboardist of the Year by the Jazz Journalists Association. An authentic master of the B3 for five decades and featured on over 70 albums, Lonnie is considered an innovator and the father of acid jazz. Lonnie Smith continues to credit his Buffalo beginnings and the generosity of Art Kubera in helping launch his career.

JOE MADISON grew up in the Jazz and R&B heyday of the late 1940s and 1950s when there was a live music club on almost every street corner along William Street on the East Side of Buffalo. He loved bebop but his first jobs were with bluesmen like Elmo "Spoon" Witherspoon and Count

Rabbit. Other early dates were with Grover Washington Jr., when he was a teen, and with Chic & the Diplomats. After Joe mastered the Hammond B3 sound, he became a fixture at The Pine Grill on Jefferson and earned the nickname "Groove" due to his similar stylings to organist Richard "Groove" Holmes. During the 1980s Madison's B3 was a permanent fixture on the stage at The Mirage at 3076 Bailey Avenue, where Holmes appeared on a regular basis. Madison also toured the country with King Curtis, and late in his career often performed at Club 1218 on Jefferson and The Calumet Arts Café on West Chippewa, before he passed away in 1995.

LUCKY PETERSON got a very early start in music. His father James Peterson was a musician and the owner of The Governor's Inn in Buffalo. During an engagement at the club in 1969, Willie Dixon saw a then five-year-old Lucky Peterson perform. Months later, Lucky was singing the song "1-2-3-4", a cover of "Please, Please, Please" by James Brown on *The Tonight Show* and *The Ed Sullivan Show*. Music journalist Tony Russel states in his book "The Blues – From Robert Johnson to Robert Cray," that Lucky Peterson "may be the only blues musician to have had national television exposure in short pants." After making national television appearances, Lucky attended the Buffalo Academy for the Visual and Performing Arts and played French horn in the school symphony. A vocalist, keyboardist and guitarist, Lucky Peterson has released over 20 albums and continues to tour extensively.

There were many other bands that could be considered in the Buffalo Sound style. Some of these groups included the bands Parkside Zoo, Parkside, Cisum Revival and The Ugly Brothers, which were a continuation of each other. It started out with Parkside Zoo, led by vocalist Mondo Galla, and was an early band for future National Trust bandleader Sam Guarino and trumpet player Ken Kauffman, a different musician from the future Road keyboardist. The guitarist in the band was Joe LoCoco. The band became Parkside, with Joe LoCoco being joined by Steve Nathan, Jim Poulin, John Grapes and Joey Scinta, who later formed the Scinta Brothers with his brother Frank. In Cisum Revival, Steve Nathan and Joey Scinta were joined by Michael Campagna and Larry Rizutto. In the Ugly Brothers, Joe LoCoco returned to work with Nathan, Scinta and Rizutto.

In the 1960s, Dolly Durante had a group called Dolly Dee and the Midnighters with brothers Tommy and Sam Burruano. She also toured across the country with the band The Truth and was a back-up vocalist with Stevie Wonder, Ike Turner and Buddy Miles.

The Venturas was one of the first bands, in which teacher and big band leader Dr. Joe Baudo (organ) performed. Other members of the 1966 band were Stanley Brown (vocals), Joe Mantione (guitar), Frank Falzone (bass & sax) and John Tomasula (drums). Lenny Licata, who became a booking agent for JR Productions, was later the keyboardist with the band.

Another early band was Chuck & the Counts, dating back to 1963. The members were Bob Passmore (guitar), Joe Ruggiero (piano), Bill Phillips (bass) and Chuck Tormeano (drums). The band started when the members were just 15 years old and they played at early Niagara Falls clubs like Keough's, DeDario's, The Strand, Defazio's, The Glass Bar, The Main, The Victory and The Club. Bill Phillips is the founder of the Niagara Falls Music Hall of Fame.

Richard Kermode played with his band Milestones at Bob Minicucci's Ontario House in Niagara Falls for more than four years during the mid-1960s. Kermond was later a member of Janis Joplin's Kozmic Blues Band and recorded three albums with Santana.

10

1960s TEEN CLUB BANDS

Teen club bands were formed by the generation of musicians who were influenced by the Beatles premier on the *Ed Sullivan Show* in 1964. Many teens purchased guitars, started taking lessons and began by playing instrumentals by surf groups like The Ventures. Most of these aspiring musicians were born in the late 1940s and early 1950s and like the name implies, started playing at teen clubs, along with school dances and community events. These groups were also known as garage bands because they rehearsed in their parent's garages. The Buffalo Sound bands were influenced by early R&B and blues radio stations, while the teen club bands were influenced by the British Invasion and surf music played on radio stations WKBW, WYSL and WNIA. There was a cross over between the two styles during the 1960s and in the 1970s they merged into a further evolution of the distinct sound of bands from the Buffalo area.

TEEN CLUBS

The first rock 'n' roll dances were held at The Dellwood Ballroom. These Saturday afternoon dances were an extension of the Hi-Teen Club, and teen bands also alternated sets with big bands at the regular Sunday evening shows. The Glen Casino presented the first teen dances on Sunday afternoons, with buses transporting the teens to Williamsville from the south towns and north towns. At the Dellwood and Glen Casino the bands performing still had more of the Buffalo Sound style. When the teen clubs began operating, that marked the beginning of the teen club band era.

In 1966, The Glen Casino moved their dances to Club Commodore at 2285 Genesee Street near Pine Ridge. This was the first large scale dedicated teen club with bands. The Club Commodore had the same management that operated the Glen Casino, and they continued the practice of having buses bring teens to the club from surrounding parts of the eastern city and suburbs. The Rogues were the house band, playing dances on Friday nights and Sunday afternoons.

Between Niagara Falls and Buffalo was the Peppermint Stick on Ward Road in North Tonawanda. They also had buses that picked up teens across North Tonawanda and brought them to the club. Kathy Lynn and the Playboys were the house band, headlining shows and being the back-up band for touring groups. The owner of the Peppermint Stick, Clive Holmes, and manager, Tony Dee, opened additional Peppermint Stick Teen Clubs at the Grand Island Casino in Beaver Island Park and Fazio's Capital Hall in South Buffalo.

Bill and Joe Jaworski opened The Volcano on Bailey Avenue near UB, The Pit on South Park Avenue in Blasdell and the Dungeon in Dunkirk/Fredonia. With these three teen clubs, they would hire national recording acts to perform one set at each club on the same night. Local bands would play before or after the national act. All three clubs had the same atmosphere; the interior was painted black, with black lights throughout the building, while the stage was painted red, with colored lights illuminating the stage.

Lou Knots owned two clubs he named The Cave. The Boulevard Cave was on the second floor of an office building on Niagara Falls Boulevard near Sheridan, with a club called Teen Town originally at this location. The Delaware Cave was in the Great Arrow Plaza on Delaware Avenue. It was later named Hullabaloo, which was owned by Larry Levite, who was later the publisher of *Buffalo Spree* magazine. Levite was also owner of WBEN AM-FM from 1978 – 1994.

In 1968, Psycus was in the former Shea's Seneca Theater at 2186 Seneca Street at Cazenovia. Prior to the club opening, the Seneca Theater, removed some of the side seating and had bands play on weekends before, between or after movies. When Psycus opened all the theater seating was removed, they retained the sloped floor, and then began extensive remodeling, which was rumored to cost $250K. Their advertising claimed they had the third largest light show in the U.S. Psycus had a capacity of over a thousand people, and they featured national bands such as Country Joe and the Fish and local bands, with a psychedelic slant. The lobby was decorated with an *Alice in Wonderland* theme, painted in day-glo colors, highlighted by black lights. The ballroom was filled with throbbing strobe lights and a liquid bubble light show, along with slides projected on all the walls and ceiling over a white cotton-like fabric. This was coordinated by Ron Plum from New York City and Robert Then from Buffalo. After opening on October 7, 1968, Psycus was short-lived and only remained open a little over a year. Other psychedelic light show clubs were The Electric Sands, on Main near Chippewa, and The Main Scene, operated by Jerry Ralston, on Main Street across from the WKBW Studios. However, they were small in comparison to Psycus.

Other teen clubs during the 1960s included: The Beatle Ballroom (267 West Utica at Elmwood), Pussycat Club (621 Main in the former Jan's Candy Cane Lounge), JB's Pendulum (Orchard Park), Sandsabarn (Perry/Warsaw), Tiki Club (1789 Whitehaven Road in Grand Island), Perry's/Marx's (Seneca Street at the city line), Rogues Gallery (1010 Niagara Falls Boulevard), Tin Pan Alley (1293 Bailey at E. Lovejoy), and the Maryvale Teen Center (Maryvale & Cayuga Road), as well as smaller clubs that remained open for a short time. Two later teen clubs were The Funnel, located near the corner of Bailey and Kensington, and The Factory, which was located on Hertel Avenue, not far from the North Park Theater. The Funnel and The Factory were open in the early 1970s marking the end of the teen club era clubs. There were teen clubs in the late '70s and early '80s, and teen nights at some of the larger clubs, along with bands at roller rinks for those under the age of 18, and later the under 21 crowd. However, they were a totally different type of operation than the 1960s teen clubs.

There were several halls that presented teen dances on a regular basis. The Strand Theater (on Clinton Street in Kaisertown, presented by Granny Go Go), Fazio's Capital Hall (on South Park), Mount Major Hall/Stadium Post (224 West Ferry at Herkimer - where future Mulligan's Cafe owner Michael Militello promoted his first events), Carpenters Hall (Kensington & Fillmore – where national groups were featured), and Leisureland (on Camp Road in Hamburg – which included everything from dances to a bowling alley and cinema).

Large events were held specifically for teen audiences. In 1966 there was a Battle of Bands at Buffalo's War Memorial Auditorium, where just about every band in Buffalo participated. In addition, the competition featured fashion shows and other activities. WKBW radio also presented the KB Fun-A-Fair in 1967 at Leisureland in Hamburg and in 1968 and 1969 at the Amherst Recreation Center.

There were some hybrid clubs that admitted those over and under 18 years old, which required a stamp or wristband to purchase alcohol. Some of these places included The Mirage (located in Transit Lanes), Lime Lake Pavilion (Delevan/Machias) and Cuba Lake Pavilion (Cuba, NY).

The bands also played at the high school, church, CYO, YMCA, legion post and community center dances, along with events in the parks. The dances at St. Joe's High School on Kenmore Avenue featured many shows by national recordings groups.

The demise of the teen clubs was two-fold. The first reason was due to the fights. Teens from the neighborhood where the club was located did not want teens from other neighborhoods coming into their turf. Often fraternities or gangs claimed a club as their territory and fought to keep others out. In addition to these nightly fights, there were stabbings or shootings at some clubs. The club owners were subjected to community disdain for running rowdy establishments. Teens who just wanted to have a good time, did not want to get beat up just for being in the wrong neighborhood. Just like teen fights were instrumental in bringing an end to The Crystal Beach Boat and inaugurating the "pay one price" admission charge to amusement parks, these fights were responsible for the closure of the teen clubs and the end of the teen club era.

Another reason for the demise of the teen club era is baby boomers were getting older. Since the legal drinking age was 18 in the late 1960s and early 1970s, the baby boomers were now becoming old enough to start going to the bars. This transition resulted in the abundance of crowded nightclubs during the 1970s.

THE TEEN CLUB BANDS

Two of the earliest teen club bands were The Buddies and Kathy Lynn & the Playboys. Both groups could be considered a crossover or hybrid of teen club and Buffalo Sound bands.

THE BUDDIES were John Culliton Mahoney's (guitar/vocals) first band. Other members were Bill Phillips (bass), Dave Matsiniak (drums) and Bob Korbit (guitar). In 1964, they recorded two songs for a 45, ("The Beetle" b/w "Pulse Beat"), both credited as written by Joey Reynolds. The DJs at WKBW liked these songs so much that the band changed their name to the KB Buddies and they played at Joey Reynolds and Dan Neaverth Road Shows. During live

THE KB BUDDIES
Bill Phillips, John Culliton Mahoney, Dave Matsinak, Bob Korbit
Photo: Courtesy John Culliton Mahoney

performances, they backed up Joey & Danny on their single "Rats in My Room." They also performed at Dellwood Ballroom dances with WKBW's Fred Klestine and Rod Roddy. Their song "Pulse Beat" became Irv Weinstein's *Pulse Beat News* theme song on Channel 7. The Buddies opened a Dick Clark Caravan of Stars concert at War Memorial Stadium. Mahoney was later a member of Barbara St. Clair and The Pin-Kooshins the John Culliton Mahoney Band, Sundance and played solo performances. He recorded several albums for Amherst Records.

KATHY LYNN & THE PLAYBOYS were formed in 1963 when guitarist Nick Ameno went to Bafo's and saw Kathy Keppen performing. With drummer Buddy (Jack) Ferraro, they started performing as a trio at a downtown Buffalo club. When they were asked to be the house band at The Peppermint Stick teen club in Wheatfield, they added bass player Denny Vellette. Tommy Shannon would often bring recording artists who appeared on his *Buffalo Bandstand* television show to the Peppermint Stick and the Kathy Lynn & the Playboys would back them up. They signed a management contract with Tommy Shannon and Carl Cisco, releasing three singles on Swan Records and opening a Dave Clark Five concert at The Aud. When their single "Rock City" began receiving airplay, they began touring in New York, Pennsylvania and Ohio.

In 1966 Tom Shannon took a position as a DJ at a Detroit, Michigan radio station. Kathy Lynn & the Playboys moved with him and Ed Bentley joined the band as their new bass player. While in Michigan the band performed and recorded as the LaSalles and Buena Vistas. They had a one

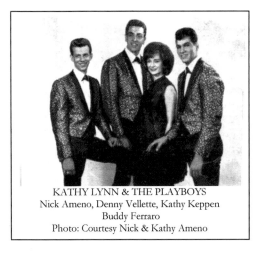

KATHY LYNN & THE PLAYBOYS
Nick Ameno, Denny Vellette, Kathy Keppen
Buddy Ferraro
Photo: Courtesy Nick & Kathy Ameno

song deal with Motown/VIP Records, being the first white artists to release a record on Motown. Kathy was offered a seven-year solo contract with Motown, but turned it down to remain with her band and to later marry her guitarist Nick Ameno.

After touring the upper U.S. and Canada for almost a decade, they returned to Buffalo in 1974 and formed Angel Baby & the Daddyo's. Kathy and Nick later joined Solid Grease, and after being inducted into the Buffalo Music Hall of Fame in 2010, they again started performing as Kathy Lynn & the Playboys.

There were teen club style bands in every part of the city and suburbs. However, many were just popular at one school or a certain neighborhood. The better bands started playing at clubs beyond their home base and built a following, and many progressed to being the early bands playing at late '60s and early '70s bars. Information on some of the most popular teen club bands follow, and mention has been made of other groups from this time.

THE ROGUES were the first teen club style band to become popular in WNY. Formed in 1963, the band was from the Amherst area with members: Jim Pierotti (vocals), Mike Spriggs (guitar), Dave Smith (guitar), Bob Radel (bass) and Gary Jaros (drums). When the Glen Casino teen dances moved to Club Commodore, the Rogues were hired as the house

THE ROGUES
Dave Smith, Gary Jaros, Jim Pierotti, Bob Radel,
Michael Spriggs   Photo: Courtesy Michael Spriggs

band and Kevin Elliott became their manager. The popularity of the band was evidenced by them opening their own teen club in 1967 called The Rogues Gallery on Niagara Falls Boulevard near Sheridan. They recorded six singles, all engineered by

Tommy Calandra and produced by Gary Mallaber of the band Raven. The most popular recordings were "Say You Love Me", which was written by Calandra and Mallaber, and a remake of "Train Kept a Rollin." During the 1960s, The Rogues played at all the teen clubs and many high school dances. In the later 1960s they began playing at area bars, including the Wa-Ha-Ki in North Tonawanda, where they worked for about two years. Michael recalled one club date at a Main Street bar, near downtown, where there was a balcony behind the stage. One night a drunk patron fell off the balcony, landing on Michael's shoulder. Michael almost dropped his guitar, but the band never stopped playing and the drunk got up, smiled and walked away like nothing happened. When Pierotti and Smith left the band, they were replaced by Glen Tate, who was previously a member of The Mixed Breed. After the Rogues broke up Tate and Spriggs formed Magnacoustic, an acoustic trio, with Nick Distefano from The Road. That trio changed its name to Good Luck and all three members moved to Nashville in 1971. Since relocating to Nashville, Spriggs has become a successful songwriter, session musician and performer. For five years he toured with The Eddie Rabbitt Band and performed on eleven #1 singles while a member of group. Spriggs has recorded on sessions with over 60 major artists, including Faith Hill, Tammy Wynette and Trace Adkins. In 2016, he celebrated his 45th anniversary as a Nashville AFM union recording session musician.

THE TWEEDS

The Tweeds were one of the most popular teen club bands. They were from the Kenmore-Tonawanda area and were formed in 1965 by Dave Constantino (guitar), Paul Varga (drums), Ted Connor (guitar) and Alan Shaw (bass). The band members had not yet or had just entered their teens. They participated in a battle of bands that was held at Memorial

THE TWEEDS
Ted Connor, Paul Varga, Alan Shaw, Dave Constantino
Photo: Courtesy Dave Constantino

Auditorium, in which almost every existing band in WNY entered. From this event The Tweeds won a recording contract with Decca Records. Jim Dunnigan (bass) joined the Tweeds in 1967 prior to the band recording in WNY and NYC. From this recording session they released several songs including the single "A Thing of the Past," which regionally charted. The Tweeds were one of the top drawing bands at all the area teen clubs, along with school, church and CYO dances. During the last year The Tweeds were together they started playing at some of the area's bars, but since the band members were still underage, they concentrated on the many available non-alcohol events. When bass player Billy Sheehan joined the band in 1969/70, it was a sign of things to come in the '70s and '80s. The band broke up in 1970, but the seeds were sown for the rise of Talas.

ROCKIN PARAMOUNTS – ROAD

The Rockin Paramounts were formed when guitarist Bob Wilcox decided to make changes to his group Digger & the Paramounts. In 1963, he was joined by Bill Wilcox (vocals), Don Rexinger (guitar), Tommy Coyle (drums) and Joe Hesse (bass). Joe was just starting out on bass, when Bob offered him the position in the band. After building a following at the Peppermint Stick and both Cave teen clubs, they started playing other teen clubs and school dances across WNY. In 1966, they entered the St. John Terrell's Rock and Roll Championship in Lambertville, New Jersey. There were over 750 bands in the competition. Music Producer Phil Spector, author James A. Michener and Don Kirshner were some of the judges. After numerous appearances in the competition, the Rockin Paramounts won second place.

ROCKIN PARAMOUNTS
Don Rexinger, Bob Wilcox, Bill Wilcox, Tommy Coyle, Joe Hesse
Photo Credit William Wilcox, Sr.

In addition to headlining at dates across WNY, the band also performed at numerous shows featuring singer Neil Darrow, who had the locally successful single called "Asphalt Jungle." Neil Darrow with the Rockin

Paramounts opened for Chubby Checkers at Memorial Auditorium.

The band often rehearsed at Joe's parent's home in Tonawanda. An aspiring young bass player who lived down the street would come to observe the band's practice sessions by looking through the basement window. He was several years younger than Joe, and he would come to Joe's house with a bass that he bought, asking for some pointers. Joe would often comment to the other Paramounts on how quickly that kid would learn. That aspiring musician was Billy Sheehan, who later became the bass player for Talas, David Lee Roth Band, Mr. Big and The Winery Dogs, and is considered one of the most influential rock bass players in the music industry.

After the Rockin Paramounts broke up, Hesse joined the group Just Us Five with Nick Distefano (drums), Chuck Mueller (vocals), Bill Bert (guitar) and Dave Bert (organ). They were thinking of making some changes to the band, so Joe and Nick went to Club Lakewood to see The Six Pact with guitarist Ralph Parker, who had previously been a member of The Madmen. During 1967, The Six Pact had been at Club Lakewood for 18 straight weeks, playing four to five nights a week. In addition to Parker, the members of The Six Pact were Steve Loncto (guitar), Dave Sands (bass), Dick Bush (drums – he was the brother of photographer Jim Bush) and brothers Phil and Jerry Hudson were the vocalists. When talking to

Road collage courtesy Joe Hesse. Most phots credit Jim Bush

Ralph they discovered that the Six Pact was in the process of breaking up, so vocalists Phil and Jerry Hudson may also be looking for a new band. The timing was right. With the addition of keyboardist Jim Hesse, who had been working with Caesar & the Romans, Joe, Nick, Ralph, Phil and Jerry decided to form a new band.

The new band's first job was at Cardinal Dougherty High School in 1967, and they performed as PMA Complex. PMA was an acronym for positive mental attitude. After that job, they went to Lum's on Sheridan for Lum's burgers and draft beer, and to discuss how their first job went. They were satisfied with their performance but not with their name. Joking around someone suggested Yellow Brick Road. To give it more of a '60s edge, that was modified to Mellow Brick Road. The name stuck but over time it was shorted to just The Road.

The three-part harmonies of The Road quickly made them a popular band at WNY clubs, special events and shows. They released a single "All Your Eggs in One Basket" on United Artists and the album *The Road – The One Less Traveled By* on Kama Sutra Records. Several singles were released from the album, including a remake of "She's Not There," which sold over 200,000 copies. In 1971 Parker and Jim Hesse left the band and were replaced by organist Jake Jakubowski and piano player Ken Kaufman. This version of the band recorded their second Kama Sutra album, *Cognition*. After five years of successful recording and performances, the initial incarnation of The Road broke up in 1972.

Other versions of the Road surfaced during the 1970s and 1980s. Nick Distefano, came out front to sing alongside Phil and Jerry Hudson, and Larry Rizzoto (drums) was added to the band. Sal Joseph was the drummer in one of the later editions. Three guitarists were also later associated with the band: Jim Catino, Dave Elder and Bobby Lebel, who besides Ralph Parker is the guitarist most often associated with The Road.

Since the break-up of the Road, Jerry Hudson had been involved in theater in LA and Buffalo, while Phil has sung with other bands, including the Three Dog Night tribute band ELI. Joe Hesse moved to LA where he was the tour manager for Chick Corea for a decade and now owns MSS Audio Services, a company that supplies audio equipment for concerts and special events. Joe is still playing bass with various projects in the LA area. Nick Distefano moved to Nashville where he is a session musician, songwriter and touring musician with numerous national acts. Ken Kaufmann owns Adsongs, a commercial jingle company. You continually hear his commercials on the radio for hundreds of clients like Cellino & Barnes, Tops and Hamburg Overhead Door. He is the organist for the Buffalo Sabres and Sunday Toronto Blue Jays games. Dave Elder is the guitarist with Party Squad. Bobby Lebel was with the rockabilly recording act The Headers and is the vocalist/guitarist with The Bobby Lebel Orchestra, along with working on a project with former Actor vocalist, Jessie Galante.

THE WEEKEND TRIP

The Weekend Trip was formed by several students who attended Bennett High School or lived nearby. Since this was an integrated school, some of their classmates started soul bands, which had an influence on the band's early sound. The members rehearsed together in various garage or basement bands for years and after months of practice, with the solidified initial members, they started playing dates as Weekend Trip in 1968. The original members were Ned Wood (keyboards), A. Mike Kobrin (guitar), Tom Ryan (drums), his twin brother Rick Ryan (bass) and Rick Ortolano (vocals). Guitarist Steve Loncto joined the band in 1969, replacing Kobrin, and vocalist Bob Culver joined in 1970, with Ortolano leaving a few months later.

Some of their first shows were at the Funnel Teen Club on Bailey Avenue and the Factory Teen Club on Hertel Avenue, near the North Park Theatre. The Factory became their rehearsal place and they alternated rehearsal days with the band, The Road. The club was owned by Harry Stewart's father and a young Harry Stewart, along with his teenage friend drummer Mike Caputi were always at the club observing band practice. They must have picked up some good pointers because Harry Stewart became one of WNY's top vocalists with Junction West and Caputi was the drummer for Junction West, along with other area bands. Caputi even purchased Tom Ryan's blue Kent drum set.

The Weekend Trip played at the KB Fun-A-Fair in 1969 at the Amherst Recreation Center,

WEEKEND TRIP
Steve Loncto, Tom Ryan, Ned Wood, Rick Ryan
Rick Ortolano, Bob Culver
Photo Credit Jim Bush

performing with Guess Who and Grand Funk Railroad. They played their own set of material and also backed up Bobby Sherman and Terry Knight during their shows. The power of WKBW Radio helped break these new artists, and Bobby Sherman had fond memories of his performances in Buffalo. When Sherman was scheduled to go on tour to support his records, he asked his manager if he could get the band that performed with him in Buffalo to be his touring back-up band. Sherman who was previously on the TV show *Shindig* and now starring in the series, *Here Come the Brides*, could only tour on weekends. This resulted in Weekend Trip leaving Buffalo on Friday mornings to perform dates in cities like St. Louis, Kansas City, various towns in Ohio and many other locations. They performed with Sherman, almost every weekend for several months during late 1969 and early 1970. The Weekend Trip played a brief set of their own material before being joined on stage by Bobby Sherman. When not on the road with Sherman, The Weekend Trip played dates in Buffalo at schools, clubs and special events.

In late 1970 Jerry and Phil Hudson temporarily left The Road and formed the short-lived group called The WET Road, short for Week End Trip Road. That group consisted of Jerry and Phil Hudson (vocals), Bob Culver (vocals), Steve Loncto (guitar), Ned Wood (keyboards), Rick Ryan (bass) and Tom Ryan (drums). With these three vocalists, they merged two of Buffalo's top rock vocal bands. A serious car accident outside of Wellsville, NY caused injuries requiring the hospitalization of the three lead singers. After recovering from the accident Jerry and Phil Hudson returned to The Road. When the Hudsons left, Steve Loncto decided to explore other opportunities, so Denny Dunkowski, who was a member of The Weekend Trip briefly before the WET Road was formed, rejoined the group. The band Weekend was born, which became one of the most popular area rock bands during the 1970s.

BUFFALO BEETLES - THE MODS

The Buffalo Beetles were another of the early teen club style bands. The band was formed in 1963 by students from Grover Cleveland High School in Buffalo. They started putting the group together to play at a Variety Show, but while they were rehearsing someone heard them and asked if they wanted to play at Tony's Place, located at 15th and Connecticut on Sunday afternoons. There was initially no pay involved but it gave the

Buffalo Beetles some exposure and eventually resulted in them getting paid to play a few nights a week, plus it got them other jobs.

THE MODS - THE BUFFALO BEETLES
Rich Sansone, Ray Hale, Dan Stupinski, Brad Gray, Rich Dromin
Bob Greco, Kenny Siracuse   Photo: Courtesy Rich Sansone

The early members of the Buffalo Beetles were vocalists Rich Sansone, Kenny Siracuse and Bob Greco, backed by Dan Stupinski (guitar), Ray Hale (guitar), Dick Cronin (bass) and Brad Gray (drums). They started playing at Twist a Thons which were held at Mount Major Hall. These shows were presented by Mike Militello and Ron Ademy. Their Grover High School fraternity, Kappa Phi also sponsored dances at Mount Major, they played Sunday afternoon shows at The Beatle Ballroom on West Utica near Elmwood, along with weddings and parties. During this time, many other musicians were members of the band, including Joe Giarrano (playing guitar, not bass) and at times they had four singers up front, making them an eight-piece band, which was a very large group for the mid '60s.

Around 1965 they signed with Great Lakes Booking, who booked them work at the area teen clubs, high school dances with Joey Reynolds or Tom Shannon, car shows, fashion shows, the KB Fun-A-Fair and two or three nights a month at a teen club in St. Catharines, Ontario, which held over 1,000 people. They also opened national shows for The Byrds and The Four Seasons, plus they were the back-up band for Jerry Lewis for a show at The Peppermint Stick. The Buffalo Beetles also were the back-up band for Chuck Berry at a Beatle Booster Ball, an attempt to finance and get The Beatles to play a concert in Buffalo, which drew about 10,000 people at The Aud.

They changed their name to The Mods in 1966 and a recording session was arranged by Joey Reynolds at a studio outside of NYC, where they recorded a song along the style of The Four Seasons. There was interest from some major labels but they had changed the sound of the song and they wanted the band to travel. A few of the members did not like the new arrangement of the song and did not want to tour. Through a contact at Buffalo State College, they were offered a date at Murray the K's World, a large club in a former airplane hangar on Long Island. They agreed to play for expenses, because The Rolling Stones were scheduled to be the headliner. The Stones never showed up and The Mods played the entire night by themselves. When the recording contract fell through, The Mods broke up in later 1967, but they had quite a run during the early teen club band days of the '60s.

THE CAVEMEN

Formed in 1963, The Cavemen were one of the first WNY teen club style bands. The group's members were Al Cretacci (vocals), Jimmy Crouse (lead guitar), Ron Gorski (rhythm guitar), Skip Miecheski (bass), Sammy Sparazza (keyboards) and Joey Calato (drums). Their popularity was enhanced by the fact they had management that provided them with top of the line equipment and the latest 1960s mod clothes. Their manager owned three of the top teen clubs in Western New York, so The Cavemen became the house band at The Volcano in Buffalo, The Pit in Blasdell and The Dungeon in Dunkirk/Fredonia. Due to this management, The Cavemen opened for national groups like The Young Rascals, The Blues Magoos and Question Mark & the Mysterians.

To expand their area of performance, The Cavemen entered and won a Battle of Bands in Rochester NY, where the first prize was a 45 released on Capital Star Records. They recorded an original song "All About Love" b/w "Hey Bo Diddley." Soon afterward, The Cavemen started playing at area rock clubs like The Inferno in Williamsville. In 1969 the band fell apart after their rhythm guitarist was in a fatal automobile accident, and their bass player was severely injured in another car crash. Around this time, their vocalist also had to quit singing when he developed nodules on his vocal chords.

After the band broke up drummer Joey Calato, who is a cousin of the Regal Tip Calato family from Niagara Falls, was drafted. He ended up in

THE CAVEMEN - OASIS CLUB IN NIAGARA FALLS
Al Cretacci, Bill Waack, Ron Gorski, Jimmy Crouse
Joey Calato   Photo: Courtesy Joey Calato

Vietnam but luck was with him. Calato was offered a job playing drums in a rock trio that was flown by helicopter to play to the troops at outlying bases, in addition to playing larger USO shows. He had to volunteer to stay in Vietnam for over a year but it was an experience he will never forget.

Since he had to take time off from singing, Al Cretacci became involved with dirt bike motocross racing. He joined the pro circuit and assisted with event promotion. When his vocal chords were healed, he changed his stage name to Al Corte and put together a six-piece show band, complete with custom tailored outfits, called Brass Tacks. During the 1970s that band toured the Midwest and Canada. A reformed five-piece version of that group started performing so often in Florida that the band decided to relocate there. Al later formed several Florida based touring show, pop and jazz groups. He later relocated to Houston, Texas, and eventually Phoenix, Arizona, where Al continued performing, working in motocross, and special event planning.

CAESAR & THE ROMANS

Caesar & the Romans was the first band for Kenmore West vocalist Chuck Vicario. When he was 15 or 16, Chuck sang on stage for the first time at The Brounshidle Post on Delaware Avenue in Kenmore. He went there with his neighborhood gang The Nobles and they asked if Chuck could sing a song with the band. The post staff looked at all the gang members and decided it would be a good idea to let him sing. Chuck sang Dion's "The Wanderer", and he was hooked. Vicario then started competing in talent shows and met his future manager at weekly dances that were being held at The Knights of Columbus on Kenmore Avenue. He eventually won the singing contest and established a friendship with Fred Caserta, who was collecting money at the door and was later instrumental in developing Chuck's career.

Vicario had been playing drums in a band called Chuck & the Roamers, but Caserta suggested he become the singing front man of the group and they should change the name of the band to Caesar & the Romans. An early version of the band in 1965 included Chuck

CAESAR & THE ROMANS
Pat Peri, Chuck Vicairo, Vinnie Parker
Dan Cooke   Photo Credit Paul Daniel Petock

Vicario (vocals), Dan Cooke (guitar), Bill Mosler, Joe DiSantis and John Sia. One of the first places the band played was at Burma Lanes at the corner of Military & Hertel. Chuck recalls that the band was getting paid $50 a night and when Fred Caserta asked for a raise to $60 a night the bowling alley fired them. When the band was leaving the club, they exclaimed "just watch, we'll show you that we were worth the extra money!"

Due to Chuck's showmanship and vocals, the band soon was performing at teen clubs across WNY. In addition, manager Fred Caserta and Fred Saia's booking agency Great Lakes Agency got them high profile jobs at schools, teen festivals and special events. It was not long until they more than proved that they deserved the pay raise requested at Burma Lanes because they quickly became one of the most popular teen club bands in WNY.

As the '60s progressed, the band changed members. Chuck Vicario and Dan Cooke remained constant members of the band but several other musicians were with the band including Dave Burt, Jim Burt, Vinnie Parker, Marty Stemler and Richard Kermode, who was later a member of Janis Joplin's band. When Jim Hesse (organ) joined the band, the rehearsal place for Caesar & the Romans also became the Hesse house where Joe Hesse's band The Rockin Paramounts were already rehearsing. The two bands alternated rehearsal nights and kids from the neighborhood would congregate outside the house to listen to the music. It was like a private outdoor teen club.

Caesar and the Romans attracted the attention of Willard Alexander, a booking agent from the New York City area, who was interested in booking the band. Alexander came to see them perform at the Oak Orchard Lanes in Albion, a club they were working at on a regular basis. He took over the booking of the band and Fred Caserta remained as their manager. This resulted in Caesar and the Romans performing at events and clubs throughout the northeast.

Jerry Meyers, from Act One Recording Studio, took an interest in the band. With him they recorded "Leavin' My Past Behind," "Green Grass Makes It Better" and "Baby Loves," with the 45s being released on Spector Records. The flip side of "Leavin' My Past Behind," was a cover of "Jailhouse Rock," a prelude of things to come from vocalist Chuck Vicario.

After Caesar and the Romans broke up in 1970, Chuck Vicario and Dan Cooke formed Friendship Train, which became Big Wheelie & the Hubcaps. More on that during the 1970s.

KING HARVEST

King Harvest is the band that released the hit single "Dancing in the Moonlight." The founder of the group was Newfane Central High School graduate Ron Altbach, who grew up in Olcott. Beginning when Ron was in the 8th grade, he played piano, trombone and bass in the Don Keller Orchestra, a big band that performed at events in Niagara County. When Ron was a sophomore, he formed the Hi-Notes with George Bridgeman (guitar), a teen band that played at Newfane and Niagara Wheatfield High School dances, along with other parties and dances in that area. The Hi-Notes booked a job to play at Cornell University in Ithaca, New York. Altbach was so impressed with the college, along with its nightlife, that upon graduation from

HI-NOTES
Ron Altbach's Newfane High School Band
Photo: Courtesy Ron Altbach

Newfane he enrolled at Cornell, where he formed an R&B band.

When he was home from college, Altbach went to The Revoilt Lounge to see Darrell Banks perform. Also on the bill was the R&B trio The Del Royals. Altbach convinced them to travel to Ithaca and perform with his band at Cornell. At this time, fellow Cornell students Ed Tuleja (guitar) and Dave 'Doc' Robison (vocals) had a Beatles and Rolling Stones style band, while Rod Novak (sax) had a blues group. Eventually these four musicians joined forces and founded King Harvest. When Altbach moved to Paris to study classical music, the other three musicians joined him in France, where they performed at European clubs and recorded the single "Dancing in the Moonlight".

In 1971 the song was released in Europe but after it did not chart, the band members returned to the U.S. In 1972, they signed with

King Harvest
St Bona 1973

KING HARVEST
Olcott 1974

Photo: Courtesy Ron Altbach

Perception Records, who re-released "Dancing in the Moonlight" and this time it became a hit. However, the record label went bankrupt. Only a year after touring the country, in 1974 King Harvest was living at Altbach's home, playing dates at The Anchor Inn and Erma's Lanes in Olcott, in addition to bookings obtained by Great Lakes Agency across WNY.

King Harvest relocated to California and formed a new version of the group, which included Buffalo drummer Richie Pidanik. The Beach Boys assisted King Harvest in obtaining a contract with A&M Records, but when the album did not produce any hits, the band again broke up. Most of the members were later associated with the Beach Boys, with Altbach touring with both The Beach Boys and Mike Love's band Celebration. In 2012 the four co-founders of King Harvest played a reunion concert at Olcott Beach.

OTHER 60's BANDS

THE TWIGGS/MAGIC RING go back to 1964 when New Castle 5 was formed by Cleveland Hill High School students Gordon Kasper, Lou Pariso, Gary Davis, Tom Karl and Bill Felger. In 1966, Gordon "Blake" Kasper (vocals) formed The Twiggs with Glen Skadan (bass), Paul Vastola (guitar), Robert Frederico (guitar) and Tom Gentile (drums). In addition to playing the teen clubs and teen dances they started working at area bars. They recorded at Brundo's in Niagara Falls, Howe Recording Studio and Select Sound, in addition to Cleveland and New York City studios. The Twiggs/Magic Ring recorded over ten songs, releasing the single "Moon Maiden", which was representative of the acid-rock era of Buffalo area bands. In 1969, the band changed their name to Magic Ring, concentrating more on recording and performing original material. The name Magic Ring was inspired by the Tolkien trilogy and promotional leather rings were made by David Uhlman's Leather Shop. Gordon, Glen and Paul were member of both groups, joined later by Derek Hillburger (keyboards) and Bill Friday (drums) and later Woody Knoblock (drums). Magic Ring was managed by Steve Goldstein, who was associated with the original Inferno that was in Glen Park and The Inferno on Walden, originally known as Gilligan's. With this connection, they played at both Infernos on a regular basis, in addition to working many University at Buffalo and Buffalo State events. Magic Ring traveled the northeast and into Canada, playing many dates in Michigan, where they opened for various recording acts. After the band broke up, Gordon Kasper moved to Los Angeles, where he works as an actor. New Castle 5 guitarist Gary Davis later formed the group Magic Mushroom, which had a similar name but was not associated with Magic Ring.

THE WARLOCKS were a '60s band that remained together and performed through the 1970s. They were formed in 1965 with the original members being Paul Englert (keyboards), Pete Englert (guitar), Bob Nowak (guitar), Victor Wawrzyniak (bass), Larry LaVorgna (drums). The band remained together until 1979, with later members including Dan Nowak (bass), Bob James (guitar), Dave Bienik (guitar), Craig Korka (vocals), Scott Case (vocals), Steve McDonald (vocals) and Joe Siragusa (drums). During 1970s and into the 1980s, Pete Englert was an employee at Kubera's Music.

THE WARLOCKS
Paul Englert, Victor Wawrzyniak
Larry LaVorgna, Peter Englert
Bob Nowak
Photo: Courtesy Dan Nowak

THE NEW BREED was formed in 1966 by Kent Miller (vocals), Mike Madden (guitar), Howie Nash (guitar), Tony Tepidino (bass), Bob Baldwin (piano) and Mike Piccolo (drums). Kent started the band but Madden, Piccolo, and Baldwin worked together from 1963-65 in The Misfits. In 1968 The New Breed won the Battle of Bands at the KB Fun-A-Fair. Mike Piccolo left the band, and later became one of the original members of Talas, Cock Robin and Jennifer's Family. In 1969 Doug Fisher (guitar) and Mark Pfonner (guitar) joined the group, along with Rick D'Amato (bass) and Mark Menge (drums). Bob Baldwin joined the Air Force in 1970, being replaced by Rick Falkowski (keyboards). Kent Miller left later that year and Craig Mangus (vocals) joined the group. When Rick joined the Air Force in 1971, he was replaced by Wally Sirotich (keyboards), later with Moonshine Express and The Toler Brothers Band. In 1978 Craig and Doug formed the country rock band Rio Grande, which evolved into a country version of The New Breed in 1983. Mark Pfonner, Doug Fisher and Craig Mangus currently perform as The Reminders, an acoustic trio.

THE FUGITIVES were another one of the cross-over Buffalo Sound – Teen Club bands. They were formed in 1964 by Tony Bellasteri (guitar), Bill Smith (guitar), Conrad Reiger (bass) and Pete Holguin (drums). From 1964 to 1966 they played many WKBW radio record hops with Rod Roddy and Joey Reynolds at legion posts, and at the pavilions at Cuba Lake and Silver Lake. They were a vocal-oriented band that played predominantly Beatles songs, but over time added songs by the Young Rascals and R&B-oriented material. In 1966, they were hired at The Club, on Falls Street next to Woolworths, in Niagara Falls. When they started this engagement, Ken Thomas (bass) joined the band, along with Doug Morgano (guitar). The Fugitives played five to six nights a week at The Club for almost three years. When they broke up in 1968 the group Parkside took their place as the house band at The Club.

THE IMPERIALS from North Tonawanda, along with Kathy Lynn & the Playboys, were two of the first bands to play at the Peppermint Stick. The Imperials started in a group called The Restless Ones that played dates at the Memorial Pool in North Tonawanda. Their claim to fame is their band picture from 1962 was included on the cover of the 2007 Fender catalogue. Bob Ambrusko (guitar) and Ed Diak from The Restless Ones formed The

Imperials, with Charlie Finsterbach (sax) and John (Majka) Samulski (drums).

Other early teen club bands included THE INVICTAS from Rochester but they often played at the Sandsabarn in Perry and other area teen clubs. Their single "The Hump" was covered by almost every WNY garage band...THE WILDCATS were the house band at The Pussycat Club in downtown Buffalo. Pat Zephro (guitar), went on to become the music director for Wayne Cochran & the CC Riders Other members were Jim Albarella (vocals), Casey Gervase (guitar/bass), Rick Falkowski (bass/keyboards) and Fred Linneman (drums)... THE MADMEN was an early band of Ralph & Vinnie Parker, which included future Road vocalist Jerry Hudson...THE MIXED BREED was a racially mixed band that included Glen Tate, later the guitarist with The Rogues. They were one of the first rock bands to perform at McVans on a regular basis...THE CHARLES was John Valby's band during the '60s, before going solo and becoming Dr. Dirty. The band relocated to Buffalo from Florida, but Valby was originally from Rochester...THE MOOD was an early band for Jim Ralston, Bill Friday and Chuck Anderson...NOBODY'S CHILDREN was Dan Gambino's first band in 65-68 and it included Could Be Wild partner Doug Dombrowski. They played the early teen clubs and won a battle of bands at The Boulevard Cave, where the Tweeds also competed. They later played steady weekends at rock bars like the Idlehour in Grand Island for a year, and the Beef & Ale on Main Street for about six months...THE AVANTIS was Rich Sargent's band from 1963 – 1967. Other members were David Parker, Frank Pirrone and Joe LoCoco. Since Sargent worked with WKBW, they played many dates with WKBW DJ's record hops, which they often played for promotion. The advertisements on the radio resulted in better pay for other engagements. They later became known as the One-Keys because, according to Sargent, they played almost all of their songs in the same key... THE CYCLONES played at The Glen Casino and assisted in opening The Boulevard Bandstand, an early teen club that was in the future location of the Boulevard Cave. The band members were Jerry Ralston (guitar), Chuck Miller (guitar) and Paul Leidelson (drums)...The NOMADS were led by vocalist Wilson Curry and The SURFERS by vocalist Steve Zdon...ARTHUR'S COURT, presided over by Art Lutz, played at Angola lake bars... THE PEEBLES were one of the first 1960s all girl bands in WNY...STREET NOISE was a Niagara Falls band with lead vocalist Mark Dixon later with Party Squad...SALT OF

THE EARTH included Calvin Nichols, later from The Little Trolls...Other groups were The Druids, London Fog, Rebel Rousers, XL's, Invaders, Shapes of Things, Vibratones, Raque, Tone Benders, Squires, Revengence, The Plague, Raiders, Maniacs, Insanes, Jaguars, Barons, Sterlings, Checkmates, Magestics, Tyrants, Symposium, Mixed Emotions, Times Syndicate, Spectres and Drastic Measures.

Other bands from the later 1960s bands include LAVENDER HILL MOB, one of the few area '60s bands with a female vocalist and included *Buffalo Evening News* reporter Dale Anderson on bass...BETHLEHEM STEEL, a progressive rock band that concentrated on Jethro Tull style material. Rich Fustino (guitar), has been teaching guitar for almost 50 years... PHARMACY JONES was one of the regular groups at Psycus. The members were Mick Thompson (guitar), John Yuknalis (bass), Rick Falkowski (keyboards) and Jim Eckert (drums). After Steve Chalmar joined the group they changed their name to SAINT HILL...Subconscious Mind was an early group of Headin On and Switch guitarist Tom Lorentz...BURNED was an early band for guitarist Don Eckel, who coordinates the Buffalo NY Garage Bands, Buffalo/Western NY Bands from the '70s and Buffalo/Western NY Bands from the '80s Facebook pages.

11

MUSIC BUSINESSES

This history of Buffalo Music and Entertainment is more than just the musicians, nightclubs, theaters and events. It is also about the businesses located in the WNY area. There were numerous companies that manufactured musical instruments and businesses operating to keep the music industry working, growing and promoted. Some of events that were occurring behind the scenes, were just as important as what was publicly keeping people entertained.

WURLITZER

The Wurlitzer Company was founded in 1853 by German immigrant Franz Rudolph Wurlitzer in Cincinnati, Ohio. Wurlitzer initially imported musical instruments from the Wurlitzer family in Germany, and during the American Civil War they were one of the major suppliers of musical instruments to the U.S. Army. In 1880 Wurlitzer started making pianos and in 1896 they started selling coin-operated pianos, which were manufactured in North Tonawanda, New York by Eugene DeKleist.

Eugene DeKleist developed the fairground (barrel) organ for use in carousels while working for a French Company called Limonaire Freres, and beginning in 1880, his own company in London. He did business with American companies, including Armitage Herschell Company in North Tonawanda. After the United States passed a tariff on organs in 1892, Herschell encouraged DeKleist to move to the U.S.

DeKleist formed a company called the North Tonawanda Barrel Organ Factory and in 1893 opened a production facility in the Martinsville section of what is now North Tonawanda. They manufactured organs suitable for a variety of fairground rides. He expanded his product line and approached other musical instrument manufacturers about creating instruments for them. Wurlitzer was not interested in the barrel organs, but they encouraged him to develop his player pianos called the Tonophone. This relationship was so fruitful that in 1897 the name of the company was changed to DeKleist Musical Instrument Manufacturing Company, with Wurlitzer making an investment in the company.

The person responsible for bringing DeKleist to Buffalo was Allen Herschell, who along with James Armitage, created the Armitage Herschell Company in 1873. That company produced carousels for which DeKleist made the barrel organs. When Herschell left the company in 1901, Eugene DeKleist bought out the interests of Armitage and Herschell. This was the plant at Goundry and Oliver Street, where they manufactured hurdy-gurdies for amusement parks, circuses, roller rinks and carnival midways. When DeKleist was seeking additional investors, discussions started with the Wurlitzer company. Due to the success of the Wurlitzer-Tonophone coin-operated pianos, to insure their continued supply, Wurlitzer agreed to purchase the company.

In 1909 Wurlitzer moved its operations from Cincinnati to North Tonawanda. The company took possession of the factory in the Martinville section of North Tonawanda and this became their manufacturing plant for pianos, organs, radios and eventually jukeboxes. The Wurlitzer company always kept its eyes open for new acquisitions and in 1910 Robert Hope Jones was employed by Wurlitzer. By 1914 his Hope Jones Organ Company, which had employed 112 workers, was moved to the North Tonawanda facility. This entered Wurlitzer into the theater organ era.

The Wurlitzer Theater Organ was conceived to accompany silent movies and designed by Robert Hope Jones as a one-man orchestra, capable of imitating all the instruments found in an orchestra. The Wurlitzer theater organ became the industry standard. It was called the Mighty Wurlitzer and was installed at many, if not most, of the major theaters in the country and in Europe. From 1914 to 1942 over 2,243 pipe organs were manufactured. The largest Wurlitzer organ ever built remains at Radio City Music Hall in New York City, where it was installed in 1932. The Wurlitzer Company utilized the four-manual organ at Sheas Buffalo and the three-manual organ at The Riviera Theater, in North Tonawanda, as their display or exhibition organs. These two theater organs are still

THE WURLITZER PLANT
Photo: Courtesy North Tonawanda History Museum

being used at the theaters, as well as about 40 other organs in theaters, and some private residences.

In the 1930s Wurlitzer started producing jukeboxes. Their sales were positively influenced by the end of Prohibition in 1933 which resulted in increasing the market for coin-operated music machines in bars and dance halls. During the late 1930s Wurlitzer was manufacturing over 45,000 jukeboxes a year. With marketing by future United States Senator Homer Capehart and the "lightup" design by Paul Fuller, Wurlitzer dominated the jukebox market to the extent that in some parts of the world, jukeboxes are called a Wurlitzer. The 1940s Fuller designed jukebox is used as a symbol for the rock 'n' roll era. When Wurlitzer's rival, Seeburg, became the jukebox industry leader, the jukebox portion of Wurlitzer was sold to a German company in 1973.

The musical instrument side of Wurlitzer was sold to the Baldwin Piano Company, which was subsequently sold to Gibson Guitar. Gibson later bought the jukebox company, which had been moved to Germany. Gibson Guitar Corporation now owns the Gibson, Epiphone, Dobro,

Valley Arts, Kramer, Steinberger, Togias, Slingerland, Maestro, Baldwin, Chickering, Hamilton and Wurlitzer brands and product lines.

The Wurlitzer plant at 908 Niagara Falls Blvd. was the manufacturing, sales and administrative divisions for the company. When it was built, the complex was one of the most modern and innovative factories in the country. Due to the popularity of its organs, radios and jukeboxes, the factory peaked at maximum employment of 3,000 workers. The organ and jukebox production was phased out in 1972, and in 1974 there were only 200 remaining employees. In 1975 all manufacturing stopped at the plant and in 1976 all operations were moved to other locations. Today the manufacturing and office buildings are the Wurlitzer Industrial Complex. It has been remodeled and is the thriving home to an assortment of 43 different businesses.

THE HERSCHELL-SPILLMAN amusement ride manufacturing company was formed after the Armitage Herschell Company was acquired by Eugene de Kleist. Armitage Herschell had manufactured barrel organ based products and steam powered portable carousels. The plant was located at the corner of Goundry & Oliver Street in North Tonawanda, the current location of the high-rise Carousel Park Apartments and diagonally across from the post office. De Kleist entered into a partnership with Rudolph Wurlitzer and concentrated on the organ business, while Herschell formed a company with his in-laws, the Spillmans, forming Herschell-Spillman Motor Company. In addition to carousels, they manufactured larger park rides and elaborate carousels with other animals besides horses. This company was located 184 Sweeney Street, and when Herschell left the company, it became the Spillman Engineering Company. The Sweeney location was later sold to Remington Rand Corporation and is now the Remington Loft Apartments. In 1915 Herchell started the Herschell Carousel Factory to compete with Spillman Engineering. That plant at 180 Thompson expanded beyond carousels to manufacture rides for children and adults. In addition to Kiddieland rides, they made the adult Twister, Hurricane, Flying Bobs and Sky Wheel rides. The Herschell amusement park rides were the rides that you found in the amusement parks around WNY, as well as parks across the country. The factory on Thompson Street is now the Herschell Carousel Factory Museum.

GEORGE A. PRINCE – MELODEON. The manufacture of keyboard instruments in Buffalo started well before DeKleist or Wurlitzer moved to

North Tonawanda. In fact, during the mid-1800s, Buffalo was the Melodeon Capital of the World. Jeramiah Carhart received the patent for suction principle of the melodeon, and in 1846 he sold the rights to George A. Prince, who had a music store at 200 Main Street in Buffalo. He later had manufacturing facilities on Pearl Street and Niagara Street. While under the employment of Prince, Carhart and George Needham invented the concept of the reed organ. Between 1847 and 1866, over 40,000 melodeons were sold across the US and exported to many foreign countries. The company, which employed over 200 workers, manufactured 40 different models, ranging from hand held single reed instruments with 49 keys to double manual organs. Constant experimentation at Prince's factory with reeds, bellows, swells and stops lead to several patented techniques, including Emmons Hamlin's refined tuning by twisting metal reeds. In 1973, musical historian Robert F. Gellerman wrote in "The American Reed Organ" that "The George A. Prince Co. was the leading manufacturer of reed organs in the U.S. from the 1850s until the 1870s, and many of the pioneers in the reed organ industry worked for Prince in the early days."

KURTZMANN PIANO company was opened by Christian Kurtzmann in 1848. At their factory, located on Niagara Street in Buffalo, they built expensive, high quality grand pianos, which were known for their old-world quality and craftsmanship. By the turn of the century they also manufactured upright and spinet pianos. Their first sales office and store was located at Batavia and Elm Street, later relocating to Main and Goodell. In 1935, the Wurlitzer Piano Company obtained control of the Kurtzmann name brand and manufacturing was discontinued in 1938. A restored Kurtzmann piano will currently sell in the low to mid five figure range.

MOOG MUSIC

Robert Moog is known as the person who developed the synthesizer for application in popular music. He has ten associated patents and is considered the inventor of the monophonic analog synthesizer. Born in 1934, when he was 19 he started building and selling Theremin kits with his father. He had always been interested in electronics, and in 1963 he came up with the basics of the modular analog synthesizer by combining voltage controlled oscillators, filters, amplifiers and a keyboard controller. At this time Moog had already received a BSEE degree from Columbia but did not receive his PhD from Cornell in Engineering Physics until 1965.

In 1967, he incorporated the R.A. Moog Company, and at a small factory in Trumansburg NY he developed the Moog Modular Synthesizers I, II and III. The 9000 Series modules were bulky instruments, that used patch chords and could only be used in the recording studio or other permanent installation. The cost of a complete Moog system was about $15,000. In 1968 the recording of the album "Switched on Bach," by Walter (now Wendy) Carlos, revolutionized classical music and introduced the synthesizer in this best-selling recording.

1969 was an important year for Bob Moog because he was granted a 15-year patent for his unique 904 "Ladder" Low Pass Filter design. Although this patent has long ago run out, it is still considered the most musical voltage controller filter ever designed. Also in 1969, four modular systems were built for a concert series "Jazz in the Garden" at the NYC Museum of Modern Art and keyboardist Keith Emerson, of Emerson Lake and Palmer, purchased one of the units after the series was completed. Emerson used it on the solo in the song "Lucky Man" on the debut ELP album, and rock music was introduced to the sounds of the synthesizer. Emerson later worked with Moog to develop a portable synthesizer that could be used on the road by musicians, and in 1970 Emerson was the first keyboardist to tour with a synthesizer. It was during this time, at the Trumansburg factory, that the Minimoog was born.

Bill Waytena was a Buffalo entrepreneur who invented the radar detector and loved electronic gadgets. He read about the synthesizer and became intrigued. When former R.A. Moog employee Gene Zumchek moved back to Buffalo, he and Waytena developed the Sonic V synthesizer. They started a company called Musonics and began manufacturing the Sonic V at the former Chalmers Gelatin factory, which Waytena purchased near the end of Academy Street in Williamsville. Sales stalled, and when Waytena found out Moog was giving a product demonstration in Rochester, he drove to event, met Moog and in 1970 Moog accepted an offer from Waytena to purchase his company.

Moog Music moved from Trumansburg to the Musonics' Williamsville factory and they worked to develop more portable, easier to play instruments, such as the Moog Sonic 6 and Moog Satellite. Norlin

Music (who also owned Gibson Guitars) purchased Moog Music in 1973. This provided the company with research and development money, and in 1975 Moog released the Polymoog, developed by Dr. David Luce, who later became president and co-owner of Moog Music. The Polymoog was a polyphonic synthesizer where you could play multiple notes like on a piano or organ, rather than just single notes on the monophonic synthesizer. The success of the Polymoog was marred by the release of Oberheim Electronics Four Voice (poly synth), which was better received and had more authentic synth sounds.

In 1976 Moog moved to 2500 Walden Ave, in the former GEX store, sharing the building with Super Flea. At the new plant, in addition to Moog Synthesizers, Moog manufactured Lab Series amplifiers and Taurus bass pedals. However, due to differences in management philosophy, Moog left his namesake company in

FIRST MEMORY MOOG
COMING OFF THE ASSEMBLY LINE
Dr. David Luce, Dr. Herb Duetsch, Rich Walborn
Photo: Courtesy Robbie Konikoff

1977. During the mid-1980s Moog worked for Kurzweil Music Systems, where he developed the Kurzweil K2000, and in the 1990s he became a professor at the University of North Carolina at Ashville. In the mid-1990s Bob Moog formed a new company, Big Briar, manufacturing theremins, most notably the Ethervox, the first MIDI theremin. He also introduced Moogerfoofer foot pedals, which incorporated his 904 Ladder Lowpass Filter into a pedal format that could be used by guitarists, as well as keyboardists.

Back in Buffalo, Norlin Music successfully operated the company, introducing many new products. However, they never achieved the level of success of the products that were developed during Robert Moog's tenure and they sold the company in 1983. The new owners went bankrupt in 1986 and ceased to exist in 1993.

During the complexities of the bankruptcy, the Moog Music trademark was not renewed and was considered abandoned. Don Martin, a

NYC keyboardist, applied for and won the rights to use the Moog Music name. Martin started manufacturing Moog branded modular systems. Litigation by Bob Moog, with the help of current Moog Music President and owner Mike Adams, won him back the Moog Music name. In 2002 Moog changed his company name from Big Briar back to Moog Music and they released a redesigned Minimoog Voyager, with the first 500 Minimoog Voyager's sold including Bob Moog's autograph in the assembly. Bob Moog passed away in 2005, but his legacy is intact and Moog Music is still operating in Ashville, North Carolina.

Moog Music will always be the other Moog manufacturing company from Western New York, often confused with Moog Inc, the engineering company in East Aurora, New York. However, Moog Music was important for providing employment to many Buffalo musicians in manufacturing, research and sales at the company. Some of these people started other music manufacturing companies after Moog Music closed.

BODE SOUND. Harald Bode was born in Germany, where in 1937 he developed the Warbo Formant Organ, an archetype of the polyphonic synthesizer. In 1940, he developed the Hohner Multimonica, and after moving to the U.S., the electric harpsichord for Estey Organ Company in Vermont. Bode was hired by Wurlitzer Organ Company and he relocated to North Tonawanda, where he developed the first transistor model of the Wurlitzer Electric Piano in 1960. Forming Bode Electronics in North Tonawanda, he created the Ring Modulator and Frequency Shifter in 1964 and Vocoder in 1977. These products later became part of the Moog Synthesizer, and after Robert Moog left the company Bode became an engineer for Norlin/Moog Music.

POLYFUSION, INC. This company was formed in 1975 by engineers Alan S. Pearce and Ron Folkman after they left Moog Music. They introduced the AS-1 analog sequencer that could automatically play musical patterns on an analog synthesizer. In 1976, they released the Polyfusion Series 2000 modular synthesizer, which had innovations and more stable oscillator designs than other modular synthesizers. Polyfusion Electronics is still in business in Lancaster, New York, where they now specialize in ultra-sophisticated electronic systems and circuitry for industrial process controls and automation.

PEARCE AMPLIFICATION. While an employee of Moog Music during the late '70s, Dan Pearce co-designed the Gibson Lab Series amp with Bob Moog. Moog manufactured 10,000 of these amps. Pearce decided to leave Moog in the mid '80s, introducing the Pearce G1 guitar amplifier. The amp alienated some traditionalists that loved the vacuum tube amplifiers because it utilized all solid-state components. However, it was much lighter than the popular Marshall tube amp heads. They later introduced the BC-1 for bass players, which was much lighter than the traditional Ampeg tube bass heads. Buffalo's Bill Sheehan embraced the BC-1 solid state dual channel pre-amp and still uses it for his distinctive distorted tones. Pearce later worked with Buffalo synthesizer player and sales rep, Vincent Michaels, to develop the Pearce G3, which included a third channel for acoustic guitar, violin or other stringed instrument. Les Paul collaborated on the development of the G3 and it was introduced at the NAMM Show, with the demonstrations presented by Buffalo's Geoffrey Fitzhugh Perry, playing violin through the third channel. Roland Japan founder Ikutaro Kakahashi championed the G3 concept and negotiated to purchase Pearce Amps. Kakahashi thought the asking price was too high, did not purchase the company, and Pearce ceased operations in 1993. Dan Pearce became an engineer at Bose Inc. and Pearce Amps still command top dollar on the high-end used equipment market.

SUNCOAST AMPLIFICATION is a division of Sluggo Music Technology, LLC, a company founded by former Moog Music and Pearce Amplifier employee and Buffalo native Jim Suchora. They are a high-end company that manufactures traditionalist tube amps and guitar/bass preamps to reproduce the classic guitar hero era sound.

EW KENT MANUFACTURING COMPANY. Kent Drums was started by Ed and Bill Kent in 1947. Bill previously worked for Gretsch Drums. They were located at 1189 Military Road in Kenmore. Kent competed with the big four of American drums (Ludwig, Rogers, Swingerland, Gretsch), but they were better known as a starter drum kit, because they were reasonably priced. However, they were made with maple shells and had a good sound. The company closed in 1977 and it was purchased by Jim Grazanowski from Edwin's Music Store, who was also the drummer from *Dialing for Dollars* duo Johnny & Jimmy. Kent no longer manufactures drum sets; they just sell accessories and parts inventory on line or by mail order. The warehouse is located across the street from the former Edwins Music Store at 1520 Broadway.

KAZOO. The patent for the metal kazoo was issued in 1902 to George D. Smith of Buffalo. In 1916 Michael McIntyne opened the Original American Kazoo Company in Eden, New York. The kazoos are made the same way they were manufactured in 1915, and the company is the only metal kazoo manufacturer, producing 1.5 million kazoos a year. The company is now owned by Suburban Adult Services and Eden is considered the Kazoo Capital of the World. Tours are offered at their plant in Eden and there is a gift shop where you can purchase kazoos on site.

HOWARD GOLDMAN MUSICIANS SUPPLY. This was a mail order company, initially offering synthesizers and recording studio equipment in the early 1980s; located in the 3 Coins Motel & Nightclub office space on Niagara Falls Blvd. When Howard Goldman started the company, the only major existing mail order catalog company for musical instruments was Veneman's Music Emporium. To promote the business, Goldman advertised in local music papers across the country and obtained authorized dealerships for numerous nation brands, eventually offering all type of musical instruments and supplies. In addition to new merchandise they also had a division that offered the sale of used equipment directly through the owners of the instruments - sort of like an early eBay or Craigslist. The company did all their business by printed catalogues, because in the 1980s the internet as we know it did not exist. At its peak, the company had eleven employees including Dick Bauerle (Select Sound), Jim Sommer (Loft Recording) and Don Missel (Denton Cottier & Daniels). Prior to closing in the early 1990s, they expanded to selling computers.

ZON GUITARS. Joe Zon started selling and repairing guitars at Ed Bentley Music and Buffalo Guitar Center on Harlem Road in Cheektowaga. In May 1981, he opened Zon Guitars, a custom guitar and repair shop on Cleveland Drive in Cheektowaga. Joe handcrafted a custom bass, utilizing a graphite neck, which is light weight and warp resistant. The graphite enhanced the sound quality and stability of the instrument. The Zon bass also had custom designed Bartolini pickups and printed circuit board active electronics, designed and manufactured by Polyfusion Electronics from Buffalo. His Signature and Standard model 4 and 8 string basses were unveiled at the 1981 NAMM show and Buffalo's Rick James

& the Stone City Band was his first endorsing artist. Zon subsequently introduced the Legacy and Scepter model (4 and 5 string) basses and his Sonus bass was dubbed the jazz bass of the '90s. In 1987 Zon Guitars moved to Redwood City, California, and the Zon Bass continues to be sold worldwide.

HAMILTONE GUITARS was a custom guitar manufacturing company run by Jim Hamilton. It was initially located on Abbott Road in South Buffalo and later moved to Tacoma Avenue in North Buffalo. Hamilton created 15 custom guitars for ZZ Top's Billy Gibbons, who Jim met when he was living in Austin Texas during the 1970s. Gibbons commissioned Hamilton to make a custom guitar for Stevie Ray Vaughan, which was presented to Vaughan during UB's Springfest on April 29, 1984. That guitar was featured in the MTV videos for "Cold Shot" and "Couldn't Stand the Weather" as well as on the covers of *Guitar Player* and *Guitar World* magazines. Hamilton later manufactured 55 copies of the Vaughan guitar, which were sold to collectors worldwide. During his career Hamilton designed and produced over 300 custom guitars and he is currently living in Florida.

JIM HAMILTON with
STEVIE RAY VAUGHAN
Photo: Courtesy Jim Hamilton

PIK STIK was developed and patented by Buffalo guitarist Casey Gervase in the 1980s. It was an extruded aluminum spring steel belt clip pick holder that clipped on to your guitar strap. Guitar picks could be stored in it, so if you dropped your pick you could get another one from the Pik Stik holder. Pik Stik came in five anodized colors and was sold in Buffalo music stores and across the world through advertising in *Guitar for the Practicing Musician* and *Guitar World Magazine*.

LUG LOCK. After playing drums with area bands since the 1960s, Vietnam veteran Phil Moodie wanted to find a way to keep his drums in tune. In 1980, he came up with the idea of Lug Lock, a plastic fabrication that holds the tuning lug in place. After obtaining the patent for Lug Lock, Phil invented Gig Rug, Quick Stand, Beat Bug and Tempo REF. These products are available at music stores worldwide or through his web page, luglock.com.

XERSTICK DRUMSTICKS was started by Tonawanda native Wil Schulmeister in 1980. They were weighted drumsticks, used as a conditioning aid to drummers. The concept is much like weighted bats for baseball players. They later added a full line of regular drumsticks and obtained endorsements from local and national drummers. However, the company could not keep up with the demand and closed in 1989, selling their remaining inventory to Music Mart.

REGAL TIP by Calato. Niagara Falls drummer Joe Calato revolutionized the drumstick industry in 1958 when he introduced the nylon tip drum stick. Prior to his invention, all drumsticks had wooden tips, which often splintered. The nylon tip also produced a uniform sound and signature clarity on drumheads and ride cymbals. In addition to the nylon tip drum stick, Regal Tip manufactures high-quality brushes, nylon-capped timbale sticks, the Conga Stick and their manufacturing techniques have established the standards in drumstick design and crafting. The third generation of the Calato family is now managing the operations of their manufacturing facilities located at 4501 Hyde Park Blvd. in Niagara Falls. In 1996, Joe Calato, the former company president and son of the founder, left Regal Tip after 26 years to start his own company. Tosca Percussion, located in Ransomville, specializes in drum brushes, which they manufacture under their name and for other drum companies.

MUSIC EDUCATION

THE UB SCHOOL OF MUSIC was patterned after a conservatory. Cameron Baird was hired by UB Chancellor Samuel Capen in 1951 to create the music department. Frederick Slee, who collaborated with Baird and Capen to form the BPO in 1935, worked with Baird to establish the Music Department at the original UB Main Street campus. Baird Hall on the Main Street campus (now known as Allen Hall and the home of WBFO, Buffalo NPR radio station) was the original music department building. It was named after Cameron Baird's father Frank Burkett Baird, who was one of the planners of the Pan Am Expo and builders of the Peace

Bridge. The Music Department was expanded with the hiring of Allen Sapp in 1961, who initially came to the college as a Slee Professor of Composition. Sapp remained at UB through 1975 and during his tenure was responsible for establishing the modern era UB Music Department. He was invited to return to the university in 1981 for the dedication of the music department's Baird and Slee Halls at the new North Campus in Amherst. The new Baird Hall houses the UB Music Library and is home to the Baird Recital Hall, one of two primary venues for Music Department sponsored concerts. The new Amherst Campus Slee Hall houses the 670 seat Lippes Concert Hall, which includes the 20-ton C.B. Fisk organ, and the Lejaren Hiller Computer Music Studios, one of the world's foremost research centers for interactive electronic music composition.

SUNY Fredonia has established a music program of applied music and music education on the undergraduate level. The Buff State music program also focuses predominantly on the preparation of music education teachers. The Eastman School of Music in Rochester provides a comprehensive high-quality performance orientated school. Villa Maria College also has a music performance centered music program.

WILLIE JAMES DORSEY graduated from Fosdick Maston Park High School and in 1950 he was one of six African American students that broke the color barrier at Fredonia State Teachers College, where he received his degree in Music Education in 1954. He attended graduate school at UB and the Eastman School of Music. After serving in the Air Force, where he was a member of the Air Force Band, he obtained a teaching position in the City of Buffalo Schools. Dorsey was the music and chorus teacher at Riverside, South Park, Lafayette and East high schools, retiring after 30 years in the school system.

SAM SCAMACCA started playing clarinet in elementary school and later switched to the saxophone. During World War II he worked at Curtis Wright riveting airplanes during the day and played music at nightclubs six nights a week. He was drafted into the Army and discharged after he was injured during training. After graduating with a degree in music education, from Ithaca College in 1949, he traveled with jazz and vaudeville bands. He began working as a music educator when he taught music at schools in Michigan for a couple years. After he returned to Buffalo, Scamacca taught at Sedola's Music, on Grant Street, and worked at The Town Casino and

Bafo's at night and on the weekends. In 1956, he obtained a teaching position at Lafayette High School, where he remained until 1990. Scamacca would recruit students in the hallways, enlisting them to become horn players or percussionists in high school orchestras or jazz combos. Some of the students he influenced and taught at Lafayette include: Don Menza, Bobby Militello, Ronnie Foster, Ernie Corallo, Joe Ford, Junnieh Booth and Gary Mallaber. While Scamacca was at Lafayette, two other Buffalo high school music teachers were having a positive influence on area musicians: Norman Weiss at Grover Cleveland High School and Don Hilliard at East High School. Scamacca concluded his education career as the vice-principal at Lafayette High School and after retirement he taught at the Community School of Music.

KENDOR MUSIC PUBLISHING was founded in 1954 by three local high school music teachers: Art Dedrick from Delevan-Machias, Les Chappell from Kenmore and Bob Hudson from East Aurora. Ramon Cornwall later replaced Hudson as a partner. In the 1950s no music publisher was producing student-level stage band music. As educators, Dedrick, Chappel and Hudson recognized that the available music charts were too difficult for school bands. Kendor started publishing student level stage band music, with arrangements by Art Dedrick carefully tailored for the abilities of school age jazz musicians. They eventually released thousands of works arranged by award-winning professional writers. In addition to jazz charts, the Kendor catalogue includes music for concert bands, choruses, string and full orchestras, instrumental soloists and chamber groups. They have also published several books on jazz improvisation, composing, arranging and performance. In 1985 Buffalo jazz musician Jeff Jarvis and his step-brother, Craig Cornwall, became associated with Kendor Music. Craig, who is the son of early partner Ramon Cornwall, purchased Jarvis' share of the company in 2015 and continues to operate Kendor Music from Delevan NY, the rural WNY town where the publishing company began over 60 years ago.

THE CHROMATIC CLUB was founded in 1898 and is the oldest music organization in Buffalo. It promotes and encourages the study, performance and appreciation of music, enriching the artistic climate of the community. They offer student scholarships for college and summer study, along with performance opportunities for student and adult members. The

Chromatic Club sponsored the first professional orchestra in the city and assisted in founding the Community School of Music.

THE COMMUNITY SCHOOL OF MUSIC was founded in 1924 and was originally called the First Settlement Music School. The mission of the school was to serve low-income individuals and families, providing music education to young people unable to pay standard prices for expert teaching. The First Settlement Music School was located at 232 Mertle Street and was chartered by the University of the State of New York. In 1948, it was renamed the Community School of Music and the school moved to its current location at 415 Elmwood Avenue in 1959. Three quarters of the students at the school are children and in accordance with the original mission, more than one third receive tuition financial assistance throughout various funding sources.

BUFFALO SUZUKI STRINGS started in 1969 by Mary Cay Neal at her home in Kenmore. She taught the methods of Dr. Shinichi Suzuki, who championed early childhood music education and the exposure to classical music starting at infancy. The organization is affiliated with Suzuki Association of the Americas. They offer classes in violin, viola, cello, piano, classical guitar and double bass. In 2001 the Buffalo Suzuki Strings moved into the former Niagara Power Company building at 15 Webster Street, on the Erie Canal in North Tonawanda. Their current enrollment is over 300 students and their Advanced Ensemble has played annually with the Ars Nova Chamber Musicians in the Viva Vivaldi Festival. The students also perform as an independent unit or with community orchestras at functions across WNY.

SHEPPARD'S MUSIC STORE – Denton Cottier & Daniels. John D. Sheppard emigrated from England in 1827. He moved to Buffalo and transported his musical instruments and piano by mule-drawn barge, along the Erie Canal; the piano he brought with him was the first in Buffalo. When he arrived in Buffalo he displayed his musical instruments in the lobby of the Eagle Tavern. He eventually moved across the street and opened his music store in the area that is now Lafayette Square, near the current location of the Buffalo and Erie County Public Library. At this store, he presented concerts, provided music lessons and had choir practice for area churches. Sheppard was the organist at St Paul's Church, where the first organ in Buffalo was installed in 1829. The Native American's in

Buffalo had never seen a piano and they came to the store to experience what they explained as, "to hear the big music box sing." Beginning in 1838, The Handel and Haydn Society was based at Sheppard's, where it remained for the next 100 years.

During the 1850s, Hugh Cottier moved to Buffalo. He became Sheppard's student, employee and eventually a partner at the store. Robert Denton joined the company in 1863 and with Sheppard's death in 1867, the name of the store was changed to Cottier & Denton. When William Daniels became a third partner in 1887, they became Denton, Cottier & Daniels. The original Lafayette Square store moved to 269-271 Main Street at Swan, where they occupied an entire five story building. In this complex they sold pianos, sheet music, a large variety of musical instruments, had a repair department and recital halls. They also had a storefront at 32 Court Street, where they were in business for over 100 years. In 1976 Denton, Cottier & Daniels moved to their former satellite store in the Northtown Plaza and in 1999 opened their current store at 460 Dodge Road in Getzville.

Since its inception in 1827, Denton, Cottier & Daniels has been in business for almost 200 years, has been operating under their current business name for over 130 years and they are the oldest Steinway dealer in the world.

ILLOS PIANO at the corner of Main and Hertel has been in business since 1961. They specialize in the restoration of pianos, with a complete staff of wood workers and piano rebuilders. Their craftsmen continue the tradition of piano building and refurbishing in Buffalo.

JOHN SEDOLA MUSIC John Sedola was one of the most influential music instructors of WNY. He also employed many of the best area private teachers to work at his store. Numerous musicians received their early training at John Sedola Music on Grant Street on the West Side. He was the saxophone teacher for Bobby Militello, Russ D'Alba, Sam Scamacca, Phil DiRe, Don Menza, Gary Keller, Sal Andolina, James Spadfore, Dave Schiavone and numerous 1950s and 1960s saxophone players in the Buffalo area. Several of Sedola's students later became music teachers. The training they received from Sedola, which they passed on to their students, contributed to Buffalo having a reputation for quality saxophone players.

KUBERA'S MUSIC STORE Art Kubera was born in 1924, started taking accordion lessons when he was eight years old, played in bands during high school and was soon leading musical groups in the WNY area. He realized there was a need for musical instruments and accessories in Buffalo, so he opened Kubera Music in 1949 at 910 Fillmore near Sycamore. When he first opened the store, he concentrated on providing music lessons. He gave accordion lessons and along with other teachers at this store, they had over 300 weekly students. The store evolved into a full service musical instruments store and Kubera's became the authorized dealer for many brands like Fender guitars and amplifiers. Kubera's Music became the 'go to' store for rock musicians and Kubera was willing to extend credit to the musicians. Every week, numerous musicians would come to the store to make payments on their equipment and Kubera would record the payments in a book that he kept in his top pocket. The efforts of Art Kubera, allowed many musicians the opportunity to purchase quality instruments and contributed to the development of the Buffalo music scene during the '60s and '70s. In addition to running the store, Kubera played in various small combos and bands and for several years led the house band at Polish Village on Broadway.

U-CREST MUSIC. Many rock musicians purchased their first instruments at Kubera's Music Store but most horn players purchased their first trumpet, clarinet or saxophone at U-Crest Music, 1268 George Urban Blvd., in Cheektowaga. The store was opened in 1968 by Art Kubera's brother Leonard. In 1971, it was purchased by Wally and Pat Pidgeon, who operated it for 41 years. Wally had been a member of the Eddie Oinski Orchestra. In addition to the sale of brass instruments, they sold a variety of musical equipment and accessories, with U-Crest Music becoming one of the areas main suppliers of school rentals. At its peak, the store sold more than 1,000 instruments a year and rented over 1,100 to students every school year. One long term employee and music teacher was Donnie Peters, guitarist from Cock Robin. Many area musicians also taught or worked at the store. U-Crest Music was in the garage attached to Wally & Pat Pidgeon's house, and the lesson studios were in their basement. When the store closed in 2012, the basement studios were removed and the store was transformed back to an attached garage.

MATTS MUSIC was started by Matthew Piorkowski in 1963 on Oliver Street, in North Tonawanda. Matt was stationed in California as a member of the Navy Band. Through a girlfriend, he met members of the Lawrence Welk band and sat in with them when they were performing at a dance. Lawrence Welk was so impressed with Matt's accordion playing that he invited him to perform on his nationally televised *Top Tunes and Talent Show* in 1957. This was two years before Welk changed the name of the program to *The Lawrence Welk Show*. The store is now owned and operated by Matt's daughter, singer Kathy Carr and his grandson vocalist/pianist Zach Carr.

ED BENTLEY MUSIC was started by Rockabilly Hall of Fame member Ed Bentley. It was located on Harlem Road in Cheektowaga, between Maryvale and Cleveland Drive. The store specialized in guitar sales and instruction but also had a drum and keyboard department. Employees associated with the store included Joe Zon, who later started the international bass manufacturing company Zon Guitars, Scott Freilich who started Top Shelf Music (vintage guitar sales and repairs) and Paul Musilli who opened Buffalo Drum Outlet in March 1980. The guitar teachers included steel guitarist Gene Strong, who worked with Bentley in one of Buffalo's first rock 'n' roll bands, The Tune Rockers.

THE STRING SHOPPE at 524 Ontario Street was opened by Ed Taublieb in 1970. Taublieb began playing guitar at folk music clubs such as The Limelight on Edward, and The Lower Level on Potomac, in the 1960s. In 1966 he began repairing, refurbishing and selling used guitars in his apartment. Soon he could not find a sufficient number of guitars to meet the demands of his customer, so he inquired about becoming a dealer to sell new guitars. The distributors would not sell to him if he was operating out of his apartment, so he opened the store. Over 50 years later, Ed is still repairing and selling guitars from the same 524 Ontario Street location.

Music stores have been an important part of the Buffalo community since Sheppards Music Store opened in 1827. The instrument manufacturers had stores in the city during the late 1880s and early 1900s. Even prior to the Beatles, when everyone wanted to learn to play guitar, music stores such as Dick's Music Store and Edwin's Music were providing combo-classes, where the students formed bands. In addition to Kuberas, U-Crest, Ed Bentley's and Matt's, some of the other early music stores were Chimes, Wurlitzer, Poppenberg's, Wally's, Premier, Helen Bell Guitar Studio, Suburban, Paramount, Keppler, Al Hemer, AAA, Buffalo Drum Outlet, Kenmore, Top Shelf, Zon Guitars, Lancaster, Limelite, Main Music Shoppe, Hamburg, Guitar Factory, Elmwood, Airport, Allentown and Music City, along with Brundo's, Grazanti's and D'Amico's in Niagara Falls. Prior to the large national stores like Guitar Center moving into the Buffalo market, these family owned stores were the providers of equipment and lessons for generations of WNY musicians. National music store chains may have moved into the Buffalo market, but several of these local stores are still serving the area music community.

RECORDING STUDIOS

BUFFALO RECORDING SERVICE was one of the first recording studios in Buffalo. Tommy Shannon and Phil Todaro operated this studio at 291 Delaware Avenue, which was the location where the Channel 2 television studios were later built. It was here that Tommy Shannon recorded many of the early bands in the Buffalo area. The equipment was sold and moved above a business, on Niagara Street. Shannon later opened a home studio in his basement in West Seneca, to control costs and allow bands more time to record their songs. It was in this basement studio that WKBW disc jockeys Danny Neaverth and Joey Reynolds recorded "Rats in My Room".

HOWELL RECORDING STUDIO – ACT ONE RECORDING STUDIO was located at 2703 Delaware Avenue, near Hertel, in North Buffalo. It was started by Dave Howell and then owned and operated by WBEN's Clint Buehlman, used mostly for recording commercials on direct-to-acetate discs. In 1969 Jerry Meyers purchased this facility from Buehlman, and opened it as Act One Recording Studio, with Bill Levy from Seneca Sound. They installed an Ampex eight-track recorder and Electrodyne 20-input mixing console in 1970. Many area bands including Ed Bentley, The Road, Lavender Hill Mob, Saint Hill and Chenango recorded there. Their sessions were engineered by Jim Barnum, Larry Swist and Mick Guzauski, with Rich Sargent assisting Meyers on production projects. In addition, Act One did remote recordings at various sites, including Big Wheelie, Isaac and United Sound at the Three Coins Nightclub.

CROSS EYED BEAR STUDIO was operated out of Mark Studios at 6010 Goodrich Road in Clarence Center during the late 1970s. At this studio, Jay Beckenstein, Jeremy Wall and Richard Calandra recorded many bands, including much of the first Rick James album. Cross Eyed Bear relocated their base of operations to Bear Tracks Studios in Suffern, NY in Rockland County, just outside of New York City. When they moved to Suffern, Buffalo's Larry Swist moved with them as an engineer at the studio.

MARK CUSTOM RECORDING SERVICE was founded in 1962 by Vince Morette. Since they had a 24-track studio, Buffalo bands from Talas to John Valby, along with many national acts, recorded there. These sessions were engineered by Vince Morette, Chuck Madden, Al Gibson Dave Bellanca, Mark Freeland and Mark Mekker (who later owned ESP CD manufacturing company). In addition to offering studio recording service, they specialize in international on-site recordings for professional classical ensembles, large music conferences, colleges and secondary schools, along with live recordings of festival events. In 1983 the studio relocated to 10815 Bodine Road in Clarence, where it is now operated by Vince's son Mark Morette. The studio operates the world's largest independently owned classical record label, which has received two Grammy nominations and various international awards.

Vince Morette was instrumental in starting the Sound Recording Technology program at SUNY Fredonia. This was the first college level recording studio programs in the country to offer a degree in sound technology recording. Vince started the program in 1981 but due to budget constraints, he personally provided and installed the recording equipment at the college. Many area and national recording engineers graduated from the program, including Armond Petri, who has recorded many national acts and produced Buffalo based national recording artists, The Goo Goo Dolls and 10,000 Maniacs.

SELECT SOUND is located at 2315 Elmwood Avenue in Kenmore, the studio was opened in 1974 by Bill and Nick Kothen, with Dick Bauerle working there since its inception as a producer and engineer. Numerous national and local bands recorded at the studio, including some top selling Latin American recordings. The studio also recorded numerous commercials and jingle recording. Starting in 1980, Select Sound offered a

Recording Workshop, which was a college accredited course at Buffalo State and Villa Maria College.

BCMK was started by Tommy Calandra and Gary Mallaber in the garage behind Tommy's home on Poultry Street, when they were still playing in Stan & the Ravens. It was here the band Raven had their first rehearsal and where several bands recorded including The Rogues. In the 1970s the studio was moved to the basement of Calandra's home on Hobmoor Avenue off Kenmore Avenue. It was at the Hobmoor studio that Calandra recorded many Buffalo original bands and his radio jingles like "Danny Moves His Fanny." This was also the location where Calandra started BCMK Records. The final location of BCMK was a combination lower level studio and Calandra's upper level home, on Delaware near Hertel Avenue. Engineer Mike Brydalski worked with Calandra at the Hobmoor and Delaware Avenue studios.

MAXWELL MUSIC was a recording studio started by Bob James in the basement of his Taft Place home in 1978. With the assistance of R. John "Alan" Oishei, grandson of the Trico Corp founder, they moved to a studio on Harlem Road near Walden Avenue. At these studios they recorded The Toys, Enemies, Vores, Jumpers and produced the *New New York* album for Pegasonics. James is still involved with area recording and coordinates Buffalo Blues, LLC, a nonprofit music campaign benefiting area veterans.

TRACKMASTER STUDIO was located on the corner of Franklin and North Street, in a turn of the century brick Allentown building. The studio was designed by John Storyk and opened by Alan Baumgardner and Kim Ferullo in 1980. Many national groups including the Buffalo recording artists Rick James, Ani DiFranco and The Goo Goo Dolls have used the studio. Being near downtown, it was often utilized by advertising agencies for the recording of commercials. The studio was purchased by the Goo Goo Dolls Robby Takac and is now known as GCR Audio Recording Studio.

LOFT RECORDING STUDIO is a home recording studio opened in 1982 by Cock Robin keyboardist Jim Sommer, above the garage behind his Cheektowaga home. Many area bands have recorded at this studio and it has remained in business for over 35 years.

AUDIO MAGIC started as a home style studio by Chuck Anderson on the second floor of a building on Hertel. After a year of success, Chuck moved the studio to the first floor, naming it ARS – Anderson Recording Studio. When he outgrew that facility, he purchased a building on Military Road in Black Rock in the mid-1980s. That facility was called Audio Magic and was managed by Robbie Konikoff. During the 1990s the company formed affiliations and joint ventures with several other recording studios. It is now a full-service audio and video recording facility called Imagine Recording Studios.

STARFIELD'S RECORDING STUDIO is located at 463 Amherst St in Buffalo, which was previously operated by David Bellanca of Communications Task Group. It was founded in 1984 and is now owned by Alan Dusel, who received his BFA from UB in 1980 and previously worked at Trackmaster. In addition to studio and remote recording, Starfield's offers recording and production workshops, along with related recording services. The studio acquired the recording console from the Record Plant in New York City, which they installed in one of their studios.

IMAGE RECORDING was an Olcott NY recording studio operated by Mitch Metzler in the 1980s. Many groups recorded there because of the laid back rural setting, located in a converted home not far from Olcott Harbor on Lake Ontario.

SESSIONS RECORDING STUDIO was located next to the Sportsman's Tavern on Amherst Street in Buffalo. It was operated by Dwane Hall and John Dikeman, with other area musicians assisting at the facility. Robbie Konikoff moved his Audio Magic operations to the studio and the name was changed to Black Rock Entertainment.

OUTER LIMIT RECORDING STUDIO opened in the early 1990s but owner Ken Rutkowski has been engineering recording sessions back to the 1980s. Local and national artists recorded at this Walden Avenue facility.

SQUIRE RECORDING STUDIOS is a South Buffalo recording studio on Clinton Street. It opened in 1980 by Paul Squire, concentrating on recordings by bands for demos and self-released albums or CDs.

RECORD PROMOTERS

Independent record promoters Jerry Meyers and Could Be Wild Promotions were based in Buffalo and were also involved with the area music scene. Meyers was more involved with early Top 40 radio, while Could Be Wild worked more with album rock radio stations.

JERRY MEYERS started out as a vocalist, recorded two records and performed at area record hops, where he assisted Lucky Pierre at some events. Meyers released the song "Please Hear My Plea" on a local label. That was followed by "Honey Bun" which was released on Vassar Records and produced by Phil Ramone at A&R Recording Studio in New York City. Future Record Theater owner, Lenny Silver was only marginally impressed with Jerry's singing ability but he was very impressed by his promotion abilities and he hired him to work for his Best & Gold Distributing Company. Meyers responsibilities were to convince area radio stations to add records that Best & Gold represented to the station playlist. Jerry became very adept at promoting an artist, song or record so he was hired as national promotion manager for Mercury Records in Chicago, later starting his own independent record promotion company. In the '70s and '80s there was an informal group of approximately six promoters called "The Network" which dominated Top 40 airplay nationally and could 'make or break' a record. Jerry was responsible for helping promote over 100 gold records by artists including Bruce Springsteen, Barry Manilow, Rod Stewart and Neil Diamond. Meyers was credited with breaking "Precious & Few" by Climax, "My Melody of Love" by Bobby Vinton, "Tie a Yellow Ribbon" by Tony Orlando, "After the Lovin" by Engelbert Humperdinck, among others. An article in *Rolling Stone* magazine named Jerry Meyers one of the top people in the music business and in Fredric Dannen's book *Hit Men*, he included Meyers among the most influential record promoters in the U.S. During the payola scandals, Jerry was one of the few promoters not implicated or called to testify before the associated congressional hearings.

COULD BE WILD PROMOTIONS was formed by two formers musicians and Record Theater employees. Doug Dombrowski was a keyboardist in the 1960s band Nobody's Children and Bruce Moser was a vocalist in The

Restless from 1967 – 1969. (No relation to the 1980s Buffalo recording band The Restless). They met while working together at Record Theater and developed a low keyed, honest, appreciation of the music approach to promotion. Bruce and Doug left Record Theater and formed Could Be Wild in 1975. Their first successes were with The Cars, followed by U2 and Bryan Adams. They concentrated on what they called The Thruway Chain which included the cities between Boston, Massachusetts and Cleveland, Ohio. Their clients presented them with sufficient gold and platinum albums to cover practically every inch of the walls in their office. In addition to working with national artists, Could Be Wild has promoted records by Buffalo artists: Willie Nile, Terry Sullivan, Billy Sheehan and The Goo Goo Dolls.

RECORD LABELS

SHAN – TODD RECORDS was owned by disc jockeys Tommy Shannon and Phil Todaro, releasing songs by Jack Scorsone & the Playboys, The Graduates and Hot Toddy's. They later changed the name of the label to Corsican. Shannon and Todaro established Mar Lee Records on which they released the original version of "Wild Weekend" by the Rockin Rebels. They had a relationship with Swan Records where "Wild Weekend" was reissued and became a gold record. When Shannon released "Rock City" by Kathy Lynn & the Playboys, it was also on Swan.

BCMK RECORDS was a label formed by Tommy Calandra and his engineer Mike Brydalski to release recordings from the BCMK Recording Studio. Several of the original music bands of the late '70s and early '80s had songs on this label, including *4 Now from Buffalo*, a compilation of songs by Pauline & the Perils, The Vores, The Cobras and The Stains. They also issued the 1982 *Airways* compilation LP. *More information on this label is in the Original Music chapter.*

BANDSTAND – ORDER – JANUARY – GJM RECORDS were labels established by Jerry Meyers, who released records in the '60s and '70s by area artists including Big Wheelie & the Hubcaps, John Culliton Mahoney, Jim Schoenfeld and Barbara St. Clair. He recorded and produced the Joe Jeffrey single "My Pledge of Love", on Scepter/Wand Records which sold over 800,000 copies in the U.S. and charted internationally. Recently he released albums by Terry Buchwald and Michael Civisca on Rhapsody Music. Meyers got Civisca signed to Michael Jackson's MJJ Records, which was distributed by Sony. Meyers also helped Hound Dog Lorenz create one of the first worldwide syndicated radio programs. Jerry owned Act One Recording Studios, which in 1970 signed an exclusive distribution deal with Mercury Records. In the December 12, 1970 issue of *Billboard Magazine* Meyers was quoted. "There's a Motown sound, a Memphis sound and I can see no reason why there can't be a Buffalo sound. This town is about to have a musical explosion."

MO DO RECORDS was a label started by William Nunn in the late 1960s, with recordings made in his home studio on Orange Street. Nunn was assisted by his son Bobby, one half of the Bob & Gene duo, who provided engineering, writing and musical assistance on most of the label's output. Bob & Gene went their separate ways in the 1970s, with Gene getting involved with the church and community endeavors, while Bobby Nunn worked with Rick James before moving to Los Angeles and Las Vegas.

ONE EYE-RECORDS was formed in the late '80's by Mighty Taco owner Andy Geravac. Mighty Taco and Andy Gerovac have a reputation of supporting area musicians and music related events in the Western New York area, dating back to when Mighty Taco first opened in 1973.

RECORD THEATER – AMHERST RECORDS was started by Lenny Silver from Rochester, New York. When he was 17 years old he started working as a stock boy at a Rochester record store. After returning from WWII he went back to that store, eventually becoming a buyer. In 1954 Silver moved to Buffalo to work for a distribution company, promoting various artists.

He founded Best & Gold Distributing which sold records for certain labels to record stores and department stores. In 1964 that was expanded to Transcontinent Records, which was a rack jobber. In that capacity, the company provided all the records, displays and advertising for the record departments of stores. Transcontinent grew to be the fourth largest record distribution company in the country.

In 1976 Lenny Silver opened the first Record Theatre at 1800 Main Street, at the corner of Lafayette. That became a record chain of 37 locations in Buffalo, Rochester, Syracuse, Cleveland, Baltimore and Philadelphia.

In the late 1970s Silver launched Amherst Records. He released records by Spyro Gyro, Glenn Medeiros, Jackie DeShannon, David LaFlamme, Solomon Burke and won a Grammy with an album by Doc Severensen & the Tonight Show Band. Amherst Records promoted Buffalo based bands, releasing albums by Gamalon, Jeff Jarvis, Jeremy Wall, Innocent Bystanders, Jim Yeomans and Stone Country, along with Jeff Tyzik and Nancy Kelly from Rochester. In 1984 Amherst Records acquired all the master recordings of the AVCO Embassy, H&L Records labels, including recordings by The Stylistics, Van McCoy, the Chambers Brothers and Softones.

Lenny Silver passed away on March 10, 2017 at the age of 90. All the Record Theater locations have closed, with the last one to close being the original store at 1800 Main Street. Transcontinent is still distributing records and Amherst Records continues to promote their vast catalogue.

CONCERT PROMOTERS

MELODY FAIR

Melody Fair was opened in June 1956 by Lew Fisher as a theater-in-the-round on Niagara Falls Blvd. in North Tonawanda. Initially the theater presented musical comedies under the brightly colored tent, with top professional performers and a full orchestra. They produced top notch shows like *The King and I, Guys and Dolls, Carousel* and *Kismet*, with performers including Nat King Cole, Ethel Merman and Ginger Rogers. During the early '60s they worked with other theaters-in-the-round, in the Northeastern United States to collectively book quality productions during the summer months.

In the late 1960s the theater moved away from musical comedies and concentrated on shows by performers like Liberace, Bill Cosby, Connie Stevens, Robert Goulet, Carol Lawrence and Bobby Vinton. These performers often came to the area for week long engagements. In the late 1960s, Melody Fair also started presenting rock groups such as The Who, Vanilla Fudge and The Byrds.

A rotating stage was installed in 1970, allowing prime viewing from every seat in the house. After a fire in 1974 a permanent fully enclosed structure was built to replace the tent. This increased the capacity from 2,000 to 3,000 people. In 1980 Lew Fisher sold the property to Rudy and David Bersani, who owned the Three Coins Restaurant and Hotel. Later in the 1980s it was operated by Ed Smith. Over its history, performers from Chicago to the Four Seasons and Johnny Cash to Tony Bennett have appeared at Melody Fair.

In 2012, a Walmart Superstore opened at the former Melody Fair location at Niagara Falls Blvd. and Erie Avenue. As Joni Mitchell once sang "They paved paradise and put up a parking lot."

FESTIVAL EAST CONCERTS

Festival East Concerts had its beginning in 1960 when Jerry Nathan with minor partners Newport Jazz Festival producers George Wein & Ed Sarkesian, presented the 1st Buffalo Jazz Festival at Offerman Stadium in 1960. The concert was produced in association with Joe Rico, a nationally respected local jazz DJ. Nathan himself played piano in jazz trios while attending Cornell University. After Nathan & his partners presented their second successful Jazz Festival in 1961, Jerry decided to begin presenting individual jazz concerts and started a company called Buffalo Jazz Festival. These shows in the early 1960s were mostly held at Kleinhans Music Hall.

Nathan established a ticket office in the Westbrook Hotel and organized ticket sales through Denton, Cottier & Daniels, the Sample Shop and Audrey & Del's Records. He shortened the name of the concert promotion company to Buffalo Festival and moved the Festival Ticket Office to the Statler Hotel Building.

Musical styles of the 1960s progressed and Nathan expanded first into folk, promoting acts such as Peter, Paul and Mary, Joan Baez, Judy Collins, Bob Dylan and others. This began to evolve into what was first called electric folk, when Bob Dylan hired The Band as back up musicians. Nathan expanded with other styles of music, beginning by being the first promoter to introduce R&B to Kleinhans and by producing soul, funk and pop concerts.

After judging a "Battle of the Bands" at Buffalo Memorial Auditorium, Nathan grasped that rock music had evolved so he began to enthusiastically promote it. Early rock concerts included the Rolling Stones at The Aud in 1966 and Jimi Hendrix at The Aud in 1968. Due to Nathan's exemplary reputation, Festival was also the first promoter permitted to bring rock acts into Kleinhans Music Hall, where they presented groups like The Who, Led Zeppelin, Frank Zappa, Santana, Traffic and Joe Cocker. They also began presenting concerts at Shea's Buffalo Theatre, which had more seating than Kleinhans.

At that time, there was little competition in the concert market and the concept of big touring acts was just beginning. The bands played for a guaranteed price and the price of talent was reasonable. Buffalo was a "must play" market as WKBW's radio signal basically covered the whole East Coast, and if WKBW added a record...it practicably assured that the record got "added" by radio stations all the way to Florida. Therefore, talent was economically priced and record companies wanted to succeed in the Buffalo market. Record Label tour support kept the tickets prices low. For example, the ticket costs were $6.00 for The Who at Kleinhans and $5.00 for the Rolling Stones at The Aud. Led Zeppelin played Kleinhans in 1972 and tickets were $2.50, $3.50 & $4.50 with reserved seats.

Jerry Nathan was established as a nationally recognized concert promoter, presenting shows in Buffalo, Rochester, Syracuse, Albany,

TWO EARLY FESTIVAL EAST CONCERTS
Presented in association with other promoters
Photos: Courtesy David & Nancy Nathan

Ithaca and Binghamton, and a Carnegie Hall date for Chuck Mangione, so he changed the name to Festival East Concerts. They also promoted 16 Superfest shows at Rich Stadium. The outdoor stadium line-ups included two more appearances by the Rolling Stones, and shows featuring The Band, Eric Clapton, Crosby Stills & Nash, Bob Seger, Foreigner, J. Geils Band, and other major acts. Additional concerts promoted by Festival included Supertramp, Bruce Springsteen, Prince, Stevie Wonder, Earth, Wind & Fire, Elvis Presley and many others.

Festival East Concerts and Festival Tickets was a family owned and operated company. Jerry was at the helm throughout the 1960s and 1970s but as the '70s progressed daughter Nancy assumed more of the artist booking and concert management, with her brother David assisting in the decision process. However, Jerry was involved with all major decisions and many entertainment industry executives acknowledged Jerry's overall knowledge of the concert promotion business. David Nathan handled the advertising, promotion and media relations, with assistance from Ed Tice, who started with the company after Jerry worked with him when getting his posters designed at Rosen Printing. Paul and Steve Nathan also worked at the company with Steve leaving to pursue his own music career as a keyboard recording session player in Nashville, where he was received awards for his contributions. Daughter-in-law Cathy Nathan managed the ticket office, handling Festival's and other promoter's ticket sales operations.

They outgrew the office in the Statler Hotel and moved to 224 Delaware near Chippewa. Other staff included David's wife Diana, who worked closely with David in advertising and Don Tomasulo, who started as a college intern, before being hired to assist David in advertising and promotions when Ed Tice left to join Harvey & Corky. Lisa Rodriguez worked with Cathy in the ticket office and in the 1980s Kevin Ketchum worked as Festival's Production Manager.

After Jerry Nathan passed away in 1987, David and Nancy continued Festival Concerts through 1989. They both remained in Buffalo, with David later working in real estate and Nancy in the hospitality industry. Festival and the Nathan family initiated concerts in Buffalo and left a legacy of producing many memorable concerts in the WNY market for almost 30 years.

HARVEY & CORKY PRODUCTIONS

Harvey Weinstein and Corky Burger began promoting a few college concerts when they were students at UB. In 1972, they arranged a Stephen Stills concert at Memorial Auditorium. When the student association got cold feet about the concert, Harvey and Corky presented it on their own. That show was the beginning of the company. In 1973, they started Harvey and Corky, with Harvey's brother Bob Weinstein. They began promoting rock shows at various facilities, especially at The Century Theatre at 511 Main Street, which they purchased in 1974. All the top touring rock acts performed at The Century, with many memorable concerts. When they did not have scheduled concerts, Harvey & Corky showed movies at the Century, called *Midnight Movie Madness.* One movie they played often was *Reefer Madness*, which was accompanied by liberal drinking and smoking by the audience. An intern to Harvey Weinstein during this time was UB Student Brad Grey. Grey later founded Brillstein-Grey Entertainment talent agency and was CEO of Paramount Pictures from 2005 to 2017.

Ed Tice was recruited from competing concert promoter Festival East in the late 1970s. Tice was hired to handle marketing, promotions and some booking for the rock concerts because Harvey wanted to concentrate on movies. Harvey and Bob Weinstein formed Miramax Films in 1979 to distribute independent films deemed commercially unfeasible by the major studios. Miramax was named after Harvey and Bob's parents, Miriam and Max Weinstein. Corky Burger concentrated on booking plays at Sheas Buffalo and touring productions of Broadway Plays like *Chorus Line* and *Annie* across New York State and the northeast. In fact, Harvey & Corky were instrumental in lobbying to get the backstage area of Sheas Buffalo remodeled. That remodeling was required because larger productions would not perform in Buffalo unless the theater could accommodate the backstage requirements of larger touring productions.

Tice recalled his first day of work with Harvey & Corky and how it set the tone for his employment with the concert promotion company. The Harvey & Corky offices were in the balcony area of the Century Theatre where you could walk out of the office area to watch the concerts or movies. After Tice selected his office location and picked his secretary, he said he would need another telephone line in the office space. Corky asked someone to call the telephone company and arrange for an additional line, when loud banging was heard on one of the office walls. Harvey entered the office next door and used a sledge hammer to knock a hole in the wall, through which he presented the extra telephone line. With Harvey & Corky, things got done quickly, in the most expedient manner, demonstrating Harvey often did things his way.

When they sold the Century Theatre, Harvey & Corky moved their offices to The Aud. Over the next decade many concerts that came to Buffalo were booked and promoted by Harvey & Corky, who later changed their name to Harvey, Corky & Tice. These concerts were held at Shea's Buffalo Theatre, Kleinhans Music Hall, Buffalo Memorial Auditorium, Melody Fair and local clubs like Sinbads, Rooftops Skyroom, Uncle Sam's and The Continental.

Touring bands were usually loyal to the concert promoter which first presented them in a market. For this reason, Harvey & Corky opened their own rock club, Stage One on Main Street just east of Transit Road. They used this club to book new up and coming bands, so they would get the rights to their future concerts in the Buffalo market. They also did a cross promotion with their concerts by roping off a table at Stage One for the artists appearing at major concert venues. Many people came to Stage One hoping to see touring groups such as Van Halen partying at the club. Some touring groups showed up and sat in with the bands performing at Stage One, while others never made it to the club but the anticipation filled the club. Two notable Stage One shows by bands early in their careers were The Police, who only drew about 14 people, and U2, who opened for Talas and were advertised and announced as V2. When U2 appeared at Stage One it was the same day that John Lennon was assassinated in New York City, December 8, 1980. Another memorable date was when Dr. J. Jones & the Interns were scheduled at Stage One. After people discovered the band was really Aerosmith playing a club date under an assumed name, the show sold out before tickets could even be made available to the public.

Rockers magazine hosted a New Wave night at Stage One, which featured original bands from the city at the suburban club. An employee of the magazine, Brian Dickman excelled as the disc jockey for this night, so he was hired by Harvey & Corky Productions, initially as the disc jockey on the Thursday New Wave nights. The regular deejay position at Stage One was long held by Jim Santella. Harvey wanted to concentrate more on Miramax Films, so Ed Tice handled most of Harvey's booking responsibilities and Brian was promoted to marketing and promotions.

Dickman later worked for Harvey at Miramax Films in New York City, and promoted roller derby with Rollermania Inc., syndicated on ESPN, with live shows from The Aud and Madison Square Garden. He also worked for Corky Burger promoting 3-D glasses for movies and television, a worldwide company with operations in Europe and Australia. Brian is now currently with Airport Plaza Jewelers. He worked with Don Hoffman to license the trademarked slogan, "...doesn't cost an arm and a leg" marketing campaign with jewelry stores across the country.

Harvey Corky & Tice and Festival East Concerts became the largest concert promoters in Buffalo in the late 1970s, but during the 1980s the concert business at large venues became corporate. National promoters like Delsener-Slater in NYC and Bill Graham Presents in San Francisco, which were both acquired by Clear Channel Entertainment, and the Canadian company CPI, which was formed by Labatt brewery, dominated the market in Buffalo and other cities. Across the country local promoters became a thing of the past and in Buffalo Harvey, Corky & Tice and Festival East, discontinued promoting shows at The Aud, Rich Stadium or other large facilities. Tice started his own company called Tice Productions but promoted the larger shows as a partner with Magic City Productions from Binghamton. Corky Burger started several low profile but very successful businesses. Harvey Weinstein's Miramax Films became one of the most successful independent film distributors, won Academy Awards and was sold to Disney. Harvey worked for Disney after the sale until he and his brother Bob founded The Weinstein Company. In less than 40 years, Harvey Weinstein had gone from cutting corners to save on the cost of adding a telephone line at a Buffalo office, to being the multi-millionaire owner of an influential international movie studio.

PATE & ASSOCIATES

Irwin and Monique Pate started promoting concerts in Buffalo around 1970. In addition to concerts, they were successful in obtaining the right to be the ticket agent for Buffalo Memorial Auditorium. They later formed Prime Seats which had an office in The Aud. and 31 satellite offices. In 1992, they won The Aud contract over Ticketmaster, who had purchased Ticketron. Prime Seats got the contract by emphasizing they were a local company and their surcharge would be $2.50 for concerts and $1.25 for family events, while Ticketmaster charged as much as a $6.00 surcharge in some other cities. Nick Giammusso, who worked for Pate & Associates, later formed VIP Seats and now operates the ticket brokerage VIPtix.com.

The WNY area colleges presented concerts on a regular basis during the 1960s and 1970s. At UB's Clark Gym, there were several multiband shows, before rock concerts were held at Kleinhans, Sheas or The Aud. UB also offered shows by bands in Norton Union at the Main Street campus. Harvey & Corky started their concert promotion career by producing shows when they were students at UB. The other colleges in the area also presented national and local bands, with many shows being available to the public. The tradition of college concerts continues with Spring Fest and Fall Fest at the UB Amherst campus.

Other promoters in the WNY area included Connie Campanao's B Shape Productions, Bobby K Promotions, Marshall Glover, Tony Billoni, Marty Boratin, Ron Mendez, Perenichols, John Scher from Rochester, Magic City Productions from Binghamton and Al Nocciolino, who produced Broadway Shows at Sheas. Many area clubs also presented shows, procuring the acts through area booking agencies or dealing directly with the national acts.

BOOKING AGENCIES

GREAT LAKES BOOKING dominated the rock music scene starting in the late 1960s and throughout the 1970s. It was founded by Fred Saia and Fred Caserta, in an office at 1455 Hertel Avenue. At one time, they were so influential with the local rock bars, that if a band wanted to play the best clubs, they had to be booked by this agency. If a band was not accepted by the agency or did not want to be represented by them, there were many clubs where they could not perform. A similar policy applied to clubs. If club owners wanted the best bands, they could only obtain them from Great Lakes. The agency often demanded an exclusive booking agreement, which meant a club had to obtain all their bands though Great Lakes. It was Great Lakes that began booking bands for one-nighters. They represented all the top bands and these were the groups that all the clubs wanted to book, so to spread them around and satisfy the clubs, the bands were booked for only one night at a club. This resulted in a band being booked at several different clubs during a given week. Prior to this practice, bands played two to six nights a week at a club before moving on to another. Although they were primarily a rock music agency, they had the Executive Hotel account and represented some commercial rock bands for booking at that club and on the lucrative out of town commercial rock market. Great Lakes was also involved in booking their bands at colleges across the state. Mike Rozniak was hired specifically to meet with college Student Activity Directors and student groups, so they would hire the agency's bands. This was when the drinking age was 18 and most colleges had an on-campus Ratskeller and all the colleges had beer blasts. Rozniak also worked with Dave Rezak from DMR Booking Agency in Syracuse and Peter Morticelli from Pelican Booking Agency in Rochester to get Great Lakes bands club dates, before or after their college dates in those markets.

STARSTRUCK PRODUCTIONS began as the artist management side of Great Lakes. When Great Lakes closed their Hertel Avenue office in the late 1970s, Great Lakes moved to office space above Mickey Rats on Main & Minnesota Streets and Starstruck moved into the office space formerly occupied by Trackmaster Recording Studio at 701 Seneca. Starstruck still concentrated on management of bands like Talas, Donna McDaniel and Big Wheelie. They also began operating a booking agency with Tom Barone starting Entertainment Services.

When Fred Saia moved out of Buffalo the Great Lakes Booking name was retired. In 1980, Starstruck moved to offices at 2650 Delaware Avenue. Starstruck Productions was on the first floor of the building, handling management of the bands, and Entertainment Services was on the second floor, handling the bookings. The administrative assistant, for both companies was Pixie. Mike Faley started working with Starstruck Productions in the management of bands, especially Talas, with Tom Barone hiring additional employees, including Sam Accordino, to assist him with the bookings. After Mike Rozniak closed Good Times

FRED CASERTA (right) - CHUCK VICARIO (center)
with MIKE CAMPBELL (left)
1969 Artists & Models Ball
Photo Credit: Paul Daniel Petock

Management, Tom Magill started working with Starstruck. The addition of Magill resulted in Starstruck directly securing more booking for their bands with Steve Simmons joining the company as an agent. In the late 1980s Fred Caserta started the Kingdom Bound Christian Music Festival at Darien Lake, which is the largest Christian Music and Arts Festival in NYS. At that time Tom Magill purchased the company, moving to offices above Mickey Rats City Bar on Main & Minnesota, where Great Lakes was located a decade earlier. Magill continues handling many bands and coordinates the entertainment calendar for several area clubs.

ENTERTAINMENT SERVICES, INC. (ESI) was originally the booking agency side of Starstruck Productions. It is owned by Tom Barone and when the Delaware Avenue office that ESI shared with Starstruck was closed, they relocated to 3690 Main Street in Buffalo. Barone booked many local bands but also concentrated on bringing national recording groups to area clubs. Dave Buffamonti from Backstage Productions, Connie Companaro from B Sharp Productions and other agents including Don Siracuse and Bob Avino, worked with ESI from the Main Street office. Artie Kwitchoff also booked original bands for ESI, before becoming the Goo Goo Dolls manager and founding Funtime Productions. With his national contacts, Tom Barone contracted the entertainment at The Tralfamadore in downtown Buffalo and is now the owner of that nightclub. Jeremy Hoyle from the band Strictly Hip, currently works with Barone in coordinating dates for area and national groups at area clubs.

JR PRODUCTIONS was started in the late 1960s by John and Frank Sansone. Great Lakes controlled the rock music market, while JR Productions controlled the Top 40 Commercial Rock market. However, just like Great Lakes booked some commercial rock bands, JR Productions also handled some rock bands. Their office was in Kings Plaza on Hertel Avenue, next to The Mug. During the 1970s they were one of the largest commercial rock booking agencies in the East Coast, providing bands for Holiday Inns and commercial rock show clubs in 24 states from Maine to Florida and the Atlantic Coast to the Mississippi River. John Sansone left the agency in 1983 to work for a national booking agency based out of Nashville. They moved their offices to The Three Coins Motel, which was one of their largest accounts and later had an office on Niagara Falls Boulevard, at the Route 290 exit. Frank Sansone handled most of the out of town dates, Lenny Licata booked the WNY area clubs and Gail Reger, who was originally the receptionist, booked the solo and duo dates. After Lenny and Gail were married they moved to Las Vegas and Franks wife assumed the administrative duties. Johnna Scime, the vocalist for Joyryde, was later hired to take over her position. Today JR Productions continues to be the largest area booking agency for weddings, private and corporate events.

ARTIST TALENT AGENCY was started by John Titak after he moved to WNY from Ohio in the mid-1970s. He represented several bands however, his main group was Rasputin. John booked local dates in the Western New York market, concentrating on securing dates for his bands across the East Coast and Mid-West. He later moved and worked for an agency in the Atlanta, Georgia area.

GREAT SOUNDS OF MUSIC was the agency Connie Stypowany formed in order to book bands at the smaller clubs in the WNY area. This agency is where many rock and commercial rock bands got their initial club bookings. Great Lakes and JR Productions were the main agencies for the A clubs but Connie handled many of the B clubs. Mike Rozniak, from Good Times Management, first started booking bands when working for Connie.

ARTISTS UNLIMITED was owned by Beth Roll. She had the initial contract to book the bands in The Pub at Darien Lake Amusement Park, when the park was still just a campground, with a beach, water slide and a few rides. Artists Unlimited also booked many of the popular country rock bands in the 1970s, handling dates for Stone Country, Backroads, Quarterhorse, Kenny Gunn & the Pistols, The Pointless Brothers and Shea Brothers, etc… for dates at clubs like Nashville North.

MARY STOCK booked commercial acts in the 1970s. She handled the early dates for the Scinta Brothers and acts like Leon Hall, Jon Kondol and Kenny Byrd. Mary was a childhood friend of Joan Baez, when she was living in the Clarence Center area, and Mary said she accompanied Joan when she was flown in by helicopter for her appearance at Woodstock in 1969.

GOOD TIMES MANAGEMENT. Mike Rozniak worked for Great Lakes Booking but represented bands through his management company, Good

Times. Starting in the late 1970s he represented Actor and Sky. Rozniak was scheduling dates for Fat Brat, Gypzy, Lebel and Strider, adding them to his roster. After he left Great Lakes, Good Times Management became a booking agency. When Tom Magill was a student at Orchard Park high school, he hired bands through Rozniak for school dances. Magill also booked Orchard Park classmate, Winnie Bergner's (Ladyfire and Anatara) first band Proteus at area clubs. To expand Good Times as a booking agency, Rozniak hired Tom Magill, to initially handle the bookings for Lebel and later his other acts.

MALLARD PRODUCTIONS. Jim Taylor created this agency in the Rochester area in the 1970s and moved into the Buffalo market. He was associated with Black Sheep and later started booking dates in Western New York for Terra Nova. In the early 1980s he represented Cheater, along with Broken Silence, Vapor Voyce and Harpo.

THE MUSIC AGENCY. Frank Michaels started this company to book his brothers group, The Vincent Michaels Band. He specialized in putting bands together, along a preplanned concept. After the Vincent Michaels Band stopped performing he represented Sudden Urge, Frank Beach, Passion, The Release, 33 West and several other acts.

BACKSTAGE PRODUCTIONS. Started in the late 1970s by Dave Buffamonti and Rick Falkowski, this agency began by representing Crossroads, Parousia, Crash Cadillac, The Keys and The John Cameron Band. When Rick left to start Buffalo Backstage Magazine, Dave was joined by Jim Schwartz and Rich Radice. In the 1980s Backstage represented The Beez, White Lies, Rock Candy, Widow, Sudden Impact, Colours and more. Dave Buffamonti later owned the rock club Rock N Roll Heaven, which was located at several different locations in WNY. The agency continues to represent area bands and Buffamonti now runs Rockstarz in the Best Western Hotel on Dingens Street.

DUNN-RITE AGENCY was started by Bob Avino. When he was still in high school, he began working as the DJ at Rooftops and coordinated the club's Rock Wars – Battle of Bands. He began handling bookings for the band Presenze and he was the first agent to begin working with Nick Gugliuzza. When Gugliuzza left the music business, Avino acquired most of the bands he handled, including Ezekial, which became Avino's main band. Dunn-Rite and Backstage Productions merged into a company called Queen City Entertainment, but later continued as separate agencies.

NICK GUGLIUZZA PRODUCTIONS was formed by Nick Gugliuzza, the former Director of Student Activities at Medaille College. While working at Medaille, Nick was approached by student Don Tomasulo, who asked if he was interested in managing his band Benhatzel. Nick had no background in music, he was a former high school health and physical education teacher, who in 1971 started Day Camps of America; a summer camp for children at Beaver Island Park that grew to 98 franchised camps across the country. He applied his business techniques to the music industry and brought Bob Avino from Dunn-Rite, Mike Rozniak and Tom Magill from Good Times, Dave Buffamonti from Backstage and Tim Gerwitz from Progressive Talent together into this company. They opened an office at 3125 Walden Avenue in Depew, where all the companies worked as a collective under the Queen City Talent name. When the bands they represented wanted more work at the lake, Nick purchased the Point Breeze Hotel, in Angola, changing the name of the club to The Beachcomber. To provide more work in the winter, he bought the former country music club The Bonnet, converting it into a rock bar called Dr. Feelgoods. However, Nick's business rather than music ambitions prevailed and in 1981 he started Empire Business Brokers, a business and franchise sales brokerage, which also provides consulting services for their clients. Now based in Philadelphia, Empire Business Brokers has 85 franchised offices, including 13 in foreign countries.

Sunshine Productions was started by Judd Sunshine from The Pointless Brothers and The Hill Brothers. Judd continues booking several bands and children entertainment, also working as an event coordinator... Mark Amo had an agency that specialized in original music bands. For many years, Sara Jo Barth assisted in booking the entertainment for Taste of Buffalo, working with Tom Barone from ESI and Frank Sansone from JR Productions on this event.

MUSICIANS UNION

In 1897 The American Federation of Musicians granted the Buffalo designation as Local #43. Prior to that affiliation, Buffalo musicians were

242

members of the National League of Musicians which was originally the Musician Protective Association Buffalo, NY #23. The office of the original association was at 551 Main Street. The union scale in the 1890s with the Musicians Protective Association was any hotel engagement up to two hours daily and terminating no later than 7:00 PM, the weekly pay was $9.00 per musician.

In 1922 The Buffalo Musicians Local was located at 2 Sycamore Street at the corner of Oak Street. This was a three-story building, with a clubhouse downstairs and offices with rehearsal halls on the second and third floor. Musicians would go to the union hall during breaks between their performances at downtown theaters. The union office then moved to 24 West Chippewa, to the Markeen Hotel on Main and Utica, 452 Franklin Street and eventually to their current offices at 374 Delaware Avenue.

During the late 20th century there were six union locals in the WNY area: Buffalo, Tonawanda, Niagara Falls, Lockport, East Aurora and Hamburg. Nearby unions were in Dunkirk, Batavia, Rochester and Niagara Falls, Ontario. If a musician played in the jurisdiction of another union local, they were required to pay travel dues to the union in which the performance was taking place. There was also a Colored Musicians Union in Buffalo. In 1969, due to integration ruling, the white local #43 and colored local #533 merged into Local #92, located in the 452 Franklin Street offices.

Pay scales for Buffalo area musicians were much different in the 1950s. In 1954 and 1957, Union Scale for a Class A engagement, large hotel or nightclub, was $4.00 per hour and for a Class B engagement, all other smaller clubs, $3.00 per hour. Musicians were paid for a minimum of three hours, earning $12.00 for a Class A or $9.00 for a Class B engagement. Any performance after three hours was considered overtime, for which the pay was $2.00 per half hour. On Saturday night, the scale was increased to minimum pay of $15.00 for a Class A club and $12.00 for a Class B club, with $2.50 per half hour overtime. These rates were for a one-night engagement. If a musician was working the same night per week for at least two weeks, it was considered a steady engagement and lower scale of $2.50 to $2.70 per hour applied, depending upon the class of the night club, with a guaranteed pay for four hours.

When recording artists performed in Buffalo, they did not always bring an entire band with them. They would often tour with their piano player, rhythm section, lead horn players and supply sheet music for the rest of the band. The concert promoter or the artists tour manager would contact the Musicians Union and local horn players would be contracted to play at the concert. This manner of touring applied to artists like Elvis Presley, Frank Sinatra and many of the other vocalists that were backed by a big band on their recordings. Due to this practice, there was a select group of Buffalo musicians that performed concerts at The Aud, Sheas or Kleinhans for these stars. The practice continues today, with area musicians being hired to be part of the band during shows at concert halls, theaters and clubs.

MUSIC PUBLICATIONS

Over the years Buffalo had several music and entertainment magazines or newspapers. The college papers led the way, along with the *Buffalo Evening News*, but several independently published papers were available across WNY. These were the days before the internet, so readers obtained information about local and national music by picking up a paper.

BUFFALO JAZZ REPORT was a monthly/bi-monthly magazine, covering the local, regional and national jazz scene. It was published and edited by Bill Wahl, from March 1974 through December 1978. The paper was distributed in Buffalo, Toronto, Rochester, Syracuse, St. Catharines, Hamilton, Niagara Falls, Lockport and Jamestown. He started a Cleveland, Ohio edition, moved to Ohio, and continued to publish it as *The Jazz & Blues Report*. In 2007, Wahl relocated to San Diego, where he continues to publish a digital version of *The Jazz & Blues Report*. Online, digitized copies of all the Buffalo issues are available at the Digital Collections of the University at Buffalo libraries.

AREA COLLEGES have also published newspapers that provided music and entertainment information. Buffalo State produced The Record, while the University at Buffalo had The Spectrum. UB published two issues of Punk, a magazine, associated with The Spectrum. It was the work of professor Jeff Nesin and featured the writing of two students, Billy Altman and Joe Fernbacher, who would write for Cream magazine later in the '70s. From 1972-1974 Shakin' Street Gazette was published at Buffalo State by Gary Sperrazza, future owner of Apollo Records. In 1976 Buffalo State printed an entertainment paper called Foxtrot. The editors were Bernard Kugel and Philip Bashe, art director was Andrew Elias and many of the staff members were later contributors at Rockers.

BUFFALO EVENING NEWS began publication in 1880, founded by Edward H. Butler. It listed entertainment events and reviews of concerts, live theater and public interest stories on area performers. In the late 1960s, in the back of the TV Topics section, the *Buffalo Evening News* began *Weekend Pause,* where they featured articles on area bands. To attract a younger readership, the News reporters lobbied for this section to be a separate insert. After Warren Buffett purchased the newspaper, Gusto premiered in June 1977. Writers for *Weekend Pause* and *Gusto* included Dale Anderson, Jeff Simon, Herman Trotter, Jim Bisco, Patricia Donovan, Sharon Fawley, Anthony Violante, Jim Santella, Mary Kunz, Tim Switala, and Toni Ruberto. For many years *Gusto* was an insert to the Friday *Buffalo Evening News* edition. Recently, it became an insert to the Thursday edition with the current music editor being Jeff Miers.

ROCKERS was published by Scott Thomas Flynn, who also owned Play It Again Sam record store. The paper started in the summer of 1979 and was edited by Andrew Elias and Geoff Copp. *Rockers* was the voice of original music bands in the city of Buffalo, but also reported on the suburban cover bands. It featured articles by area writers Tony Billoni, Brian Dickman, Dave Meinzer, Bill Poczik, Steve Ralbowsky, Scott Schiller and Tim Switala.

In June 1980, after *Rockers* ceased publication, *New Beat Magazine* premiered. The staff of this paper included many of the former editors and contributors of *Rockers*, but it was only published for a few months.

MAGAZINE MAGAZINE was a short-lived publication published in 1980 that focused on local music. The staff included Craig T. Kosinski (Publisher-Editor), Bruce Pilato (Rock Music Editor), James Drummond (Jazz Music Editor) and business manager Jim Taylor.

BUFFALO BACKSTAGE MAGAZINE published its first issue in April 1981 as an 8 ½ x 11, fold-over offset print magazine. The covers were drawn by artist Chas Gillan, who also illustrated some ads for Mighty Taco. Published and edited by Rick Falkowski and Marsha Falkowski, it later evolved into a newsprint monthly. *Buffalo Backstage* featured articles and reviews by a variety of contributors, including Bob Ballentine, Dick Bauerle, Barry & Gerry Cannizzaro, Kenny Page Czworka, Tracey DeGeorge, Andy Scott Dikens, Bob Evans (Southern Tier), Metal Mike Faley, Harold Goldman, Kevin Hosey, Rose Ann Jankowiak, Jeff Johns, Dave Johnson, Craig Kosinski, JR Letterman, Anne Leighton, Mark Marcaccio, Pat Maren, Kim Markel, Paul Marko, Dawn Mullen, Ken Rybarczyk, Mindy Schlez, Susan Slack, Snoop & Scoop, and Ted Alan Sterns. *Buffalo Backstage* focused on covering local bands and was known for its extensive monthly music calendar, listed alphabetically by the entertainer, not the venue. The Buffalo Music Awards and Buffalo Music Hall of Fame were started by the publishers of this magazine. It discontinued in 1984, but later printed several special edition local music yearbooks, in conjunction with the Buffalo Music Awards – which was initially called the Buffalo Backstage Music Awards. The last *Buffalo Backstage Yearbook* associated with the publication ceased with the tenth anniversary issue in 1990.

NIGHT-LIFE MAGAZINE is a weekly paper that has been in publication since the early 1980's. Published by Ed Honeck, in the early 1980s it merged with *Street Beat* which was published by Dave Koester, who remains associated with *Night-life*. They present the Night-Life Music and Club Awards.

ARTVOICE MAGAZINE has been in publication since 1990. It was previously called *Arts in Buffalo*, which publisher Jamie Moses premiered in the 1980s. They produced the annual Arties, an awards show for the local theater community now sponsored by WNED/WBFO. *Artvoice* still presents The Best of Buffalo competition, which covers a variety of categories including music. In 2014, some members of the staff launched a competing alternative newspaper called *The Public*.

FREETIME MAGAZINE began publishing a bi-weekly Rochester paper in 1977. They covered the Rochester arts and entertainment scene. For several years in the 1980s they printed a Buffalo edition of the paper, managed by Dan Deutsch. After nearly 40 years of support for the community, they ceased print publication in February 2016, another casualty of the digital assault on print media.

12

1960s & 1970s CLUBS

During the 1940s and 1950s there were taverns in all parts of the city that had live music. Most of these were small bars, where there was a piano on a little stage in the back room. You could often walk from one club to another and see different bands. Most of the music clubs at that time were in the city of Buffalo because over two thirds of the population of Erie County resided within the city limits.

Starting in the mid-1960s the first wave of the baby boom generation began to reach the legal drinking age of 18. The population of Buffalo was already starting to decrease but the number of young adults that were going to bars increased, due to the baby boom after WWII. The population shift to the suburbs was starting and more clubs were being opened in the suburbs. By 1980, only one third of the population of Erie County resided within the city limits.

The first rock clubs that opened in Buffalo during the early to mid-1960s, featured bands that played the R&B style of rock referred to as The Buffalo Sound. As the '60s progressed the bands playing the style of music referred to as The Teen Club Bands started getting older and these bands also started playing at these bars. In the early 1970s the two styles of bands from the 1960s started to merge, with bands now separated into the rock or commercial rock styles.

Two of the first rock music clubs in Buffalo were LuLu Bells and The Hideaway. LuLu Bells was on Humboldt and Best and was owned by Bud and Pauline Tower, where Stan & the Ravens and The Vibratos played early dates. The Hideaway was on East Delevan across the street from the Chevy Plant, which was also an early home for Stan & the Ravens. Other early clubs were The Pastime on Grant Street, Ivanhoe on Forest Avenue, Shells Lounge on Broadway, Silhouette on Fillmore & East

Delevan and The Colony on Hertel. Rock bands also played the front bar at the Town Casino but it was the other club owned by Harry Altman that got the reputation as the main rock club of the mid-1960s.

The Inferno was in the Glen Park Casino, located in the Glen Park amusement park on Main Street in Williamsville. The Glen Casino was the summer home for the shows that were presented at The Town Casino during the 1940s and 1950s. In the 1960s, it became a rock club on a scale that was never seen before in WNY. There were two stages, one in the main room and another in the smaller bar, which was totally separated from the larger room. Top local bands like The Vibratos, Stan & the Ravens and The Rising Sons performed there along with early touring rock recording groups like the Bob Seger System, The Boxtops, Union Gap, Sly & the Family Stone, Wilson Pickett, Paul Butterfield, Jackie Wilson and Rare Earth. The band that was considered the house band and drew the biggest crowds was Wilmer & the Dukes. They were from Central New York but played in Buffalo so often that they were considered a Buffalo band. The band had the hit single "Gimme One More Chance" and played soul-oriented versions of rock songs, with one their most popular cover songs being "Reach Out." Wilmer played at the Inferno every Wednesday night. The club was usually sold out and lines to get in extended over the bridge on Glen Avenue. On September 23, 1968 a fire totally destroyed the Inferno. Barbara St. Clair and the Pin-Kooshins played there the night before the fire and were scheduled for the next night, so they left their equipment at the club. Everything was destroyed in the fire and a benefit, to assist in replacing their musical equipment, was held for them a couple weeks later at The Mug on Hertel Avenue.

In addition to The Mug, which was in Kings Plaza, there were two other popular rock clubs on Hertel – The Bona Vista and Aliotta's. The Bona Vista at 1504 Hertel Avenue was the home club for Ash & Campagna. For four years, they played every Monday on acoustic night and with their band on Tuesdays. When Ash & Campagna moved to Los Angeles, Dillon & Brady continued the Monday acoustic nights, performing with Pollo Milligan. The Shakin Smith Blues band played at the club every Wednesday. Weekends would feature bands like The Houserockers, Shakin Smith Blues Band, Argyle Street Band, Posse, Billy Bright Band and more. The club was managed by Frank Sperrazza and began featuring bands in 1971, continuing music until it closed in late 1970s. It was later the location of The Shadow Lounge.

Aliotta's was at 1180 Hertel Avenue, which was home to area bands like Raven and Flash, but also featured touring national groups. On April 29, 1970 The Allman Brothers, who were into the fifth month of touring to support their debut album, were scheduled to play two shows. The crowd was smaller than anticipated and club owner Angelo Aliotta claimed the band started late, so he only offered them $500 instead of the contracted $1,000. An argument resulted in the Allman Brother's road manager Twiggs Lyndon fatally stabbing Mr. Aliotta. Lyndon hired the Buffalo law firm of John Condon, who claimed a defense of "temporary insanity induced by the burnout of a rock 'n' roll lifestyle." Twiggs got a sentence of 18 months (time served) and six months in a psych ward. Greg Allman retained Condon's law firm for his legal representation and returned to the Buffalo, on a regular basis, to consult with his attorney. For that reason, Allman and Cher, his wife at that time, were often seen at Buffalo area nightclubs. After Aliotta's closed it became Hotel California and in 1990 the Comedy Trap, comedy nightclub.

During the 1970s, one of the most popular clubs was the Belle Starr in Colden. It was located up a winding country road in a large barn style building, which was once part of a riding stable. In addition to area blues, R&B and country rock bands, the club featured many touring national acts like BB King, Muddy Waters and .38 Special. The club was destroyed by a fire on August 20, 1980. Ironically the sign on the top of the building, which was not burned in the fire, read "This Place Cooks."

After the Belle Starr burned down, many of the bands that performed there began appearing at The Longbranch Saloon on Jamison Road in Elma. This club was also one of the first county bars in WNY to feature a mechanical bull, made popular in the 1980 movie *Urban Cowboy*. After presenting concerts by groups like The Winters Brothers, Black Oak Arkansas and Stevie Ray Vaughan, The Longbranch, which was also an old wooden building, was closed by a devastating fire.

During the summer time in the '60s and early '70s both the R&B and teen club style bands were performing at the lake clubs in Angola. Lerczak's and Bill Millers were so crowded every weekend that the clubs and surrounding businesses would charge cars to park in their lots. Next door to these two clubs was the Southshore and just around the corner was Bruce Jarvis'. Down the street was the Du Drop Inn, The Big Ten Club and Point Breeze Hotel. It was a tradition to stop at Connor's Restaurant for a hot dog or ice cream before going to the clubs. The location of Lerczak's and Miller's is now Mickey Rats Beach Club. This site has been sold and it is uncertain if the location will remain a beach party bar in the future.

THE LATE 1960s & 1970s ROCK & COMMERCIAL ROCK CLUBS

In the city of Buffalo during the late 1960s, new clubs were opening and older ones were being reinvented, with bands playing at venues previously mentioned and at clubs like the Beef & Ale on Main Street, the Beef & Ale on Grant Street, the C Lounge on Dewey and smaller bars in all neighborhoods. One intriguing club was Chopin Singing Society on the East Side, where polka bands were featured in the back room and rock bands at the front bar. With the population movement to the suburbs, live music clubs started opening across Western New York. Popular places for music included, the Wa-Ha-Kie on River Road in North Tonawanda, Old Barn in East Aurora, Idlehour in Grand Island, Edgewater in Grand Island, Astro-Lite in Lackawanna, Mil-Sher Lanes in Tonawanda, Club Lakewood in Youngstown, The Ranch House in Chaffee, The Caboose in Fredonia, Trivit House on Genesee Street, Melanie's on Main Street, Keystone 90s in Lockport and smaller bars with names that faded in memory.

In the late 1960s and early 1970s, the largest club in WNY was Gilligan's at 2525 Walden Avenue in Cheektowaga. After the Inferno in Williamsville burned down, former owners and manager, the Goldstein family with Kevin Elliot, opened Gilligan's in March of 1969. Many of the bands that played at the Inferno moved to Gilligan's, including Wilmer & the Dukes. One difference is Gilligan's was larger and since more baby boomers were of drinking age, the crowds were bigger.

The club had a stage which was large enough to accommodate two bands, that alternated sets. One band was usually from out of town and the other from the Buffalo area. Most of the out of town bands performed for a full week, with different area groups working each night. Gilligan's featured many national acts including shows by Three Dog Night, Alice Cooper, Fleetwood Mac, Chicago Transit Authority, Blood Sweat & Tears, Joe Cocker and The Crazy World of Arthur Brown. The Club remained open until 1972 and it was later reopened by Kevin Elliott as the "new" Inferno, which became Uncle Sam's.

Another large 1970s club was The Yellow Monkey, which was located at Main & Transit also owned by the Goldstein family and Kevin Elliott. This club was previously called The Mauna Kai and later became the first location of The Salty Dog. Some other clubs included, as you were traveling to Keystone 90s in Lockport, you passed The Attic. The Poor House East, which later became Patrick Henry's, was just east of Main & Transit. The Crossbow was on Sheridan Drive and the Scene was on Niagara Falls Blvd. When you drove down the Youngman toward the numerous Niagara Falls clubs, He & She's, formerly Mother Tuckers, was at the Colvin exit. Back in Cheektowaga/Depew, The Zodiac was in the former Fridays & Saturdays and Bowinkles, which was originally called Big Bertha's, was at Broadway & Transit. The Hideaway was in Darien Center and The Primitive Scene was in Batavia. In the southtowns there was the Barrelhead, Poor House West, Fast Annie's, The Southtowner and The Purple Moose. If you drove further south, during the summer the lake clubs were still operating in Angola and Sunset Bay, with The Surf Club in Bemus Point featuring music on Lake Chautauqua.

As the 1970s progressed, more of the baby boom generation continued to reach the legal drinking age. The population pool frequenting area bars just kept growing. There were so many people going out, it seemed like all you had to do is get a liquor license, hire a band and when you opened the doors people would be lined up to come in.

With so many places to go, an unwritten hierarchy of clubs developed. There were A, B and C levels of clubs in both the rock and commercial rock (top 40) markets. Plus, there was still the corner drinking bars and party bars (that did not have live music), where people often met to start out the night and make their plans about what bands they wanted to see and what music clubs they wanted to visit.

Initially there was little or no difference between the rock and commercial rock bands, but they became more divergent over time and often progressed in different directions based upon the clubs where they were performing. What differentiated rock clubs and bands from commercial rock lounges and bands? As their names indicated, rock bands played rock, while commercial rock bands played more dance oriented music. The age groups were basically the same, but the rock bars may have been a little younger and may have had more underage people with false sheriff cards or altered licenses. The most obvious difference, other than the music, was the way that the bands and the people dressed. At the rock clubs, the attire was usually jeans and t-shirts. The commercial rock clubs often had a dress code of no regular jeans (designer jeans were OK) and shirts with collars. The bands were also louder in the rock clubs, with stacks of Marshall Amps, a huge PA system and roadies to move their equipment. The commercial bands had professional stage and PA equipment, but performed at a lower volume and were often dressed in matching outfits. The commercial rock bands usually featured a female vocalist and the larger groups included a horn section. Another difference is at rock clubs the bands often only played one night, but at the commercial rock clubs a band was hired to play perform for the entire week.

The A level clubs, were larger, had big sound system and lights. They had music 4 -7 nights a week and usually charged a cover. This is where you would find large crowds, even during the week. Newer groups or bands moving up in the hierarchy would often first have to play several week night dates at these clubs before they were given the opportunity to play on the weekend.

B Level clubs were smaller and had music 2 or 3 nights a week. It was not unusual for A bands to play at these clubs and some of the B clubs were former A clubs that fell out of favor with the crowds, either because of their location or because new larger clubs opened.

C Level clubs were more of the neighborhood bar type locations. This is where most bands started out. Sometimes these clubs would hire an A band for a special event or to bring in new customers.

The clubs at which a band played determined the hierarchy of the band. Bands know where they ranked in the hierarchy and strived to move up to the next level. There were no arguments about who were the most popular bands, you just had to look at where they played and how many nights a week they worked. Most bands would play their first dates in the C clubs, move into the B clubs and especially for rock bands, play some week night dates at an A club before finally getting weekends engagements at the top A clubs.

When a band was established at the A level clubs, if they broke up they would often form a new group with members of other former A level bands. The best musicians tended to merge together or interchange in bands. A musician could progress up the levels with their band, but the easiest way was to audition for a vacancy when someone left an A level band. The bands and club owners all talked to each other. When a good new musician started performing at clubs, the word spread quickly and he would start receiving offers to join better known bands. Some of the better players stayed with their B or C level bands because the comradery with his band mates was more important than being in one of the most popular bands.

The largest commercial rock club in the WNY market was the Executive at 4243 Genesee Street across from the Buffalo International Airport. It was opened by James Cosentino in 1961. Originally the lounge featured light dinner music but as time progressed they began featuring Top 40 show bands. During the 1970s The Executive garnered the reputation as the nightclub to see the foremost commercial rock bands in the region. The Dining Room presented national and local show bands, while the Cabaret Lounge featured dance bands. With the groups alternating sets, you could always make The Executive your last stop of an evening out, as the bands would still be performing after music ended for the night at most other nightclubs. Some of the featured bands at The Executive included, The Scinta Brothers, Lance Diamond, Big Wheelie, Junction West and National Trust. Natalie Cole performed at the nightclub with a Top 40 rock band before embarking on her recording career.

SHOWBOAT NIGHTCLUB ON THE NIAGARA RIVER – FOOT OF HERTEL AVENUE
Photo: Courtesy Paul Preston

The Showboat was one of the most unique clubs in Buffalo. It was a Mississippi River style paddlewheel boat, that was converted to a restaurant and was moored at the foot of Hertel Avenue on the Niagara River. It was opened in 1970 by John Piazza, who had it towed to Buffalo. The ship featured entertainment on four levels; the basement engine room, 1st floor dining room, 2nd floor dining room and a banquet area on the roof. Piazza sponsored the steel band Caribbean Extravaganza, from Trinidad & Tobago, to move to Buffalo and perform on the ship. Caribbean

Extravaganza usually played on the roof and after moving to Buffalo, the band traveled the world on USO and private tours. The Bar-Room Buzzards performed on the ship during the entire four years it was open, playing all floors, especially the Engine Room. John Valby was a regular performer on the Showboat, along with small Top 40 Dance bands. Hundreds of people would pack the ship, to enjoy the dinners they served and the four floors of entertainment. Eventually the ship started to take on water, but did not sink because the water was not very deep where it was docked on the river. The costs of operating the Showboat caused the third owner to file bankruptcy and the ship was sold to another city.

Some of the other Top 40 clubs included Jerry Korabs on Sheridan, which was also known as Magoos and the Yellow Balloon. The Spectrum in North Buffalo. The Three Coins on Niagara Falls Blvd. featured touring and area bands, along with other clubs on the boulevard like The Holiday Inn, Canterbury, Scene, Crossbow and Mean Guys East. Eduardo's on Bailey and The Landmark, in the former Sloan Lanes, also featured touring acts. Other clubs in the Cheektowaga area included The Poets Lounge in the Airport Holiday Inn, Passport Europe on Union, The Town & Country, Rogues II, Four Stallions, Port Shark, Sheraton Lounge and Sestak & McGuire's. In Williamsville Page One was on Main Street, Suburban House on Main and Schony's was in the Evans Plaza. In the Southtowns, Jacobi's was on Abbott Road and the McKinley Park Inn in Blasdell.

DISCOS

Many Top 40 bands played some disco material during their shows, but it was the disc jockeys who ushered in the disco era. It was the loud pulsating music and light shows that defined disco music. Everyone was dressed to kill and took to the dancefloor attempting to imitate the routines of *Saturday Night Fever*.

FRIDAYS AND SATURDAYS advertised itself as the first disco club in Western New York which was located at 207 Youngs Road in Cheektowaga, behind the airport. It opened in 1971 and featured an 82-foot stained glass bar, the largest Electrophonic lit dance floor in Western New York, along with slides and film that were projected on multiple TV sets before the advent of videos. This later became the location of the rock clubs Septembers, Sinbad's and Blind Melons.

CLUB 747 was inside a Boeing 747 jetliner, located next to the Executive Entertainment Complex across the street from The Greater Buffalo International Airport. It opened in 1975 and was the inspiration for a string of discotheques in other cities. Patrons purchased a "boarding pass" as admission to the club. The dress code barred street wear such as sneakers, jeans and sweatshirts. The DJs included Shane Brother Shane, Super Shannon and Dr. John Bisci who played the dance tunes. The TV show *Disco Step-by-Step*, hosted by Marty Angelo, was filmed at Club 747. The show was aired initially on local access Cable TV but due to its success, it was moved to Channel 4 and weatherman Kevin O'Connell joined as co-host.

MULLIGAN'S CAFE AND NIGHTCLUB on Hertel Avenue was a hotspot where many celebrities hung out and where the patrons dressed like they were going to Studio 54 in New York City. The back room often featured live music but the front room was the area where you had the opportunity to possibility rub elbows with OJ Simpson, Rick James or members of the Buffalo Bills and Buffalo Sabres.

UNCLE SAM'S at 2525 Walden Avenue was known as a club with live music, in its previous incarnations as Gilligan's and The Inferno. When it opened as Uncle Sam's the club became a disco, complete with a lighted dancefloor and space for over 1,000 dancers. It was not until the disco trend started to phase out, later in the 1970s, that Uncle Sam's returned to featuring live bands.

Other disco era clubs included the Charter House on Transit Road, near the Thruway exit, which catered to a more adult disco crowd. The Elmwood Village was located above Casa di Pizza on Elmwood and advertised itself as the club where "you had to go up to get down." Many of the Top 40 live music clubs featured disc jockey's and disco music between the bands sets. Some of these clubs included Korab's, Schony's, Jim Kelly's, The Three Coins, The McKinley Park Inn, The Marriott Inn, The Sheraton Inn and Poets Lounge.

THE WORLDS LARGEST DISCO premier was held in 1979. The Buffalo Convention Center was transformed into a 64,000-square foot disco, with a

30,000-watt sound system and a $25,000 light show designed by Litelab from Angola NY; Litelab created the bar scene lighting in the *Saturday Night Fever* movie. "Captain Disco" Buffalo's Charles Anzalone was one of the featured DJs, Gloria Gaynor was at the event to sing her hit "I Will Survive" and The Trammps were on hand to play "Disco Inferno." The estimated crowd of 13,000 in attendance was confirmed by *The Guinness Book of World Records* as the largest disco crowd of all time. In 1994, on the 15th anniversary of the original event, The World's Largest Disco returned with costumes and hairstyles transporting the attendees back to the 1970s. The event continues, annually during Thanksgiving Weekend, at the Convention Center. It now provides an advertised 500,000-watts of sound and lights, is one of the world's largest retro-dance parties and the proceeds benefit Camp Good Days and Special Times.

DINNER CLUBS AND ENTERTAINERS

During the 1960s and 1970s the rock and commercial rock clubs were filled with the under 30 crowd. However, there were dinner clubs, supper clubs or cocktail lounges, that catered to clientele over 30. The bands performing at these clubs played light jazz, standards and very light rock material. Many of the schooled musicians played in these groups which often consisted of piano, bass and drums, with a male or female vocalist. Some groups added a guitarist or sax player and sometimes the keyboardist played the bass parts or the guitarist switched between guitar or bass, depending upon the song. One constant is the groups were laid back and more background, than foreground entertainment.

COINCIDENTALS
Photo: Courtesy Pete Haskell

THE COINCIDENTALS were one of the first successful lounge bands. They started playing in 1961 at LuLu Bells on Best & Humboldt. The original group included Peter Haskell (bass), Ed Blodgett (guitar), Sally Huffer (piano) and Phil Kordos (drums). Sally was a Sophie Tucker style singer who later played the Borsch

Belt Circuit in the Catskills and eventually in the Caribbean. Other members of the band were Joe Ferrara (drums), Lee Carroll (guitar) and Nick Salamone (sax). The Coincidentals are often recalled as the version in this photo, which included twin sisters Sandy and Dee Ann Baret (vocals), and played six nights a week on a regular basis at Joe Martino's Page One on Main Street in Williamsville.

Some of the other popular lounge groups included: Lou Powers Quartet with Marilyn Mann, Al Vino & Friends, Small Society, Gus Broncato Quartet, Lenny Mann Quartet, Stardust Quartet, Charlie Briggs Quartet, Beau Hannon & the Mint Juleps, Tony Dee, Al Dilivio, Frankie Manne, Crosswinds with Carol Craig, Great Day, Manhattans with Arlene Banan and New Era (Chuck Roast Jack O Lantern Show).

Many lounge clubs offered music two to six nights a week in Western New York. Some started out as a lounge club and later became commercial rock rooms. Others retained and expanded upon more up-scale cocktail lounge atmosphere. Some of the establishments that started out as lounge clubs were: David's Table, Victor Hugo's Wine Cellar, Park Lane, Gabriel's Gate, Manny's, George's Table, Cloister, Jack's Cellar, Sebastian's, Shayleen's, Hourglass, Romanello's Roseland, Roundtable, Royal Pheasant, 31 Club, Candlelight, Friar's Table, Executive Lounge, Town & Country, Zodiac, Little White House, Red Carpet, Colonial Inn, Mauna Kai, Big Apple, Orchard Down's, Saratoga, Regency Motor Inn, Grandmother's Closet, Scotch & Sirloin, Red Lobster, Three Coins, Canterbury, Safari Room, Bedell's, Daffodils, Best Western (Niagara Falls) and John's Flaming Hearth (Niagara Falls).

In addition to lounge bands, solo piano players or piano trios were also popular in the dinner clubs.

JACKIE JACKO. When he was 12 years old John Giaccio started playing piano at taverns on Hertel Avenue. Before forming his duo, he had a 10-piece orchestra. By the early 1950's he adopted the stage name Jackie Jacko and with Joe Peters on drums, they performed at The Statler Hotel and Town Casino. After recording a few albums, they left Buffalo to headline at Birdland in New York City, worked on the Caribbean island of Aruba and played at The Sahara in Las Vegas for five years. Upon returning to Buffalo in 1972 he started a long-term engagement at The Cloister on Delaware Avenue. Jackie had a distinctive style that entertained

JACKIE JACKO & JOE PETERS
Photo: Courtesy Howard Goldman

generations of fans and he had the ability to remember the name of almost everyone that came to see him perform. Jacko probably knew every song in The Great American Songbook, which consists of the popular songs and jazz standards of the early 20th century. For example, one-night songwriter Ray Evans came unannounced to one of Jackie's club dates and Jacko played an entire set of Evans compositions. After the death of his partner Joe Peters, Jackie retired from his regular performances at E.B. Greens in the Hyatt in 2016.

GUY BOLERI was a piano player/vocalist at area lounge clubs. An Art Education graduate from Buffalo State, while still in school, Guy started playing at The Black Magic at Delaware near Virginia. This club preceded the rowhouse basement bar that became Manny's Supper Club, operated by Norm and Rosemary Besso, who previously ran the 132 Club at Oak and Genesee. Boleri then worked at Esmonds Supper Club at Wherle and Union in Williamsville. In the early 1960s, he moved to Los Angeles, where he obtained work as pianist and vocalist at various supper clubs. Guy eventually secured the position playing piano at Martoni's in Beverly Hills. This was the dinner club where everyone from the Los Angeles music industry hung out. On a typical evening, Frank Sinatra and the members of the Rat Pack would be seated at one table, while executives from Warner Brothers Records would be entertaining at another. When the music industry changed and rock 'n' roll began to replace the standards, Boleri moved back to Buffalo, playing solo dates at various lounges. He had a long-term engagement with his trio, which included Joey Giambra, on trumpet and vocals, at The Saratoga Restaurant on Delaware near Kenmore. Boleri has also performed for special lounge music events at Buffalo State's Burchfield Penny Art Center and The Buffalo History Museum.

ANNE FADALE. In 1944, Anne Hudec graduated from SUNY Fredonia with a degree in music education. She taught in the Lackawanna schools for a year and realized it was music performance, not education, that would be her career. She became a professional piano player and entertained Western New York audiences for the next five decades.

She was hired for the house piano player position at WBEN, performing on both radio and television programs. On WBEN's *Uncle Jerry's Club* she was known as the piano player Aunt Annie. Fadale was also the piano player that accompanied many of the vocalists who appeared on local television shows, including the early telethons.

Fadale often worked as a solo pianist, but is remembered for her work with piano trios. For many years that trio was Anne Fadale on piano, her son Bud on bass and her son Charlie on drums. One of Anne's regular engagements in the 1980s was at E.B. Green's. She was also an in demand accompanist for jazz vocalists, during their Buffalo engagements.

In 1983 WBFO-FM aired a series of live jazz broadcasts from Select Sound Recording Studio, hosted by disc jockey John Hunt. The trio of Anne, Bud and Charlie Fadale performed several of these shows and the broadcasts were recorded. After Anne's death in 1990, her son released a three CD set of her jazz stylings.

NORM WULLEN was a solo piano player and organist who performed in Buffalo for 70 years. In 1916, when he was 12 years old he was playing on one of the old Crystal Beach Boats and working at Canadian dance halls. He joined the Musicians Union when he was 13 years of age. Wullen played for silent films and vaudeville at the early theaters like the Court Street, Hippodrome and Sheas Buffalo. In the 1920s, he was a contemporary of Harold Arlen, performing at many of the same restaurants on alternating dates. Starting in the 1930s he was on WBEN radio, playing duets with his brother Charles, and in the 1950s moved to WBEN-TV with singer Ruppel Lascelles and hostess May Jane Abeles. During the 1950s he was the in-house organist at Laube's Old Spain, on Main Street. When the Buffalo Sabres obtained the NHL franchise in 1970, he was hired as their organist, and continued to play at hockey games until 1985. Wullen performed at restaurants until he was in his late 80s and when he was approaching 100, he continued playing piano at area Senior Citizen Centers. Wallen passed away in 2004 a month before his 100th birthday. He lived a lifetime of performances, where he was heard playing at theaters or restaurants, on radio or television or at hockey games and other events.

13

THE 1970s

The 1970s were a very diverse time in Buffalo music. The bands referred to as The Buffalo Sound continued their R&B influenced music at clubs on Hertel, the West side, the Angola lake bars and the legendary Belle Starr in Colden. The teen club bands evolved into more rock oriented groups. Many new bars opened because baby boomers, who were born in the late 1940s and early 1960s, reached the legal drinking age of 18 years old.

Top 40 commercial rock bands performed a mix of the Buffalo sound and the 1960s music played at teen clubs. This created a style with a feel that was unique to Buffalo. These groups toured clubs across the eastern part of the country, from New England to Florida.

Country rock bands took country music to a new level, merging it with a Southern rock feel but traditional country bands still filled area bars. With the advent of disco, former clubs featuring live music now featured disc jockeys. However, there were so many people going to the clubs there were lines to enter discos as well as all styles of live music venues. One of the consequences of disco was the punk music backlash, bringing music back to the basics. In WNY, specifically in the Kenmore West high school area, original music bands were being formed. These bands played songs they wrote and their home base became McVans.

Even with all these options of music available and no matter what style of music a person preferred, most people in WNY would probably agree the most popular Buffalo area band was Talas.

TALAS

Talas was formed in 1971 by Dave Constantino and Billy Sheehan who had played together in the final version of the popular area teen club band The Tweeds. Their first drummer was Mike Piccolo, who had been the

TALAS AT KLEINHANS MUSIC HALL
Bill Sheehan, Paul Varga, Dave Constantino   Photo: Courtesy Dave Constantino

drummer and vocalist with The New Breed. One of their early jobs was at one of the first M&T Bank lunchtime concerts in downtown Buffalo. From the very beginning of Talas, they picked up where they left off and expanded upon the popularity of the Tweeds.

When Mike Piccolo left the band he was replaced by Rocco Oliveria from Olean, NY. Rocco's brother Danny joined the group, resulting in a dual drummer configuration. Danny also played guitar and sometimes joined Dave up front.

Paul Varga had been the original drummer with Dave Constantino in the Tweeds, going back to when they formed the group in 1965. Paul was playing with The Hard Times when Talas formed, but he left that group to become a member of Talas in 1973. When he returned to work with Dave and Bill, this formed the power trio that is most remembered as the band Talas. These were the days of He & She's in Tonawanda and Tuesday nights at The Barrelhead, where the band was so loud your hair would blow back just from the soundwaves.

Then for about a year in 1977 Bill left the band to play in Light Years, with drummer Ron Rocco. During that time Talas added Rochester bassist Dale Croston and guitarist Michael Marconi. Marconi had been a member of Alice Cooper's Billion Dollar Babies band and was a big song writing influence on Dave. In fact, Constantino wrote many of the songs on Talas' first album during this period.

When Sheehan returned to the band, in 1978 Talas released their self-titled first album, which included the hit regional single "See Saw."

The release of this album catapulted Talas from being a local club band to larger facilities and regional dates. They played a concert at Kleinhans Music Hall in 1979 and in 1980 they opened a 30-city national tour headlined by Van Halen. During one of their steady Monday night performances at the club Stage One, U2 opened the show as part of one of their first U.S. tours.

However, even when the "glam band" and "hair band" style grew in popularity during the early 1980s, for some reason that all elusive national contact evaded them. Sheehan took a leave of absence from Talas in 1982 to go on a European tour with the band UFO. When that record contract, which would elevate them from a regional to national act never materialized, Talas broke up.

Bill Sheehan retained the name and formed a 'new' Talas with Phil Naro (vocals), Mike Miller (drums) and Los Angeles based guitarist Mitch Perry, the group that released the album *Live Speed on Ice*. When Mitch Perry left he was replaced by Rochester guitarist Johnny Angel. That was the version of the band who opened the 1985/86 Yngwie Malmsteen's Rising Force tour. Another album called *Lights, Camera, Action* was planned but never released because Sheehan joined David Lee Roth's solo band with guitarist Steve Vai. Sheehan was later a member of Mr. Big (who recorded the #1 single "To Be with You"), Niacin and is now with Winery Dogs.

When Sheehan formed a later rendition of Talas, Dave and Paul returned to their roots, reforming the band The Tweeds with bass player Randy Satz, later being replaced by former Watchers bassist Alan Thompson. The Tweeds became so popular they had to schedule a day off months in advance so their booking agent, Starstruck Productions, would not fill that open Monday or Tuesday night. The Tweeds later became Shyboy, named after the Talas single, when former Fare Trade and Stryder member Mike Runo joined the group on bass. Dave now plays with The Dave Constantino Band and Paul is with ASP – The All-Star Project, a band consisting of several members of the Buffalo Music Hall of Fame.

Talas played a sold-out reunion concerts at Kleinhans in 1997 and 1998, a tour of Japan to support the release of the *If We Only Knew Then What We Know Now* live CD, an outdoor waterfront show in 2001 during the Buffalo Niagara Guitar Festival and a 2012 a reunion show at The Hard Rock Café in Niagara Falls with The Road and Fat Brat.

From 1978 to 1983, Talas released three albums *Talas, Sink Your Teeth into That* and *Live Speed on Ice*. They released three compilation or live albums between 1990 and 1998. A tribute to the popularity of the band Talas, in 1983 Bill, Dave and Paul were the first three people inducted into the Buffalo Music Hall of Fame. Their induction could also be considered the induction of the band Talas, but the first band formally inducted in the Buffalo Music Hall of Fame was The Tweeds in 1990.

WEEKEND

As covered in the '60s Teen Club Band section, the band Weekend was formed from the band Weekend Trip, after the short lived WET Road. They shortened their name to Weekend and began to play dates in January 1971. The members were Bob Culver (vocals), Ned Wood (keyboards), Denny Dunkowski (guitar), Rick Ryan (bass) and Tom Ryan (drums). This unit of five musicians remained together until 1978.

Their first job was a one-month engagement at The Gallery in Niagara Falls, where they performed four nights a week. That was followed by other club dates and many school dances. Being a group of younger musicians, whenever they had a night off they often went to Alliotas and The Bona Vista on Hertel, the Wa-Ha-Ki in North Tonawanda or the Niagara Falls bars to observe the bands and to learn from veteran performers like Stan Szelest, Gary Mallaber, Steve Nathan and Joe Scinta.

In June 1971 Weekend was one of the bands appearing at an outdoor Reservoir Park show in Niagara Falls. Many of the top bands in WNY were on the bill, with over 20,000 people in attendance. Their performance impressed WKBW program director Don Berns and arrangements were made for Weekend to record at Jerry Meyer's Act One recording studio with Rich Sargent and Ken Gorka producing the sessions, and engineered by Larry Rizutto, Larry Swist and Mick Gazauski. The song "Everyday" was released in July 1971 and became a regional hit. With airplay on the 50,000-watt WKBW, Weekend was heard along the Atlantic coast of the U.S.

A year later in 1972, Weekend recorded a demo of "Together" at A&R Recording Studio in NYC, where Paul McCartney had just completed his album titled *Ram*. That session was produced by Peter Schekeryk, husband of '60s recording artist Melanie. The band's management turned down Schekeryk's record offer and re-recorded "Together" at Act One in Buffalo. When it was released WKBWs Don

Berns played it nine or ten times in a row as a WKBW World Exclusive. The song charted regionally across the U.S. and in foreign countries. It would have reached the top of the WKBW charts,

WEEKEND
Tom Ryan, Rick Ryan, Bob Culver, Ned Wood, Denny Dunkowski
Photo Credit Jim Bush

but Paul McCartney's "Uncle Albert" from the *Ram* album held on to the number one spot. WKBW radio presented a contest called Champion/Challenger. "Together" won as the most requested song in the contest, topping hits by many major artists.

The song "Coming Home to Mrs. Jones Garden" was released in 1973 and getting airplay on WKBW helped Weekend obtain dates in New Jersey, Pennsylvania, Massachusetts, Florida, Ohio and Canada. When their album *Weekend at Last* (recorded at Act One and completed at Trackmaster on Seneca Street) was released in 1976, they continued their full schedule of out of town and local dates, appearing at clubs, high schools and colleges. They opened concerts at Sheas and The Century Theatre for Fleetwood Mac and Styx.

Weekend's success during the 1970s and their strong song writing, musicianship and harmonies were attracting attention across the East Coast. However, due to their popularity and the money they were making locally, they believed their agent wanted to keep them in the Buffalo market. Booking Weekend at clubs and schools in Western New York, helped the agency secure dates for other bands at those venues. On the verge of being signed as the first group on the Warner Brothers new label, Bearsville Records, Foghat was chosen over Weekend. Devastated, the band signed with new management. That agency did not have the contacts to keep them working on the road, so Weekend announced the breakup of the band in November 1978.

Twenty years later Ned, Bob, Tom and Rick got together to record a song. They enjoyed working together and decided to play a reunion show. When their original guitarist Denny Dunkowski was not able to play the reunion show, Niagara Falls guitarist Frank Grizanti joined them. They played two sold out shows in November 1998 at The Tralfamadore in

Buffalo and with the help of their original producer Rich Sargent they released *Weekend at Last* on CD, adding six new songs. Other reunion shows followed and in 2001 they released a live CD of these shows. The special shows continued until founding member Ned Wood was diagnosed with cancer and passed away in 2011 at only 57 years old. Weekend played a couple songs at benefit concerts in 2014 and 2015, with former Road keyboardist Ken Kaufman, but decided without Ned, the band Weekend would be permanently retired and remain a memory of the nostalgic days of the 1970s.

THE HARD TIMES – TOPAZ – EMERALD CITY

The beginning of The Hard Times goes back to 1966 when Dick Bauerle formed The Raves with fellow students at Benjamin Franklin Junior High School. Typical of teen club bands, they played at the Delaware and Boulevard Cave, Peppermint Stick, Strand Ballroom and at school, club or skating rink dances. They learned by watching the other bands while continuing to practice, play and rehearse. All vastly underage, they even played a bar gig in May 1967 at the Old Barn in East Aurora.

When he was a junior at Kenmore East, The Raves disbanded and Bauerle joined up with Jim Kam and Joe Pici, forming the Hard Times in May 1969. They performed often at The Funnel on Bailey, high school dances and numerous fraternity or sorority parties. Later in their senior year they started playing at area bars like Mil Sher, the former bowling alley at Military and Sheridan. This club had two stages and they often played opposite fellow Kenmore area band, Caesar & the Romans.

The Hard Times were forever evolving; alternating members as a 5, 6 or 7 piece band. Permanent members included guitarist Dick Bauerle (guitar), bassist Joe Pici (bass), keyboardist Sal Azzarelli (keyboards), and Jim Kam (drums), who later became the lead vocalist and front man. Considering themselves a pop rock band, they performed the most popular songs on the radio concentrating on vocal-oriented material. Heavy

THE HARD TIMES
Jim Cameron, Joe Pici, Jim Kam, Sal Azzarelli, Gary Dieboldt, Phil Drum, Dick Bauerle   Photo: Dick Bauerle

rock and/or obscure albums cuts were purposely left out of their repertoire. When the band members graduated from high school in 1970 they started playing the larger rock clubs like Gilligan's on Walden Avenue and the Attic, which was on Transit Road, near Keystone 90's, both of which featured two bands on separate stages. More personnel changes occurred in 1971.

In 1972 the band came into their own. Former Road drummer/vocalist Nick Distefano joined the band in February, being replaced a few months later by former Tweed's drummer/vocalist Paul Varga. They played all the top clubs like The Barrelhead, Crossbow, Surf Club and Orange Monkey. An indication of how much work was available for the top Buffalo rock bands in 1972 and 1973, they played over 330 dates each year.

It is very seldom that the same members remain together in a band due to changing musical tastes, new opportunities and personal circumstances which result in members leaving. Such was the case with The Hard Times. Sal Azzarelli left in the fall of 1973 and became a national B3 Hammond Organ technician, traveling the country servicing equipment for organists such as Jimmy Smith, Keith Emerson, Felix Cavaliere and Stevie Winwood. He was replaced by former New Breed keyboardist Wally Sirotich, who later worked with The Toler Brothers. Paul Varga left in February 1974 to join Talas and the group The Hard Times disbanded. Joe Pici joined United Sound, other touring Top 40 bands and eventually moved to Las Vegas where he ended up being Gene Simmons personal party deejay. The Hard Times reformed three months later in April 1974 as a three-piece unit with Bauerle, Kam and bassist Don Nuttle. The name was changed to Topaz a few months later, when Tim Hacker was added as keyboardist/vocalist. In 1975 Topaz was the first Buffalo band to be signed to Amherst Records, initially called Lu Ann Records. Then when the number of available dates for rock bands started to be reduced, due to the popularity of disc jockey's playing disco, Dick Bauerle decided it was time to take time off from performing to concentrate on his work at Select Sound Recording Studio.

From the ashes of one popular band, another popular group is often formed. In 1975 Jim Kam (now back on drums), Don Nuttle and Tim Hacker continued as the band Topaz with Gary Calvaneso (guitar) and former Road member Jerry Hudson (vocals). When Jerry decided to leave in 1976 they changed their name to Emerald City and added Phil Sims and

Frank Cascino. With this line up, they could cover all the popular music of the late '70s and early 80's. Both Sims and Casino played keyboards, giving them three keyboardists; and Sims also played trombone, while Cascino played sax.

In 1978, Emerald City created a unique arrangement of the Harold Arlen song "Over the Rainbow" which became the anthem for the band. Alan Parsons of the Alan Parsons Project saw the band performing at The Executive Lounge and told them he was impressed with their arrangement of the song. Shortly thereafter, Emerald City was approached by Gold Leaf Management who offered them a contact with RCA Records and a one-year concert tour opening for a major act. Due to personal commitments and ties to the WNY area, the band declined the contract.

Emerald City remained one of the most popular bands in WNY for almost a decade and won the Best Top 40 Band Award in the first three Buffalo Backstage Music Awards. After most of the original members left to work on other projects, they broke up in 1984. Ironically, the original Topaz (Bauerle, Kam, Nuttle and Hacker) reunited as the '60s band Pastime in 1985. That group, with various configurations and under different names continued until 1996, when Bauerle joined Joyryde. That was the end of a long musical line that began in a study hall at Kenmore East in 1969.

COCK ROBIN

The name Cock Robin comes from an old English nursery rhyme. "Who killed Rock Robin? I, said the sparrow, with my bow and arrow....". Some entertainment guides and newspapers purposely misspelled their name and some Catholic schools refused to hire them, due to the perceived sexual connotation. The band claimed that there was no ulterior meaning, but you must ask, why was their slogan "Rock with the Cock?" With this marketing concept, once you heard the name – you remembered it.

The origin of the band goes back to 1973. After playing at Dirty Dick's Bath'ouse for almost two years in a band called Court, with Victor Marwin (later of Rodan), guitarist Dave Bienik met bass player Steve Keenan, who was originally from Rochester. They decided to put a band together and answered a newspaper ad placed by vocalist Bill Shaver and keyboardist Jim Sommer, who had been working with the band Shadowfax. Mike Piccolo, the original drummer with Talas, was looking for a new group. They had a rehearsal and the five musicians clicked. Their first job of consequence was at Keystone 90's, when they were asked to fill in when a member of Weekend was ill and the band had to cancel. This was an interesting turn of events since Cock Robin filled in for Weekend and Mike Piccalo was formerly with Talas, it was a convergence of what many

COCK ROBIN
Don Peters, Bill Shaver, Peter Militello, Jim Sommer
Dave Dunkowski   Photo: Courtesy Peter Militello

followers of 1970s music consider the top three rock bands of the era.

Cock Robin classified themselves as a British rock band, that also covered many B side or album cuts, but they also played material by American rock groups, the song "White Punks on Dope" by The Tubes was their anthem. Throughout the entire career of Cock Robin, original material had always been a priority, with them performing as much as 25% original songs. Their first recording was a single "Very Fine", released by Amherst Records in 1974. They also recorded an album for Amherst Records at Trackmaster in Buffalo, completed in Nashville, and produced by Chip Hawkes from The Tremeloes, but it was never released.

In June 1975 Cock Robin became a full-time band, packing clubs in WNY, along with clubs west to Cleveland and east to Albany. It was in 1975 that Steve Keenan decided to move to Boston and was replaced by former Waverly Brothers bass player Dave Dunkowski. Additional changes occurred in 1977 when Dave Bienik and Mike Piccolo decided to relocate to Nashville and work with Chip Hawkes.

The 1977 changes resulted in the best remembered version of Cock Robin. Don Peters joined on guitar and Peter Militello, the former drummer with Windfall, joined the band. This was the group that played steady Tuesdays at Stage One and steady Wednesdays at The Barrelhead, playing 5 or 6 nights a week from 1977 through 1980. It was in 1979 that the biggest change happened with the band when lead singer Bill Shaver left the group, being replaced by Jim "Buzz" Rummings, who worked with Pete in Windfall. When Jim joined the group Cock Robin also added second guitarist Dick Grammatico, to cover the guitar parts that Shaver provided while with the group. Grammatico was from Rochester and is the brother of Foreigner's vocalist Lou Gramm. This version of the band celebrated New Year's Eve 1980/1 at The Barrelhead and they played their final show at The Sundown Saloon in Chaffee NY on January 3, 1981.

Cock Robin played many memorable shows, one being an outdoor show in the parking lot behind Knickerbockers on Walden Avenue. The bands set up on the roof of the club and the music carried to all the houses in this suburban Cheektowaga/Depew neighborhood. One of the first acts performing on the roof was Dr. Dirty – John Valby. His expletive lyrics were heard by people barbequing and children playing in backyards surrounding the parking lot. Complaints began to be called in to the police station and when the police arrived they discovered the club owner never obtained a permit for the concert and they shut it down. The only consolation for hauling all their PA speakers, the Hammond B3 organ, the Marshall amps and all their other equipment up to the roof, is they still got paid for the concert.

The final version of Cock Robin was formed in early 1981 and had a Buffalo and Rochester connection. Jim Sommer (keyboards), Don Peters (guitar) and Dave Dunkowski (bass) were from Buffalo. Dick Grammatico (guitar) from Rochester remained with the band, adding Rochester's Jim Patrick (drums) and Joe Pullara (vocals), who had a vocal style very much like Dick's brother Lou Gramm. They played dates in the Buffalo and Rochester areas, performing the last show of Cock Robin in August 1981 at Stage One.

There were revolving musician doors after Cock Robin, through which many individuals and band names seemed to pass. After Dave Bienik and Mike Piccolo left the group in 1977 they remained in Nashville, with Dave touring the southeast with The Legendary Panama Red and Lynxx. Mike changed his name to Mike James and started working as a singer/guitarist, which he still does in Southern Ontario. When Dave returned to Buffalo in 1979 he joined The Warlocks and then formed Dear Daddy with Cock Robin vocalist Bill Shaver and Weekend keyboardist Ned Wood. Dear Daddy was an all original band that opened several area concerts, including The Kinks at The Aud. In 1981 Bienik (who currently lives in Texas and returns to Buffalo during the summer to perform some acoustic dates) formed Daring Hearts with Dan Nowak from The Warlocks and Doug Fisher from The New Breed. That was followed by X-Dreams with Jim Sommer, guitarist Denny Dunkowski from Weekend, bass player Rich Farmer from Shiner and Rick Miller. Jim Sommer and Don Peters opened Loft Recording Studio and Don worked at U-Crest Music. When Cock Robin decided to have a reunion in October 2002, Jim, Don, Pete and Buzz were joined by former bassist Dave Dunkowski, who was later replaced by Rich Farmer, who worked with Jim in X-Dreams. After Buzz decided to leave the band he was replaced by former Warlock's vocalist Steve MacDonald. The revolving door of Cock Robin is more like a musical circle and they continue to perform periodic shows in the WNY area.

JAMBO – SKY - RUFUS – PEACE BRIDGE – FAT BRAT – CHEEKS

These bands cover the time from approximately 1970 until the present. They shared many of the same members, while some of the groups were formed with musicians from other bands. However, they were all interrelated.

Jambo was a popular rock band from 1973 through 1978. The band having its roots in a band called Rufus that played in the early 1970s rock bars. That group included Tom Makar (guitar), Don Eckel (guitar), Russ Costello (keyboards), Ted Seramac (bass) and Rich Vanni (drums). Initially the members of Jambo were

RUFUS
Top Row: Ted Seramac, Don Eckel
Bottom Row: Rich Vanni, Russ Costello, Tom Makar
Photo: Courtesy Don Eckel

Tom Makar (guitar), Russ Costello (keyboards), Frank Pusateri (bass), Rick Collins (drums) and Rufus Campbell (guitar). When Rick Collins left he was replaced by Bob Makar on drums and Ken Wilczak replaced Rufus Campbell on guitar.

Jambo usually played six nights a week, including steady nights performing every Sunday at The Barrelhead in West Seneca, every Monday at Super Bar, Lake near Abbott, and every Wednesday for "Drink and Drown" night at After Dark in Lockport. During their career, they released one 45-record although they had 32 original songs in their repertoire. Many nights they played one full set of originals and at some

JAMBO
Top Row: Bob Makar, Frank Pusateri
Bottom Row: Ken Wilczak, Tom Makar
Photo: Courtesy Frank Pusateri

out-of-town dates they played just their own material. They came close to signing with A&M Records but could not come to contract terms.

When Jambo disbanded in 1978, Ken Wilczak and Frank Pusateri joined the band Sky. Formed in 1977 the members were David Keith (guitar/vocals), Sherry Hackett on (keyboards /vocals), Al Hury (drums), Doug Townsend (bass) and Bob Tomaskovich (guitar) who were replaced by Pusateri and Wilczak. As Sky, they continued steady Sunday nights at The Barrelhead where they performed a lot of original material. They broke up in April 1981 when David and Sherry decided to move to NYC, where they worked for the next 14 years. David and Sherry were very successful as studio musicians and recorded many national commercials, for clients like Coca Cola, Crest and Burger King. One of the most recognizable commercials was the "Meow Mix Theme" song. Sherry was one of the vocalist in the Meow, Meow, Meow, Meow chorus. David and Sherry moved back to Buffalo and still perform dates as Sky.

Formed in 1972, Peace Bridge was the name of the group that preceded Sky. They were originally a folk-rock band with Sherry Hackett (vocals/keyboards), Don Hackett (guitar), Al Rizzatto (drums) and Sandy

SKY
Ken Wilczak, David Keith, Sherry Hackett
Al Hury, Frank Pusateri
Photo: Courtesy Sherry Hackett

Shire (bass), who was the brother of movie score composer David Shire. When Bob Radel (formerly with The Rogues) joined as bass player they began playing pop-rock songs at Holiday Inns, Mean Guys East and Sestak & Maguire's. Drummers that also worked with the band were Jim Palys and Al Hury. The band switched to a rock format when David Keith became the guitarist in 1975, changing their style to the extent that resulted in the name change from Peace Bridge to Sky in 1977.

In 1981 Ken Wilczak formed Fat Brat and continued the steady Sundays at The Barrelhead. With his various bands, Ken performed at the club almost every Sunday for over nine years, ending the steady night when the Barrelhead closed. Fat Brat members were Ken Wilczak (guitar), Bob Maggio (vocals), Greg Priester (bass), Paul Rizzo (keyboards) and Pat Brayman (drums). After taking some time off from performing, Wilczak joined the Shakin' Smith Blues Band. Wilzak reformed Fat Brat and they continue to play area club dates. Ken's brother Bob Wilczak, formerly of Actor, has been with the Fat Brat for over a decade.

After leaving Jambo Tom Makar (guitar) formed the band Cheeks with Gary Wagner (guitar), Randy Preksta (bass) and Howard Wilson (drums). With the assistance of Jerry Meyers and David Kahn they secured a deal with Capital Records to record the soundtrack for the *Mad* magazine movie *Up the Academy* from which the single "Boney Maroney" was released. Their song "Coquette" was also included on the soundtrack. They played local clubs dates performing "new wave" covers and originals, and signed a demo deal with Elektra Records. However, before Elektra decided on releasing the record, the band broke up.

This version of Cheeks should not be confused with another band called Cheeks that performed in the 1970s, which was a commercial rock band and included Tom Bucur (guitar), Jay Dzina (guitar), Bob Ambrusko (bass), Terrie George (vocals) Dave Cress (vocals) and Tim Barraclough (drums).

Tom Makar has been active in the theater community for over 25 years, as a sound designer, composer, actor and director for over 300 local theater productions in WNY. Tom also plays solo dates, doing much of the material he performed with Rufus, Jambo and Cheeks, and is billed as "The Wild One."

After Sky, Frank Pusateri played in Lions prior to forming Only Humen, with previous Two Hills member Ray Wood (guitar) and Bruce Morgan (drums). Many musicians have been members of Only Humen including Paul Varga (Talas), Jerry Augustyniak (10,000 Maniacs) and blues recording artist Mick Hayes. Primarily a cover band, Only Humen has released three albums of original material. Various musicians performed dates with Only Humen including Ken Wilczak (who worked with Frank in Jambo and Sky) and Al Hury (who was also in Sky). It is almost a continuous circle as Frank also currently plays some acoustic dates with David Keith and Sherry Hackett, who were the founders of Sky.

ROCK BANDS AT McVANS

During the 1930s through the 1960s McVans was known for its floor shows and in 1963 it was purchased by former Buffalo mayor Steven Pankow, who operated it as a supper club. As the 1960s progressed the dining area on the second floor was closed and on the first-floor McVans started featuring rock bands. They presented rock groups including Bill Haley & the Comets, Little Anthony & the Imperials, The Inkspots and Ruby & the Romantics. One of the highlights was when Joey Dee & the Starlighters played at the club for a week in November 1965. The guitarist was a then unknown left-handed guitarist named Jimi Hendrix. In addition to the week at McVans, Joey Dee & the Starlighters, with Hendrix, played at Club Commodore, during one of their Sunday afternoon teen shows.

McVans in the late 1960s, may have appeared at times to be somewhat dysfunctional. Management seemed to be unsure on what direction they wanted to take. It offered a combination of everything and anything they could do to attract an audience. There could be a rock band playing on stage, then the MC would entertain with a burlesque comedy routine and then introduce the floor show acts. When the show was over, the rock band would go back on stage for another set. While these shows were being presented in the show room, in the front bar there were go-go dancers.

This changed in the 1970s when the club started featuring cover rock bands on a regular basis. Several groups performed at McVans during the cover-rock band era, but the act predominantly associated with this era of the club was Rasputin.

RASPUTIN

In 1971 Rasputin was formed by John Schmidt (guitar), Dave Yax (guitar), Chris Enlert (bass), Paul Steinbruckner (drums), Pete Morath (vocals) and Ted Pawlak (keyboards). The band rehearsed in the building next to the grocery store that Ted's parents operated at the corner of Young and

Alexander Street in the city of Tonawanda. They began playing heavy rock but after a year Ted left the band, with Johnny Gonzales replacing Enlert and becoming the new bass player.

Johnny Gonzales had previously played at McVans so they went to talk to Joe Terrose about Rasputin playing there. In the early 1970s, McVans was experimenting with country bands but Joe was open to the offer and Rasputin became the house band. After working at the club for approximately a year, all the members remained except they were now on their fourth bass player; Ralph Phillips, who had replaced Victor Marwin, who was later with Rodan. With the club having two stages, Rasputin often played five nights a week, with various other bands performing on the second stage. Rasputin played a variety of hard rock material and their roadie, Mike Faley (now manager for Billy Sheehan and executive with Metal Blade Records) suggested adding some songs by the band Kiss. In 1975, they decided to apply Kiss makeup for the McVans Halloween costume party. It was such a big success that McVans owner Joe Terrose offered to give them a raise and pay for the make-up if they continued performing the Kiss show.

By forming the Kiss show, Rasputin became one of the first tribute bands in the Buffalo area and one of the first Kiss tribute bands in the country. Rasputin was different from other Kiss tribute bands because they also played songs by other artists like Alice Cooper, David Bowie and Ted Nugent. They also differed from other Kiss bands because they had five members. This required guitarist Dave Yax to create his own character, opting for a court jester look, which matched his jovial personality. Vocalist Pete Morath grew tired of wearing make-up, even applying it over his full beard, so he left the band. He was replaced by Doug Kalosza, who in addition to being a member of Rasputin attended UB Dental School, later opening a dental office in Buffalo.

Along with being the house band at McVans, Rasputin played at most of the other large Buffalo rock rooms and on weekends

RASPUTIN
Top: Dave Yax, Doug Kalosza, Ralph Phillips
Middle: Paul Steinbruckner , Bottom: John Schmidt
Photo Credit Mary Carner

often traveled to other parts of New York, Pennsylvania, and Ohio. The original Rasputin broke up and a new four-piece version was formed by John Schmidt (guitar), Doug Kalosza (vocals/guitar), Art Wall (bass) and Mic Walker (drums). They played their final date as Rasputin in 1979 and formed a new group called Video, sans the make-up. Currently John and Mic play in NY2LA, John and Paul play together in Stonehouse and Art Wall was later a member of the band Actor. Both Doug Kalosza and Dave Yak have passed away.

RODAN

Rodan was formed in 1974 by Ted Reinhardt (drums) and Bruce Brucato (guitar) who had played together in groups since they were teens and were in the band Opus One with Billy Sheehan. They wanted to perform progressive rock material by bands on the line of Genesis, King Crimson, Emerson Lake & Palmer, Gentle Giant, and mixing in some Mahavishnu Orchestra jazz fusion. Bassist Bill Ludwig started rehearsing with them, word of the project spread and keyboardist Rick McGirr joined the band. Rick worked at Transcontinent Records on Harlem Road with vocalist Victor Marwin, who had left Rasputin because he wanted to play progressive material. In addition to playing flute, Victor played electric violin, taking classical lessons since 4th Grade, which allowed Rodan to cover a wider range of progressive rock material.

In addition to steady Sunday nights at McVans, for an extended period Rodan played every Monday at the Barrelhead and every Wednesday at He & She's, along with dates at other area rock clubs. This

RODAN
Bruce Brucato, Ted Reinhardt, Rick McGirr
Bill Ludwig, Tom Reinhardt
Photo: Courtesy Rick McGirr

was during the time of disco music and Rodan drew an audience that did not come to dance; they came to enjoy the bands flawless reproduction of the complex progressive material. On the day that Genesis was playing at The Aud, they conducted a live radio interview at the WPHD radio studio.

Rick McGirr heard the interview with Tony Banks and Mike Rutherford and went to the station. He told Genesis about his band Rodan and invited them to come to McVans after their concert. Genesis came to McVans and it was reported that this was one of the first times they had the opportunity to watch a band play their material. All the Genesis members except Bill Bruford came to the club and during the break they joined Rodan backstage. Phil Collins was full of compliments for drummer Ted Reinhardt and it is rumored he asked Ted if he wanted to join Genesis, as their touring drummer. Bruford, who was the touring drummer on the tour and did not come to see Rodan at McVans, was replaced by Chester Thompson for subsequent tours. When Genesis came to the club, they were obviously in the market for a new touring drummer.

The backstage dressing room area of McVans has many stories to tell, most of which cannot be told. However, one that can be shared is the night when Rodan and Black Sheep were playing a night together at the club and of course sharing the dressing room. Victor Marwin threw a cigarette butt towards the garbage can but an ash flew off and landed in Lou Gramm's hair. His hair started smoldering, Lou poured cup of water on it, smiled, got up and went on stage to play Black Sheep's next set.

Rodan never recorded their originals at a recording studio but bootleg live copies may be found on You Tube and Facebook. Andy Gerovac, the owner of Mighty Taco, sponsored a 90-minute live concert that was broadcast on WBUF-FM. This was the closest they came to professionally recording their material. After Victor Marwin left Rodan in 1976, he was replaced as vocalist by Tom Reinhardt. They opened a concert at the Century Theater for Gentle Giant, playing a set of all original material. It was a three-band concert and they had so little room to set up, they were almost falling off the front of the stage.

This version of Rodan continued until the fall of 1977. For a short time in the early '80s Rodan coexisted with Gamalon. That group included all the members of Gamalon except George Puleo. Victor Marwin was one of the first electric violin players in Buffalo. That sound had an influence on Gamalon because they later added Geoff Perry on electric violin.

PEGASUS. The first job that Pegasus played at McVans was opening for Rodan on a Sunday night in October 1975. The previous night Pegasus played a live concert of their rock opera *Alienation* on the UB radio station WBUF. At this show Pegasus played all original progressive music, while

Rodan played progressive covers. Later Pegasus started performing a live rendition of Genesis *Lamb Lies Down on Broadway* album, presenting it in concert at The Granada Theatre. However, the performance by Pegasus, opening for Rodan, introduced original material and paved the way for original music bands performing at McVans. *More information on Pegasus and original music at McVans will follow in chapter 14 on the Original Music Scene in Buffalo.*

BLACK SHEEP was a Rochester based band that played at McVans on a regular basis in the mid-1970s. The group featured lead vocalist Lou Grammitico, (later known as Lou Gramm – the vocalist for Foreigner) who had been playing drums and singing in the band Poor Heart. When Black Sheep initially formed, Lou was playing drums but when his grammar school friend Ron Rocco (later with Terra Nova, Light Years, and Cheater) joined the group, Gramm became the lead vocalist. Another future member of Cheater, Don Mancuso, was the guitarist with the band. They released two albums on Capital Records but disbanded just before Gramm was asked to join Foreigner in 1976. Other than a date at the Belle Starr and one other small club in the WNY area, McVans was the only Buffalo club where Black Sheep performed.

PAROUSIA was a progressive rock show group that included a lot of original material in their sets, making them a combination cover and original band. During the early 1980s the band included Pat Connolly (vocals/flute), Kim Watts (vocals), Garth Huels (guitar), Barry Cannizzaro

Barry Cannizzaro, Bob Lowden,
Pat Connolly, Gerry Cannizarrio,
Garth Huels, Kim Watts, Eric Scheda
Photo Credit Marsha Falkowski

(guitar), Eric Scheda (keyboards), Bob Lowden (bass) and Gerry Cannizzaro (drums). Parousia was formed in 1975 by the Cannizzaro brothers and Pat Connolly, with Steve Soos (keyboards) and Rich Kollmar (keyboards). Dave Matlbie (keyboards) was a member in 1978 and 1979. Several of the members of Parousia relocated to Los Angeles in 1986, where they performed and released video and audio compositions, along with presenting some Los Angeles shows with the former Buffalo art/rock band Green Jello.

CROSSROADS was based out of the Tonawanda area and the members were Tom Geraci (guitar/vocals), Frank Iacono (guitar), Dan Patrick (bass) and Kevin Henneman (drums). *Information on them in 1980s as The Beez.*

SHEFFIELD was together from 1974-1978 and was a regular performer at McVans. The band featured vocalist Bob Maggio, later with Tyrant and Fat Brat, and bass player Joey Cristofanilli, who was later a member of California metal band Ratt and toured with LA based bands Rough Cutt and Jagwire. Cristofanilli is now a member of Silver Xtream and Radio 9, with his wife Patsy Silver, who during the 1980s was a back-up vocalist for Lou Rawls and a lead vocalist with the Las Vegas based band, International Fox, who toured nationally and recorded in Nashville.

DIAMOND AXE was a Jimi Hendrix tribute band that often played at McVans. Formed in 1976, the members of Diamond Axe were John Cameron (guitar), Doug Cerrone (bass) and Gary Stegmaier (drums). In 1980, they changed the name of the group to The John Cameron Band with John Cameron

DIAMOND AXE
John Cameron, Gary Stegmaier, Doug Cerrone
Photo: Courtesy John Cameron

(guitar), Brad Towart (guitar), Joe Martucci (bass) and Gary Stegmaier (drums), which was a hard rock cover band. Doug Cerrone was later a member of the band Benhatzel.

GRIM REAPER was a McVans band that concentrated on Alice Cooper material. Kevin Kalicki (drums) and his brother Alan Kalicki (guitar) then formed the band Aunt Helen, which gravitated more towards playing original songs. Bob "Bob the Record Guy" Paxon was also a guitarist in Grim Reaper. Kevin and Alan were later the founders of the original group The Toys.

McVans closed in late 1984 and the building was demolished in 1986. When driving from downtown Buffalo on the I-190, along the Niagara River, look to the right when passing the foot of Hertel Avenue. The former Wilson Farms, now a 7-11 Store, is where McVans once stood.

OTHER 1970s BANDS

IAN QUAIL

In 1970 Ian Quail started out as a Tonawanda based high school band called Rush. The nucleus of the band was Stuart Ziff (guitar), James Flynn (keyboards/vocals), Tom Tripi (bass), Craig Korka (vocals), Ted Reinhardt (drums) and three keyboardists – Chet Folger, Carl Bundshu and John Jarvis, who played in the group at different times. They eventually expanded to a ten-piece horn group in early 1971. In 1972, they discharged the horn section and became a six-piece rock cover group. The band broke up but reformed in the summer of 1973 to compose and perform their own material. Their all original sets were not well received at the rock clubs where they had regularly been performing.

In the summer of 1974 Stuart met with John Sansone of JR Productions, who told him about an agent he knew out of Atlanta who was looking for rock cover bands to tour the Midwest and the South. They decided to go on the road and began rehearsing cover material. However, before their first dates in the fall of 1974 a situation arose concerning their name. The Toronto-based band Rush released their debut album "Rush" in 1974 and were starting a United States tour, so the band changed their name to Ian Quail. The reformed group included Ziff, Flynn, Tripi, Korka, Folger with Howard Wilson (drums) and Duane Skibinski (sax/vocals).

Successfully touring the college town club circuit in the Midwest, they became known for their funky, danceable, vocal-oriented, rock music. They would travel for eight weeks, play in each town for one or two weeks, and then return to Buffalo for three or four weeks. When back in Buffalo, their home base was the Poor House West, where they began filling the club to capacity. As the years progressed, they would remain in Buffalo for longer periods of time, performing at

IAN QUAIL
Back Row: George Doty, Dewey Campbell, Chet Folger, Tom Trippi Front Row: James Flynn, Stuart Ziff
Photo: Courtesy James Flynn

all the top rock clubs, before going back on the road.

Ian Quail had the distinction of being one of the few rock-oriented bands that toured outside of Buffalo on a regular basis. Ziff, Flynn, Tripi and Folger were together, with various other band members for over five years but in 1979 decided it was time to go in different directions. Stuart Ziff moved to NYC to work as a sideman and session musician before becoming a member of the band War in 2002, a group he still tours with. The other members played in Buffalo area bands, with James Flynn, Duane Skibinski and Howard Wilson now performing with The Informers.

TERRA NOVA – LIGHT YEARS started out as a band called Targa which was based out of Rochester. The band changed their name to Light Years and developed a Buffalo connection when they added Billy Sheehan as their bass player. Whenever they were booked in Rochester, it was considered drummer Ron Rocco's band and when they played in Buffalo, it was looked upon as Billy Sheehan's band. After Sheehan left to rejoin Talas, they changed their name to Terra Nova. Their manager, Jim Taylor, booked them in both Buffalo and Rochester on a regular basis. At one point in the late 1970s their schedule was every Sunday at Parliament Lounge in Rochester, every Tuesday at The Salty Dog on Main & Transit, every Wednesday at The Penny Arcade in Rochester and every Thursday at After Dark in Lockport. Weekends were at various clubs across the state, working at least six nights a week. After Terra Nova broke up Rocco joined the band Cheater.

NIGHT SHIFT was not a regular headlining band at the larger clubs in Buffalo, but they performed some dates with bands that were later very successful. On New Year's Eve 1976/7 they shared the billing at Pease Air Force Base in Portsmouth, New Hampshire with a band that was playing their first job. They called themselves The Cars. In November 1978, they were offered a Wednesday booking at Patrick Henry's (later Stage One) because a band from England needed a routing date in Buffalo and did not have their own PA system. No one was familiar with the band because they just released their first album. According to Night Shift vocalist Tom Gariano, there were less than 10 people at the club and he thinks that band was only paid $250. That band was The Police and Miles Copeland was their soundman. Night Shift played the Point After, in North Tonawanda, on a regular basis. Their booking agency asked if a band from Detroit could share a Friday night with them. That touring band was too much of a new wave/punk band so they did not go over that well at the Point After, which was more a harder rock bar. That band was The Romantics. In 1979 Night Shift did a six-week tour of New England posing as The Kingsmen, playing "Louie Louie" and other songs that The Kingsmen recorded. In 1980 Night Shift moved to Milwaukee, where they played clubs in the Midwest and were managed by the same agency that managed Cheap Trick, opening several concerts for them. Tom Gariano returned to Buffalo and was the lead vocalist with Looker and Broken Silence in the 1980s. He is currently the vocalist for A-List.

ASG – The Alyn Syms Groups was formed by former Rick James guitarist Al Szymanski. It was an original band that differed from the McVans/Continental original bands by being a suburban, rather than a city band. They started out by playing their original music at the small suburban rock bars and worked their way up to the larger rock clubs. In 1979, they released an EP "You Can't Keep a Good Band Down" and in 1981 the album *The Offering*. ASG headlined concerts at Sheas Buffalo and Melody Fair. Members included Alyn Syms (guitar), Peter Davis (vocals), Eric Boyd (guitar), Tom Marvich (bass) and Michael Simonson & Lenny "Potts" Potwora (drums & percussion).

LITTLE TROLLS were formed in 1974 by brothers Guy Nichols (bass) and Calvin Nichols (guitar), along with drummer Pete Gomez. They were known for their crazy antics as well as for their music. Guy or Calvin would often play their guitars, with wireless connections, walking on the bar, pouring shots into the open mouths of eager fans. Since the group was based in Batavia, they played both the Buffalo and Rochester markets. Guy Nichols also worked as a guitar technician for touring national acts, currently works in concert production management and is a member of the band Hit N Run. Calvin Nichols still performs in The Trolls and bills the group as an "American Biker Band".

OPUS 1
Photo Credit Robert Raithel

OPUS 1 was a Kenmore East area high school band in 1971. The band included several musicians that became prominent in the area music scene or became music teachers at area schools. Opus 1 included Billy Sheehan, Jim Elmore, Ted Reinhardt, Bruce Brucato, Bill Nice, Chet Folger, Ron Mendola, Dick Fron, Mike Migliori and Jim Board.

FARE TRADE was formed in 1968 by Mike Runo (guitar) and Mark Terreri (drums). David Lee Frost (bass) joined later in 1968, David Buxton (guitar) in 1969, John Kensinger (keyboards) in 1972 and John Pokrandt (guitar) in 1978. They were known for their Southern rock, with three guitarists and for their steady gigs every Tuesday for years at The Barrelhead. In 2010 all the original members reunited and they annually produce the Cabin Fever concert every February.

SWITCH was originally named Yesterday but decided to become a Beatles Tribute band. In 1976, they changed their name to Switch, playing exclusively Beatles material and changing their costumes every set. John Connelly (bass) was an original member and in 1980 the other members included Vic Paselle (guitar), Russ Muscato (guitar) and Steve Connelly (drums). John Connelly still performs The Beatles material in WNY with the band, The BBC.

THE KEYS were another one of the early Beatles tribute bands in Buffalo. They were led by Jo Perez (guitar) and often played at Graffiti's, the former Elmwood Village, above Casa di Pizza, on Elmwood Avenue. The other members were Manny Campos (guitar), Ron Greco (bass) and David Lloyd (drums). When not performing the Beatle Tribute Show, they were known as JPB (The Jo Perez Band) played rock-oriented material and released two singles.

Some other 1970s rock bands included: Sniper, Woodbridge, Arlanza, Iron Priest, All About, Pearl, Lamont, Choo Choo Mama, Looking Back, Tyrone, Foxy, Oasis, Pinnacle, Heaven, Jetz, Moxie, Monolith, Waverly Brothers, Gypsy, Denison Stars, Edge, Rotary Bed, Beowulf and Jonsie & the Cruisers.

Junction West and Jerry Hudson's band After Dark were two of the bands that consciously made the transition from the rock music scene to the commercial rock clubs. One of the other early bands making this transition was Friendship Train, which included former members of Caesar & the Romans.

JUNCTION WEST

Junction West is best remembered as a dance show band fronted by singers Harry Stewart and Joey James, but they started out as a straightforward rock group. The original Junction West was formed in the summer of 1970 by vocalists Paul Campanella, Frank Ricchiazzi and Peter Calieri, with Pete Viapiano (organ), Mike Kucharski (guitar), Joe Secchiarolli (bass) and Ron Sutliffe (drums). With the three vocalists, they put on a rock show similar to the early Three Dog Night.

In late 1969, the original rendition of the band came together in a round-about manner. Mike Kucharski from the Maryvale area and Pete Viapiano from the Cleve-Hill area, had played together in Cheektowaga bands throughout most of their teenage years. They were looking for serious musicians who were interested in putting together a top-flight band, so they answered a newspaper ad placed by a Buffalo band. The audition went well, but they were not totally satisfied with the lineup. Bass player Joe Secchiarolli, who also auditioned for the same group that day felt the same way and suggested the three of them form a band. Mike, Pete and Joe, teamed up with other North Buffalo musicians that Joe knew to start Soft Stone with Frank Palumbo (drums), Dave Dickash (vocals/drums) and Bob McManus (vocals).

After playing a few jobs in early 1970, by summer Frank, Dave and Bob decided they were still dissatisfied. Joe contacted musicians he knew from another group, Mixed Bag. Paul Campanella and Ron Sutliffe from that group joined Mike, Peter and Joe in Junction West, along with vocalists Peter Calieri and Frank Ricchiazzi. This completed the initial

JUNCTION WEST
Steve Camilleri, Kevin DellaPenta, Harry Stewart, Joey James
Andy Rapillo, Pete Holguin
Photo: Courtesy Joey James

formal rendition of Junction West and their first notoriety came from winning a Battle of Bands at St Barnabas in, Cheektowaga in November 1970. Soon they were playing the top area rock clubs like Keystone 90's, The

Mug, Crossbow, Yellow Monkey, Night Owl, The Zodiac, The Scene, Poor House and high school dances.

In mid-1971, Peter Calieri and Frank Ricchiazzi decided to pursue other interests and Joe heard that another area band, Amber Hill was breaking up. Rob Horvatits (vocals) and Mike Kobrin (guitar) from that group joined to form the second version of Junction West. This rendition started performing some mid-1960s soul, which included a very well received full set of Young Rascals covers.

Mike Kucharski and Peter Viapiano left Junction West in October 1972 to join After Dark a/k/a The Jerry Hudson Group, which was formed by former Road vocalist Jerry Hudson. Paul Campanella wanted to travel and left in late 1972 to join Freedom's Fare, a touring show band. This resulted in a third version of the band, when they added guitarist Dave Bellanca and changed to a harder rock repertoire. This group included Dave with Joe Secchiarolli, Robbie Horvatits, Mike Kobrin and drummer, Howard "Fleetwood" Wilson. Pete Viapiano rejoined on keyboards after he left After Dark.

In 1973 Junction West continued their evolution and ventured into the funk/disco movement, when they auditioned vocalists Harry Stewart and Joey James Gajewski. They were both still in high school and in their early teens had played together in the band First Light. Joey drove Harry's mother's car to the audition because Harry was not yet old enough to drive at night.

By 1974 the band consisted of Harry Stewart (vocals), Joey James (vocals), Mike Kobrin (guitar), Ronny Burrano (keyboards), Joe Vertino (bass), Mike Caputy (drums), Tom Adcock (trumpet) and Jimmy Witherspoon (sax). It was this rendition of Junction West that people remember for their funky dance style and as the band that played at their senior prom, formal, homecoming or high school dances in the mid-1970s.

In the late 1970s Junction West was performing at The Executive and The Buffalo Playboy Club on a regular basis and touring the East Coast all the way down to Key West. The touring continued throughout the early 1980s when Joey James decided to leave the music business. Since its inception, Junction West had about one hundred different members and by the mid-1980s the group included Harry Stewart (vocals), Bruce Brucato (guitar), Ricky Briggs (keyboards), Tom Reinhardt (bass) and Ted Reinhardt (drums). Bruce, Tom and Ted were also members of the jazz fusion band Gamalon.

Harry Stewart was affectionately called "Dancin' Harry" by his co-workers at UPS; the company where he worked after returning to Buffalo after years of touring with Junction West. Backed by The Hitmen Horns, he later produced special reunion shows, until his untimely death in November 2010.

AFTER DARK – JERRY HUDSON BAND

After Jerry Hudson left The Road, he formed a group called Jerry & the Hornets with some former members of the band Flash. They performed heavier rock material but only remained together for one gig at St. Joe's High School. His next group Alacazam, with former members of Parkside, played lighter rock material but only stayed together for a short period of time.

Jerry decided he wanted to pursue the lucrative commercial rock club market that was growing in popularity. He placed a newspaper ad which was answered by guitarist Mike Kucharski and keyboardist Peter Viapiano from Junction West. They were trying to soften the harder rock element of Junction West so Jerry's concept appealed to them. The group was completed by drummer Eric Malinowski, who had played with The Country Gentlemen and bassist Mike Romano, who was with in Alacazam.

AFTER DARK
Front: Jerry Hudson, Donna McDaniel
Back: Mike Romaro, Eric Malinowski
Mike Kucharski, Peter Viapiano
Photo: Courtesy Mike Kucharski

Their agent Fred Caserta, from Great Lake's Booking, suggested they add a female vocalist, which was preferred by commercial rock club owners at that time. He recommended Donna McDaniel, who had vocal and acting experience but had never sang in a rock group. She and Jerry's vocal styles complimented each other and after rehearsing for a couple of months and purchasing matching white suits, they premiered at The Crossbow on October 24, 1972. When Jerry's single "Gillian Frank", on Big Tree Records, started to receive airplay they changed their name to The Jerry Hudson Band.

That group was short lived and the members went their separate ways in February of 1973. Jerry reunited with former members of Flash and formed another version of The Jerry Hudson Band. Donna McDaniel and Mike Romano remained in that group, with the other members being: Jimmy Ralston (guitar), Jimmy Poulin (keyboards) and Richie Pidanick (drums). The group After Dark, in its short existence, was an example of rock musicians moving towards a commercial rock style and it marked the rock music debut for Donna McDaniel.

DONNA McDANIEL & WINDFALL was the evolution of the Jerry Hudson Band after Jerry left the group. The group which opened for KC & the Sunshine Band, at Kleinhans in 1977 was Donna McDaniel, Tyrone Williams, Lou Carfa, Richie Pidanick, Kevin DellaPenta and Jim Poulin. Donna recorded the Buffalo Sabres song "We're Gonna Win That Cup" and was a regular performer at The Executive Lounge. The members of a later version included: Donna McDaniel, Jim Poulin, Lou Carfa, Mark Dunham, Jim Rummings, Pete Militello and Jim Witherspoon. After moving to California, Donna became an actress in Hollywood films and a back-up singer for many recording acts. She accompanied Motley Crue, Billy Idol and Toto on world tours.

FRIENDSHIP TRAIN – BIG WHEELIE

In the fall of 1970, Fred Caserta of Great Lakes Booking Agency had the inspiration to form a unique commercial rock show band. Fred got the idea after he and Chuck Vicario went to see a band called Glass Bottle at Eduardo's on Bailey Ave. Utilizing a base of three members from the popular 1960s rock band Caesar & the Romans, Caserta placed an ad looking for female musicians and vocalists.

Soon Chuck Vicario (vocals), Dan Cook (guitar) and drummer Pat Perry (Pat was replaced by Guy French before they started playing out) were joined by Carol Jean Fremy (keyboards), Diana Fremy (bass), Judy Ware (vocals) and Linda Socie (vocals). Vicario, Cook and French had been with Caesar & the Romans; for the previous six years, sisters Carol Jean and Diana had worked together in The In Crowd, Storybook and Blues Forum, Judy was with the band Lemon Sky, and Linda performed with Ed Bentley's country recording band. Starting in mid-October, these

FRIENDSHIP TRAIN
Standing: Guy French, Carol Jean Fremy, Chuck
Vicario, Diana Fremy, Dan Cook
Seated: Judy Ware, Linda Socie
Photo: Courtesy Carol Jean Swist

seven members were rehearsing five or six nights a week in the Fremy sisters' town of Tonawanda living room. They were still rehearsing their show when they were displaced by the Fremy's Christmas tree. All the group members put in a lot of work on the project that would transform them from a rock band into a commercial rock show band.

Fred Caserta booked their first date at Russo's Trophy Room on South Park in January 1971, which was followed by eleven weeks at Williamsville's Page One on Main Street and a six-night-a-week extended engagement at The Scene (now the location of the Classics V Banquet Room) on Niagara Falls Blvd. This was in the days that bands still had long-term bookings at a club. The music of Friendship Train was arranged by Carol Jean and featured up to five-part harmonies. Their material included songs that featured vocals comparable to The Fifth Dimension, Three Dog Night, Sly & the Family Stone, Brasil '66, including a complex vocal arrangement of the Edwin Hawkins Singers "Oh, Happy Day".

Throughout 1971, Friendship Train was performing six nights a week, quickly becoming a top draw at commercial rock clubs across Western New York. To retain their popularity, they regularly learned new material, expanded their show, and continued rehearsing a few times a week. One slow weeknight, they played some oldies songs that they were working on, and soon people were requesting more '50s songs. It went over so well that Friendship Train rehearsed and added an entire set of oldies. The reception continued to grow after they added a costume change for their 1950s set. They created the name Big Wheelie & the Hubcaps as an alter ego, and soon the band played as Big Wheelie for two sets a night.

In October 1972, an oldies show was booked at Memorial Auditorium featuring The Chiffons, The Coasters, The Shirelles, Roy Orbison, Joey Dee, The Skyliners, Little Richard, and headlining Chuck Berry. At this concert, Chuck Berry pulled one of the typical Chuck Berry stunts before a show. He often asked for more money if he saw there was a good crowd, but at The Aud he walked out of the building because he did not have a private dressing room. That was quickly arranged, he came back in the building and performed his set. One of the opening bands dropped out and Big Wheelie was hired to fill in at the sold-out concert. The audience was so impressed with Big Wheelie's show that they returned for an encore; and after the concert, the show's promoters offered the group a spot on the road tour package. They accepted the offer, playing major concert halls across the country, ending the tour in Los Angeles.

Upon returning to Buffalo, in late 1972 Big Wheelie & the Hubcaps recorded a live album "Solid Grease" at The Three Coins on Niagara Falls Blvd in Tonawanda. This live recording session was engineered by Mike Gazauski and Larry Swist, who later formed a world-class studio design company, the studio monitor speaker firm Gazauski-Swist Audio Systems and collectively worked on many award-winning recording sessions (including Rochester's Chuck Mangione and Buffalo's own Spyro Gyra). It was at this recording that Carol Jean Fremy first met Larry Swist, about a year later becoming Carol Jean Swist. By the time of this recording, the personnel of the band solidified their classic line-up, with Angelo Monaco joining on bass. Some later members of the band included: Nick Veltri (bass), Sam Guarino (sax) and Nick Salamone (sax). The popularity of Big Wheelie was such that they set attendance records at area clubs. The band went back to Hollywood to play dates at top Los Angeles nightclubs and audition for the Tony Orlando television show. They were offered a contract to perform a five-minute segment for the next season of the television show, but the series was not renewed and Big Wheelie & the Hubcaps did not have the opportunity to become national television stars. After the death of Elvis Presley, Big Wheelie presented an Elvis Forever show at various area concert

BIG WHEELIE & THE HUBCAPS
Chuck Vicario, Diana Fremy, Dan Cook, Judy Ware, Guy French
Carol Jean Fremy, Linda Socie   Photo Credit Paul Daniel Petock

facilities. That series was promoted by Harvey Weinstein of Harvey & Corky.

Leaving Buffalo behind, Big Wheelie & the Hubcaps went on the road and played at clubs across the country. Chuck said members of Sha Na Na would show up in various cities when both groups were playing in the same town. He became acquainted with several members of Sha Na Na, but even though some promoters tried to book a date with both bands, they never played a show together. Big Wheelie decided to make Florida his new home, becoming the house band at a Sarasota club, and continued performing there for several years. Chuck met one of the producers of the *Sha Na Na* TV Show, who confided that he wished he had seen Big Wheelie & the Hubcaps before casting the TV show; because the concept of a mixed male and female band may have made a more interesting, longer lasting TV series. Still, for Wheelie and his colleagues, that national television exposure continued to evade the band.

Eventually, the band returned to Buffalo, and at one point in time, it seemed like Big Wheelie was the entertainment at every church lawn fete in Western New York. Now, over 50 years since he started performing, after playing shows across the country and releasing five albums, Big Wheelie is still periodically appearing at special concerts in WNY. He is no longer just Chuck Vicario, he is Da Wheel – Big Wheelie, while original founding members Diana Fremy and Dan Cook are now in Rock and Roll Heaven.

TOURING COMMERCIAL ROCK TOP 40 BANDS

In 1972 JR Productions was asked to book a band at Saints & Sinners, a large lounge club in Cleveland, so he suggested the band United Sound. The club owner was so impressed that he asked the owner of a popular Akron, Ohio club called Reds to come to see the band. Not only did Reds hire United Sound they inquired if JR Productions had other groups that could play in Ohio. During 1973 JR Productions obtained the booking contract for a chain of Holiday Inn's in Ohio and several clubs in Florida. By 1975 they were booking bands in 24 different states and groups from Western New York were performing at all these clubs. Fred Saia and Fred Caserta, from Great Lakes Booking Agency, primarily booked rock

UNITED SOUND
Photo: Courtesy Frank Sansone

bands but they also scheduled the commercial rock bands at The Executive. This provided them with a roster of Top 40 acts which they booked throughout the East Coast.

United Sound was not only the first area commercial rock show band to start performing out of the area, they were also the first racially integrated band to play at upscale suburban Western New York clubs. The band had four vocalists: Dottie Hooks, Larry Gilbert, Bill Miller and Ike Smith, who was later replaced by Johnny Martin. In addition to guitar, bass, keyboards, drums, they added a full horn section. United Sound was a show as well as a dance band and for ten years they performed at area clubs, along with touring the U.S., Canada and Europe. It was after they added the horn section that they obtained larger dates and it was the horn sections that identified the larger WNY touring commercial rock shows.

One of the best ways to highlight the touring commercial rock show bands from WNY is to list the bands that had horn sections. They were the larger bands and they played the larger clubs. Due to the efforts of JR Productions and Great Lakes Booking, commercial rock touring show bands were one of the main exports from WNY during the 1970s. These were bands that performed Top 40 shows and played at clubs along the East Coast from New England to Florida and west to the Mississippi River. If you went to a hotel or club that featured Top 40 touring bands in this half of the country, there was a good chance the band was from Buffalo or at least included musicians from Buffalo or was scheduled by a booking agency from Buffalo.

From the beginning of the jazz days, the "Queen City" always had many proficient horn players. During the big band era, when bands performed in the city, they often left with a new member from the WNY area. Buffalo got the reputation as one of the places where you could find quality musicians. In rock and commercial rock bands, the names of these horn players were often overlooked. However, these were the members of the band that possibly had a college degree in music and they were often the music teachers at area schools.

In the appendix, there is a listing of Buffalo bands that had horn sections. Bob Meiers, who established the Hitmen Horns in the early '90s, with musicians he worked with during the '70s, assisted in compiling this comprehensive listing. See Appendix B.

Another important element of the touring Top 40 band was the inclusion of a female vocalist. During the '60s there were very few bands with a female vocalist, but with the advent of commercial rock dance and show groups, the female vocalist became the focal point of many bands. Following are some of the female vocalists from the Buffalo area and the groups they worked with. This identifies more of the Top 40 Commercial Rock bands from Buffalo. Most of the groups mentioned are touring bands, but some primarily performed in the WNY market.

Cindy Reinhardt was the vocalist with Reasons, Pure Pleasure, The Headliners, Windsong, Splash, Hernandez and Destiny…Dee Ann DiMeo was with Freefall, London Fog, Trick, The Move and NRG…Carol Blenker sang with Fantasy, Visions and National Trust… Cheryl Baer was with Raintree, Fantasy, Body Heat and Shinin' Star…Kathi Miller was with Eclipse, The Joel Dane Show, Headliners, Visons, Second Wind and Junction West…Debbie Schebel was with Transition, Shayde, Freeway, Ike Smith & Free Spirit and Night Magic…Suzi Rose performed in road groups in Pittsburgh and other cities before relocating to Buffalo to work with Obsession and 20/20.

Following are some of the Top 40 commercial rock bands that toured the East Coast, Canada, nationally and at times toured overseas. Some bands that primarily played in Buffalo are also included in the listing. Groups that started out as rock bands like Junctions West, Windfall and Friendship Train, which evolved into Big Wheelie, were covered earlier in this chapter.

NATIONAL TRUST was formed by Sam Guarino in 1969 and played some of their first dates at McVans. They initially had a different name for the band but since no one could remember it, took the name National Trust from a line in "Happiness is a Warm Gun" on the Beatles *White* album. They started doing their Sammy Slicker & the Black Jacks 1950s show at The Kings Inn in Angola during 1971. During this time, National Trust often also played at Bill Millers on the Lake and The Telemark in Ellicottville. From 1973-1975 Sam Guarino was a member of Big Wheelie's band and in 1975 he reformed National Trust as a Top 40 touring show band. Their regular clubs in the Buffalo area were The Three Coins, Landmark and Executive. In addition to touring the U.S. they had many dates in Quebec and Ontario, Canada. Over the years over 100 musicians have been members of the band and the personnel in this late 70's photo was a group that worked together for an extended period.

NATIONAL TRUST
Seated Sam Guarino, Carol Blenker
Standing Steve Way, Al Albano
Joe Grisanti, Dan Hull
Photo: Courtesy Sam Guarino

Other members of National Trust included Paul Weitz (guitar), Rick Johnston (guitar) and Pete O'Donnell (drums). In the later '80s Sam formed a smaller group for area club dates, which continues to perform, and with Nick Veltri he currently presents several R&B Revue, an all-star band of almost 20 members, special events annually.

HEADIN' ON was a three-piece show group that performed at all the top area clubs and lounges from 1971 to 1984. These were the times when area musicians could make a living playing 5 to 6 nights a week at area clubs and the nights when many musicians congregated at Holiday Showcase on Union for breakfast after their shows. The band began at The Tack Room on Walden in Cheektowaga, worked three or four nights a week at The Lockport Sheraton for 5 years (1974-8) and started the Bong Show at the Three Coins with MC Tony Oddie. Due to the amount of work they had in WNY, Headin' On did not travel but they played one summer on the strip in Las Vegas, at the same club with The Osmonds. The Headin' On show included all styles of music, costumes with sequins, Don Lorentz with seven keyboards, Tom Lorentz with 8 or 9 stringed instruments and Ernie (Grzankowski) Grant surrounded by drums and percussion instruments. After the band broke up Tom Lorentz became a member of the Beatles tribute band Switch and Don Lorentz later joined The Boys of Summer.

THE BETTER WAY
Dominic Mitro, Bob Ambrusko, Jim Hanusin,
Donna Pecoraro, Pete Zito, Dick Rey
Photo: Courtesy Bob Ambrusko

BETTER WAY. Formed in 1968, Better Way was one of the early Top 40 Commercial Rock Bands. The band was started in Niagara Falls and played Holidays Inn's in Massachusetts almost more often than they appeared in Buffalo. They were regular performers during the early commercial rock days at The Executive and Three Coins, and they were known for their vocal arrangements. The members were Donna (Rose) Pecoraro (vocals), Bob Ambrusko (bass), Jim Hanusin (guitar), Pete Zito (organ), Dominic Mitro (piano) and Rich Rey (drums). They broke up in 1972 but 45 years later, Donna and Bob still perform together in bands at area clubs.

FOUR UM released the album *Just Us* in 1972. It was released on the Buffalo label Libra 7 Records and was engineered by Wes Owen who previously worked with John Lennon. The members of Four Um were Diane Taber (vocals), Frank Campanella (keyboards) and Dennis Schooley (guitar) and Buddy Hinds (drums). They changed their name to Forum and released a live CD, which was recorded in 1973 and included bass player Al Zielinski. The CD *Smile Live* was recorded at the Statler Lounge in Buffalo and Speakeasy in Niagara Falls, and included vocalist Linda Campanella. Drummer Buddy Hinds was on the road from 1971 to 1988, performing across the U.S., on cruise ships and in Central America.

ISAAC was one of Lance Diamond's early bands. There were several different versions of this band, which in 1975, in addition to Lance, featured female vocalist Many Jane Burruano with Guy French, Rick Guadajna, Tom Burruano, Sam Barruano Glen Thomas and Frank Marini.

Some of the other Top 40 commercial bands in WNY included Raintree, a mid-70's touring group with members Greg Janus, John Boyana, Bob Bumker and Butch Kania...The Lonely Souls, who became Chenango, included keyboardist John Mancuso who later owned The Shadow Lounge on Hertel and Macaroons on Dick Road & George Urban in Cheektowaga...Hernandez with the the Hernandez brothers...The Party Time Band included Marsha Falkowski (vocals), Rick Falkowski (keyboards), Chet Gary (guitar), Steve Kosinski (bass) and Bob Price (drums). They later became Essence…Trick was a touring 1970s group led by bassist Joe Pici. The band included Dave Bondzio (guitar), Dee Ann DiMeo (vocals), Lori Richert (vocals) and Mike Licata (drums), who was later a member of Jermain Stewarts Band. The female vocalists were later Patsy Silver and Tasha Williams…Destiny included Joe Vertino and Pete Holguin…A number of touring R&B groups included Sabata, Last Days of Time, Exoutics and UST Topaze…Other touring groups and bands that played often in WNY included Déjà Vu, Magenta, Bourbon N Spice, New York West, Primetime, Rhymes, Brothers Plus, United We Stand, Coalition, Jetz, Pure Gold, Rubberband, Carnival, Time Square, After Five, Reunion, Great Day, Friends, December, Transition, Pale Fire, Reasons, Good Guys Revue, Fantasy, Good Tymes, Calaband, Visions, Sound City Express, Crystal Revelation, Sasafrass, Lookin Back, Patchwork, Good Feelings, The Joel Dane Show, Lance Diamond Show and Top Banana.

Some entertainers from Buffalo became popular on a national level, with The Scinta Brothers and Clint Holmes becoming regular acts in Las Vegas, while John Valby toured as a solo act.

SCINTA BROTHERS

In 1976 Frankie Scinta was at his father's house talking to his brother Joey who already had his van packed getting ready to move to Florida, where he had a job waiting for him to sell home security alarm systems. The telephone rang and it was Paul Maguire, former Buffalo Bills player and NBC television color commentator, who owned the Kenmore restaurant/nightclub Maguire's Arches on Elmwood Avenue. He told Frankie that he needed a piano player at his club and offered him the job. Frankie explained to Maguire he did not work alone, and only performed with his brother Joey. Paul repeated he just wanted a solo for his piano bar and Frankie reiterated that he only worked with Joey. Eventually, Paul relented and offered them an audition as a duo.

Frankie said he only worked with his brother to stop him from leaving for Florida. They had not previously worked together as a duo, but they both had an extensive musical background and performance experience. When he was seven years old, Frankie was on the *Uncle Jerrys Club,* televised on Channel 4, and when he was eleven years old he appeared on *The Merv Griffin Show.* Joey played bass with Steve Nathan in the band Parkside at The Club in Niagara Falls and toured with the show

FRANKIE & CHRISSI SCINTA
Photo: Courtesy Frank Scinta

band Top Banana. In fact the only time Frankie and Joey played together on stage was when Frankie played piano with Top Banana for two months in Hawaii. The other members of Top Banana decided to stay in Hawaii but Frankie & Joey came back to Buffalo.

After two or three days of constant rehearsal, the brothers went to the audition. Paul Maguire was impressed and hired them to play five nights a week. Their pay was $200.00 each a week. They thought they had hit the lottery. With Frankie on piano and string ensemble, along with Joey's percussive bass playing, their singing and showmanship was soon packing the club. Within six months, you could not get in Maguires Arches. Their sister Chrissi was around 15 years old at that time, but she wanted to sing with her brothers. Due to her age, Chrissi had to be accompanied by her parents to sing the first set every Friday and Saturday night. She brought the house down. Frankie and Joey completed the night as a duo and played the other three nights just two piece.

Good news travels fast, especially in the Buffalo music community. Jimmy Cosentino, the owner of The Executive Hotel on Genesee Street, came to Maguire's Arches to check out The Scinta Brothers show. After seeing them perform a few times he offered them a job at The Executive. Consentino did not ask what they were getting paid, he just said he would pay them double of what they were making at Maguire's. In 1977, The Scinta Brothers started at The Executive, making $400.00 a week each. There were two stages in the ballroom at The Executive. The Scinta Brothers, were performing as a duo, with special guest Chrissi Scinta on one stage and Top 40 show bands like Junction West were on the other. It was not long until The Scinta's were attracting 600 to 1,000 people at The Executive every night.

Taking the engagement at The Executive was a wise decision by The Scintas. The club obtained a Playboy Club franchise in 1981 and Jimmy Cosentino helped the Scinta Brothers get booked at other Playboy

Clubs. They first played in St Louis and then at the Atlantic City Playboy Club. By the early 1980s they were touring the country, still performing as a trio (with Chrissi now a permanent member of the group), appearing at large show clubs and special events. They eventually added a drummer, adopting Buffalo's Pete O'Donnell into the family, and worked their way into Las Vegas clubs and concert halls.

In 2000 The Scinta Brothers signed a multi-million-dollar contract to perform at Rio All Suites Casino. Frankie's singing and multi-instrumentalist talents, coupled with Joey's celebrity impressions, along with their humor and brotherly banter, has made the Scinta Brothers one of Las Vegas' first families of entertainment. When sister Chrissi had to leave the band due to medical reasons, Buffalo native Janien Valentine joined the group. A horn section now augments The Scinta Brothers high energy show, which features a huge variety of all styles of music.

The Scinta Brothers have not forgotten their Buffalo roots. Every year they come back home to host *The Variety Club Children's Telethon*, for several years they performed at The Italian Festival on Hertel Avenue and they annually sell out a several Christmas concerts at The Riviera Theater in North Tonawanda.

CLINT HOLMES grew up in Farnham, NY, not far from Angola on the lake. His father was an African-American jazz musician and his mother was a classically trained Caucasian opera singer from Great Britain. When Clint was 12 years old, his father would take him to the Sunday afternoon Jazz jam session at the Colored Musicians Club in Buffalo to introduce him to authentic jazz. In high school, he played trombone in the Lake Shore High School Band and he sang in a rock band called Clint Holmes & the Cavaliers. Clint's mother did not like him playing rock 'n' roll and encouraged him to add Doug Morgano to the band as another singer and guitarist. During the early 1960s this gave the band a unique twist because on some songs Clint added trombone, Doug added sax and the bass player added trumpet. When Clint left the group to attend SUNY Fredonia and then join the Army, the Cavaliers became the house band at The Colony on Hertel in 1965. After serving three years in the Army, where he sang with the U.S. Army Chorus, Clint started performing at nightclubs along the East Coast. In 1973 Clint's song "Playground in My Mind" reached #2 on the U.S. charts and was #1 in some other countries. This launched a career in Las Vegas and television, including being the announcer on the *Joan*

Rivers Late Show and the *Honda All-Star Challenge* on the BET Network. Currently Holmes is still a star attraction in Las Vegas and on cruise ships. He annually returns to Buffalo to co-host the *Variety Kids Telethon* on Channel 7.

JOHN VALBY started playing in Buffalo during the 1960s as a member of the Florida based rock band The Charles. A classically trained piano player, ironically Valby received his first piano lessons from catholic nuns while in grammar school in Rochester NY. In the early '70s John was playing ragtime and standards during solo piano dates at The Showboat, which was docked at the foot of Hertel Avenue. One night, to liven up the crowd, he played a couple R rated songs that he had performed while in college, to mirror the debauchery of college frat parties. The audience loved the songs and asked for more of what he called "dirt" songs. After experiencing a performance at the Showboat, future manager Paul Lamanna persuaded Valby to create an entire night of dirt songs. He coined the moniker of "Doctor Dirty" and started booking him at WNY clubs like The Red Balloon, After Dark, Merlin's, Gilligan's, The Trivit House and Melanie's. In 1975 Lamanna booked Valby for six weeks in Daytona Beach during spring break, when the town was overflowing with partying, hormone driven college students. It was a perfect match. After presenting a showcase for the NEC college concert booking conference, during the 1975-6 school year, Doctor Dirty started performing at colleges from Vermont to Florida. Everyone knows Valby for the over 30 albums of dirt that he has released. However, he has also recorded a Christmas album, a rock CD by the Krakup Quartet, new age album, produced an album by Buffalo Sabres alumnus Jim Schoenfeld and believe it or not, a children's album. During his career, Doctor Dirty has sold more albums than many established national recording acts and is still touring the college circuit that he established over 40 years ago.

14

ORIGINAL MUSIC SCENE

The punk/new wave music scene was begun by musicians who rejected the perceived excess of mainstream 1970s rock and started producing short, fast paced songs with hard edged melodies and stripped-down instrumentation. It was influenced by the proto-punk bands or garage bands from the 1960s, like The Seeds, Standells, Shadows of Knight, Question Mark & the Mysterians, 13th Floor Elevator, and in some respects, early Kinks songs. During the late '60s and early '70s the garage bands became groups like the MC5, Iggy Pop & the Stooges, New York Dolls and The Velvet Underground, which had a more direct influence on the punk scene. By 1976 bands like The Sex Pistols, Clash and Damned started performing in London, while groups like The Ramones, Television, Talking Heads, Mink DeVille and Blondie were playing in New York City at the legendary club CBGB.

Buffalo musicians were introduced to this music by fanzines published in NYC and London, that profiled the bands and their music. Area bands performing new wave/punk music were started by musicians that lived near Buffalo State and UB campuses. The early local punk bands, like Lip Service, with guitarist Jamie Carlson, played mostly covers. Many of these bands and aspiring musicians congregated at Play It Again Sam record store, which was opened by Scott Thomas Flynn in 1976. It became Home of the Hits, when his sister Jennifer Flynn Preston purchased the store from him in 1982 and moved it a couple doors down Elmwood Avenue. This store became mission control for punk records, fanzines and info on the Buffalo punk scene. It was the first place where you could buy new wave punk records in Buffalo, and people that wanted to be part of the punk movement started hanging out at the store to become involved with the scene.

THE ENEMIES
Fred Mann, Peter Secrist, Sinister, Joe Bompczak
Photo authors collection, Photo credit Gene Witkowski

After seeing the New York Dolls open a concert at Kleinhans and watching the local punk cover band Lip Service perform, Joe Bompczyk put an ad in the paper to form an all original band. He recruited bass player Bob Guariglia and drummer Peter Secrist, with singer Fred Mann completing the band in 1976. They are considered by many to be Buffalo's first original punk band and the band members took the personas of Billy Pirahna (Bompczyk), Rocky Mann (Mann) and Sinister (Guariglia). The first club to offer performances by punk bands was McVans, and The Enemies were the among the first bands to play there. In true punk fashion, if a fight broke out while they were playing at McVans, Bompczyk would put down his guitar, join in the ruckus, knock out some of the participants and return to the stage to finish his set.

The enemies released two singles "No Reason" b/w "Secret Agent Man" and "Capital Idea" b/w "Political Sod" and a six song EP *Products of the Street*, with the cover artwork produced by Marvel Comics artist Gene Colon. One of the songs on the EP "Disconnected" was covered by the Goo Goo Dolls and was included on their *A Boy Named Goo* album.

Many of the early original bands were based in Kenmore or included members from the Kenmore area. During the mid '70s at Kenmore West High School, students were as involved with original music bands, as they were with the school's sports teams. Musicians like Mark Freeland from Pegasus or Bill Manspeaker from Green Jello would attend school in outrageous stage attire. Students at the school were either in a band or followed a friend who was in a band. There were band practices in basements across the village of Kenmore and parties attended by all the band members, along with their friends. A camaraderie developed and all the musicians and their followings were connected.

McVans had been featuring cover rock bands since the early '70s and had a past history going back to Prohibition. The bartender, Bambi, was even one of the exotic dancers going back to the burlesque floor show days. It was in this dark, dank club that all the original bands came together to create the original music scene in Buffalo. Pegasus was one of the first original bands to perform at the club, and vocalist Mark Freeland began coordinating shows at McVans with his side projects and other Kenmore area bands. He would put on some shows with 13 different groups. Freeland felt individually the bands would not be able to draw a large crowd, but collectively, if each of the bands brought their friends, the club would be packed. This would allow each group to play a few songs before a large crowd, which may interest some of the audience to come and see them when they played later dates. Some of the other Kenmore area bands involved in these McVans dates or with the early Kenmore West scene were Electroman, The Scooters, Factor (Jimbo Freeland's Band), More, Cherry Bombs, Kicks, Secrets, Plastics, George, Avatar, Indians, Atones and many more that lasted for only a few dates. The band Atones included Marc and Rachel Weinstein (children of WKBW's Irv Weinstein) and Tony Billoni, who was later one of the founders of the annual Artists & Models Affair.

The original music bands became the main style of music featured at McVans. Goo Goo Dolls bass player Robbie Takac remembers playing early dates at McVans when he was still in high school. During the cover rock days, Rodan had played Sunday nights at McVans but during the original period, Oil of Dog DJ Gary Storm played there with his band Extra Cheese. Other groups that played at the club included Davey & the Crocketts (Dave Meinzer's country rock influenced band), The Vores, Jumpers, Factor, Bernie Kugel & the Good, Toys, Pauline & the Perils, The Stains and Tourists, Bob James' group from 1979 which included Mark Lukich, Jef Allen, Bob Kozak and Tom Hauptman.

The early new wave punk bands also played dates at Art Galleries such as Hallwalls on Essex Street and other similar venues. At these shows they often had four bands, each playing a different style of music. There could be a show with one band playing hard core punk, another doing pop, another country orientated and the last having a jazz influence. The audience equally appreciated what each band performed, regardless of their style, because it was original music.

Other clubs like The Masthead, Pastime, City Lights and Schupper House, featured original bands but the entire scene changed when The Continental opened at 212 Franklin Street in February 1981. People following original music immediately gravitated to this club which had bands on the first floor, a deejay spinning dance music on the second floor and an enclosed outdoor patio. The club also featured television screens that showed the band performing on stage or MTV style videos. Since owner Bud Burke was not certain if bands would draw crowds, he initially paid the bands the door. The crowds were beyond expectation and the bands were getting the largest pay they had ever received. Soon Burke changed his policy and started paying the bands a fixed fee. The success of The Continental resulted in the McVans bands all moving their base from Riverside to Downtown Buffalo. Some of the bands that performed at The Continental included many of the groups that had worked at McVans, along with Gary Zoldos & the Method, The Cobras, Elements, Bud Redding's Funk Monster & Woman, Viceroys, Chesterfield Kings, Paperfaces, Splatcats, Lumens, Moment, Fems, Scott Carpenter & the Real McCoys, Quakes, Pinheads, Beaumonts (Johnny Rzeznik's former band), Sinatra Test, Third Floor Strangers, Stiff Mitten, Remote Control, David Watts Great Train Robbery, Walk Don't Walk (with Brian Mann & Bruce Cranston), and many touring national recording groups. The downtown Buffalo original scene thrived and the crowds at McVans continued to diminish until it eventually closed. This opened the door for other clubs like Mr Goodbar, Cabaret, Marshalls, The Hat Trick on Military near Kenmore and Peppers on Hertel near Delaware, along with shows by promoters Marshall Glover, Bud Redding and Marty Boratin.

In addition to playing parties, events and clubs, most if not all of the original bands released records. Many of these records were do it yourself (DIY) projects but some were released on major labels and several on Buffalo's BCMK Records. BCMK was a recording studio owned by former Raven bass player and commercial jingle writer Tommy Calandra. Bands were recording at the studio, engineered by Calandra and Mike Brydalski, so they formed a label to release some of these songs. The first releases were in 1979 by Bernie Kugel & the Good, and Dave Meinzer's Davy & the Crocketts. In 1982 they released *4 Now From Buffalo*. This was an EP with one song each by four different Buffalo original bands. Pauline & the Perils contributed "See for Yourself," The Vores "New Aesthetic," The Cobras "One Way Street" and The Stains "Of Life." These bands played local and out of town shows together to collectively promote their individual groups and the record. *The Airwaves – Showcase Volume 1* album was released in 1982. This compilation album included one song each by the following artists: The Elements (I Can't Help Myself), Coffee Scare (Scare Song), Bob Kozak (Waste My Time), UST Topaze (Our Love Has Gone), Kathy Moriarty & Liars (Mary), Pointless Brothers (Hyper Space), Madcaps (Airwaves), The Good (Message From My Heart), Nick Angelo & the Killing Floor (Sorry Boys), Cold Water Flat (Never Let It Stop), Russell Steinberg & Mike Brydalski (Water Dub) and The Detours (Everybody's Got Soul.)

In addition to the BCMK compilation album, compilation albums were also released by radio stations 97 Rock and WPHD. These albums were a combination of the city original bands and suburban bands that were primarily known for their cover, songs but included some originals in their sets. The first WGRQ 97 Rock *Buffalo Rocks Volume One* was released in 1981. The bands on the recording were Mike Mazur & the Blue Collar Band (Queen City Bound), Secret Savior (First Love), Raven (Baby Go Away), Stross Fletcher (Susan Bannister), Benhatzel (Undeniable), Dear Daddy (We'll Be on Our Way), Cheater (Ten Cent Love Affair), John Hilliard Band (Someone Else's Eyes), Parousia (Miss Ogyny) and Mike Mazur (Blue Collar City).

97 Rock *Buffalo Rocks Volume 2* was released in 1982. It contained the following bands and songs: Cheeks (This Is Rock and Roll), Pauline & the Perils (Lauren Bacall), Lou Rera (Why Bother), Broken Silence (High and Dry), The Alyn Syms Group (Rock and Roll), Big Fun (Do What You Want), Cheater (We Came Here to Rock), Actor (Checkin' Out), Buxx (Take You Back Anyway), Bob Campbell & Gibralter (Suicide Hotline), Sturr (See It All) and Cheeks (Honey Slow Down). After the album was released 97 Rock presented a concert with all the bands at Melody Fair.

WPHD 103.3 released the *Homegrown* album in 1981. Included on this album was Cheater (Back Road), Gibralter (You), Benhatzel (I Know), Mary Anne O'Shea (Time After Time), Gary Greco & Alan Mangus (Never Let You Down), Pete Howard & John Valby Band (Why Did You Hesitate), JDM Hybrid (By Man's on the Road), The Glass Band (Move It), The Rouges (It's Just Another Lie) Louise Lambert (Time for Love), The Hostages (Nasty Girl) and Broken Silence (Love for The First Time.)

There were later compilation albums by 97 Rock, 103.3 and 107.7. These releases are not included because they featured material which was not recorded within the timeline of this book.

During the 1950s many bands recorded original songs and during the 1960s that was a goal of most groups. Starting in the 1970s there was always a difference between the predominantly city based original bands and the bands from the suburbs that played mostly cover songs. There were some original bands that were from the suburbs, but if they concentrated on playing their own songs, they usually performed at the city clubs. The suburban bands did some originals, but usually the suburban club owners demanded that they play the popular songs which people heard on the radio. It was OK to play a few of your own songs at the suburban clubs, but the club owners wanted that to be the exception, not the rule. Of course, there were some variances to these guidelines. There were occasional original music nights at suburban clubs and some suburban cover bands released records with original songs. However, the original vs. cover dichotomy was an accepted reality.

These differences were illustrated in the *Music Is Art* benefit CD that was released in 2006. This recording was considered a time capsule of Buffalo recordings from the late '70s and early '80s. The record differentiated the groups as bands from the original scene at McVans & The Continental and bands from the cover scene at The Barrelhead, He & She's, etc.

There were eight songs from each category of group. The original groups and songs were Mark Freeland (My Baby's Got a Thing for Me), Third Floor Strangers (The Long Letter), The Enemies (Contender), The Elements (Hurtin'), The Jumpers (South of the City), The Restless (It's Over), Davy & The Crocketts (Stage Zero) and The Vores (Forget that Guy). The cover groups and songs were: Talas (See Saw), Weekend (Everyday), Actor (Checkin' Out), The Road (Night in the City), Cheater (Ten Cent Love Affair), Benhatzel (Undeniable), Alyn Syms Group (Can't Keep a Good Band Down) and Mike Mazur's Blue Collar City (Queen City Bound). A review of the names of the bands on the CD, provides a good example of which type of groups were considered belonging to either the city or suburban category.

In 2003 there was a CD released on the Musicians United Label titled *This is It! Greater Buffalo's Greatest 1977-1984*. This was a two CD package which included 46 songs. Some groups had more than one song on the CD and that is annotated on the following list. The groups included were: Scooters, Jumpers (3), Lip Service, Davy & the Crocketts (2), Tourists (3), Enemies (3), Blue Reimondoz, Vores (2), Bob Kozak, Extra Cheese (2), Good (2), Toys, Third Floor Strangers (2), Pauline & the Perils (2), Cobras, Detours, Stains, Lou Rera, Beez, Method, Edge, New Toys,

Throbs, Jetsons (2), Moti, Bob James & the Restless, Elements, Pauline & the Third Floor Strangers, Paper Faces, Riddlers (2), Splatcats and The Restless. There was a listing on Amazon offering a used copy of this CD for $99.95. This recording was released to benefit several area youth leadership organizations. In 2002 there was a benefit concert at The Tralf. and some of the bands on the CD performed, including The Jumpers, Pauline & the Perils, Vores, Davy & the Crocketts, Third Floor Strangers, Stains, Lip Service, Method and Riddlers.

Mark Freeland, Kent Weber and David Kane were three musicians that were involved in the original music scene starting in the early 1970s. There were many groups that included one, two or all three of these musicians, but collectively they have been at the forefront of the original music scene for almost 40 years.

PEGASUS 1972
Steve Trecase, Kent Weber, Chuck Cavanaugh, Vince Cooper, Mark Freeland
Photo Credit Jim Cavanaugh

The band Pegasus was initially formed by Kent Weber (bass) and Chuck Cavanaugh (drums) in 1970, with John and Peter Schmid (guitar). They were at a party where they met Steve (Trelaine) Trecase (bass-keyboards) and Vince Cooper (guitarist). After a few rehearsals, they asked Steve and Vince to replace the Schmid brothers in Pegasus. All four of these members went to high school in Amherst. Trecase and Cooper had worked in another band with a vocalist Randy Singer, who they recommended as a vocalist for the group. During a rehearsal Singer went outside to take a break and his friend, Kenmore West student Mark Freeland sang a song. The band members were so impressed with Freeland's vocals that Mark became the new lead singer. That was the summer of 1972, and in the fall Weber switched from guitar to bass and Trecase, a classically trained piano player, switched from bass to keyboards. The basis of Pegasus was intact and they started to work on creating their identity.

Pegasus started as a cover band playing The Stones, Alice Cooper and other '70s rock bands. In 1973, they embraced glam rock and in 1974, they started writing their own progressive rock-oriented, original material.

In October 1975, they performed their *Alienation Rock Opera* live on UB's WBUF radio station on a Saturday night and the following night, on Sunday, they opened for Rodan, All the members were under age, so the owner of McVans required they each get letters from their parents giving them permission to play at the bar. At this McVans date Pegasus performed all original material, while Rodan played progressive covers. However, in 1976 Pegasus created a Genesis cover show, complete with costuming and artistic scenery created by Mark Freeland. This show, which featured *The Lamb Lies Down on Broadway* album, assisted Pegasus in obtaining dates in the larger cover-oriented suburban clubs and securing performances at theaters and halls.

McVans became the home base for Pegasus, where they played every Thursday for four years. They often used both stages, with Freeland setting up performance art or side projects on the smaller stage. The tenure of Pegasus at McVans was the basis of changing McVans from being a rock cover club to becoming the first home of original music in Buffalo. During their career Pegasus released several records and the same personnel performed together for eight years, until 1980. The tradition and spirit of Pegasus was continued after the band broke up with Mark Freeland, Chuck Cavanaugh and Steve Trecase forming the recording trio Pegasonics. That band released the album *New New York* on their Trelaine Records label.

In 1978 one of Mark Freeland's side projects was Electroman. This began as a solo act and over time became a full band, with a forever evolving group of musicians. During performances, you never knew what to expect or who would be with the band. Sometimes they started off with a riff, upon which they improvised and it continued for an entire set. Electroman became an actual band in 1981 and in 1985 core basic line up was Mark Freeland, David Kane, Kent Weber and Bill Moore (drums). The band did many recordings including the songs like "The Vegetarian Song," "Girl Power" and "Go Go Go."

From 1980 to 1982 Kent Weber and David Kane worked together in The Celibates, with Terry Sullivan (vocals) and Bill Moore (percussion). The Celibates were one of Buffalo's first original electronic synth pop bands. They also made extensive use of drum machines, which were coming into vogue

CELIBATES
David Kane, Kent Weber, Terry Sullivan, Bill Moore
Photo: Courtesy Kent Weber

around this time. They released an independent album *A Shameless Fashion* which received airplay at college radio stations across the U.S. and in Europe. The Celibates spent half of its time in New York City and half in Buffalo, disbanding when Terry left to join The Restless.

The Fems was another Mark Freeland project that featured John Walters and Bob Weider. They released the single "Go to a Party" in 1982 and later a reunion cassette and CDR. There were several renditions of the band with one version including Freeland, Walters, Weider, Lou Mang and Kent Weber.

David Kane was with the progressive original band Masque in 1979. He then formed Trek with Quintronic with Paul Wilcox, who was the guitarist/vocalist from Masque. They released two albums *Landing* and *Trek W/ Quintronic* on Bi Plane Records, which were both produced by Chuck Madden. After working with Kent Weber in The Celibates, Kane worked on several projects, including Electroman and Erectronics before starting the electronic trio Nullstadt with Donald Kinsman (vocals) and Stephen Collins (guitar). Nullstadt was expanded with the addition of Kent Weber (bass), Bart Mitchell (Guitar) and Greg Gizzi (drums). They released the video *Mayday,* which

NULLSTADT
Bart Mitchell, Greg Gizzi, Kent Weber, David Kane
Seated: Steven Collins, Donald Kinsman
Photo: Courtesy: Kent Weber

received airplay on MTV's Basement Tapes, with former Electroman guitarist Cage replacing Bart Mitchell. Kane's group Decay of Western Civilization evolved into Them Jazz Beards, who released four albums and included sax player Jack Prybylski.

Mark Freeland died of cancer in 2007. With his passing Buffalo lost a true Renaissance Man: as he was an actor, musician, singer and artist. In addition to the bands previously mentioned, Freeland was also a member of Pageantry of Weens, the Jamie Moses Band, Our Daughter's Wedding (in NYC), Industry of Life Divine and others. He was active with his music projects until just prior to his death and before he died he had an exhibition of his artwork at The Albright Knox Art Gallery. Kent Weber is currently working on several projects, including performing with John & Mary and the Valkyries. David Kane is working on theater/dance projects and continues performing with Them Jazz Beards and The David Kane Quartet.

OTHER ORIGINAL BANDS

THE JUMPERS. In 1977 Terry Sullivan was one of the founding members of The Jumpers with Scott Miklasz (guitar), Craig Meylan (bass), Roger Nicol (drums), songwriter Bob Kozak and manager Steve Ralbovsky. The band was from the Hamburg area and they were one of the earliest Buffalo original underground groups who paved the way for other area power pop and alternative bands. They were one of the first original bands from Buffalo to tour colleges and clubs outside of the WNY area and they opened shows for many of the early national alternative bands like The Ramones, B52s and Talking Heads. The Jumpers released a single "You'll Know Better (When I'm Gone)" b/w "I Wanna Know" in 1978 and in 1979 released "This is It" b/w "Sick Girls." They also contributed "Hello Girl" to the 1980 *Waves* compilation album. "You'll Know Better" was recorded at Select Sound Record Studio, with production assistance from Dick Bauerle and engineered by Robbie Konikoff. The 45-sleeve was designed by Andrew Elias (*Rockers* magazine editor & art director). Other people credited on the record included Maurice Narcis (cover photo), Dave Meinzer, Nancy New Age, Stu Shapiro, Bruce Eaton and Bob James.

After The Jumpers broke up in 1979, Sullivan formed The Celibates in 1980 with David Kane and Kent Weber. This group divided its time between NYC and Buffalo. Sullivan was signed to a management agreement with record promoters Bruce Moser and Doug Dombrowski of Could be Wild. They assisted in creating The Restless (initially named The Edge) with Terry, Bob RM James (guitar) from The Third Floor Strangers, Joe Bompzck (guitar) from The Enemies,

THE RESTLESS
Bob James, Frank Luciano, Joe Bompzck,
Guy Polino, Terry Sullivan
Photo: Courtesy: RM James

Guy Polino (bass) from Paper Faces and Frank Luciano (drums) from Empty Desks. The Restless signed a long-term contract with Mercury Polygram Records and released a self-titled LP produced by Eddie Kramer, who also produced Jimi Hendrix and had engineered The Rolling Stones and The Beatles. A video to promote their record, which received medium rotation on MTV, was produced by Susan Seidelmen, who had previously worked on Madonna videos. After The Restless, Sullivan was a member of Terry & the Headhunters, who released an album (produced by Mike Sak) on the Eureka/Capital label, and Dollywatchers, who recorded an independently released CD.

PAULINE & THE PERILS were one of the first original bands with a female vocalist. They were originally a four-piece band with Pauline Digati (vocals), Geoff Copp (guitar), Tim Switala (drums) and Russell Steinberg (bass). After about a year they added Jeff Helmick (sax). The Perils were regular performers during the original music period at McVans and were one of the first bands to play at The Continental. They released "I Can't Walk Away" b/w "She's Just a Picture" in 1980, "See for Yourself" in 1981 on BCMK Records and "Lauren Becall" on a compilation album. The group broke up in 1982. Guitarist Geoff Copp was the associate editor of the magazine *Rockers,* while drummer Tim Switala was a writer for *Rockers* and later for the *Buffalo News.*

After Pauline & the Perils, Digati started The Throbs with Dan Patrick (bass) and Kevin Henneman (guitar), who had been members of both Crossroads and The Beez. The Throbs included Adam Gearing

PAULINE & THE PERILS
Jeff Helmick, Geoff Copp, Tim Switala,
Pauline Digati Russell Steinberg
Photo authors collection, photo credit Adam Burgess

(guitar), with either Jim Celeste and David Lloyd on drums. They were together during most of 1983 and when the group broke up Partick, Henneman and Lloyd formed Western Voice. They recorded a 15-song demo at BCMK engineered by Mike Brydalski. The group relocated to New York City, where they showcased at CBGBs and the Peppermint Lounge. Not attracting the interest of a major label, they returned to WNY where they started a cover song side-project called the Skiffle Band. After Dan Patrick (now with NBC-TV for almost 30 years) and Kevin Henneman (who owns KMH Audio Video) permanently moved to New York City, David Lloyd changed the name of the Skiffle Band to Bleeding Hearts, a group which still performs in Western New York.

Pauline formed The Promise, which released an album in 1985. The group members were Pauline Digati (vocals), RM James (guitar), formerly with The Restless, Marty Stevens (keyboards), Bill Guercio (bass) and Howard Wilson (drums), formerly with Cheeks. They played showcases in NYC and when The Promise did not obtain a record contract, Digati, Wilson and James formed The Rain, with bass player Spike from The Lumens. That group later included Kyle Brock (bass) and Marc Feliciano (guitar), a version that recorded and released several songs

In addition to Pauline & the Perils, there were several bands that featured female vocalists in original music groups. Natalie Merchant was the lead vocalist with 10,000 Maniacs, Doti Hall was the bassist and vocalist in both The Stains and The Elements, with Pat Kane and future 10,000 Maniac drummer Jerry Augustyniak. Kathy Moriarty performed solo dates and later in the 1980s formed Beat City, which also included co-vocalist Sue Kincaid. Kathy and Sue previously worked together in True Beat. Michelle Weber was with House of Usher, but primarily performed solo dates. Almost 30 years ago, Mary Ramsey began singing with John Lombardo, forming John & Mary. Rita Seitz recorded and played some original songs with Watchers and later performed as an original music artist in England. Gretchen Schulz was the vocalist with Shaking Hands before joining The Pine Dogs with Jim Whitford (guitar), Don Vincent (guitar), Tom Fischer (bass) and Jim Celeste (drums).

THE TOYS were a suburban based band that found its success as a city original band. The group was formed by Kevin Kalicki (drums) and his brother Alan Kalicki (guitar), who were from Pendleton and had been in the band Aunt Helen. In The Toys they became Kevin Starr and Rocky Starr. They were joined by Lewiston natives Doug "Mick" Tyler (guitar) and Joel (Meat Cleaver) Slazyk (bass). The group released a 45 and an album *Say It* under the name New Toys, which was more power pop material. The band moved to NYC, where they changed their name to The Lone Cowboys. Over the past 30 years, Kevin K has been releasing albums and touring in Europe. He continues to perform and has separate European and American bands to back him at shows.

THE EMPLOYEEZ were together from 1982 to 1984, with the group members being Roger Hooven (vocals), Dave Camarda (guitar), Michael Jackson (guitar), Bill Mason (drums) and various bass players – Sal Ianello, Dave Rosenburg or Rick Ipolito. They were one of the few Buffalo bands that had the opportunity to play a concert at The Aud, when they opened for Culture Club. They also opened the Inxs concert at Rooftops. Roger later formed Roger & the Standards with Dave Camarda and former Stiff Mitten bass player Paul Mordaunt.

THE FANS were another original band which had success in the suburban market. Members included Gary Kowalski (drums), who is now with Tom Stahl & the Dangerfields and Mark Dux (keyboards) who is now in The Informers. Test was a band that wore white makeup, with keyboardist Tom Trigilio now with the Italian music band The Formula. In the mid '80s there were many suburban original bands including SS Thunder, Boy Girl Boy, TDM, Tokyo Rose, Rif Raff, Izzy Rex, Beat Goes Bang, Stealin', Baby Blue and Rockcandy

GREEN JELLO was formed in 1981 and featured outrageous on-stage antics, bizarre theatrics, sophomoric humor and intentionally bad musicianship. They billed themselves as "The World's Worst Band." They encouraged the audience to throw food at them and this often got them in trouble with the venues. One of their earliest shows was at the Masonic

Temple in Kenmore, where the crowd broke into the kitchen and threw ice cream sandwiches they found in the freezer at the band. The stage was ruined and the band had to reimburse the temple for the damages. At a YMCA, they spilled fake blood on the carpets and had to pay for the rug cleaning. Joe Terrose, the owner of McVans, banned them from the club for smashing television sets on stage with a sledgehammer. They changed their name and successfully got rebooked at the club, only to be banned again for destructive behavior. The epitome of their antics was an outdoor show at Buffalo State college where they were opening for The Ramones in 1984. The audience threw Jell-O, whipped cream and pudding at the band. Unfortunately, all the food also covered The Ramones equipment, which was set up behind them on stage. Green Jello found a supporter in Bud Burke from The Continental. He encouraged their bizarre shows, which now included sadomasochism, gravity boots, arrival in stretch limos and incompetent musicianship, which resulted in shows that regularly played to sold out crowds. The band reached what they considered the pinnacle of its success, when they performed on *The Gong Show*, playing as bad as they could so they were immediately gonged. This provided them with national exposure.

Green Jello moved to Hollywood, California in 1987 where they became a fixture in the LA underground scene. They established a friendship with the band GWAR, solidified by their mutual love of costumes and props. The band was sued by Kraft Foods for trademark infringement and had to change their name to Green Jelly, with an umlaut over the "y" so, according to the band it is pronounced as an o. Although Green Jello established a reputation of being terrible musicians, members of the band went on to play in several successful bands, including a few members joining the band Tool.

GOO GOO DOLLS

The Goo Goo Dolls were not formed until 1986 but their roots go back to earlier in the '80s. Johnny Rzeznik (guitar) was with the Beaumounts, while Robby Takac (bass) and George Tutuska (drums) were with the Beat Mongers. Robby had also been a member of the hard-rock original band Cromagnen. At first, they were going to name the band Sex Maggot, but after paging through *True Detective* magazine they saw an ad for goo goo dolls and the name stuck.

GOO GOO DOLLS
Robby Takac, George Tutuska, Johnny Rzeznik
Photo Authors Collection

When they started playing early dates at The Continental, Johnny was also a part time employee at the bar and Robby was working as an assistant at Trackmaster Recording Studio (a studio he now owns). After playing early dates in Buffalo, they recorded their first album on a very limited budget at Trackmaster. Constant touring got the band signed by Metal Blade Records. In 1987 the band was set to go on tour with The Ramones, Suicidal Tendencies and some headlining independent dates, when misfortune struck. The band was walking down Elmwood Avenue with their manager Artie Kwitchoff, when a car came careening towards them. To get out of the way, Rzeznik jumped over a parked car and landed on his arm; the broken arm resulted in the cancellation of the tour. 1987 was the beginning of an interesting relationship between the Goo Goo Dolls and the Buffalo Music Awards. In 1987 the band won the best new original band award; in 1988 Johnny was ejected from the awards show when he protested the lack of recognition for original artists by throwing a bottle in the direction of 97 Rock DJ Carl Russo on stage; In 1989 the band played a high energy set at the awards show with guest vocalist Lance Diamond; in 1989, they also won the best original band award and in 1990, Johnny was one of the hosts, presenting the original music awards.

On their first album Takac was the lead vocalist, with the band having an alternative edge. On subsequent albums Rzeznik, increasingly covered more of the lead vocals, eventually becoming the primary singer.

When Rzeznik took over more of the lead vocals and songwriting, the band changed from being an alternative rock band to more of a pop AOR (adult orientated rock) group.

Additional Buffalo connections regarding the Goo Goo Dolls include their first five albums recorded in full or partially at Trackmaster Studio. Their second and third albums were produced by Buffalo's Armand John Petri. The representative from Metal Blade Records that signed the group was Buffalo native Mike Faley. The cover of the *Jed* album was named after and painted by Robby's Medaille College art teacher Jed Jackson. *Superstar Car Wash* was an actual car wash on William Street in Buffalo. They recorded a live album on July 4, 2004, during a pouring rain storm on Niagara Square in front of Buffalo City Hall. Buffalo lounge singer Lance Diamond was guest vocalist at Goo Goo Dolls concerts and on albums. When George Tutuska left the band after the release of *A Boy Named Goo,* he became the drummer for the South Buffalo Irish Rock band Jackdaw and Buffalo keyboardist Dave Schulz became a touring member of the band starting with the *Dizzy Up the Girl* album. Schulz had a falling out with the band after the airing of a secretly filmed hidden camera episode of *Taxicab Confessions* in 1999. Schulz remains an in-demand live and session musician for groups like Berlin in LA returns to Buffalo for dates with his band C.O. Jones.

During their career, The Goo Goo Dolls have released eleven studio albums, had 19 top ten singles on various charts and has sold over twelve million albums. Their most successful singles were "Iris", "Slide" and "Name." The Goo Goo Dolls have not forgotten that Buffalo is their home. Robby is the founder of the Music is Art Foundation, which was started in 2003 to support music in Buffalo schools, donates instruments to schools, awards scholarships and produces the Music is Art festival on the second Saturday of September, presenting artists, dancers, over 100 bands and drawing tens of thousands of people annually.

10,000 MANIACS

10,000 Maniacs were formed in Jamestown in 1981. Before becoming the Maniacs, they played a job in a band called Still Life at Molly B's in Erie, Pa. The members of Still Life included future 10,000 members Steve Gustafson (bass), Dennis Drew (keyboards), Rob Buck (guitar) and Natalie Merchant (vocals), along with Rob's wife Teri Newhouse and Chet Cardinale (drums). They were fired by the club owner after their first job in

January 1981, so they knew they had a good thing going. John Lombardo was playing with another Jamestown band called The Mills, that shared the bill with Still Life for some dates. Eventually Lombardo joined the band as guitarist/vocalist, Tim Edborg (soon replaced by Bob "O'Matic" Wachter) took over on drums and when Newhouse left he group, Merchant became the principle vocalist. They played some dates as Burn Victims and performed the first date as 10,000 Maniacs on Labor Day 1981 at the club Mothers in Jamestown.

Initially 10,000 Maniacs performed cover songs but they tired of playing other people's songs and started to write their own music, Merchant usually handling the lyrics and Lombardo contributing most of the music. Their first release was the EP *Human Conflict Number Five*, which was recorded at SUNY Fredonia in 1982. 10,000 Maniacs started playing Buffalo clubs in 1981, with their first date being at The Pastime. Marshall Glover assisted the band in obtaining Buffalo dates at other clubs like The Schuper House, Continental and special events. During 1982, with the release of their EP, the band started playing out of town. They established contacts in Richmond, Virginia and while playing there, musicians in that city told them they could find a lot of work and exposure in Atlanta. While in Atlanta the jobs dried up and the The Maniacs were sleeping on the floor in a rented house and resorting to selling plasma or doing yard work to get by. They decided to return to Jamestown.

When back in WNY, they came up with a new game plan – record and tour, tour, tour. The band returned to SUNY Fredonia and recorded the album *Secrets of I Ching*, with Marshall Glover assisting with the financing. 1983 was also again time for a new drummer. John Lombardo suggested Jerry Augustyniak, who had opened some 10,000 Maniacs shows with his band The Elements. The band offered Jerry the drummer position, which he still occupies 30 years later. With the release of this album, on the bands own Christian Burial Music label, they started contacting college radio

10,000 MANIACS AT BUFF STATE 1983
Steven Gustafson, Rob Buck, Jerry Augustyniak, Natalie Merchant
Dennis Drew, John Lombardo
Photo: Courtesy Steven Gustafson

10,000 MANIACS BUS IN FLORIDA
Dennis Drew, Rob Buck, Natalie Merchant, Steven Gustafson
John Lombardo, Jerry Augustyniak
Photo: Courtesy Steven Gustafson

stations on the East Coast to get airplay and inquire about places to perform. Many colleges had on-campus clubs during the early '80s and they obtained dates at the schools or clubs near the campuses.

The band bought an old 1979 school bus and started performing at colleges or college towns up and down the east coast. Gustafson's parents had moved to Florida, so the band would travel down the coast to their home in Florida. They would stay at his parent's home for a few days, get some sleep, eat all their food and drink all their beer before heading back up the coast. The band was not interested in the amount of money they were earning; they were interested in building a following. During club appearances, the band would ask if anyone had a place where they could stay. This often ended up being at musician's homes, who then helped them get additional bookings and promote those shows the next time the 10,000 Maniacs came to their town. The touring continued through 1983 and 1984. Everything started to change when agent Frank Reiley got them a date in NYC, where Elektra Records A&R man Howard Thompson saw the band and signed them to a contract.

All the hard work paid off. Their 1985 Elektra album *The Wishing Chair* received critical acclaim and their 1987 album *In My Tribe* established the 10,000 Maniacs as a successful recording act. They were especially popular with college rock radio, a market they devoted years establishing and along with REM are considered the first wave of alternative rock bands. They played President Clinton's 1993 Inauguration Ball. Their appearance on MTV's *Unplugged* helped establish that show. During their career, 10,000 Maniacs have sold tens of millions of albums.

Other connections for the 10,000 Maniacs to Buffalo include when John Lombardo left the band in 1986, he moved to Buffalo where he formed the duo John & Mary with vocalist and viola player Mary Ramsey. One of the biggest dates the band ever performed was opening for the Grateful Dead before 80,000 people at Rich Stadium in Orchard Park on July 4, 1989. When Natalie Merchant left 10,000 Maniacs in 1993, John Lombardo rejoined the band and Mary Ramsey became the lead vocalist.

On September 28, 1996, the 10,000 Maniacs were the first band to perform at HSBC Arena during a concert which also featured Barenaked Ladies and The Goo Goo Dolls. When Rob Buck took a break from the band in 1999, Buffalo attorney and Animal Planet guitarist Michael Lee Jackson was his replacement. Jerry Augustyniak has played with Only Humen and other Buffalo bands when 10,000 Maniacs are not on tour. Maria Sebastian was a back-up vocalist and played acoustic guitar with the band in 2010 and 2011. John & Mary and the Valkyries play regular Buffalo dates when the 10,000 Maniacs are not on the road, with the current members being John, Mary, Kent Weber (bass), Pat Kane (guitar) and either Rob Lynch or Jerry Augustyniak on drums.

The path that the 10,000 Maniacs followed to success should be the example that independent bands follow to build a local, regional and even larger following. The 10,000 Maniacs proved success does not come overnight; it must be earned and, if properly gained it will remain with you. That is why after 35 years, the 10,000 Maniacs are still playing sold-out concerts across the country.

CANNIBAL CORPSE was the merger of several Buffalo death-metal or thrash bands, that performed in the mid '80s. They were formed in 1988 by Alex Webster and Jack Owen from the band Beyond Death and Bob Rusay, Paul Mazurkiewicz and Chris Barnes who were in Tirant Sin. Barns was also previously in Leviathan. They played their first date at River Rocks Café in March 1989, shortly afterward recorded a five-song demo and within a year of that first date they were signed to Metal Blade Records. The band's album art and lyrics are highly controversial and the sale of their recording have been banned in several countries. Cannibal Corpse has released 13 studio albums, two box sets, four video albums and two live albums. Worldwide they have sold over two million units, probably making them the top selling death-metal band of all time.

15

JAZZ, BLUES AND R&B
1970s – 1980s

Jazz has always been a dynamic and intriguing form of entertainment in the Buffalo area, and numerous nationally-acclaimed jazz artists are from WNY. As previously documented, Big Band Jazz was the dominant form of music during the 1930s and 1940s. In the late 1940s to early 1960s, many nightclubs and bars in WNY featured jazz groups. Buffalo was one of the major stops on the Chitlin' Circuit, with all of the top black jazz artists performing at Buffalo clubs like The Pine Grill, Revilot and Bon Ton on a regular basis. That era ended with the advent of rock 'n' roll during the late 1950s to early to mid-1960s. During the 1970s, there was a jazz resurgence in Buffalo spearheaded by Phil DiRe's Buffalo Jazz Ensemble. This inspired many Buffalo musicians to focus on becoming successful in the Jazz genre, resulting in national recording acts like Spryo Gyra and various other Buffalo musicians that toured with internationally renowned jazz groups, like Bobby Militello's long-standing performance relationship with Dave Brubeck.

BUFFALO JAZZ ENSEMBLE

The roots of the Buffalo Jazz Ensemble go back to the Marine Corps Band that performed at The White House in the late 1960s. After playing at Buffalo bars and studying music at Fredonia, Berkley, and Toronto, Phil DiRe was drafted into the army in 1963. During basic training, the unit commander had Phil form a band to march the recruits. Phil's military aptitude test revealed his musical talents, and he was assigned to the Navy School of Music and then three years in the Army Field Band, one of four special military bands. He was informed of an opening in the "President's

BUFFALO JAZZ ENSEMBLE – ALBRIGHT-KNOX 1975
Tom Walsh, Al Tinney, Phil DiRe, Joe Ford, Jay Beckenstein, Sabu Adeyola,
James Clark, Nasar Abadey, Jeremy Wall   Photo: Courtesy Phil DiRe

Own" United States Marine Band that performed jazz at The White House, but it required that he transfer from the Army to the Marines and re-enlist for four more years. The opportunity was too good to pass up. When he arrived for his posting at The White House, he was happy to reunite with two friends from Buffalo - bass player Nick Molfese (with whom he worked Buffalo club dates before he was drafted) and drummer Justin DiCioccio (who is now the head of the Manhattan School of Music in NYC).

After being discharged from the military, DiRe enrolled in the Music Department at UB, where he received his BA in performance. While teaching summer courses in Jazz History and Theory, he met student Jay Beckenstein, who introduced him to the area blues scene.

In 1972, he formed a jazz group, The Buffalo Jazz Ensemble, which played its first performance of original compositions at The Buffalo Public Library. The initial members of the ensemble were Phil DiRe (tenor sax), Tony Carere (alto sax & flute), Nick Molfese (bass), Maurice Sinclair (drums) and Johnny Gibson, a piano player that a teenage Phil worked with playing burlesque shows at The Billboard Lounge. Other early members of the band, which performed at area bars from 1972 to 1975, included Louie Marino, Jim Calire, Jay Beckenstein and Joe Azarello.

To obtain funding for the Buffalo Jazz Ensemble's first performance at the downtown library, DiRe needed to form a not-for-profit corporation. He started the Association for Jazz Performance (AJP) so he could apply for grants, and this became the sponsoring organization behind the CETA grant, as well as other sources of funding.

In 1973 the CETA – Comprehensive Employment & Training Act - was passed by the federal government to train workers and provide them with jobs in the public service. Inspired by the WPA programs in the 1930s, CETA initiated the Neighborhood Arts Program, where musicians and performing artists were employed to work at schools, community centers and prisons. It was envisioned as a 12 to 24 month long program, with employment at public agencies or not-for-profit organizations.

Phil was told about the CETA Program, and since he was teaching part time at The Community School of Music and performing nights at area clubs, he met the qualifications for the program. The stars were properly aligned because the day before he went to City Hall to report for work, Phil DiRe's photo appeared in the *Buffalo Courier Express*, along with an article on the Buffalo Jazz Scene. With his credentials from the Marine Corps Band, a degree in music from UB, and this recent newspaper article, he was invited to meet with Buffalo Mayor Stan Makowski to discuss the creation of a special music program.

In 1975 the Buffalo Jazz Ensemble was approved for the CETA program, and with the assistance of Mayor Makowski, they were assigned as employees in the Parks Department. Thirteen CETA jobs were established, which included the musicians, two equipment managers, and an artwork/marketing position. The Buffalo Jazz Ensemble office and rehearsal space was the Delaware Park Casino, and the thirteen members were paid and received full benefits from the City of Buffalo. Some of the initial members were Phil DiRe, Al Tinney, Lou Marino, Joe Ford, Jeremy Wall, Jay Beckenstein, James Clark, Sabu Adoyola, Nasar Abadey and Tom Walsh.

To obtain additional funding for performances, DiRe negotiated arrangements with the New York State Council on the Arts, National Endowment for the Arts, Association for Jazz Performance, and Musicians Local #92 (all the participants had to be union members). They held performances at grammar schools, high schools, community centers, cultural centers, parks, and prisons. They also ran clinics, attended by young and old aspiring musicians. DiRe's purpose for all this activity was to create awareness for the music as well as a fertile bed for future musicians and their music.

The CETA version of the Buffalo Jazz Ensemble played their first formal concert on the steps of the Albright-Knox Art Gallery. This was a significant first concert because it was the inception of the ever-popular Jazz at the Albright-Knox concert series.

When DiRe moved to the West Coast in 1976, Sam Falzone assumed leadership of the Buffalo Jazz Ensemble and the CETA program. Falzone put more emphasis on clinics, thus the name of the organization was changed to the Buffalo Jazz Workshop. African drummer Emile

"Papa" Latimer got involved and inaugurated his drum clinics at Delaware Park. The CETA funding was expiring in the early 1980s; the musicians lost their full-time employment from the city of Buffalo, and the Albright-Knox series was also in jeopardy of ending. *Buffalo Evening News* publisher Stanford Lipsey, who happened to also play sax, worked with Falzone to arrange funding by the *Buffalo News* to continue the Sunday summer concerts at the art gallery. These concerts continue to be a popular summer destination for the people of Buffalo.

After the Buffalo Jazz Workshop, Sam Falzone put together the Sam Falzone Quartet with himself on sax, Al Tinney (piano), Jim Coleman (bass) and John Bacon (drums). Several other musicians were members of the group including Mike Royal (piano) and Buddy Fadale (bass). The band was often expanded with Susan Slack or Geri Peters as female vocalists. For much of the early 1980s, they hosted the Sunday afternoon jam at The Cloister.

A group that was an extension of the Buffalo Jazz Workshop was Birthright. This group included Joe Ford (sax), Paul Greshan (sax), Nasar Abadey (percussion) and Greg Millar (guitar). Birthright was a John Coltrane/Miles Davis influenced jazz group that released two albums. Another group that was an extension of the project was Sweetball, which was a combination of members from the House Rockers and Jazz Ensemble. They played instrumentals, including some original compositions by Phil DiRe and Jay Beckenstein.

SPYRO GYRA

In 1974 Spyro Gyra started out as a group simply called Tuesday Night Jazz Jams. When the club owner purchased a new sign for the club, he told them they needed an actual name. They jokingly suggested spirogyra, a type of green algae. The owner misspelled it as Spyro Gyra, the name stuck, and over 40 years later Sypro Gyra is still one of the top jazz groups in the country.

Jay Beckenstein was born in Brooklyn. His mother was an opera singer and his father loved jazz, so he grew up listening to the music of Louis Armstrong, Charlie Parker, Sonny Rollins, and Dizzy Gillespie. He started playing piano at age five and was given his first saxophone at seven. He first enrolled at UB as a biology major but changed to music performance and received a degree in 1973. His high school friend and early bandmate keyboardist Jeremy Wall attended college in California, but they played together in bands on Long Island during summer breaks. After Wall graduated from Cal Arts, he joined Beckenstein in Buffalo to participate in the thriving 1970's Buffalo Music Scene. Both were involved with the Buffalo Jazz Ensemble and they performed with various R&B and jazz bands.

Tuesday was a night when most Buffalo musicians were not working, so Beckenstein and Wall started a jazz jam session at Jack Daniels on Forest Avenue, just off the Elmwood Strip and close to Buff State College. At that time, the original Spyro Gyra consisted of Jay Beckenstein (sax), Jeremy Wall (piano), Jim Kurzdorfer (bass) and Tom Walsh (drums). It did not take long until crowds packed Jack Daniels, and many musicians came to either experience the band or sit in on the jam. One regular musician who came to play at the club was 16-year-old keyboardist Tom Schuman, who forty years later is still a member of the band. The success on Tuesday nights led to other engagements, including regular dates at the venue which became known as their birthplace, the basement club at Main and Amherst, the original Tralfamadore Café, which was owned by Ed Lawson. Soon the group was headlining and opening for touring jazz groups in Buffalo, Rochester and Cleveland.

While performing at area clubs at night, Beckenstein formed a production company called Cross-Eyed Bear with Richard Calandra, the former drummer with the original rock band Posse. Calandra was confined to a wheelchair due to a car accident. Using the insurance money from the accident claim, they bought block recording studio time, which they sold to other Buffalo acts. They made agreements to produce these groups in the studio. One of the groups they sold time to was Buffalo's Rick James, with Beckenstein also played in the horn section on James first album. That album *Come and Get It* is listed as recorded at Cross-Eyed Bear Recording studio in Clarence and included studio work by several Buffalo musicians.

In 1977 the band self-released their first album *Sypro Gyra*. Their popularity from appearing at The Tralfamadore and other area clubs earned them airplay in Buffalo. They pressed 500 copies of the album and distributed copies from Jay's car in Buffalo, Rochester and Cleveland, even creating a TV commercial to self-promote the album. The album caught the attention of Lenny Silver, who re-released it on Amherst Records with new artwork. Their second album *Morning Dance* was financed by Amherst Records and released on Infinity Records, a subsidiary of MCA Records.

Two of Spyro Gyra's most successful albums were their first two releases, which included several musicians from Buffalo and were recorded by Buffalo's Larry Swist. A summary of the Buffalo musician's contribution to Sypro Gyra follows. When Tom Walsh left the band, he was replaced on drums by Ted Reinhardt, who was later replaced by Eli Konikoff. Freddy Rapillo became the guitarist and when he left the group Rick Strauss took his place. Rapillo again returned only to be replaced by Rochester's Chet Catallo. Bass player Jim Kurzdorfer was with the band until 1980, Konikoff until 1984 and Tom Schuman continues as a member, since joining the group in 1977.

During their 40-year career, Spyro Gyra has performed over 5,000 shows, toured on five continents, released over 30 albums, sold over 10 million records and received one platinum and two gold records... impressive credentials for a band that started out without a name and adopted a name derived from a misspelling of their flippant suggestion.

1970s/1980s JAZZ GROUPS AND MUSICIANS

DICK BAUERLE GROUP. While getting material together for a Select Sound Recording Studio Workshop in 1980, instructor Dick Bauerle's scheduled band was not available for a class where the students were going to work on mixing an instrumental song. Dick called the musicians that made up the Select Sound house band, who worked on sessions and commercials at the studio. They played a funky jazz song called "Juicy" that the students practiced recording during the class and completed as a demo.

Jazz DJ John Hunt started playing the song on the radio, it was well received and John asked for additional material. More songs were recorded, with either Jim Witherspoon or Sal Andolina on sax. The Dick Bauerle Group (DBG) was born, and their first job was a radio performance, broadcast live worldwide on the NPR Network. The initial "live" lineup consisted of Dick Bauerle (guitar), Jim Witherspoon (sax), Joe Bellanti (keyboards), Vanik Aloian (percussion), Joe Hesse (bass) and Jim Zeams (drums). They later played dates at the Central Park Grill (CPG) and other venues through late 1983.

The first DBG album was recorded in 1985 with a new group of musicians: Dick Bauerle (guitar), Bob Volkman (keyboards), Tom Reinhardt (bass) and Ted Reinhardt (drums) and released on MCA Records in 1986. It did not receive much support from the record company, but several of the songs were used on a regular basis on the *Entertainment Tonight* television show. The musicians on the second DBG album were Dick Bauerle (guitar), Sal Andolina (sax), Bobby Jones (keyboards), Jerry Livingstone (bass) and Eli Konifoff (drums). This CD was on the Atlantic Jazz label and reached #5 on the national Smooth Jazz charts. After 26 years, in March 2016, the DBG reunited for a date at the Sportsman's.

TAXI was formed by Sal Andolina, who was also a member of the Buffalo Philharmonic and Amherst Saxophone Quartet (ASQ). The members included Sal Andolina (sax), Steve Parisi (keyboards), George Puleo (guitar), Jim Kurzdorfer (bass), and Ted Reinhardt (drums); Rick Fadele (bass) and Bobby Jones (keyboards) later joined the group. The band stopped performing after Gamalon, formed by Puleo and Reinhardt, began playing on a regular basis, and Sal began concentrating more on his classical performances with the BPO and ASQ.

GAMALON was formed in early 1982 by Ted Reinhardt and George Puleo, when they wanted to perform heavier fusion material than they were playing with Taxi. The group was completed by Bruce Brucato (guitar) and Greg Piontek (bass & chapman stick), playing their first dates at Jingles on Main Street. Much of the material they wanted to cover had a prominent keyboard presence, so they added Rick McGirr. Tom Reinhardt took over on bass in 1984 and after McGirr left, Geoff Perry started playing violin and piccolo bass as a guest performer, eventually joining as a permanent member in the late 1980s. Gamalon later

GAMALON
George Puleo, Ted Reinhardt, Greg Piontek, Bruce Brucato
Photo: Courtesy George Puleo

performed at clubs and concerts across WNY and toured to support their albums. However, they are remembered for their steady Tuesday nights at the CPG on Main Street where they played for almost ten years. Gamalon released three albums on Amherst Records which charted nationally, another album with saxophonist Ernie Watts on MCA and a self-released album. The band continued with various members and performed on a periodic basis until Ted Reinhardt died in a tragic plane crash in March 2015. Guitarist Bruce Brucato passed away from cancer in January 2014.

BOBBY MILITELLO'S RPM. Bobby Militello is probably the best nationally known sax player from Buffalo. From 1975 to 1978 he played with Maynard Ferguson, he was a member of the Dave Brubeck Quartet for 20 years, performed with Doc Severinsen's Tonight Show Band and was a featured soloist with the BPO. His most consistent Buffalo-based group was RPM from 1982 to 1983. The original RPM was Bobby Militello (sax/flute), Paul Viapiano (guitar), Bobby Jones (piano), Bill Steubel (bass), and Paul Fadale (drums). In 1983, Bobby released the album *Bobby M Blow* on Motown Records, with Buffalo's Rick James listed as the executive producer. After that album was released, Rick Strauss (guitar) joined the band. Bobby Militello and his brother Michael Militello were part-owners of The Bijou Grill, a restaurant where they featured jazz groups. He was later the owner/manager of the Tralfamadore Night Club, where he presented performances by touring jazz artists.

BOBBY JONES & RUSHOUR was formed by Bobby Jones (piano) after Bobby Militello moved to LA. The group included Sal Andolina (sax), Tony Scozzaro (guitar), Rich Fadale (bass) and Paul Fadale (drums). The members of the band performed with other projects, but they played steady Sundays at Amandas in Lewiston.

THE SAM FALZONE QUARTET hosted the Sunday afternoon jam sessions at The Cloister for over three years in the early 1980s, with Sam Falzone (sax), Al Tinney (piano), Geri Peters (vocals), Jim Coleman (bass) and John Bacon (drums). A later version of the band included Falzone and Bacon, with Mike Royal (piano) and Buddy Fadale (bass). In addition to the Sundays at the Cloister, they performed at other clubs on weekends and broadcast several live shows from The Cloister on WEBR. Prior to forming this group, Falzone was a member of the Don Ellis Orchestra, for thirteen years. With Ellis he toured the world, recorded several albums, appeared on TV specials and played at many major Jazz Festivals.

CORONA performed at The Anchor Bar every Friday, Saturday and Sunday in the early 1980s. The members were Mark Mazur (keyboards/trumpet), Dave Marcewicz (sax), James Clark (guitar), Geoff Morrow (bass) and Mark Horning (drums).

MAGNITUDE was an outgrowth of Jimmy Gomes & the Jazz Example, who had previously performed steady weekends at The Anchor Bar. The group was led by Jamaica native, Carroll McLaughlin, who before moving to Buffalo was the music director on Caribbean cruise ships for over a decade. Magnitude included Jammal (piano), Gil Pease (bass) and Shirley Harris or Geri Peters (vocals). Their single "I Saw You Now" b/w "Marcia" received extensive airplay on WEBR and WBFO. McLaughlin still performs with a current version of Magnitude and he leads a big band that rehearses at The Colored Musicians Club.

C.Q. PRICE BIG BAND. When saxophonist, songwriter and arranger C.Q. Price returned to Buffalo in 1977 he put together a 16-piece big band to perform a show at the Statler Hilton Terrace Room, which included some of the top musicians in Buffalo. Price had returned after four years working as the alto sax man and arranger for Count Basie's Band. Other members were: Eddie Inge (tenor sax) from the Don Redman and Andy Kirk bands, Albert Riding (trombone) who worked with Roy Eldridge and Billy Eckstine, Leroy Johnson (trumpet) from the Charlie Mingus band, Bill Mosny (trumpet) from Fats Waller group, Prince Moss (vocals) who worked with Nat Towles and Al Tinney (piano) who was director of the Buffalo Jazz Ensemble, after years playing in NYC, influencing the early bebop jazz scene and working with Charlie Parker. Other members were James Young

C.Q. PRICE BIG BAND
M&T PLAZA CONCERT SERIES
Photo: Courtesy Buffalo Musicians Union

(tenor sax), Bob Crump (baritone sax), Art Anderson (alto sax), Max Thein (bass), Cubby Copland (drums), Stanley Day (trumpet), John Hargrave (trumpet), Maynard Wright (trombone), Willy Dorsey (trombone), Jimmie Legge (trombone) and Doristene Tydus (female vocalist). C.Q. Price remained in Buffalo and later led the Colored Musicians Club Big Band.

PHIL SIMS & THE BUFFALO BRASS was a 16-piece big band that Sims formed when he returned to Buffalo in the mid-1980s, after touring with the Tommy Dorsey Band. Phil Sims (trombone) was the conductor and arranger for the band. Other regular members were Sal Andolina (alto sax), Ron Palidino (alto sax), Dave Schiavone (tenor sax), Joe Compagna (tenor sax), Jim Pudini (baritone sax), Lon Gormley (trombone), Stewart Easter (trombone), Fred Secor (bass trombone), Dennis Tribuzzi (trumpet), Glenn Lista (trumpet), Nelson Starr (trumpet), Jeff Jarvis (trumpet), Mike Royal (piano), Jim Coleman (bass) and Louie Marino (drums).

LOOSLEY TIGHT included Tony Genovese (guitar), Dave Genovese (guitar), Al Monti (sax). Tim Wells (keyboards), Geoff Perry (bass/violin), Jim Zeams (drums), and Kevin Roth (percussion). Tony was the owner of Elmwood Music, located next to Home of the Hits record store on Elmwood near Forest.

67th AVENUE was a fusion group led by Stu Weissman (guitar). Other members included Cliff Spencer (keyboards), Russ Carere (sax), Zach Colbert (bass) and Reggie Evans (drums).

THE DAVE SCHIAVONE GROUP was Dave Schiavone (sax), Susan Slack (vocals), Jim Beishline (piano), Jim Coleman (bass) and Harri Pender (drums). They were the group that backed vocalist Susan Slack on her *Sunrise* album in 1981.

JR WEITZ BAND was a fusion trio that John Weitz put together after the break-up of Raven. They played various area clubs including regular dates at the Beef & Ale on Main Street. Members were John Weitz (guitar), Gary White (bass), John Opat (drums) and later adding Erie Traud (sax). After recording an album produced by Billy Cobham, the band relocated to California

RONNIE FOSTER was an early keyboardist who performed in Buffalo with jazz and R&B groups. A student of Buffalo organist Joe Madison, Foster is considered an important contributor to the Acid Jazz style, of which Buffalo organist Lonnie Smith is consider the father. He released five albums on Blue Note Records from 1972-1975 and recorded for Columbia later in the '70s. In the later '70s he toured and recorded with George Benson. Foster is currently the director of musical productions at The Venetian Hotel & Casino in Las Vegas.

EMILE LATIMER was a conga player and percussionist who toured and recorded with Nina Simone and Richie Havens. During his career, he performed world-wide and worked the major festivals. Affectionately known as "Papa," he moved to Buffalo in 1976, where he performed with the Buffalo Jazz Workshop, led drum workshops and mentored aspiring musicians. Emile worked with various dance groups and African percussion ensembles. He also led a band that performed at area clubs. Latimer passed away in October 2013 at age 79.

AL TINNEY. While still in his teens, Tinney was cast as an actor in George Gershwin's *Porgy & Bess*, and worked as the rehearsal pianist for the Broadway play. From 1939 to 1943, he was the leader of the house band at the NYC nightclub Monroe's, where he was instrumental in influencing the early bebop jazz scene. Tinney moved to Buffalo in 1968 and was considered the godfather of the Buffalo Jazz scene. You could find him mentoring younger musicians at The Colored Musicians Club, performing as one of the initial members of the Buffalo Jazz Ensemble or appearing at his long-standing performances at The Anchor Bar or Fanny's. At the Anchor Bar, he was joined on a regular basis by Buffalo native and Blue Note Records artist, Dodo Greene. Shortly after his passing in 2002, the portion of Broadway from Elk to Michigan leading up to the Colored Musicians Club was designated Dr. Al Tinney Way.

AL TINNEY & DODO GREENE
Photo Credit: Marsha Falkowski

JAZZ CLUBS IN THE 1970s AND 1980s

TRALFAMADORE. In 1975 the original Tralfamadore Café was opened in a basement location at 2610 Main Street near Fillmore. It was owned by Ed and Bob Lawson and is considered the birthplace of Spyro Gyra. They performed there every Thursday and the cover charge was only one dollar. National bands and top area bands, also performed at this basement nightclub. In 1982, The Tralfamadore was moved to downtown Buffalo and became the anchor of Theater Place. The club design emphasized site lines and acoustics, creating what was considered one of the top jazz clubs in the Northeast. Opening night featured, Sypro Gyra, who had become an internationally known, Grammy nominated band. In addition to Lawson, other owners and/or managers of the club have included Ed Smith, Alan Dewart, Bobby Militello, Tony Marfione, Peter Goretti and Tom Barone.

ONTARIO HOUSE at 920 Ontario Avenue was a jazz club in Niagara Falls, during the 1960s to 1980s. Owner Bob Minicussi presented area jazz groups and for several years featured the organ trio of Richard Kermode, who later became Janis Joplin's keyboardist.

THE STATLER HOTEL was owned by William D. Hassett Jr. in the late 1970s, featuring jazz in both the Rendezvous Room and the Terrace Room. In September 1977 Hassett presented a three-day Jazz & Pop Festival, with performances primarily at The Statler. He was also the promoter of the Artpark Jazz Festival in both 1977 and 1978. In addition to featuring jazz at The Statler and at the festivals, he was the co-owner of Improv Records, with Tony Bennett. In 1979, he became the New York State Commerce Commissioner, where his responsibilities included the I Love New York campaign and the 1980 Winter Olympics in Lake Placid. In the 1980s Hassett was the president of the Boston Bruins, working for Buffalo's Jeremy Jacobs of Delaware North Corporation.

RENAISSANCE II was the second club opened by trumpet player Sam Noto, the first Renaissance was on Pearl Street during the mid-1960s. This club was in the former Frank's Casa Nova at Bailey and East Ferry. Starting in 1981, Noto brought in top name jazz artists and featured the top local jazz musicians. However, the economically depressed neighborhood continued to deteriorate, resulting in the closure of the club.

THE CLOISTER was a fine dining restaurant at the corner of Virginia and Delaware, on the site where Mark Twain's home once stood. It opened in 1964 and for several years entertainment was provided by pianist/vocalist Jackie Jacko, accompanied by drummer Joe Peters. In the 1970s and 1980s it was home of jazz by the Sam Falzone Quartet and the Sunday afternoon jam sessions.

THE ANCHOR BAR at 1047 Main Street had live jazz groups years before they became known for their chicken wings. Of the many jazz clubs that featured live music in Downtown Buffalo and on the East Side during the 1940s, the Anchor Bar is the only one that remains open, with the same name and continues to have music. Many top area jazz groups performed at The Anchor Bar including Corona, Jimmy Gomes & the Jazz Example, and Carroll McLaughlin & Magniture. Al Timmey and Dodo Greene were also headliners at the restaurant.

ST GEORGE'S TABLE opened in 1975 at 675 Delaware in the former location of David's Table, which was in the basement of the Westbrook Hotel. It was owned by jazz promoter Frank St. George, who operated the Jazz Center on Washington Street in the early 1960s. Jazz vocalist Mark Murphy often performed at this club and at Papagayo located at 124 Elmwood.

Additional clubs featuring jazz on a regular or periodic basis during this time included Joe Rico's Milestones, Quincy's Pub, Vinei-Su, Bagatelle, Danny Sansone's, The Library, Revilot, Fieldstone Manor, Front Room, Johnnie's Old Time, Tara Manor, Jafco Marine Restaurant, Bourbon Street, Jack Daniels, Kaleidoscope, Odyssey, Pierce Arrow, Checkerboard, The CPG, The Bona Vista, The Blue Note, owned by Andy Vitello and big band rehearsals on weeknights at The Colored Musicians Club.

One later club was the Calumet Café on Chippewa. It was purchased in 1988 by local historian and author Mark Goldman. In the early 1990s the club was featuring live jazz and started the transformation of Chippewa Street. For many years Chippewa was a street dominated by bars with topless dancers and streetwalkers; it was considered Buffalo's Red-Light

District. Some of the clubs were House of Quinn, Silver Dollar, Erin Go Braugh, The Cosy Bar and Fishermans Wharf (Drums A go-go) and Radices. The one exception was Ciro's Lounge, which at times had go-go girls but also featured bands playing in the front window. The Calumet featured live jazz and ultimately had three separate rooms for dining and entertainment, along with an outdoor patio where they showed movies. The success of The Calumet and efforts of Mark Goldman changed Chippewa Street into the current thriving entertainment district that it is today.

Jazz Radio & Jazz Disc Jockeys had a history going back to when WEBR broadcast shows from the Town Casino and Dellwood Ballroom during the 1940s. Joe Ricco programmed jazz at various radio stations during the 1950s and 1960s. In the 1970s, WEBR continued its jazz programming with Al Wallack's *Jazz in the Nighttime*, which broadcast from several jazz clubs. WBLK featured *The Sound of Jazz* with Carroll Hardy and WADV broadcast nightly jazz with DJ George Beck. WBFO-FM featured daily jazz programs with DJs including Jim Santella, Bill Besecker and Pres Freeland. John Hunt was the program director at WBFO from 1976 to 1985, increasing the stations jazz broadcasting to 72 hours per week.

BLUES GROUPS

Blues Groups were the bands that performed what is referred to as Chicago-style blues, released on labels like Alligator, Cobra and Chess Records. Music by artists like Muddy Waters, Willy Dixon, Buddy Guy, and Howlin' Wolf. Musicians will refer to this style as 12-bar blues, with the basic 1, 4, 5 chord progression.

There was a vibrant black blues music scene in Buffalo, with many national artists performing, on a regular basis, at The Governor's Inn, Pine Grill and other area clubs. The

SHAKIN SMITH BLUES BAND – BONA VISTA
Joe Zappo, Phil Smith, Rob Schurer,
Clark Finn, Shakin Smith
Photo: Courtesy Joe Zappo

early Buffalo area black blues musicians included James Peterson, Count Rabbit, Matt "Guitar" Nickson and Elmore "Spoon" Weatherspoon.

THE SHAKIN SMITH BAND was the first predominantly white band to popularize the 12-bar blues style in Buffalo. Shake started playing in 1970 and had steady nights at The Bona Vista. Gary Gollisano, who later legally changed his name to Shakin Smith was an authentic Chicago-style harmonica player. He gained such a reputation in the WNY area that, even without a nationally successful album or touring with the early blues masters, he was endorsed by Hohner Harmonicas and featured on their company-issued calendar.

The Shakin Smith Band had many members over the years, but the early band was Shake (harmonica/lead vocals), Phil Smith (guitar), Joe "Dr Z" Zappo (guitar), Clark Finn (bass) and Rob Scheuer (drums). Shakin Smith was the first blues band that many people in WNY were exposed to. Many of the '70s and '80s blues musicians apprenticed with the band. In addition to the Bona Vista Shake played at all the WNY blues clubs and opened shows for numerous national blues artists. Among the many musicians that worked with him was former Jambo and Fat Brat guitarist Ken Wilczak.

THE STEADY ROLLIN BAND was formed when guitarists Phil Smith and Joe "Dr Z" Zappo left the Shakin Smith Band. They were together for three or four years and it grew to a nine-piece band, complete with a female vocalist. Some of the band

THE STEADY ROLLIN BAND
John Jacobs, Joe Zappo, Rob Schurer
Jack Prybylski, Mitch Robinson, Norman Duzen, Phil Smith
Photo: Courtesy Joe Zappo

members included Jimmy Wozniak (organ), Pete Howard (sax), Harmonica John (harmonica) and Jack Prybylski (sax), who worked in the band when he was a freshman in college.

THE RHYTHM ROCKERS were an early '80s blues group that included Harmonica John "Wielgus" (harmonica), Stevie B "Berezink" (guitar), Joe Skinner (bass) and Rob Scheuer (drums). They split up in late 1982, with the members forming two different bands, Stevie B & the Rhythm Rockers (which was continued by Stevie B) and Kingsnake.

KINGSNAKE was led by guitarists Phil Smith and Dr Z from The Shakin Smith and The Steady Rollin Band. They were joined by Pete Howard (sax), Clay Stahlka (piano) and Joe Skinner (bass) and Rob Scheuer (drums) from The Rhythm Rockers.

DR Z & THE BLUES REMEDY was formed by Joe "Dr Z" Zappo after he left Kingsnake in the early '80s. The original members of the group were Dr Z (guitar/vocals) Steve Sadoff (bass) and Richie Wieglus (drums). They were the first band to perform at Marshall's on Main Street and remained together, with various members, for about 30 years. Dr Z still currently performs some dates in the WNY area.

THE BLACK CAT BLUES BAND was an early blues group led by vocalist and guitarist John Brady. John previously performed solo at acoustic clubs and was a member of the duo Dillon & Brady, who recorded an album produced by Gary Mallaber. Brady has written material recorded by other artists, including Albert Collins. Other members of the band were Willy Haddath (guitar), Ken Zemke (bass), Jeff Breloff (sax) and Ivo Renner or John Waite alternating as the drummer. Willy later formed the group Willy & the Reinhardts, with Tom Reinhardt (bass) and Ted Reinhardt (drums). Dave Constantino (guitar) from Talas and The Tweeds often joined them for select shows.

THE WILLY MAY BLUES BAND concentrated on original blues material. They did not consider themselves a traditional blues band, calling their selections party barroom blues. In the early 1980s, they released several albums and toured to support them. Members were Willy May (guitar/vocals), Ronnie Kain (guitar), Larry Cheeley (sax), Kevin Espinosa (harmonica), Tom Corsi (bass) and Randy Corsi (drums).

Two other Chicago-style blues groups during the 1980s were the Excello's, led by guitarist Mr Conrad, and the Hurricanes, led by bassist/vocalist Harvey Murello. The Peer Pressure Project was more of a southern rock blues band, led by vocalist/harmonica player Ron Mendez. Ron later promoted the Belle Starr Annual Reunion shows for several years, and The Peer Pressure Project was one of the first bands for guitarist/vocalist Jack Civiletto.

Stan Szelest formed various bands during the 1980s, when he was in town after touring with various acts. They were not strict Chicago blues bands, but that style was represented in their music. His bands during the 1980s included Ernie Corallo (guitar), Doug Yeomans (guitar), Al Monti (sax), Nick Veltri (bass) or Andy Rapillo (bass) and Sandy Konikoff (drums). When Szelest was on tour and not available, Barbara St. Clair and Paul Campanella covered the vocals. That was the foundation of Barbara St. Clair & the Shadows, a group that was formed after Stan discontinued regular performances in WNY.

Billy McEwen's bands covered some Chicago blues but had a variety of material that they performed and they could not be considered a traditional blues band. There were several other groups that performed more of an R&B blues or Southern rock blues style. The traditional blues bands also included some R&B material, but concentrated more on the authentic blues structure and sound.

The most popular blues clubs during the '70s and '80s were The Bona Vista (Hertel), Aliottas (Hertel), Belle Starr (Colden), The Longbranch Saloon (Elma), The Imperial Garage (Niagara Falls) and Lafayette Tap Room in downtown Buffalo. There were also a number of smaller clubs that featured blues bands and rock clubs that had blues nights. Some of the other musicians that performed blues during the early blues days, many of whom still perform, include Donna Rose, Patti Parks, Carol Jean Swist, Dolly Durante, Paul Ianello, Tony Grisanti, Jack McArdle, Greg Zark, Dan Sterner, Bob Falk, Joseph Michael Mahfoud, Hoagy de la Plante, John Rose, John Wade, Dave Keller, Andy Romanek, Dan Gambino, Dan Harper, Paul Siwula, Guy Nigelli, Tommy Z, Jony James, Robert "Freightrain" Parker, Greg Leech, Kent Leech, Frank "Sonny" Mayo and Rod Nickson.

The popularity of blues bands in WNY has waxed and waned over the years, but there has always been a blues presence and a loyal fan base. In 1992 the Western New York Blues Society was formed and they are active in promoting blues and blues events in the area.

EARLY BUFFALO R&B GROUPS

R&B began during the early 1960s at the organ trio bars on the East Side. These were clubs that featured music by a trio consisting of an organist playing a Hammond B3, a guitarist and drummer. Some of the first Buffalo performers were Chick Carrol Davis at Holly's Lounge (Michigan & Best), The Bobby Hall Trio, Charles Bailey Trio, Roy Cobb Trio and piano player Jimmy "J-Man" Manuel. The organ trio was an extension of the jazz trio, leaning more toward hard bop or soul jazz, giving it the R&B flavor.

WUFO 1080AM went on the air on November 2, 1962 as the first Buffalo radio station programmed for the African-American community. Cleveland DJ Eddie O'Jay moved to Buffalo and started broadcasting a Rhythm and Blues (R&B) format. The gathering place, with a big WUFO billboard above the restaurant, was Burger Land at Southampton and Michigan. WUFO would broadcast live from the roof at Burger Land, where you could buy a 13-cent hamburger, around the same time that McDonalds revolutionized the fast food industry by offering 15-cent hamburgers. The Dellwood Ballroom (Main & Utica) started Friday night R&B dance nights, sponsored by WUFO. The Friday night R&B dances drew a black audience, while the Saturday afternoon rock 'n' roll dances drew a white audience to the ballroom that previously featured big band dance music.

Another popular dance venue for black youths in the early to mid '60s was Skateland at 1300 Main Street near Riley. Owner Trunnis Goggins would play records for skating from 7:00–11:00 followed by dancing until midnight. The most popular dances were the James Brown, rubber legs and circle dances, where couples would try to out-do each other during their turn in the center of the circle. Skateland also featured live entertainment by national acts like Stevie Wonder, Gladys Knight, Dionne Warwick and James Brown. The rink moved to New Skateland at Main and East Ferry, where the Vermillion Room nightclub was on the second floor. The slogan of the club was "get up to get down" and Mr. Goggins closed every skating session at his rinks by saying "Yes Baby, it's time to go home."

With the popularity of R&B, the organ trios began including a sax player. The classic combination for the early R&B Group was piano, two guitars, bass and drums. Adding the sax to the organ trio gave a new feel and dimension to the groups, taking them back more to the roots of rock 'n' roll and R&B. The sax was featured on what was considered by many to be the first rock 'n' roll song, Rocket 88 by Jackie Brensten & his Delta Cats, which was really Ike Turner & his Rhythm Kings. This song went to #1 on the R&B charts in 1951.

James Brown changed it all with the release of the TAMI Show in 1964. Based upon the format of the James Brown Band, groups started putting on a show, complete with trumpets, trombones, female dancers and back-up singers. The bands started to dress for their performances wearing flamboyant clothing and shiny shirts. James Brown set the standard, with area bands working to replicate his show and the excitement level of his performance.

CARL LaRUE & HIS CREW were one of the first Buffalo groups that performed R&B. In 1960, they started playing at Buffalo clubs like The Markeen Hotel on Main Street and Padlock Social Club on East Ferry, the Dellwood Ballroom and the Apollo Theater, along with dates at Buffalo State and UB college functions. LaRue was a piano player in the vein of Ray Charles. His Crew included Alvester "Pig" Jacobs (guitar), Willie Earl (drums) and Arlester "Dyke" Christian (bass). In 1963, they released the single "Please Don't Drive Me Away." After receiving an offer to back up The O'Jays, they relocated to Phoenix, Arizona in 1964. LaRue returned to Buffalo, but Dyke stayed in Phoenix where he formed Dyke & the Blazers. More on that later.

EL TEMPOS were another early Buffalo R&B band. They were a Lackawanna based band that played at Maxie's in Lackawanna in the early 1960s. In 1963, they released a song "My Dream Island" on Vee Jay Records, which preceded and sounded very similar to Bunny Wailer's (from Bob Marley & the Wailers) signature song "Dreamland." The El Tempos were Al "Bunk" Johnson (guitar, lead vocals), Willy "Fish" Lowe (keyboards), Leroy Brown (drums) and Otis "OT" Tolliver (bass), who was later a member of Dyke & the Blazers.

THE NEW SOUNDS were formed in 1964 and could be considered one of the first R&B Showbands in WNY. The group was led by Otis Tolliver who had been a member of El Tempos. Other members were Willy "James Brown" Rogers (vocals), Ronnie Amos (vocals), Cheno Rodriguez (guitar), Jerry Hodges (drums), Stanley Lee (sax) and Maurice Jones (trumpet).

MILTON SALTER & THE NEW BREED BAND was formed in 1966 by Milton, along with Chuck Chester Colverhouse (guitar), Bee Bop (drums) and Randy Turner (bongos). They Played at a Club on High & Jefferson, called The New Breed Lounge. This group included The All Night Workers - Ansel Cureton (trumpet), Arthur McBride (trombone), Danny Spidell (keyboards) and Robert Garrett (drums). The band was managed by Johnny Young from Wings 'n' Things. Like the Anchor Bar, Wings 'n' Things also started serving chicken wings in 1964. According to an article in New Yorker magazine, Johnny claimed he was the creator of the chicken wing. Young served his wings whole, not cut into flats and drumsticks, and prepared them breaded with his special mambo sauce. A Buffalo poultry company confirmed both the Anchor Bar and Wings 'n' Things purchased chicken wings in the mid '60s. For his contributions, Young was inducted into the National Buffalo Wing Hall of Flame at the 2013 Buffalo Wing Festival.

PROMO FOR EARLY R&B SHOWS BY THE SALTER BROTHERS
Photos: Courtesy Larry Salter

THE NEW BREED split into two separate bands. Early vocalist James Hunt had number of bookings in the Niagara Falls area so he formed a Niagara Falls version of the group. The All Night Workers segment of the group became the Buffalo version. They hired vocalist Alphonse Yousef who sang with Norm Bernard's Soul Chargers. The given name for this vocalist was William E. Shingles but he began using the name, Lance Diamond, and he became known as the best dressed and the hardest working man in Buffalo show business. Lance later toured with Isaac and The Lance Diamond band, performing across the U.S. and in Japan. He also performed and recorded with The Goo Goo Dolls. With the 24 Karat Diamond Band, he was a regular performer at The Elmwood Lounge and various high-profile Buffalo events until his passing on January 4, 2015.

LANCE DIAMOND
Photo Credit: Bob Mussell

In the late 1960s and early '70s some of the early R&B clubs included The Sands, Jans, Brownies Upper Terrace, Pine Grill, Maxies, Club Carousel, Shalamar, 133 Club, Holly's, Reviliot and Johnny's Ellicott Grill. A couple other early R&B bands were Full Measure and Dynamic Souls. The New Breed changed their name to Pheu Breed Productions in 1971. The amount of available R&B clubs was diminishing and during the summer of 1972 The Pheu Breed played at The Big Ten Club in Angola, and they were the first all-black band to play at The Suburban House in suburban Williamsville. However, in Buffalo there were fewer clubs where black groups could perform, so the bands started successfully traveling on the road.

HANK "SOUL MAN" MULLEN was the leader of a soul-R&B band called the Avengers, performing in Buffalo clubs during the 1960s. Guitarist Alan Syms, later a member of Rick James Stone City Band, was a member of Mullen's band. Syms remembers wearing tailor-made suits and playing four nights a week when he was still a junior in high school. The Avengers had three vocalists, Mullens, Moe Jones and Carlena Weaver and toured the Midwest and South as the backing band for Eddie Floyd, Arthur Conley, Betty Wright and Betty Swan. Hank "Soul Man" Mullens released a single "Listen" b/w "He Upset Your Dreams." In Macom, Georgia they recorded another single "Heart Break" which was credited to The

Avengers vocalist Carlena Weaver (who later sang with the Ikettes). Both singles were issued on Audel Records, operated by the Buffalo record store Audrey & Dells. Mullins career was cut short in the early 1970s when he tragically died of a heart attack while still in his mid-20s.

THE EXOTICS was a five-piece vocal group that disbanded in 1971, but later become known as The Exoutics. They released the regionally successful song "Here We Go Again" and performed predominantly in Southern Ontario. In the 1990s, the group members later released songs as the band Paradyme.

UNITED SOUND was formed in the early 1970s. They were a racially mixed band and the first group to break the suburban color barrier. The group had four vocalists up front, four instrumentalists and later added a horn section. United Sound was one of the first WNY bands to tour the East Coast Top 40 Show clubs and they established the practice of Buffalo R&B bands performing more out of town shows than WNY area dates. In addition to dates on the East Coast, United Sound also toured the entire United States, Canada and Europe.

UST TOPAZE had its roots with the Lackawanna band Unique Sound, which was formed in 1973. The members included Anthony Viterna (guitar), Derrick McAlister (drums), Jerry Morero (percussion), Andre Morrow (bass) and Henry Wright Jr. (vocals), with Van Taylor

UST TOPAZE
Photo: Courtesy Van Taylor

(keyboards) joining in late 1973. The group included a horn section and during 1974 and 1975 they played music in the style of Chicago and Tower of Power. During the fall of 1975, they merged with the vocal group Topaze, which included singers Raymond McCastle, Joey Diggs and Vanesa Brooks. They decided to choose the combined name of Unique Sounds and Topaze, which was shortened to UST Topaze, and they finalized the line-up with Kelvin Knight (bass), Brian

Freeman (trumpet), Robert Tatum (sax) and Anthony Ceasar (vocals).

A musician who later became internationally famous, was a regular spectator at UST Topaze shows. James Johnson, attended their shows at Erikson's Lounge, the former Royal Arms on West Utica. Johnson obtained a recording contract with Motown Records and when he recorded his first album in 1978, he used the vocals of Joey Diggs, Vanesa Brooks and Anthony Ceasar from UST Topaze to back up his lead vocals. The name of the album was *Come Get It* and with the release of the record, Johnson started using the name of Rick James.

UST Topaze performed primarily outside of the Buffalo area and many different musicians were part of the band including Kenny Hawkins (guitar), Thomas Rodgers (drums), Carl Christian (trombone) and Shawn McQuiller (guitar/vocals). Before joining the band, Lackawanna native McQuiller had an area band called Pleasure Secrets; and after he left UST Topaze, he formed a band called Traffic Jam, which included his wife as the vocalist. Traffic Jam also mainly played outside of the Buffalo area, and when they were working a two-month engagement in Singapore, they opened a show for Kool & the Gang. After that show in 1991, Kool & the Gang asked McQuiller to join them as lead vocalist and guitarist, a position he still retains today.

Keyboardist Van Taylor started Taylor Made Jazz in 1987, with members from UST Topaze and other musicians from the Buffalo R&B community. Over the past 30 years the band has traveled hundreds of thousands of miles performing for the military at USO functions, for government officials at American Embassy events and at educational seminars throughout Europe, Asia, Africa, the Caribbean and Pacific Islands.

SABATA was another 1970s Buffalo-based R&B band that traveled extensively. They were originally known as Sabata and the Cause, with their Buffalo home club being the Vermillion Room, above New Skateland. The original members were Larry & Curtis Patterson, Stacy Lattimore, Sharon

SABATA & THE CAUSE
Photo: Courtesy Sharon Banks

Banks, Grady Tatum, Anthony Anderson, Finell Steel, Elgy Fleming and Zondra Yarborough. They are the members is this photo. When Sabata and the Cause split up, some members of The Cause become part of Rick James first band. Sabata performed more dates in Canada, Japan and the Pacific Rim than they did in the immediate Buffalo area.

THE UNITY BAND was formed by bass player Tommy Flucker after he returned to Buffalo from a national tour with The Whispers in 1983. The group featured a horn section, choreography and tight musicianship. Lisa Rushton and Cynthia Moore from The Unity Band later became members of James Brown's backing band. Other members of the group toured with The Coasters and Marvelettes. Thirty-five years later, founder Tommy Flucker still leads the band and is now the owner of two East Side Nightclubs, Mikes Lounge and Arthur's Pub.

Other R&B bands and musicians during the 1970s and 1980s were The Last Days of Time, Kenny Berry Band, Marshall Badger Band, Momentz Notice, Pressure, Inflyte, Pulse and Harold Travis & Variations of Love, which was an integrated disco/funk band, that included Tom Reinhardt and Rick McGirr from the progressive rock band Rodan. These bands performed at clubs like The Little Harlem, Cotton Club, Poor Man's Castle, Caesar's Lamplight, Vermillion Room, Eriksons Lounge, Club Virgoan, Wall Street, the New Golden Nugget, Green Ghetto, Kilimanjaro and Le Club Etcetera.

Some Buffalo R&B performers achieved national recognition without ever performing in Buffalo area clubs or by just appearing in town on a limited basis.

DYKE & THE BLAZERS. In 1964, Carl LaRue & His Crew relocated to Phoenix, Arizona to be the back-up band for The O'Jays, a job offered to them by former WUFO DJ Eddie O'Jay. After playing some dates backing up the group, The O'Jays decided to leave Phoenix. Carl LaRue's band had established itself in the city and started playing the Phoenix clubs, but Carl decided to return to Buffalo. The bass player/vocalist in the band was Alester "Dyke" Christian, who attended Burgard High School and grew up in the Fruit Belt. Dyke, along with Buffalo guitarist Alverter "Pig" Jacobs and saxophonist J.V. Hunt, decided to stay in Phoenix and joined an Arizona band called The Three Blazers, which was renamed Dyke & the Blazers. They released "Funky Broadway" in 1967, a hit for them, as well as Wilson Picket's cover version which reached #1 on the R&B charts. After the release of "Funky Broadway" and a series of dates at NYC's Apollo Theater, Dyke returned to Buffalo and formed a new touring version of Dyke & the Blazers, including Buffalo musicians Willie Earl (drums), Wardell "Baby Wayne" Peterson (second drummer), Otis Tolliver (bass), Ray Byrd (keyboards) and Maurice "Little Mo" Jones (trumpet). This version of the band performed at Memorial Auditorium in 1967, only one day after the line-up was solidified. That group gradually disintegrated; and by 1969, Dyke was recording with various LA studio musicians. It was that rendition of the group that recorded "We Got More Soul" and "Let A Woman Be a Woman," both top 10 R&B hits. During their career Dyke & the Blazers had seven singles that charted. Dyke had experienced some drug problems but cleaned himself up and was preparing for a tour of England, along with new recordings with Barry White. The recordings and tour never happened, because Dyke was fatally shot in front of a Phoenix bar on March 13, 1971. He is buried in Buffalo's Forest Lawn cemetery.

DARRELL BANKS was born in Mansfield, Ohio in 1937, but he grew up in Buffalo. Darrell began singing gospel music at Buffalo churches but decided to follow a career in secular music. His biggest hit was "Open the Door to Your Heart", which peaked at #2 on the R&B charts in 1966. The song was recorded in Detroit, but after it was released the Buffalo connection intensified. The record was released on Revilot Records, a label Banks created along with a production company. This label was named after the Revilot Lounge, the club where he often performed in Buffalo. "Open the Door to Your Heart" was listed as written by Darrell Banks, but it was actually written by Donnie Elbert, who was a member of the Buffalo band the Vibraharps. Banks knew Elbert when he lived in Buffalo and Elbert wrote the song for Banks. When Elbert did not receive any writer's royalties for the song on his BMI statement, he sued and received 50% writers credit. The courts ruled in Elberts favor because he had over 100 songs listed in his BMI catalogue, while "Open the Door to Your Heart" was the only song Banks ever claimed to have written. Banks had another hit with the song "Somebody (Somewhere) Needs You" but none of his subsequent releases charted. Darrell Banks was an exciting performer known for his soulful voice, but off-stage he evidently did not retain that pleasant personality. In 1970, he was shot in an alleged love triangle, cutting short his very promising career at only age 32.

FRANK BRUNSON was born in 1929 and started singing at his father Rev. John Brunson's church in Dunkirk. He graduated from Hutchinson High School in Buffalo and released his first single "Charmaine" in the mid-1950s. Bruson was called Little Frankie during his early days of rock 'n' roll but after he signed with Jackie Wilson's manager, he became Big Daddy, due to his powerful voice. He released the classic R&B album *Big Daddy's Blues* and one of his songs "I Believe in You" was recorded by Jerry Lee Lewis in 1965. His real success came in 1971 when he formed the American funk band, People's Choice, based in Philadelphia. Brunson was the keyboardist and vocalist and ten of their songs, mostly instrumentals, reached the Billboard R&B Charts. The song "Do It Any Way You Wanna" reached #1 on the R&B charts and was a gold record. People's Choice broke up in 1984, and when Frank Brunson returned to Buffalo, he went back to his roots and started singing at St John's Baptist Church. He continued singing with the choir, even after a stroke confined him to a wheelchair. Bruson sang with that choir until just before his death at age 78 in 2007.

RICK JAMES

Rick James was born James Ambrose Johnson Jr. in Buffalo in 1948, one of eight children. His father left when Rick was young, and he was raised by his mother, who was a dancer and later ran errands or numbers for organized crime. When accompanying his mother to nightclubs, he got to see performances by jazz and R&B performers. James was arrested in his early teens and to avoid jail and the draft, he joined the Navy Reserve when he was only 16. Since he was playing drums in a band, he kept missing his Reserve meetings. This resulted in him being ordered to active duty and assigned to serve in Vietnam.

In 1965, rather than go to Vietnam, James want AWOL and relocated to Toronto, Ontario, Canada. In Canada, he assumed the name of Ricky James Matthews and befriended then local Toronto area musicians Neil Young and Joni Mitchell. He formed a band, the Mynah Birds, who were signed to Motown Records in Detroit and recorded in LA. His Toronto friend, Neil Young later became a member of that group. When Motown found out about his AWOL status, they told James to turn himself in and serve his time. He surrendered to the Navy, eventually serving five months.

When James was released from prison, he returned to Toronto, to Detroit and to LA. He again signed with Motown Records and returned to Buffalo, where he put a band together; that played their first job at East High School. His first album was primarily recorded in Clarence, with additional parts and mastering in NYC. James realized that the talent was available in Buffalo for the project. He recalled seeing Dyke & the Blazers perform in Buffalo and hearing "Funky Broadway" on the radio. That had an effect on James career because he recalled, "...it showed me somebody from Buffalo could make music that was new and fresh and funky."

Rick James utlized many Buffalo musicians when recording his first album *Come and Get It* in 1978. These musicians included Billy Nunn (keyboards), Bobby Nunn (keyboards), Freddie Rapillo (guitar), Andy Rapillo (bass), Mike Caputy (drums), Richard Shaw (bass), Lorenzo Shaw (drums) and the Williams brothers Flick, Berry and Steve as the horn section. The album was engineered by Chuck Madden. On the second album, additional Buffalo musicians were Oscar Alston (bass), Al "Syms" Szymanski (guitar), Lanise Hughes (drums) and Jackie Ruffin (percussion). Kenny Hawkins was later Rick James' music director and guitarist. The band that recorded on the album and toured with Rick James was called the Stone City Band, including mostly Buffalo musicians. On later albums, when James was no longer recording in Buffalo, more LA musicians were members of the Stone City Band.

During his career Rick James recorded 13 studio albums, and four of his singles reached #1 on the R&B charts: "You and I", Give It to Me Baby", "Cold Blooded" and "Loosey's Rap." However, his most successful and signature song was "Super Freak," which was later sampled by MC Hammer in the song "You Can't Touch This" which won a Grammy Award. James best-selling album was *Street Songs* which went seven times platinum.

MARY JANE GIRLS were a group formed by Rick James as his vocal back-up band. The original members that sang on James' albums were Joanne "JoJo" McDuffie, and sisters Maxine and Julia Waters. McDuffie was the primary vocalist and she had previously worked with Buffalo bands at area nightclubs. For live performances, the members were JoJo McDuffie, Cheryl "Cheri Wells" Bailey, Candice "Candi" Ghant and Kimberly "Maxi" Wuetich, with Yvette "Corvette" Marine replacing Cheri Wells. In 1983 James was successful in getting The Mary Jane Girls signed to Motown Records, with himself as the songwriter and producer. Their first album yielded the singles "Candy Man" and "All Night Long". The second album was released in 1985 and included the single "In My House", which reached #3 on the R&B Charts. The members of The Mary Jane Girls, they were basically just part of the stage show. On the recordings, McDuffie was usually backed by the Waters sisters. After the group disbanded, JoJo also sang back-up for Barry White and Anita Baker. The Waters sisters continued as back-up vocalists and toured with various recording artists including Paul Simon and Neil Diamond.

PROCESS AND THE DOO RAGS were another project by Rick James, to establish his back up vocal groups as stand-alone acts. The group was reminiscent of a '50s doo-wop group, with their processed hairdos, zoot suits and dance routines by legendary Buffalo choreographer Cholly Atkins, best known for his work with The Temptations and Supremes. The members were led by James' primary back-up vocalist James "Process" Hawkins, along with Stacey "Wave" Lattimore, Henry "Grumps" Graham, Dennis "Shorty" Andrews and Michael "Smooth" Gibson. On recordings and during performances the band was supported by Rick James' music director and James Hawkins' brother, guitarist Kenny Hawkins and the Stone City Band. The band played their premier showcase of six sold-out shows at the Cotton Club in Buffalo. Process and the Doo Rags released two albums on Columbia and their most successful single was "Stomp and Shout", with its video being featured on MTV, VH1 and BET. In addition to their recordings, Process and the Doo Rags were the backing vocal group on several of Rick James albums.

TEENA MARIE was not from Buffalo, but her 1979 album Wild and Peaceful was produced by Rick James. James composed six of the songs on the album, which featured Buffalo musicians including Oscar Alston (bass), Lanise Hughes (drums) and Levi Ruffin (keyboards). Guitarist Kenny Hawkins also worked with Teena Marie on several projects. Rick James and Teena Marie had a close working relationship, but Teena Marie's daughter (Alia Rose) revealed in November 2015 on the radio show "2 Black Girls and A Mic" that there is no truth to the rumors that Rick James is her father. One of Rick James' last television appearances, was singing the duet "Fire and Desire" from his Street Songs album, with

Teena Marie at the 2004 BET Awards. James died of a heart attack on August 6, 2004 and is buried at Forest Lawn Cemetery.

BRIAN McKNIGHT was born in Buffalo on June 5, 1969. He began performing during his childhood as a member of his church choir and started a gospel quartet with his brothers. In 1980, while at Oakwood College, a Seventh-day Adventist university in Huntsville Alabama, his older brother Claude V. McKnight III formed Take 6, an a cappella gospel music sextet. Since 1988, Take 6 has won a total of ten Grammy Awards. His brother's success encouraged Brian to pursue a recording career. However, rather than performing gospel music, Brian concentrated on popular music, resulting in several million-selling R&B albums. Brian McKnight is classified as a leggero tenor and is recognized for his strong falsetto. During his career, he has been nominated for 16 Grammy Awards, the third highest amount of nominations by any performer without a win. He is only surpassed in that distinction by Morten Lindberg and Snoop Dogg.

GOSPEL. In addition to Brian and Claude McKnight, there have been other successful gospel performers from the Buffalo area. A young Aretha Franklin sang at a church were her father, Minister C.L. Franklin was the pastor. Pastor Jerome L. Ferrell of the Lighthouse Choir released several records and recorded other Buffalo area gospel artists. Ella Robinson began her career in the 1960s, performing with her father Rev. John H. Monroe at the Greater Hope Baptist Church and was a vocal music teacher in the Buffalo School system from 1972 to 2007. She founded and directed The New Beginnings Choral Ensemble.

JOE PUBLIC did not release their first album until 1992, but the band members started working together in Buffalo in 1984. Joseph 'JR' Sayles and his brother Nathan, were members of Ice Band. Isaac Scott and Joe 'Jake' Carter were in the group New World. They won a Battle of the Bands contest and producer Lionel Job signed them to a recording contract. These musicians became the band Atension, releasing an album on Island Records and the single "Let Me Push It to Ya." Kevin Scott, Joseph Sales, Joe Carter and Dwight Wyatt, along with Lionel Job and Keith Sweat, wrote the song "Keep It Coming" for Keith Sweat, a #1 R&B single. They changed their name to Joe Public and signed with Columbia Records. The line-up of Joe Public was Kevin Scott (vocals/bass), Jake Carter (keyboards), JR Sayles (guitar) and Dwight "Mr. Dew" Wyatt (drums). Their single "Live and Learn" reached #4 on the Billboard Top 100 in 1992. Classified as a "new jack swing band," Joe Public was the first R&B band to perform on MTV Unplugged, where they were also the back-up band for Boyz II Men and Shanice. Joe Public was also the backing band for Kris Kross on The Arsenio Hall Show. It all began when the members of Joe Public were young and they would sneak into the Buffalo East Side clubs, to learn from veteran Buffalo R&B groups and sometimes sitting in with UST Topaze, Last Days of Time and Sabata.

16

ETHNIC MUSIC IN BUFFALO

When ethnic groups immigrated to Buffalo they brought their culture and music with them. The Germans were the first ethnic group to settle in the Buffalo area and nationally, more people have immigrated to the U.S. from Germany than any other country in the world. In the 1840s over a third of the Buffalo population was German and prior to the Civil War, there were twice as many Germans than Irish in Buffalo. According to the 2000 Buffalo census, the top four ancestries in Buffalo were German, Irish, Polish and Italian.

The Germans brought their beer halls and singing societies to the Fruit Belt and East Side area near Genesee Street. The Irish brought their songs and dancing to the many pubs and local bars that opened in the South Buffalo area. The Polish settled on the East Side of Buffalo and Polish Singing groups and taverns featuring polka bands opened around the Broadway Fillmore area, expanding into the suburbs.

Other ethnic groups contributed to the diverse music scene in Buffalo. Many of the early musicians working at WNY theaters and playing popular music were Italian. Jewish immigrants also became members of early orchestras and bands, along with playing a prominent role in live theater. Greek musicians played at Hellenic Festivals and other Slavic immigrants performed at their church or neighborhood events.

GERMAN

The German population of Buffalo started to substantially increase around 1850, when liberal working-class German immigrants began leaving Germany after losing the Revolution of 1848 to the conservative aristocracy. They formed the Turn Verein, which was a German American social club, community center and gymnasium. Members were called the Turners due to their emphasis on gymnastics, together with health and physical education activities. Their community centers also featured German musical and theatrical productions, with an emphasis on German singing associations.

The first German singing society in Buffalo was the Leidertafel formed in 1848. It had several music directors including John Dossert and Joseph Mischka. In 1853, Das Liederkraenzchen was formed, later becoming the Saengerbund. Other singing societies were Harugair-Maennerchor, Orpheus (Ernst Schultz and Carl Adams directors), Arion Singing Society (August Goehle director), Harmonie Singing Society (John Laux director), East Buffalo Maennerchor, St. Stephens Maennerchor (J. Eitelman director) and the Helvetia Saenger Verein (William Lutz president).

The Buffalo Turn Verein was formed at Roth's Hall at Michigan & Cypress in 1853. They moved into Gillig's Hall at 249 Genesee in 1854 and Turner's Theatre in 1858. There were two separate factions of the group. The Manner Turn Verein remained at Gillig's Hall, which they renamed the Stadt Theater in 1858. The Turn Verein Vorwarts moved their activities to the Turner Theatre. In 1869 the first Saengerbund made its home at Turner's, remaining there until the Saengerhalle was completed in 1887. German theater and musical performances were associated with many other theaters and halls in the Genesee Street area through the early 20th century. For a listing of all the theaters and additional information, see the Early Theaters section in Chapter 1.

In 1855, the Buffalo Saengerbund was formed at the home of Charles Dorn, who lived at the corner of Cherry & Maple Street. The first music directors were C.W. Braun and Professor Friedrich Federlein. The Saengerbund and Buffalo Glee Club participated in the song festival in Cleveland, Ohio in 1859 and offered to host the song festival in 1860. However, so many singing groups agreed to perform in the 1860 Saengerfest (Feast of Song) that Buffalo did not have a hall large enough to accommodate all the participants. An opening ceremony was held at St. James Hall, conducted by Julius Moevius, and the great depot of the New York Central Railway was transformed into a concert hall for the main concert. The acoustics of the depot were perfect for the singing festival, and railway business was conducted at the terminal during intermissions.

A second Saengerfest was scheduled to be held in Buffalo in 1883. For this festival the Saengerhalle, The First Music Hall, was built on the corner of Main & Edward, across the street from St Louis Church. The property was on the site of the former estate of previous Buffalo Mayor, Judge Ebenezer Walden. The music

FIRST MUSIC HALL 1883-1885
Photo: Picture Book of Earlier Buffalo

hall was built by then Buffalo mayor Philip Becker and businessman Jacob Schoelkoph, who were also responsible for securing the Saengerfest in Buffalo. A grand parade progressed from the downtown train station through a decorated Main Street to the Saengerhalle. The festival was a success, and Buffalo had a grand music hall, but the hall and adjoining St. Louis Church were destroyed by a fire in 1885.

The Saengerhalle was rebuilt and reopened as The Music Hall on October 18, 1887. The new concert building had an auditorium that held 2,500 people, a second concert hall held 1,100, parlors, banquet rooms, meeting rooms, a store, restaurant and library. This building housed Buffalo's first symphony orchestra and hosted concerts by Jan Paderowski and John Phillip Sousa. Jacob Schoelkoph remodeled the building, and it reopened as the Teck Theatre in 1900.

During the Pan-American Exposition, the third Saengerfest was held in Buffalo. It was a series of concerts offered by the North American German Singing Society, which was a group of 105 choruses from across the country. This event was so large that it had to be held at the Connecticut Street Armory, at that time known as the 74th Regimental Armory, at the corner of Connecticut and Niagara Street. The main concert at the Armory was comprised of 40 societies and 2,000 singers, with room for a capacity crowd of 10,000 people. This festival was financed by forming the Buffalo Saengerfest Company, with 1,600 shares being sold at $25 each.

German music was featured at the Pan-American Exposition in the beer gardens. There was plenty of beer to go around because at this time Buffalo was one of the brewing capitals of the country. There were almost

100 breweries in the Buffalo area, and almost all of them were of German origin. The first person to open a brewery in Buffalo was Rudolph Baer in 1826. Later breweries included: Iroquois Brewery owned by Leonard Burgwerger, Magnus Beck Brewery, Gerhard Lang Brewing Co., the German American Brewing Company, Ziegele Brewing Co., John Schusler Brewery and the William Simon Brewery. In 1900, the U.S. Brewmasters Association held its convention in Buffalo and voted to continue the exclusive use of German as the official language of the group. There were 29 operating breweries in Buffalo on the eve of Prohibition in 1920 and it was estimated that two years later, there were still an estimated 8,000 locations in WNY where you could illegally buy alcohol. In 1921, Francis Schwab, a former brewmaster and opponent of Prohibition, was elected mayor of Buffalo.

The German American clubs like Turn Verein provided entertainment but also emphasized physical fitness and German patriotism. With the beginning of WWI, the general population of WNY looked suspiciously upon the German clubs that were advocating German values and culture. The clubs started to decline, but people of German ancestry were still a dominant population group. Due to the wartime attitude, German-Americans had to assimilate into the general population. Prohibition started soon after the end of WWI, so the drinking of beer went underground to the speakeasys and there were no longer any beer gardens to feature German bands.

When prohibition ended in December 1933, the attitudes from WWI had subsided; and since the beer was flowing again, German music was again in demand. German music was popular in all parts of the city, and three to five-piece bands, including the popular Frank Radl Band, were performing at places like Braun's Park on Genesee, Mann's Restaurant on Bailey, Casino Restaurant on Genesee & Kieffer, George Doyle's Restaurant on Genesee, Café Heidelberg on Bailey & Genesee, Hans Geyer's Chateau on Main near Edward, and George Troidl's Tavern on Olympic. German bands were even playing at Hotel Worth, The Statler and Hotel Lafayette. The standard pay for musicians performing at these taverns in the 1930s was usually $3.00 each per night and $4.00 each on Saturday. In 1933 The German American Musicians Association was formed with some of the early members being Kurt Wissing, Al Feustel, Frank Schwindler, George Troidl and Carl Fassel. In 1939, with the advent of WWII, public sentiment again turned against anything German, and there were only two or three bands still playing German music in the Buffalo area.

There was a rebirth of German music after WWII and it became apparent that German music was not just played by people of German heritage, it was also performed by people of Irish, Polish, Italian, Ukrainian and Spanish decent. In 1961, Dick Silva met with Louis Beer and Al Feustel at the Genesee Park Restaurant. Silva became the treasurer of the German American Musicians Association and later served as president from 1976 to 1981. In 1964, Silva with George Hinterbichler, Al Odenbach and Kurt Wissing from the German

FRANKFURTERS 1982
Glenn Call, Geoff Richter, Jim Pace
Bob Bieger, Dick Rine, Clint Koetzle
Wendy Pace, Bobby Prigl, Jan Richter
Photo: Courtesy Jim Pace

American Musicians Association and Frank Bihler of the Germania Sports Club, co-sponsored the first area Octoberfest at the Chuckwagon Banquet Hall in Lackawanna. It was a sell-out and Octoberfests became regular events on the WNY entertainment calendar.

George Hinterbichler received his degree in music from the Music School in Salzburg Austria and was a member of the Saalfelden city band from 1937 to 1956. He moved to Lackawanna in 1956, and in 1963 he assumed directorship of the German American Musicians Association. The highlight of his tenure was taking the Association band on a 16-day tour of Austria and Germany in 1979. The band played concerts in twelve cities, including George's hometown of Saalfelden.

During the 1950s and 1960s, German Bands were performing at clubs like Scharf's Schiller Park, Gillitzers on Broadway near Smith, Maxl's Brau Stuberl on Main and East Ferry, Deutsche's Haus, Strinkas Tavern, Alpine Village and Troidl's. In 1974, the Auslanders were formed by Frank Wailand, and in 1982 the seven-piece Frankfurters were formed by Jim Pace. Together with the German American Musicians Association Big Band, these groups currently perform all year long at German events and especially at Octoberfest celebrations across WNY.

THE BUFFALO SILVER BAND 1915
Photo: Courtesy Martha Neri

OTHER ETHNIC

The First Hungarian Baptist Church Band was formed in 1915 but had its roots in 1909, when the First German Baptist Church on Spruce Street reached out to the Hungarian immigrants and helped them establish a meeting place where they could worship. They established their own church in 1912 and had sufficient members to form the band in 1915, which accompanied the congregation by playing hymns and other works of religious nature.

The band was a British style brass band, also called a silver band, because they do not use any reed instruments. They were allied with the style of the Salvation Army Band and in 1981 officially changed their name to the Buffalo Silver Band. The organization has been performing for over 100 years and one of the prominent members was Nelson Starr, who played in touring big bands and Legion bands in WNY.

IRISH MUSIC

The Irish started arriving in Buffalo to assist in building the Erie Canal, which opened in 1825. Many workers remained in Buffalo after the canal was completed, obtaining jobs on the waterfront, scooping grain at the grain mills or building the railroads. In 1845–1852 the Irish Potato Famine resulted in many people leaving Ireland for the United States and by 1855 there were over 10,000 people of Irish descent living in Buffalo.

When the Irish moved into the First Ward near the Buffalo waterfront, they brought their pub culture with them. Many taverns became the gathering places for the dock and grain workers, with some serving as a union hall for the hiring of day laborers. Irish music often filled the back rooms of many of these bars. Michael Shea began his career as a South Buffalo tavern owner before opening his music halls, vaudeville and movie theaters.

Many of the early performers were solo artists, playing fiddle, accordion or guitar. They sang or played Irish folk songs at taverns, clubs, social events and house parties. In 1948 fiddler Martin Wynn emigrated to Buffalo and started playing traditional Irish music at parties, accompanied by other members of his family. Patricia McCarthy played piano at the Knights of Equity Hall and for the Irish Friendly Sons. Pat Collins

STUART MONTEITH
Photo: Courtesy Stuart Monteith

played the concertina for the Quealy School of Irish Dance and at social functions, while Paddy Herlihy was known known as a fiddler for dancers and at the Gaelic Football games. Stuart Monteith could be seen performing solo or with his trio at the Bishop Duffy Center and with his band at Sparfield Hall. Many would come to hear organist Mary Jane Moran sing her signature song "Down in the Old Neighborhood" and other Irish-American songs at the Top Hat Grill, the old Fitzgerald's in Tonawanda, Hotel Lackawanna and the Carriage House. Other places with Irish music during the 1950s, 1960s and 1970s were the Chuckwagon, McGinty's, Doherty's Pub and The Buffalo Irish Center.

One of the cornerstones of the Buffalo Irish-American community and a showplace for hearing Irish music is the Buffalo Irish Center. The center had its roots in the late 1960s when St Patrick's Irish American Club, under the direction of president Michael Bryne, began a quest to find a place where all the Irish groups in Buffalo could share as a meeting place. The Knights of Equity Court 5 had decided to sell their building at 493 Delaware Avenue. They partnered with the St. Patrick's Irish American Club, who had been meeting at the Bishop Duffy Center, located at Main and Riley. In 1970, they purchased the former South Buffalo YMCA at 245 Abbott Road. They formed the Gaelic American Athletic Association of Buffalo NY Inc. d/b/a Buffalo Irish Center to oversee the building and operations. Currently the center is home to over 15 non-profit organizations including traditional Irish Dance schools, Adult Ceili classes, language classes and the Fenians Gaelic Football Teams, for both adults and children.

THE PLOUGHBOYS
Jack Bonner, Brian Bonner, Bob Beckley
Eddie O'Neill
Photo: Courtesy Brian Bonner

In 1968, one of the first Irish folk groups in Buffalo was the Ploughboys, formed by accordion player Brian Bonner. The initial members were guitarist Bob Beckley and vocalists Eddie O'Neil and Jack Bonner. Vocalist Liz Tynan later joined the group. The Ploughboys played their first dates and their home base was McGinty's on Seneca Street, near the Larkin Center. They performed functions around WNY until 1971.

In 1971, The Blarney Bunch was formed by Frank Finn and Tootie Stark, with the other original members being Eileen O'Sullivan and Cathy Beecher. Over the years, Mary Pat (Maracle) Stark, Jeanne Stackpoole, Jim O'Dea, Denise O'Dea, Bernie Stack, Dan Bonner. Rich Bonner, Tome Hennessy, Frank Hilliard and Tom Jordan were members of the band. The Blarney Bunch first started performing at Rielly's Bar and since 1973 has been led by Dan Bonner. They have released six albums and the band continues to perform at Irish festivals and community events across WNY.

Other performers in the 1970s and early 1980s were the acoustic duo Gerry McCrudden & Sheila McCrudden, solo performer Mike Brennan and vocalist Niall O'Donoghue. Other clubs featuring Irish music were the Buffalo Irish Center, Niall Donoghue's Irish Singing Pub, The Wilton Arms on Abbott Road and The Shannon Pub.

BLARNEY BUNCH
Frank Finn, Cathleen Beecher, Frank Hilliard
Eileen O'Sullivan, Dan Bonner
Photo: Courtesy Dan Bonner

In February 1982, The Shannon Pub opened in the Airways Hotel, located on Genesee Street in front of the Airport. They featured live Irish Music four nights a week, with the initial entertainers being The Blarney Bunch, Sheila & Gerry McCrudden, Niall O'Donoghue, and the Dady Brothers and The Emigrants from Rochester. Entertainers from Ireland also performed at the club playing what was termed "Rebel" Music, centering around the troubles that were, happening in Ireland and Northern Ireland at that time. The Shannon Pub remained at the Airways Hotel until the building was razed for airport expansion in 1993. They reopened in the Lord Amherst Hotel on Main Street in Snyder in 1994 and again relocated in 2005 to their location at 2250 Niagara Falls Blvd (in the former Canterbury Restaurant), which closed in 2017.

In 1982, Kevin Townsell of The Shannon Pub presented the first Buffalo Irish Festival at Weimer's Grove in Lancaster. It featured local Buffalo and Rochester Irish performers The Blarney Bunch, McCruddens, Dady Brothers and Emigrants, regional bands such as The Shenanigans, Seamus Kennedy, Tom O'Carroll and Canadian entertainers Kevin Kennedy, Jimmy Carton and The Descendants. The Buffalo Irish Festival has been presented annually since 1982 and for the first 20 years it was held at Weimer's Grove. It was then held at various locations and is currently held at the Outer Harbor.

POLKA MUSIC

The first style of polkas to gain popularity in the 1940s–1960s was the Eastern Style. It originated in the NYC, New Jersey, Massachusetts and mainly the Connecticut area of New England. It featured big bands playing charted, up-tempo, 2-4 beat music. This was the style of polka bands that first played at the big band ballrooms, like Crystal Beach, and included Gene Wisniewski, Frank Wojnarowski, Bernie Witkowski, Walt Solek, Happy Louie, the Connecticut Twins and Jimmy Sturr, who is still performing and has been the winner of 18 Grammy awards.

The Chicago Style Polka, next to emerge, is slightly slower and is played by smaller bands. It has a connection to '50s rock n roll because it features what is called the Push Style, the bellow shaking of the accordion. The earliest Chicago Style Polka artists, originating in the Chicago area, were Li'l Wally (Jagiello), Edie Zima, The Ampol Aires and Marion Lush, followed by Lenny Gomulka and Eddie Blazonczyk.

The Buffalo Style Polka is a mix of the two other styles. The bands are sometimes smaller than the Chicago style bands and usually include one or two trumpets, one or two sax players doubling on clarinet, accordion, bass and drums. They may also include a concertina or violin. In addition to polkas, the bands perform waltzes, obereks and Rhinelanders. The early popular Buffalo style bands were Joe Macielag (Pick-A-Polka Orchestra), Walt Jaworski Orchestra, The New Yorkers, Big Steve & the Bel-Aires, The Valients and The Musicals.

A derivative style of polka was the Honky Polka, which came from the Chicago style but had a Dixieland feel and featured the harmonica sound of the concertina. It was usually performed by five-piece bands consisting of a concertina, trumpet, clarinet, bass and drums. This style was made popular by Chicago's Li'l Wally, Stas Golonka and Buffalo's Wanda & Stephanie.

Polka music was featured on the early '50s radio program by Stan Jasinski on WKBW, which was broadcast in Polish and was sponsored by Lucki Urban Furniture Store. Stan Jasinski later owned WMMJ, which was predominantly a Polish music radio station. When he started Channel 29, he sold the station to Ramblin' Lou, who renamed the station WXRL which featured country western music, but still included polka programs. In the late '60s and early '70s, there were a number of Polish music DJs on the radio, including: Stan Jasinski, Stan Sluberski, Big Steve and Walt Jaworwki on WXRL, Danny Lesniak on WADV, Happy Harry on WNIA, and Bob Mycek on WWOL. Early polka clubs and ballrooms were The Stand Ballroom, Adam Plewacki Post, Polish Falcons, Chopin Singing Society Clubrooms, Polish Village Restaurant, Polka Town Park, Dom Polski on Broadway and St John Kanty's Lyceum. Polka music was also featured at church lawn fetes and at Polish weddings in halls across WNY. Polka Town on Cayuga Creek Road in Cheektowaga had a large tent for performances and hosted the largest outdoor summer events. As a promotion for one show, a helicopter landed Polka king Marion Lush on the Polka Town grounds before his performance.

Polka music is associated with the East Side of Buffalo, but it also had an early history in North Tonawanda.

Topolski's Restaurant at 747 Oliver Street was one of the earliest polka music clubs in WNY. They were in the center of the North Tonawanda Polish neighborhood, in the vicinity of Our Lady of Czestochowa Church, Dom Polski Hall and the Third Warders Social Club.

The restaurant was opened by Julian Topolski in 1940. Starting in the mid-1940s they had their own house band which was called "Its Own Orchestra." In addition, they booked guest bands like Doc (Joseph Penksa) Penkson from the Black Rock area, Edward Ogorzaly and his Knights of Melody and Stan Sojka and his ten-piece orchestra. Topolski's was also one of the first clubs where Joe Macielag started performing. He worked here before he formed The Melody Bells, which became the Pic-A-Polka Orchestra. Julian would occasionally book out-of-town bands like Eddie Rogers and his Orchestra. Large crowds packed Topolski's for these dances, and the bar ran buses to bring people in from other Polish neighborhoods. Across Oliver Street from Topolski's was The Mirror Room, operated by Mrs. Palka, which often featured polka bands on weekends. This was back in the days when Oliver Street in North Tonawanda had the distinction of being one of the streets in the U.S. with the most bars per mile...some intersections had a bar on each of the four corners.

The control center for polka music in Buffalo was Ruda's Records, started in 1950 by accordion player Don Ruda and his wife Virginia. During the late 1940s, Don was a member of the Polka Trio, the band that released the Mruk Polka, written for Buffalo mayor Joseph Mruk. Ruda wanted to make a larger contribution to Polish music, so in 1950 he opened Ruda's Music Store at 733 Ridge Road in Lackawanna. Here he gave accordion lessons, had teachers that gave lessons on other instruments and sold popular and foreign records. In 1961 he opened Ruda's Records at 915 Broadway, just west of Fillmore. This store became the center of the Buffalo Polka community. If you wanted to know anything about polka music, you went to Ruda's Records. In addition to selling Polish records, he booked bands, scheduled dances, had info on all events, organized trips to polka festivals and helped organize International Polka Association conventions at the Thruway Plaza in Cheektowaga and other locations. Ruda assisted many Buffalo polka bands in releasing records. He always told the bands that they first needed to release a 45 so it could be played on jukeboxes and on the radio. Don helped the bands get their records placed on jukeboxes in Polish neighborhoods and talked to the DJs about playing their songs on the radio. Don felt that only after their 45-single was a hit should a band consider releasing an album. Through Ruda's connections many Polka bands from the WNY area obtained work on the national polka circuit. In 1993, Ruda moved the Broadway Fillmore area store to the downsized Ruda's Polkas and Polish Gifts at 2445 Williams Street in Cheektowaga, which closed in 2007.

Edwins Music Store first opened on Broadway near Bailey Avenue, and in the early '60s they moved to 1515 Broadway. The store was opened by accordion player Edwin Grazanowski and his wife Victoria. Edwin's focused on providing music lessons on accordion, button box, drums, trumpet, sax and guitar, along with selling musical instruments. The store began providing combo lessons, where students rehearsed as an entire band. These lessons gave aspiring musicians the opportunity to play with other musicians and not just practice on their own. It also resulted in some new young polka bands. Dick's Music on Clinton Street in Kaisertown, Wally's Music on William Street in Cheektowaga and studios by Johnny (Banaszak) Johnson and Dave Gawronski also started combo lessons at their stores, but Edwin's was the main combo lesson center. Edwins Music later became the sheet music headquarters for WNY. The sheet music section took up well over half the store and was the most complete selection of sheet music for all styles of music. Managing the sheet music became a full-time job for Edwin's son Greg and daughter Doreen, while his other son Jimmy purchased The Kent Drum Company and operated a nationwide music equipment sales outlet across the street from the store.

After a fire at Edwin's Music in the early '70s, the salvaged instruments and sheet music, along with the music lessons, temporarily moved to Ruda's Records Store at 915 Broadway. Later, Music City opened on Broadway near the Broadway Market and Sattler's Department Store. It was opened by Johnny Banaszak from Johnny & Jimmy, along with his manager, Pat Pantonini, who also managed The New Yorkers and The Musicals. Music City sold all types of musical instruments and equipment and was like a prototype for the music super stores (Music Connection, Music Mart, Guitar Center, etc...) that would later open in WNY. Music City closed after Edwin's Music Store was rebuilt.

Chopin Singing Society was started in 1899, by Boleslaw Michalski. Their first rehearsal facility was at 1210 Broadway. At that time, there were three other Polish Singing societies is Buffalo: Moniuszko, Lutnia and Kolo. Chopin Singing Society commissioned artist Jozef Mazur to create a bronze bust of Frederic Chopin in 1925, which stood in front of the Museum of Science in Humboldt Park until it was moved to its permanent home on Symphony Circle, after Kleinhans Music Hall opened. In 1947, The Chopin Singing Society moved to a new club house and rehearsal facility at 18 Kosciusko Street near Broadway. Membership was reduced to only 15 male singers in the 1950s, but in 1958 Ted Mikoll and his wife Judge Ann Mikoll were recruited and successfully revitalized the society. In addition to choral rehearsal by an expanded membership, the club became known for having live music and carrying on Polish traditions. Dyngus Day was a Polish tradition brought over from the old country, but it was at Chopin's in 1963 that Dyngus Day parties started to be celebrated on the Monday after Easter. These celebrations have grown to be the World's Largest Dyngus Day party, drawing thousands to the Central Terminal on Paderewski Street. The Dyngus Day celebrations extend across WNY with polka bands playing at numerous locations on the East Side, Cheektowaga, North Tonawanda, Niagara Falls, etc.... There is now a Dyngus Day parade from the Broadway Market to the Central Terminal, featuring over 120 floats and attended by over 40,000 people.

The Adam Mickiewicz Library & Dramatic Circle, located at 612 Fillmore Avenue near Broadway, is the oldest Polish American organization in WNY. The Dramatic Club was organized in 1895 and started producing amateur productions at the Mickiewicz Hall. The upstairs library at the non-profit organization contains over 12,000 volumes and over 400 hand-written scripts for Polish plays. Currently the building is a private club but visitors are welcome. They serve the largest selection of Polish beer outside of Chicago, along with Polish vodkas and Krupnik, a Polish honey liquor. The Circle is the home to most of Torn Space Theater's productions, a large Dyngus Day party, along with cultural events and readings of Polish poetry.

A new generation of Buffalo Style polka bands started to become popular in the 1960s. The period from the late '60s through the early '80s was the heyday of polka bands. These bands continued to perform at weddings, church lawn fetes and polka festivals, along with the early clubs, ballrooms and dance halls. They also played at The Broadway Grill, Warsaw Inn, Ray's Tavern on Clinton, New Clinton Lounge, Town Edge Bowling Lanes, Gay Way on Broadway, Franks Market Restaurant on Lombard, Ben Lees on Woltz Avenue, The Jolly Roger, Union Casino, Sportsman's Tavern in Depew, Zasada's Restaurant, Club 77, Evening Star, Anchor Inn, Wiechecs, Eddie & Carries and the Hearthstone Manor. The Broadway Grill was purchased in 1976 by Henry Mazurek (who played sax and clarinet in The New Yorkers), while the Warsaw Inn was owned by the Eddie Kutas Sr., whose family later owned the Polish Villa I and II in Cheektowaga.

The New Yorkers were a popular area polka band from 1960 to 1967. In 1965, they were on a Channel 7 TV Show called *Polka Time* with The New Yorkers. This is not to be confused with the 1962 Channel 7 TV Show *Polka Time* with Eddie Yankovic, where they also appeared. In 1965, The New Yorkers were at the height of their popularity because that year they released "Hello Dolly Polka" which sold 250,000 copies. During the 1960s, The New Yorkers also had live radio broadcasts from the Warsaw Grill and Polish Village, which were on WADV-FM. The members of the New Yorkers were John Banaszak, Henry Mazurek, Gene Martin, Edward (Whitey) Mazurek, Gino Kurdzeil and Jimmy (Edwin) Grazanowski. In 1964, Johnny & Jimmy from The New Yorkers began performing as a duo on *Dialing for Dollars*, broadcast on Channel 7 weekday mornings for 14 years. In 1978, the name of the show was changed to AM Buffalo, which is still on the air every weekday at 10:00 AM.

Wanda & Stephanie were a mother and daughter team that were called "America's Polka Sweethearts." Wanda was born in Lackawanna but grew up in the polka capital of Chicago. During the 1950s she sang Polish music with her mother at house parties. Her family moved back to Buffalo, where she met her husband Henry Pietrzak. Their daughter Stephanie showed musical talent and Wanda taught her how to play the accordion and her grandmother taught her Polish vocals. Wanda took Stephanie to see Li'l Wally perform in Buffalo and she was fascinated by the sound of Wally's playing of the concertina. During a trip to Chicago, they went to Li'l Wally's Jay Jay Music Store and the concertina Stephanie liked the most was a red one on display at the store. Wally said it was not for sale

WANDA & STEPHANIE
"America's Polka Sweethearts"
Photo: Courtesy Stephanie Pietrzak

because that was the concertina he played on the Lawrence Welk Show. Stephanie was persistent and Wally eventually relented after she promised to become proficient on the instrument. Ironically, Li'l Wally and Stephanie are considered two of the most prominent artists in making the concertina-driven, Honky Polka style popular.

When Marion Lush was performing at the International Polka Association (IPA) Festival at The Hearthstone Manor in Depew, Wanda & Stephanie played some songs with him. The audience enjoyed their performance and Marion Lush asked Wanda & Stephanie to go on tour with his group. Eddie Blazonczyk signed Wanda & Stephanie to record for his Bel-Aire Records in Chicago. Their first song "Come Back My Johnny" was a hit, but their 1971 single "Lover Oh Lover" was a #1 Polka song and was the IPA Song of the Year. They formed a band, Wanda & Stephanie & the Golden Stars, and were soon performing across the U.S. and Canada at ballrooms, polka conventions, festivals and on Caribbean cruises, along with appearing on radio and television programs. Locally they opened several concerts for Bobby Vinton at Melody Fair in North Tonawanda. After Wanda's death in 1996, Stephanie stopped performing but after two years of retirement she returned with Stephanie & Her Honky Band. Both Wanda & Stephanie have been inducted into the IPA Polka HOF, Wanda in 1999, Stephanie in 2010 and they were the first polka artists inducted into the Buffalo Music Hall of Fame in 1999. Stephanie continues to extensively tour, has released almost 20 albums, is considered one of the premier Honky Style Polka performers in the country and on occasion she plays the same red concertina she bought from Li'l Wally.

The Goral Boys were formed in 1969 by members of several other popular area polka bands. Ken Machelski (trumpet, concertina, vocals) from the Buffalo Hi-Notes, John Gnojeck (trumpet) from Big Steve & the Bel-Aires, Hank Krzykowski (drums) from The Musicals & Hank Pajak Band, Joe Grenda (accordion, vocals) from The Dynatones, Ted Darlak (sax) from The Hi-Notes, Steve Michaels (bass, guitar) who previously played in country bands and Harry Burdick (violin) who was a 30- year veteran of various area polka groups. Goral means mountaineer in Polish; they chose that name to suggest the old country to their audiences.

In 1972, the band had a radio show on WXRL, which remained on the air for several years. That program was recorded every Sunday night at The Polish Village Restaurant and broadcast on Sunday afternoons at 4:00. They would promote that evening's recording on the show, and a variety of

THE GORAL BOYS
Ken Machelski, John Gnojeck, Ted Darlak, Harry Burdick
Hank Krzykowski, Joe Grenda, Steve Michaels
Photo: Courtesy Ken Machelski

members from the Polish American community would come to Polish Village to be interviewed on the program, including many sports figures. Most Sundays there was a line around the corner waiting to get into the club. During the mid-1970s, The Goral Boys changed their name to the New York Six and in addition to traveling to perform at national polka festivals, they appeared on a regular basis at The Jolly Roger on Harlem Road. In 1975, Ken remained on trumpet and vocals, Steve switched to guitar and they added Jimmy Edwin (drums) from The New Yorkers, John Hill (sax), Dave Kalota (keyboards) and Tadj Symczak (bass). They became New York Transfer, who only played a few polkas, but remained one of the in-demand society and party bands in WNY for the next 30 years. Ken Machelski is now the leader of the Buffalo Touch, founded by IPA HOF member Jerry Darlak, and a group that was nominated for three Grammy Awards in the Polka music category.

There were many other polka bands that released albums and played weddings, clubs and festivals in the WNY area. Formed in 1968, Dyna-Tones were a polka band with a rock 'n' roll feel and attitude, led by drummer Larry Trojak and featuring concertina player "Scrubby" Seweryniak. They were a road touring band, still occasionally play a reunion show and members have spun off several bands like Sunshine Polka Band the The Knewz...The G-Notes included the Miesowicz and Karas brothers, with leader Gino Kurdziel. Some of the Karas brothers later joined the Jimmy Sturr Band...The Krew Brothers were the seven Krupski Brothers: Tony, Donny, Dennis, Rickie, Kenny, Alan and Gary, who still play reunion shows and perform individually...The Jumping Jacks from the 1960s were Bob Nowicki, Ed Grabski, Gerald "Mousey" Miesowicz, Don Zak and Dick Sczykowny...Steve Krzeminski led Big

Steve & the Bellares from the '60s until his passing in 1998, along with being the polka voice of WXRL radio and TV's *Polka Saturday Nights*. Other bands were: Happy Richie & the Royalaires, Modernaires, Polecats, Silvertones, Musicals, Buffalo Hi-Notes, Varitones, Associates, Hotshots, Tom Karas' New York Sound, Steel City Brass, New Tones, Dave Gawronski Band, Twylites, Ampoltones, BlueBells, Pachulski Brothers and from Southern Ontario, the Canadian Polka King of the early '60s through today – Walt Ostanek, who won two Grammy Awards and had the *Polka Party* TV show on CHCH-TV in Hamilton. Ontario.

Currently the International Polka Association, which has its Polka Hall of Fame in Chicago, holds the International Polka Festival in Buffalo on a regular basis. The Polka Boosters and Polka Variety Club meet monthly to support and present Buffalo polka bands. Ron Dombrowski features Polish programming during his daily Monday–Saturday Drive Time Polka Show on WXRL radio and Sundays on WECK-AM radio. George and Mike Pasierb's *Rockin Polkas* have been on WXRL each Saturday and Sunday for over 25 years. The Polka Jammer 24-hour internet network features programs originating in Buffalo. WBBZ-TV telecasts the *Polka Buzz* television show, which is filmed at Potts Banquet Hall on Clinton Street. Polka music remains alive and well in Buffalo. It always puts a smile on your face, but after years of investigation, still no one knows "Who Stole the Kishka?"

17

COUNTRY MUSIC

Traditional country music was popular in the Buffalo, NY area reaching back to the late 1940s and early 1950s. During that time, there were not any permanent clubs featuring country bands but there was a group of musicians that traveled from club to club playing for tips. This was called club busking or passing-the-hat at restaurants, bars and cafes, like the concept of busking by street performers.

In the 1940s and early 1950s, the club busking scene included musicians such as Patsy Loveless (vocalist), Billy Custard (bass), Larry Smith (fiddle, guitar), Fiddlin' Zeke (fiddle), Wings (guitar), "Two-Ton" Tony (later the owner of TNT Western Paradise), Adele Dickey (vocals), Slim Lee (vocals) and Tennessee Buck. They would meet at one club and proceed to other bars, like Mulligans on Allen, performing for patron's contributions. This would usually just be on weekends or what they thought might be a busy night during the week. These groups did not yet have a drummer, so it was the responsibility of the upright bass player to add a percussive feel to the music.

In the mid to late 50's, clubs started featuring country & western bands. A few of these earlier clubs were Club Utica, TNT Western Paradise and The Roseland at 490 Rhode Island Street. Earl Overholdt began promoting Country Jamborees on Sunday afternoons at the Bellevue Hotel (on Como Park Blvd.), Popular Inn (on Broadway in Alden), Rose Garden (on Wehrle in Williamsville) and at other rural and suburban locations. Country bands would perform as the jamborees exposed them to a new audience and resulted in work at other clubs. Some of the early bands, through the 1960s included Walt Weber & the Double Clutchers, Happy Mann & the Country Squires, Jimmy Kay & the Mountain High, Al Porky Withrow, Larry Smith, Cliff McCarthy & the Wranglers,

Frontiersmen, Melody Mountaineers, Boots Hanner, Sally Bishop, Al Aiken, Bobby Willard, Dick Lobdell & the Wanderers, Ed Bentley and Ramblin' Lou Schriver.

During the late 1960s and early 1970s, many of the earlier clubs continued with live country music and many of the early bands continued performing. Some of the other establishments that began featuring country music included Harry's Mil Sher, Hank's Fairways, Janiks, The Galaxy Lounge, The Bonnet, Club Romway, Al-E-Oops, Christy's Lounge, Shveedee's, Rosie's Clinton Lounge, Tony's Union Casino, Globe Hotel in East Aurora and Luders Log Cabin in Elma, NY.

The country rock and Southern rock music of the 1970s introduced country to many followers of rock music. During the disco era, many musicians were looking for an alternative to disco, progressive rock or hard rock music, so they turned to the more authentic harmony-oriented new country music. A new legion of country music fans was initiated, but there was still the division between the older traditional country and the newer country music stylings. This section will cover some of the traditional, bluegrass and country rock bands, clubs and events in WNY. The country scene in WNY peaked in the mid to late 1980s so the time line will be extended a little to mention the country bands through the 1980s.

RAMBLIN' LOU FAMILY BAND

Ramblin' Lou Schriver was a performer, concert promoter, country music tour provider and radio station owner. Together with his wife, Joanie Marshall, and children, they are the areas First Family of Country Music.

Lou began his country music radio career at WJJL in 1947, when he was 18 years old. During the 1950s he performed at The Grand Ole' Opry in Nashville and on the WWVA Jamboree, the fabled country music radio station in Wheeling West Virginia. When WJJL changed formats, in 1964 Lou moved to WWOL in Buffalo, with WJJL allowing him to take all the country music records from the stations music library with him. In 1970 WMMJ was put up for sale by Stan Jasinski because he was starting WUTV–Channel 29. Lou purchased the station and changed the name to WXRL (WX Ramblin' Lou) in 1970. After purchasing the station, Lou started providing bus tours to Nashville and country concerts/festivals across the country. Since 1970, WXRL has been the home of traditional country music in WNY and Lou was on the air until a couple weeks before his death in January 2016. The Schriver Family continues to operate the station.

Schriver started performing with The Twin Pine Mountaineers in 1951. With his wife, Joanie Marshall on guitar, Lou and Joanie formed the Ramblin' Lou Family Band. The early band was Lou (rhythm guitar/vocals), Joanie (lead guitar), Accordion Jake (accordion), Don Juan (drums) and Bashful Eddie (bass). This group later included their children; Lou Jr. (drums), Lori Ann (violin), Lynn Carol (keyboards), Linda Lou (bass) and five of their grandchildren. Linda Lou is a distinguished performer in her own right, graduating from The Eastman School of Music and performing for 25 years on Jamboree USA. Lou has the distinction of performing at the Erie County Fair for 51 years. His Family Band was also annual performers at the noontime M&T Downtown Buffalo Concerts and at the bandshell during Canal Fest, in his hometown of Tonawanda.

RAMBLIN' LOU FAMILY BAND
Photo: Courtesy Linda Lou Schriver

He began his career as a country music concert promoter when he was 22 by booking Hank Williams in Niagara Falls. This concert was on April 25, 1952, less than a year before Williams died of a heart attack. Sixty years later, Lou received a call from Time/Life because a recording of that concert turned up, which Time/Life released on a CD called *Hank Williams: The Lost Concerts*. This CD was only one of two recorded Hank Williams shows known to exist. Lou later brought concerts to Buffalo and Niagara Falls by artists including Buck Owens, Merle Haggard, Dolly Parton and Johnny Cash. Many of the early shows Lou presented in Niagara Falls were at the State Theater on Portage Road, before moving to Kleinhans Music Hall in Buffalo. Promoting concerts and performing were so much a part of Lou's life, that he proposed to guitarist Joanie Marshall just before they were about to go on stage in Niagara Falls at a Ray Price concert. Combining radio and concerts, Ramblin' Lou had a disc jockey booth at Earl's Drive Inn Restaurant in Chaffee, NY where he would broadcast, while Earl Northrup held country music concerts behind the restaurant.

As a tribute to his accomplishments, Schriver was inducted into the national Country Radio Broadcaster Hall of Fame, was a second-year inductee into the Buffalo Broadcasters Hall of Fame and he was the first traditional country musician inducted into the Buffalo Music Hall of Fame.

ED BENTLEY

Ed's mother Patsy Loveless was an early Buffalo area country vocalist and guitarist. When Ed was 15 his aunt and uncle took him to a Johnny Cash/Marty Robbins concert at the State Theater in Niagara Falls. After his mother taught him some chords on guitar, in 1957 he entered a talent contest, performing a Marty Robbins song at a country music bar which was located on the corner of Jefferson and Eaton Street in Buffalo. Bentley won the contest, received $5.00 and a white cowboy hat. He was hooked...he wanted to be a musician.

ED BENTLEY
Photo: Courtesy Ed Bentley

After winning the contest, Ed started playing guitar with an early Buffalo rock 'n' roll band called the Tune Rockers. Teaching his bandmates, the guitar chords his mother showed him, they were soon playing record hops with radio DJs. Bentley was torn between country and rock music. He decided to leave the band to play country and the Tune Rockers went on to be the first Buffalo RNR band to have a song that reached the national Top 100. Bentley was looking for that combination of country and rock.

In the late 1950s, Ed Bentley formed a band with Joanie Marshall (guitar & fiddle) with her father on bass. After Joanie left the group to play guitar for her future husband, Ramblin' Lou, Bentley was heartbroken and decided to move to Memphis. In 1961, he worked for DJ and singer Eddie Bond, at his Little Black Book nightclub in Memphis, where Bentley opened for Carl Perkins and Charlie Rich. Returning to Buffalo, in the early 1960s, Bentley continued playing at area country music bars, but performed country with a rock music edge. He even toured with Kathy Lynn & the Playboys, adding his country flavor to their rock 'n' roll show. Drawing from his experiences in Memphis, Bentley finally found that merger of country and RNR – it was the style of music called "Rockabilly."

In 1971, Bentley started a five-year engagement at former Buffalo Bills offensive lineman Al Bemiller's Turf-side Restaurant in Hamburg, NY. Ed Bentley & the Memphis Sound played at the club four nights a week and Sundays after the Buffalo Bills home games. The band

ED BENTLEY & THE MEMPHIS SOUNDS
Stan Szelest, Barb Meeker, Ed Bentley
Photo: Courtesy Ed Bentley

merged country, rock and pop musical styles and over the five years, many Buffalo musicians were members of the band including: Stan Szelest, Mickey Kipler, Don McGreevey, Barb Meeker and about a hundred more.

During his career, Ed Bentley created many recordings, including several at Jerry Meyers studio and more recently at Duane Hall's Session Recording Studio. He continues composing new material, on his own or with song writing partners such as Ernie Corallo. His songs have been included in several television shows and he was inducted into the national Rockabilly Hall of Fame in 2005. Ed Bentley still performs at special-events in the WNY area.

STONE COUNTRY

Stone Country's Dwane Hall was introduced to country music by his father who played fiddle and accordion in country music groups. Dwane's mother would record country songs that Ramblin' Lou played on his radio program with a reel-to-reel tape player, so he could learn the country standards. When he was nine years old, Dwane started on lap steel guitar and to indoctrinate all the Hall children into country music, Dwane's father formed what he called the Circle D's Family Band. The name was inspired by the fact that all the Hall children's first names began with the letter D.

STONE COUNTRY AT THE BONNET 1980
Top Row: Buffalo Zew, Randy Bolam, Carl Eddy
Dwane Hall, Rich Kilmer, John Dikeman, Bud Webber
Photo: Courtesy Dwane Hall

In 1974 Stone Country was formed by Dwane Hall (guitar), D. John Hall (guitar), Bud Weber (bass) and Randy Bolam (drums). Other members of the early Stone Country Band were Carl Eddy (guitar) in 1976 and Jim Yeomans (guitar) in 1980. Many other musicians were members of the group during the four decades they have been performing. Some of the other long-term members included Mike Meany, Rich Kilmer, Buffalo Zew and John Dikeman.

They began and remained a traditional country band, with the heaviest country rock being material by Commander Cody or New Riders of the Purple Sage. However, in the mid 70's to the early 80's, they were one of the only country bands to perform at rock clubs on a regular basis. They hosted country night at the Buffalo Playboy Club, played steady Thursday at The Belle Starr, being the last band to play at the Belle Star on the night that it burned down. Stone Country first recorded in Nashville in 1979 and in 1983 they released the successful "Rodeo Song". In 1984, they recorded the *Curly Shuffle* album for Amherst Records, which broke the Top 200 on the national album charts.

As a promoter Hall presented the Sunshine '79, '80 and '81 Festivals. These were outdoor events featuring the top bluegrass, country and country rock bands of Western New York. The first show was a huge success but the last show was a disaster, due to drenching rainstorms. However, presenting these shows set the precedent for Dwane's promotion of bands at The Sportsman's Tavern, which he and his wife Denise opened in 1985. The club presents all styles of music but focuses on Americana, even forming the non-profit Sportsman's Americana Music Foundation, to promote Americana music. They feature the type of music that was played at The Belle Starr; a mix of national, reunion and local shows. The Sportsman's Tavern features over 50 live music shows every month.

TWO HILLS

Two Hills began when guitarist/vocalists Ray Wood and Jeff Munzert met in the early 1970s. They started playing shows at UB and other locations as a duo. In 1978, they met guitarist/vocalist George Doran, at a show in Hamburg, and decided to form a trio. That trio was expanded to a complete band with the addition of Doug Fields (bass) and Tom Fronczak (drums). This initial version of Two Hills performed strictly country rock, adding many of their original songs to sets at area clubs such as Nashville North, The Belle Starr, The Longbranch Saloon and Frank's Casa Nova.

In 1982 George Doran decided to concentrate on his solo performances, so Ray & Jeff restructured the band with Mike Marriott (guitar), Chris Marziale (keyboards), Lloyd Soderholm (percussion), Paul Warner (drums) and Rick Ellis (bass), with Tom Lema soon replacing Rick on bass. This group performed a more diverse style of music, but because of their roots they were always considered country rock, even playing a steady country night at the rock club Stage One. Two Hills paved the way for other country rock bands to break into the rock club market.

The band released an album *Worth the Wait* in 1983 and a holiday single "He Does It All the Time" which they continue to promote every Christmas season. One of their most memorable shows was being one of the few Buffalo bands that opened a major concert at Buffalo Memorial Auditorium, playing before a crowd of 17,000 people at a Charlie Daniels show.

After the band broke up in 1986, Ray Wood was one of the founding members of Only Humen and original member George Doran, released several recordings with his group Winterwood.

JC THOMPSON

The JC Thompson band was formed in 1983 by Jim Thompson, who was the vocalist in various bands at the rock club McVans. One night in 1981 he went to the Playboy club to watch the Stone Country Band and decided to form his own country band. He performed country rock and country music, giving it a rock edge from his earlier performance days. The band was like a Buffalo version of Garth Brooks, who added rock showmanship to his country repertoire. JC Thompson band opened concerts at Kleinhans, Melody Fair and the Erie County Fairgrounds for acts like Charlie Daniels, Diamond Rio, Willie Nelson, Marty Stuart and Dwight Yoakum. Members of the original group were Jim "JC" Thompson (vocals/guitar), Steve Serwinowski (bass), Phil Serwinowski (guitar), Jeff Kershner (guitar) and David "Beav" Nizol (drums). The band reached the height of their popularity in the late 1980s through the early 1990s. All the original members of the group remained except Phil, who was replaced by Chris Panfil (fiddle/guitar) and Chris Marziale (keyboards). That group broke up in 1998 and after taking a short hiatus, JC returned to performing. Thompson still performs with his band and plays solo dates, along with hosting an open mic.

KEITH ALLEN & THE CROSS COUNTRY EXPRESS was an '80s country group that worked full time at Buffalo area country music clubs. Starting in 1983, brothers Steve and Gary Edmonds, were members of the band and continued performing with Keith Allen even after they formed The Boys of Summer, which began as a part-time summer project in 1991. During the mid '80s there were several full-time country groups and many of the members would meet at The Golden Nugget on Seneca Street, for last call and to exchange stories about the show they performed at that night.

BECKY HORNING & NY ROCKIN RODEO. Becky started working with Al & the Alley Cats when she was 12 years old. She then played with Del Sylor & the Country Hobos. In 1982, she met her future husband, Dan Horning, who was with the touring country band Aurora. Dan formed NY Rockin Rodeo, a Top 40 country band, and asked Becky to join. That group toured western Canada for five years and then contracted with the Department of Defense (DOD) to entertain US troops around the world. Through the DOD, NY Rockin Rodeo performed for the military in 31 different countries. Becky and Don still work together in NY Rockin Revue, with Eric Zak (keyboards) and Michael Trig Lehmann (drums), which now performs all styles of music.

MOONSHINE EXPRESS was a country rock band, with diverse influences from rock, blues, R&B, jazz and reggae. The band members were Butch Kania (organ & guitar), Bob Falk (guitar), Wally Sirotich (piano), Pete Crisman (bass) and Mike Phelps (drums). In addition to playing WNY clubs, for several years they were Bo Diddley's back-up band at The Lone Star Café in NYC. As the house band at The Lone Star they backed up Elliot Randall (from Steeley Dan), Richie Havens, Odetta and in 1981 filmed a TV pilot, for the USA Network, *Live from the Lone Star Café* with Levon Helm and Johnny Paycheck.

LONE STAR EXPRESS was together from 1976-1979. The band members were Doc White (vocals, guitar), Roger Schlee (bass), Tom Allen (lead guitar), Tom Bath (steel guitar) and David Green (drums). Both David Green and Tom Bath moved to Houston, Texas in 1979 where they performed with many of the top country bands of that time.

VANISHING BREED played at Christy's Lounge on Clinton & Union, every Friday and Saturday, from 1974 to 1978. This was the first band for future Boys of Summer guitarist Gary Edmonds. He joined the group when he was 16 years old and the lead singer of the band was his mother Jeanne Marie.

VANISHING BREED
Photo: Courtesy Gary Edmonds

DALE AND THE PIONEERS were Dale Thomas (guitar), Wally Weber (bass) and Mickey Bechtel (drums). They were Porky Witherill's band at Club Utica until Porky left to join the WWVA Jamboree in Wheeling, West Virginia. In 1970 the band toured Japan.

Other '70s country and country rock bands were: Sheri Lane & Lenny Nast, Billy Lee & the Bad Companions, Clyde Bonnas & His String Men, Dick Moore & the Country Playboys, Loveless Singers, Steve Scott & the Country Music Circus, Dody Lynn & the Guitarmen (from the Southern Tier), Wild Bill & the Sweet Clover Boys, Bud Perry & Western Union, Kenny Gunn & the Pistols, Country Cousins, Clearwater, Rio Grande, OK Corral Band, Bud Perry, Paul Zittel, Longriders, Hole in the Wall Gang, Old Salt, and The Shea Brothers.

Many of the country bands and country rock bands from the 1970s continued performing into the 1980s. These bands and some of the groups formed in the 1980s included Backroads which was led by vocalist Buffalo Zew...Quarterhorse with guitarist/vocalist Roger Kowerko...Ozone Rangers started as a country rock band before they became a ZZ Top tribute band, featuring guitarist Bob Muhlbauer...Houston was Willy Haddath's first band but most remember him starting with 10

Gauge...Union Transfer featured an Elvis set by singer Ted Siwy...Curtis Loew was a Southern rock band, which was the first group for future Watchers/Pretty Poison guitarist Tim Fik. Eileen Smith was the lead singer of Curtis Loew but Rita Seitz of Watchers/Pretty Poison also sang with them.

Other groups from the '80s included: New Breed, Underground Country, Cotton Mouth, Gene Hilts & the Back Side of Thirty, Cherokee, Sweet Honey & the Badmouth Boys, Country Company, Jim Yeomans Band, Smith Brothers Band, Crossfire, New Country Team, Country North, Colt, OK Corral, Mason Dixon, Cross Country Express, Badlands, Silver Line Express and The Farrell Brothers.

The number of country bands and clubs probably peaked in the mid to late 1980s. Bands played at the remaining early clubs and the newer country bars from the late '70s and '80s like The Belle Starr, The Longbranch Saloon, Get-A-Way Saloon, Wagon Wheel, Kitty's Dodge City Saloon on Hertel, Nashville North on Niagara Falls Blvd and The Golden Nugget on Seneca Street. Some of these newer clubs featured bands four to six nights a week, with the Belle Starr and Longbranch bringing in national country acts. Melody Fair in North Tonawanda featured big name country artists and when WYRK started broadcasting modern country in 1981, national country artists performed at the major WNY concert venues, including the Aud, and currently at KeyBank Center and Darien Lake Performing Arts Center.

BLUEGRASS

Bluegrass Music was originally performed in Appalachia and is defined as Irish and British ballads that were influenced by Irish fiddle music and African-American blues and jazz. It is characterized by breakneck tempos, sophisticated vocal harmony arrangements and impressive instrumental proficiency in solos on mandolin, banjo and fiddle. Bluegrass and country western both evolved from old time mountain music. They were very similar until the introduction of drums and electric instruments in the 1940s. Country music is played primarily on electric guitar, electric bass and drums, while bluegrass uses all acoustic instruments and no drums. Bluegrass music is performed primarily for listening or rural dancing known as buckdancing, flatfooting or clogging. Country music is performed more for dancers, who prefer two-step or more recent country line dancing.

Mandolin player Bill Monroe is considered the "Father of Bluegrass Music". In 1938, he assembled the first version of his band The Bluegrass Boys, and in 1939 he became a regular performer at the Grand Ole Opry in Nashville. In 1945 the classic version of The Bluegrass Boys was formed with the addition of Earl Scruggs on banjo and Lester Flatt on vocals/guitar. This rendition of the band set the formula for the traditional bluegrass instrumentation of: mandolin, banjo, fiddle, guitar and bass.

Bluegrass moved north after WWII, and one of the first prominent bluegrass performers in WNY was Bob Schneider, a self-taught banjo player from Elmira, New York who settled in South Buffalo. Bob was influenced by Bluegrass musicians from West Virginia who had taken jobs at Harrison Radiator in Lockport, New York. Bob taught many of the early bluegrass players in Buffalo who would make weekly pilgrimages to his house in search of the southern Bluegrass sound. To many, he was the local father of Bluegrass. In the 1960s, he started playing banjo and dobro (resonator guitar) and in the early 1970s formed the Border City Bluegrass Band. That band included a West Virginia fiddle player Kenny Bennet and the McCarthy brothers from Canada, hence the name The Border City Bluegrass Band. Bob moved to the Southern Tier in the late 1980s but periodically returned to play in the Buffalo area.

Billy Hamilton & the Bluegrass Almanac were a mid-1970s bluegrass band, led by mandolin and fiddle player Billy Hamilton, that performed often at The Library on Bailey Avenue. He attended graduate school at Yale in the late '60s, where he had a bluegrass band, The Ohio River Boys. Hamilton took a job at UB as a professor of Russian and formed the Bluegrass Almanac, with another UB professor Dick Menn (guitar). They were joined by Dave Soda (banjo), a bass player, and Hamilton's wife Cindy. In addition to appearing at nightclubs and colleges in WNY, they won first place at the Canadian National Bluegrass Festival in 1974. Hamilton left Buffalo in 1982 to take a position at Wake Forest University, where he remains a professor and Associate Dean.

When Billy Hamilton left Buffalo, some musicians that were associated with the Bluegrass Almanac formed The Queen City Cut-Ups. UB students at the time, Dave Haney (guitar), Tom Cook (mandolin), Marv Pfleuger (guitar) and husband and wife team, Steve Aby (banjo) and Martha Aby (bass) played Pandee's, located in Depew at Broadway and

Bordon Road, and Johnnie's Old Timer on Delaware Avenue in Kenmore. Dave Haney left town to teach and play Bluegrass music in Boston MA, and some of the members of the band went on to form Poplar Ridge. They played local bars including a steady Tuesday night stint at Pandee's. The line-up was Dick Menn (guitar), Dave Soda (mandolin), Mike Wahl (banjo), Marv Pfleuger (bass) and Bob Schnieder (dobro).

ERIE LACKAWANNA RAILROAD 1976
Mark Gannon, Chris Panfil, Mark Panfil, Bill Matthews
Photo: Courtesy Mark Panfil

In 1975, The Erie Lackawanna Railroad (ELRR) was formed by brothers Mark Panfil (banjo) and Chris Panfil (mandolin/fiddle), along with Bill Matthews (guitar) and Mark Gannon (bass). The band played at clubs and festivals in WNY and southern Ontario, including steady Thursday nights at Johnny's Old Timer on Delaware. During the late 70s, Ted Lambert and Scott Leighton joined ELRR, replacing Bill Matthews and Mark Gannon. Years later, the Erie Lackawanna Railroad Band was started up again by Mark's children, Scott Panfil (bass) and Katie Panfil (fiddle). They also play with their father and uncle Chris, along with Katie's husband Jayson Clark, in the Panfil Family Band.

In 1977, Jerry Raven and Don Hackett started the folk/bluegrass group The Hill Brothers with a third member that changed throughout the early years. That third members included musicians Stu Schapiro, Steve Moscov, Mark Panfil, Rich Schaefer, Judd Sunshine, Dave Ruch and Sue Rozler. The Hill Brothers played bluegrass for an entire generation of students in school assemblies throughout Erie and Niagara County. In 1983 the Hill Brothers were the featured soloists in a joint Bluegrass Symphonic concert with the Orchard Park Symphony Orchestra.

The band Creek Bend was formed in 1978 by Ted Lambert (banjo), Ted Lambert Sr. (bass) and Rick Schaefer (guitar). Very soon after the band started, the line-up settled on Ted Lambert (banjo & fiddle), Rick Schaefer (bass), Dennis King (guitar), Tom Vaughn (mandolin) and Mark Panfil (dobro & harmonica). Ted was a natural-born Bluegrass picker, switching effortlessly from banjo to guitar, mandolin, fiddle or bass. He also worked as a promoter to bring national Bluegrass acts to Buffalo. Mark Panfil joined the band after performing with The Hill Brothers and obtaining a degree in music education, later teaching for 30 years

CREEK BEND
Rich Schaefer, Carl Eddy, Chris Panfil, Ted Lambert, Mark Panfil
Photo: Courtesy Mark Panfil

at elementary schools in the Frontier School district. Chris Panfil joined Creek Bend on guitar/mandolin after performing in country and bluegrass bands in Florida, Nashville and playing tours of the Caribbean and Europe. After Ted Lambert passed away in 2015, Phil Banazsak joined Creek Bend as fiddle player. Phil is a former New York State Fiddle Champion and was inducted into the North American Fiddler's Hall of Fame, located in Osceola NY, north of Syracuse. Carl Eddy and Doug Yeomans have played extended stints with Creek Bend. Over the past 40 years Creek Bend has performed in WNY and at bluegrass festivals across the country.

Ramblin' Lou's Schriver Family may be the first family of country music in WNY but the first family of Bluegrass Music in WNY is the Weber Family. The Weber band included Ernie Weber (fiddle and banjo), Wally Weber (mandolin) and Fritz Weber (banjo and dobro), all also played guitar. They started performing in the early 1950s and they recruited their children and grandchildren to work with the family band, as soon as they were old enough to hold instruments. Some of the Weber children included Wally Weber Jr. (guitar, bass and drums), Judy Weber (bass), Wendy Weber (vocals) and Cindy Weber (banjo & guitar). The Weber Brothers Band played regularly at the Club Utica, TNT Western Paradise, Rinaldo's, later at Luder's Log Cabin in Elma. Almost every Sunday they could be found performing at Jamborees all over WNY.

Dr. Peter Mirando, a self-taught banjo player and Hamburg HS teacher, began offering a Continuing Education class in Bluegrass instruments in 1975. Over the past 42 years, in his weekly classes, he has taught hundreds of people how to jam and sing Bluegrass songs on banjo, mandolin, guitar and bass. In the late 1970s, Andy Cushing, a Hamburg native and music business program graduate from Belmont College in Nashville, started offering banjo lessons on tape to aspiring banjo players. He used national magazines to market his Bluegrass banjo lessons all over the world.

In 1976, four students from Buffalo State College started the Pointless Brothers Band. Mike Stern (guitar), Pete Seman (fiddle), Charlie Ranney (banjo) and Judd Sunshine (bass) started the band to fulfill a class project and have continued playing to this very day, with only a few personnel changes. From 1977- 1984 they played every Sunday night at the Central Park Grill on Main St. in Buffalo.

Another bluegrass band that played in WNY from 1977 to 1984 was the Boot Hill Boys. The members included Paul "Slim" Norris (mandolin), Steve Stadler (banjo), Jim Zaprzal (guitar) and Jim Cooke (bass). Bob "Buffalo Zew" Palaszewski (fiddle) later joined the band. Zew went on to form The Buffalo Zew Review and was a member of both Backroads and The Stone Country band. The Boot Hill Boys played every Thursday night at Good Time Charlie's in Town Line, NY. They had regular gigs at Grover's Old Ale House (Franklin & Tupper) and the Bullpen on Main Street in Clarence. When Jim Zaprzal and Jim Cooke left the band, they changed the name to Night Watch, with Bob Webster (guitar) and Tom Jackson (bass) joining the group.

City Fiddle brought Bluegrass to Allentown in the late 1970s, when they began playing a weekly happy hour at Nietzsche's. Fiddlein' Phil Banaszak was in the band with Ron Hinton (mandolin), Steve Pevo (guitar) and Ed Woods (bass).

Around 1982, one of Bob Schneider's banjo students, Sue Galbraith put together a Bluegrass band with her sister, Kathy (guitar), Craig Kellas (fiddle), Jennifer Cooke (mandolin) and Jim Lynch (bass). They called themselves Dempsey Station. This group played together until 1999 but seldom played bars. They preferred playing local farm festivals, People Art, Buffalo Friends of Folk Music Concert openings and Historical Societies. Dempsey Station also played out of town Bluegrass Festivals, including the Panama Rocks Folk and Craft Festival in Panama, near Jamestown N.Y.

WNY has had several Bluegrass Festivals over the years. In 1977 The first Creek Side Bluegrass Festival took place in Akron, NY. This Festival had national bluegrass acts like Larry Sparks and the Lonesome

Ramblers, and area groups like the Erie Lackawanna RR, the Pointless Bros., Night Watch, The Dady Brothers from Rochester, Border City Bluegrass, the Queen City Cut Ups and The Shea Brothers, featuring future Nashville performer Pat Shea. This festival continued through 1980.

The Kissing Bridge Country and Bluegrass Festival started in 1980 and continued until 1984. Area bands that played this festival included Stone Country, The Erie Lackawanna Railroad, Creek Bend, Jimmy Kaye Review, the Pointless Brothers and Two Hills. National acts included the Seldom Scene, the Johnson Mountain Boys both from the Washington, DC area and Joe Val and the New England Bluegrass Band from Boston, MA.

You could hear live and recorded Bluegrass music on WBFO, the NPR station from the University of Buffalo, every Sunday night from 9 pm till midnight from 1965-1995. Over the 30 years of that radio show, some of dedicated bluegrass disc jockeys that took to the air and kept the local scene alive were Steve Abby, Marv Pfleuger, Rose Haney, Mike Wahl, Craig Kellas, Rich Schaefer, Randy Keller, Rob Campbell, and Keith Zehr.

1 8

THE 1980s

Clubs featuring all styles of music remained crowded and the popularity of many bands from the '70s carried forward into the '80s. Rock, Top 40, R&B, original, country, jazz and ethnic musical groups all continued to have a loyal fan base. Musicians from styles other than rock were covered in previous chapters, so this chapter will primarily concentrate on bands performing rock music. Several popular bands were already covered in the 1970s, so following is information on groups that began playing or became popular in the early 1980s, the period through which this book covers.

ACTOR

Actor is remembered as Jessie Galante's first band. However, the initial version of the group had a male vocalist. They were formed in 1979 by Bob Wilczak (guitar) and Leon Hopkins (bass). The first lead singer was Bob Maggio, who later sang with Fat Brat. Other members of this version of Actor were Dave Gramza (keyboards) and Frank Christofanilli (drums) who was later with Curtis Loew/Pretty Poison.

Jessie became a member in 1980, when she and guitarist Brian Marche joined Actor after leaving their former group Evidence.

ACTOR AT THE BARRELHEAD
Bob Wilczak, Jessie Galante, Rick Proctor, Leon Hopkins, Brian Marche
Photo: Courtesy Jessie Galante

Rick Proctor and Dave Forte were the drummers, until David Joel permanently filled the position. By 1981 Jessie was known as "Buffalo's First Lady of Rock". Their self-released, EP Actor featured the single "Checkin' Out." A&M Records was impressed with the EP and signed them to a recording contract, negotiated by Actor's management of Mike Rozniak and David Cahn.

The A&M album was being recorded in Toronto and during the sessions Leon Hopkins left the band, and was replaced by Art Wall. During the middle of recording the album, artistic differences arose that separated the members, resulting in Jessie leaving Actor and moving to California. A new group was formed by Bob Wilczak with former touring Top 40 vocalist Lori Richert, Tom Lema (bass) and Todd Turner (keyboards). That was a short-lived project and David Joel and Art Wall returned to the band. This version of Actor with Lori remained a popular group through 1984.

After Actor broke up, Bob Wilczak joined Lions and Rock Rats, before reforming Fat Brat with his brother Ken Wilczak. David Joel was a member of the hard rock group Rock Candy. Leon Hopkins started touring as a road crew member for national sound reinforcement company Showco, and 30 years later is the Road Staff Manager for Clair Global Sound Company. Leon still plays bass with local bands in Texas, where he now resides. When Jessie returned from California, where she was a member of the band Fire, she relocated to Europe. While in Europe Jessie toured with her band, releasing Italian and rock albums.

CHEATER

Cheater was based in Rochester but most considered them a Buffalo based band. Led by Jeff Cosco (vocals), it included Don Mancuso (guitar) and Ron Rocco (drums), who were both members of the band Black Sheep, which featured vocalist Lou Gramm, later with Foreigner. Other members were Blayne Pierce (keyboards), Chris Mawesley (guitar) and Kevin McKee (Bass). Cheater released several songs and their EP, featuring the single "Ten Cent Love Affair," was a regional hit, selling over 10,000 copies. The band established a touring circuit that included Buffalo, Rochester, Ohio and Michigan, playing each market on a regular basis, but only a couple times a month, always resulting in large crowds at all their dates. Their follow up single "We Came Here to Rock" was also a regional hit but they broke up soon after. Cosco, Pierce, McKee and Mawesley joined forces with Jimmy Fox from the band Toronto and Ashley Mulford in the new band Easton West. Mulford was a former member of the English band Sad Café, which included vocalist Paul Young who was later with Mike & the Mechanics, a group Mulford toured with after leaving Easton West. Ron Rocco joined the band Freehand with guitarist Dick Grammatico (Lou Gramm's brother), Joe Pullaro (vocals) and Lee Brovitz (bass). When Rocco joined the band, they changed their name to Silver. Currently, Jeff Cosco is still performing in Rochester, Ron Rocco moved to Lockport and is the drummer with Widow Maker and Don Mancuso is the guitarist with Lou Gramm's touring band.

BUXX

Buxx relocated to the Buffalo area with the members being originally from Hawaii, Rochester and Ontario, Canada. The band was formed in Rochester and performed there often, as well as touring the east coast from Quebec to Florida. Members of the group were Bob Norman (guitar), Martin Victor (keyboards), Paul Gallop (bass) and Alan DesGrange (drums). Formed in 1980, Buxx released the album *Knickers Down* and a single "Not This Time" b/w "Hanger 18" which were released on the independent label Panther Records. In addition to their recordings, which received regional airplay, the band was known for their concert level sound

and lighting during performances at all the area major clubs. After the band broke up, Bob Norman moved to LA where he became an agent with Creative Artists Agency (CAA). In this position, he handled the bookings for many national artists, including being the agent for Buffalo's Cory Wells from Three Dog Night. Martin Victor also relocated to

BUXX
Martin Victor, Bob Norman, Alan DesGrange, Paul Gallop
Photo: Courtesy Martin Victor

LA where he became an actor and voice over artist for national commercials. Their album *Knickers Down* was remastered and released as a CD in 2012.

THE BEEZ/WHITE LIES

The Beez were formed from the band Crossroads, which started in 1978. The formation was basically a name change because the final version of Crossroads and the first version of The Beez included the same members: Tom Geraci (guitar), Dan Macaluso (guitar), Dan Patrick (bass) and Kevin Henneman (drums). Dan Macaluso assumed the name of Mac James so there would not be any confusion with two Dans in the band. The difference between the two bands was Crossroads played heavier material and The Beez were more 60's and 70's oriented, with an emphasis on original material. Their first date was on April 1, 1980 at Stage One.

At the time of their premier show, The Beez released the 45 "Me and My Girl." Gene Jacobs, who had managed Cory Wells in The Enemys, before Cory formed Three Dog Night, placed that song in the TV movie *Return of the Rebels*. The Beez obtained the reputation of being the Bad Boys of Buffalo Rock; a title they gained by destroying their equipment on stage, their defiant attitude, and a running feud with the band Talas. Tom Geraci often insulted the audience when they did not show, what he thought was, proper appreciation of their original songs.

An example of how their reputation got them in trouble includes one night at The Sundown Saloon, in Chaffee. After insulting the members of a gang, the band members had to sneak out of the building. Their sound company pulled the equipment truck up to the back door, they got into it and drove away. They waited until the following day to go back and pack their equipment. Another time, at The Red Lantern in Salamanca, due to a

THE BEEZ
Dan Macaluso, Dan Patrick, Kevin Henneman, Tom Geraci
Photo: Courtesy Dan Macaluso

snow storm there was a smaller than normal crowd and the owner did not want to give The Beez their full pay. An argument escalated into a fist fight between the club owner with his bar staff and the band with their equipment roadies. The fight progressed from inside the club, out into the parking lot and ended when the police arrived. A few days later the owner called the band, apologized, offered them their full pay and gave them another date at the Red Lantern. Fearing they were being set up, The Beez brought several truckloads of friends with them, ready to rumble. All went well and they continued to return to the club for many future dates.

In 1982 the band moved to Florida, for dates during Spring Break. Dan Patrick left the band before they departed and the new bass player they hired to replace him quit shortly after they got there. Stranded without a bass player, they flew drummer David Lloyd (from The Keys) down to Florida, Mac James switched to bass and drummer Kevin Henneman started playing guitar. After a short period of time in the Sunshine State, they returned to Buffalo and in late 1983 they were offered the opening spot to go on tour with Badfinger. They were packed and ready to leave for the tour when they received word that the tour was cancelled because a member of Badfinger committed suicide.

Bob Andolora (guitar) and Mike Cox (drums) joined The Beez in 1984. A disagreement arose with Tom Geraci and he left the band in June 1984; they changed their name to White Lies. That group, with various personnel, remained popular until the late 1980s. Tom Geraci is currently playing with the band Rio Bravo in California and Bob Andolora is in Nashville. Dan Patrick and Kevin Henneman formed Western Voice (original) and The Skiffle Band (cover) with David Lloyd, with Dan and Kevin relocating to New York City where they both are employed in the national broadcast television industry. Lloyd expanded the Skiffle Band concept into Bleeding Hearts, a band that still performs in WNY. Mac James changed his name back to Dan Macaluso and is playing in a band called Hypnic Jerks, with two of his daughters.

THE VINCENT MICHAELS BAND

The Vincent Michaels Band (VMB) was formed when Vincent returned to Buffalo from Florida in 1980. In Florida, Vincent presented his original material to Tom Dowd and to the Beatles engineer Ken Scott and attorney Nat Weiss. Previously, in 1966, his songs were presented to Morris Levy of Kama Sutra Records. Vincent Michaels (keyboards/vocals), was joined by former Weekend members and twin brothers, Rick Ryan (Bass) and Tom Ryan (drums), along with Dave Elder (guitar), formerly with The Road. They invested six months of rehearsal, before their premier at Mean Guys East on December 18, 1980.

VINCENT MICHAELS BAND
Dave Elder, Tom Ryan, Vincent Michaels, Rick Ryan
Photo: Courtesy Vincent Michaels

During the 1970s Vincent was the area representative/demonstrator for internationally known synthesizer brands such as Moog Music, Polyfusion, Oberheim and Sequential Circuits. MTV was on the upswing and were featuring the synth-pop sound that the Vincent Michaels Band was already performing. Vincent had the top of the line synthesizers and effects from his previous employment and the band members had over a decade of experience playing at the top area rock clubs. It was the bands intentions to feature their original music, but due to the positive audience reaction to their MTV style dance covers, they were immediately in demand at area clubs. Vince's brother Frank Michaels (The Music Agency) booked the band five nights a week at the top area clubs. The club owners demanded the recognizable covers, not the originals the band wanted to feature. They were playing until 3:00 AM every night, so the recording of their originals was put on the back burner.

Since the original objective of the band was to record, despite their popularity, frustration started to set in. Tom Ryan left the band and was replaced by Howard Wilson (drums). Soon afterwards, Rick Ryan left the band and was replaced by Geoffrey Fitzhugh Perry (bass). Later members of the group included: Les Bowman, Joe Santi, Ted Reinhardt and Kevin Roth. The album they recorded at Image Recording Studio in Olcott NY was well received, but with no contract, the Vincent Michaels Band disbanded in 1988. Frank Michaels continued with his company, The Music Agency, Vincent worked for Illos Pianos and Pearce Amplifiers, where he helped develop a new amplifier with guitarist Les Paul.

OTHER POPULAR EARLY 80's BANDS

There were many other popular early '80s bands. Following is information on some of these groups. Benhatzel recorded an album produced by John Nagy who produced George Thorogood and they also placed songs on the 97 Rock, WPHD and Z98's albums. Band members were Paul Benhatzel (guitar), Doug Cerrone (bass) and Don Tomasulo (drums). Tomasulo also worked for Festival Concerts and is now a sales manager for Entercom

388

Radio. Doug Cerrone relocated to LA where he worked for MCA Records...Lebel was the trio that guitarist Bobby Lebel formed with Danny Sawyer (bass) and Gary Tracy (drums). Bobby Lebel moved to WNY from Vermont to join The Road. After working with Lebel for several years he rejoined The Road. He later formed The Headers and The Bobby Lebel Orchestra...Broken Silence was a Niagara Falls based band with Tom Gariano (vocals), Jim Jeckovich (guitar), Jeff Jeckovich (keyboards), Marty Lewars (bass) and Kevin DeDerio (drums). Tom Gariano now leads the band A-List...Songbird was previously known as Cisco Ducks and Ice Nine. They changed their name to Songbird when vocalist Robin Rinkerman joined the band. Tom Fenton (guitar), Jim Iarocci (bass), keyboardist Craig Allen (keyboards) and Mike Binda (drums) rounded out the group. Fenton and Iarocci were also members of The Fibs...Rred was formed by former Lamont vocalist Mike O'Mara and Road drummer Sal Joseph. They had several different guitarists, Rick Dittmar, Paul Palisano, Don Mancuso and Bobby Lebel, and bass players Dan Patrick and Dave Forrest. Mike O'Mara is currently the vocalist with several rock bands in LA, including the nationally touring Def Leppard tribute band Pyromania, Motley Crue tribute True2Crue and as a member of Tracii Guns Band...Lions was formed by Steve McDonald (vocals) from Network, Tom McGurrin (guitar) from Bishop, Bruce Decker (keyboards) from Stross Fletcher, Frank Pusateri (bass) from Jambo/Sky and Rick McEvoy (drums) from Fat Brat. Currently, Frank Pusateri is the leader of Only Humen, Bruce Decker is with Breakaway and Steve McDonald is the vocalist with the reunited Cock Robin...Shiner included three former members of Weekend who were Denny Dunkowski (guitar), Ned Wood (keyboards), Rick Farmer (bass) and Tom Ryan (drums) ...Doors tribute band, Lizard King was a Niagara County based touring group, featuring vocalist Craig Sandish...Gypzy was fronted by vocalist Glenda Chausse, who later formed the band Strider with Mike Runo (guitar), Matt Young (keyboards), Joe Martucci (bass) and Johnny Magnum (drums)...Vapor Voyce was led by former Off Hour Rockers vocalist Wendy Lasker...Pretty Poison featured Rita Seitz (vocals), Tim Fik (guitar), Alan Thompson (bass) and Frank Christofanilli (drums), later replaced by Tom Ryan (drums). They changed their name to Watchers and became known for saran wrap and electrical tape stage wear. Tim is now with the Florida blues group The Bridget Kelly Band and Reeta performed in England... Additional bands were Insomniax with Sue Kolaga, Zillion with drummer Mike Terrana, Tobias with guitarist Kenny Andrews Kanowski, along with Ezekial, Siamese Eyez, Third Street, Elliott, Sass, Lix, Onyx, Voyager, Savoire Faire, Kiki Birds, Assailant, Izzy Wilde, Tarkus, Jade and Colours. Many bands had rehearsal rooms at Ultimage Storage in Kenmore or Keith Gregor's Music Mall in Cheektowaga.

NON-LOCAL CLUB BANDS

During the late 1970s and early 1980s Buffalo became known as an area with an active live music club scene. Work was available six nights a week and it was centrally located for dates in the Ohio, Central New York and Toronto markets. In the early 80's members of the band Buxx moved from Rochester and Ontario, Canada to Buffalo and made it their home base. In the mid-1980s the hair band Rock Candy moved here from New England. The band Cheater, only had one member from the area but since they played steady nights at clubs like Stage One, they were considered a WNY band.

Some groups performed in Buffalo so often, they were thought of as area bands. Examples of these groups were 805 a Syracuse based progressive-rock band, led by guitarist Dave Porter, who had a regional hit with "Stand in Line" on RCA Records. Duke Jupiter was a Rochester band that released the single "I'll Drink to You". Paul Pope, with Billy Sullivan, was from Ohio who are remembered for their theatrics and Big Mac Attacks. Paul was previously with Molkie Cole, an Ohio band that played at Western New York clubs in the 1970s. The band Clevelend was from Cleveland and were known for their theatrical rock shows. The hard-rock band Harpo was from PA. Moonlight Drive brought their Doors show from Ohio to Buffalo, with their lead vocalist Bill Pettijohn portraying such an authentic Morrison impersonation that he was offered a film role to play Morrison in a movie. Blotto was a comedy-rock band from Albany who had the hit MTV video with "I Wanna Be a Lifeguard".

Canadian bands that performed in Buffalo on a regular basis included Kim Mitchell, who was in Max Webster and had the hit single "Go for a Soda." Triumph played dates at After Dark when they first formed in the mid-1970s and guitarist Rik Emmett has been appearing in Western New York ever since. The Rick Santers band, from Toronto, were regular performers in WNY during the early 1980s, along with Toronto heavy-metal vocalist Lee Aaron.

RADIO IN THE 1980s

FM radio began playing rock music in the 1970s, with the first progressive rock station being WYSL-FM, which became WPHD 103.3 FM in 1970. In 1975 96.9 FM became the Album-Oriented Rock Q-FM 97 and eventually 97 Rock WGRQ-FM. By the time the 1980s began, FM had become the radio dial location for music, while AM was starting to feature talk radio.

The early '80s DJs at 97 Rock included Larry "Snortin" Norton, Bruce Barber, JC Corcoran, Lauri Githens, Cindy Chan, "Slick Tom" Tiberi, Jim Pastrick, Paul Hein and Carl Russo. On January 4, 1985, the station changed to an Adult Contemporary format as WRLT and released most of their on-air staff. That decision was reversed on September 20, 1988 when the station rehired most of its staff and returned as 97 Rock.

103.3 FM was known as the progressive rock WPHD during the 1980s, becoming WUFX in 1989 and the alternative rock WEDG in 1995. The morning team on WPHD from 1978 to 1989 was Taylor & Moore, remembered for their comedy routines including the Land of Fa. The program director was John McGhan and DJ's included Brian J. Walker and Tony MaGoo.

98.5 FM or Z98 was known as WZIR. In 1981 it was knows as Wizard FM and featured a free form format. Management changed it to a more classic rock format with the DJs at the station including Dean Matela, Bob Kramarik, Janet Merrian, Tony Florentino, Jim Nowicki, Mike Brown, George Prentice and Anne Leighton.

107.7 FM was known as WUWU–The Rock of Western New York. The DJs were Bob Allen, The Unknown, Justin Case, Georgine, Bill Nichols, Jeff Gordon, Gary Storm and Jim Santella, many of whom were at 98.5 FM when it was the free form Wizard format. A memorable event was in May 1983 when station manager Bob Allen took over the transmitter site and hijacked the radio station. The station also broadcast the *BCMK Local Music Show*, hosted by Tommy Calandra. Later in the 1980s the station became WBYR.

A criticism of the radio stations was they did not play local music on regular rotation. Buffalo city councilman David Fronczak even started a committee, which met at City Hall, to investigate if Buffalo could initiate a local content policy, comparable to Canadian Broadcasting which mandates the playing of Canadian artists. Disc jockeys at area stations contended that they wanted to play local songs on regular rotation but it was contrary to the corporate programming policy of the stations.

The programming policy of the radio station was not a local decision and the stations supported local musicians by starting music shows. The radio stations also released compilation albums by area groups and the DJs promoted area groups when possible during their radio shows.

The radio station that played the most local music was WBNY-FM broadcast on 91.3 FM at Buffalo State College. It was a station policy that regardless of the programming of a show, they had to play at least one recording by a WNY group every hour.

BUFFALO MUSIC AWARDS & BUFFALO MUSIC HALL OF FAME

BUFFALO MUSIC AWARDS. The first Buffalo Music Awards was held on Monday, November 23, 1981 at Rooftops, 2186 Seneca Street in Buffalo. The awards show was initially called The Buffalo Backstage Music Awards because it was started by Buffalo Backstage Magazine. Over 1,000 people attended the first awards show and the bands that performed that evening were Benhatzel, Vincent Michaels Band, Beez, Backroads, Parousia, Stross Fletcher, Cheater and an impromptu blues duo by Dave Constantino from Talas and Mark Freeland from Electroman.

BUFFALO MUSIC AWARDS POSTER
Photo Authors Collection

Air personalities from 97 Rock and Z98 presented the awards, the local television stations covered the event, International Cable videotaped the night for future broadcast and Mayor Griffin proclaimed November 23, 1981 as Buffalo Music Day. The entire WNY community got together to honor the musicians performing in the Buffalo area, which was the objective of Rick and Marsha Falkowski publishers of *Buffalo Backstage* magazine.

At the first event, there were awards for seven groups, seven individual musicians, recorded album, recorded single, DJ and club. There was no differentiation for musical styles, with all musicians grouped together regardless of the type of music they performed. Over the 30-year history of the Buffalo Music Awards, the award categories were

1st BUFFALO BACKSTAGE MUSIC AWARDS
Dave Constantino, Fred Caserta, Paul Varga
Photo Authors Collection

expanded to cover the diverse styles of music being performed in WNY and there were individual musician categories for vocalists and all instrumentalists for rock, Top 40, blues, original, country and R&B.

Due to the many changes in the music industry, the Buffalo Music Awards were retired after their 30th Anniversary show in 2010. For information on The Buffalo Music Awards and a listing of all the annual award winners, go to *buffalomusicawards.com*.

THE BUFFALO MUSIC HALL OF FAME was founded by Rick and Marsha Falkowski to further honor and bring additional attention to the musicians of WNY. It was initially patterned after the policy of other awards events, where after an individual won their musical category for several years, they were placed in a Hall of Fame. In 1983, the first three musicians inducted into the Hall of Fame were Dave Constantino, Billy Sheehan and Paul Varga, essentially inducting the band Talas.

During the first two decades of the Hall of Fame individuals could be inducted by two different paths. If a musician or group won their category in the Buffalo Music Awards for three consecutive years or it was determined

1st HALL OF FAME INDUCTION TALAS
Dave Constantino, Bill Sheehan, Paul Varga
Being presented by Rick Falkowski
Photo Authors Collection, Photo Credit Peter Henley

they were a dominant member of that category, they were inducted. The other path was an individual could be inducted by a vote from the already inducted members of the Hall of Fame. At first the Buffalo Music Hall of Fame concentrated on rock music musicians and emphasis was placed on local, rather than national accomplishments. As time progressed, individuals from all musical styles were considered for induction and national accomplishments were prioritized. Eventually the automatic induction after winning a Buffalo Music Awards category was discontinued and induction was based upon review by a committee, with various criteria being factored into consideration for induction. The Buffalo Music Hall of Fame annually inducts new members at a ceremony that takes place every Fall.

In the Appendix there is a listing of the members of the Buffalo Music Hall of Fame, with the year in which they were inducted. For more information on the BMHOF and its inductees go to buffalomusic.org.

EPILOGUE - END OF AN ERA

During the 1970s and early 1980s bands of all musical styles had a multitude of clubs and events where they could perform. The most popular groups had more work than they could handle and had to determine in advance when they wanted to take time off. Everyone was going to nightclubs on a regular basis.

The attendance at area clubs started to decrease when the legal drinking age was increased to 19 on December 4, 1982. An entire year of potential customers could no longer be admitted to bars, which meant their friends, who over 19 years old, also stopped going to the clubs. Then on December 1, 1985 the legal drinking age was increased to 21. This removed another two years of potential clientele. In addition to the changes in the drinking age, drinking driving laws began to be strictly enforced. Anyone who was ticketed no longer went to the clubs, while customers drank less due to their concerns when driving home. Enforcement of the laws was good for public safety and accident prevention, but had a negative effect on the bottom line at the clubs.

During the early 1980s more factories were closing in the WNY area and pay raises were not being provided to keep pace with the standard of living. Baby boomers did not have the disposable income to go out as often as they did in the 1970s. The baby boom generation was getting older and many former club regulars were now staying home in favor of raising a family. They were also staying home to watch MTV, play video games and enjoy other new forms of entertainment. With the closing factories, lack of pay raises and expenses of a growing family, many others were leaving WNY for other markets where better paying jobs were available. Now that there were fewer people going out, clubs cut back on the number of nights they offered live music and some nightclubs closed. There were still many talented bands available to perform at the clubs, but the problem is there were now fewer clubs and fewer dates available for them. It became more difficult for professional musicians in the WNY area to make a living by performing at area clubs.

Some date had to be arbitrarily selected as an ending date for this book, so the mid-1980s was picked. The above factors contributed to that decision because they signaled an end to the glory days of Buffalo Music & Entertainment. For all the talented musicians that began performing after the early to mid-1980s, an entire book could be and probably will be written on the mid-80s and 1990s.

The mid-1980s was over 30 years ago. If someone was just turning the legal drinking age at that time they are now in their 50s and if someone was in the mid-30s, they are now probably retired. However, everyone has many memories of that time. The music from the 1950s to 1980s is still very popular and outdoor shows in WNY often feature music from that period. It could be said that the music featured in this book is still with us today.

APPENDIX

APPENDIX A - POSTSCRIPT

When researching the information for this book, some items did not specifically fit into one of the chapters. To create a space for this information, this postscript was added.

Steele Mackay (James Morrison) was born in Buffalo in 1842. In addition to writing over 30 plays and opening the first acting school in the United States, he invented flameproof theater curtains and folding chairs.

Mark Dixon, from the band Party Squad, recorded the vocals for Boston's Second Album *Don't Look Back*. After Boston vocalist Brad Delp decided to return to the band, Delp re-recorded the vocals. However, Mark was paid for the sessions.

David Boreanaz, star of the television series *Bones*, is the son of Dave Thomas, who was the host of *Rocketship 7* and *Dialing for Dollars* on WKBW TV from 1962 – 1978.

Stephen Nathan is a television writer and producer, and Steve Nathan is a Nashville studio keyboardist. They were both born in Buffalo, but they are not the same person.

The Buffalo Zoo's Reptile House was designed in 1942 by Marlin Perkins, who was originally the reptile curator and then the director of the Buffalo Zoo from 1938 to 1944. From 1963 to 1985 he was the host of the TV nature show, *Mutual of Omaha's Wild Kingdom*.

Buffalo native Frank Mancuso first worked in the entertainment industry as an assistant manager at The Lafayette Theater. He was later the chairman and CEO of Paramount Pictures from 1984 to 1991 and MGM from 1993 to 1999.

The Variety Club was founded as a private club for theater owners and showmen, where they could have dinner, socialize and enjoy an after-hours cocktail. The Buffalo clubhouse was on Delaware Avenue which included slot machines and card games, with the proceeds going to charity. As more locally owned theaters closed, the Variety Club by-laws were amended to include members who were not part of the entertainment industry. In 1962, they worked with Dr. Robert Warner to form the *Variety Club Telethon* to benefit Women's and Children's Hospital, with all the donations staying in Buffalo. The telethon was originally on Channel 2 and is now broadcast on Channel 7. It was held at various locations, at The Executive for years and is now telecast from the Seneca Niagara Events Center. The Buffalo chapter is # 2 in the per capita dollars raised in the US and # 6 worldwide.

During the 1950s, Buffalo was known for its gay bars and people would travel to Buffalo from Toronto to be part of the scene. In the '50s the police would look the other way, but that changed when Nelson Rockefeller was governor in the early '60s. Males could be arrested for dancing with another male. Gay rights groups began working toward political goals and building community meeting places. *5th freedom* was a paper published at the gay center, located at Main & Utica, above a tire store and in the current site of McDonalds. They offered dances on weekends and it was the location where the first gay produced musical was presented. This center was instrumental in paving the way for openly gay entertainment venues in Western New York.

Actor Vincent Gallo wrote, directed, composed the music and starred in the movie *Buffalo '66* during 1998. When growing up in Buffalo he played bass in the bands Blue Mood in 1971, Zephyr with Danny Rowland (guitar) and Barry Height (drums) which played a battle of bands at Delaware Park in 1974 and The Plastics, who played at Hallwalls in 1976. Gallo moved to New York City when he was 16 years old and was a member of a band called Gray before concentrating on acting.

Footnote to the Scinta Brothers section. In the 1890s and at the turn of the century, The Scinta's Band were regular performers at parks and gazebo concerts, including being one of the bands performing at the Pan Am Expo in 1901. The leader of this group was Serafino Scinta, who emigrated to Buffalo after leading bands in his native Italy. Serafino cannot be directly traced to The Scinta Brothers, but their grandfather Joe Scinta played a multitude of instruments and had each of his nine children learn an instrument. Joe also worked at Trico in the early 1900s and was involved with the invention of the windshield wiper blade. There is another Joe Scinta that plays in the band eXit and owns Ken-Ton Electronics, a company that develops and manufactures electronic circuits for many companies, including Lazertron. There is also another cousin, Frank Scinta, who is a professor of music at a college in California.

Hide in Plain Sight, May 1978. left to right, Jim Kipler, Tony Galla, Carolyn Ferrini, Mickey Kipler. James Caan, Tony Grasso, Fred Saia, John Licata. Dick Riederer and Jiggy Gelia.
Photo: Courtesy Dick Riederer

When filming *Hide in Plain Sight,* a music scene was filmed at the Mount Major Banquet Hall on West Ferry & Herkimer Street. This was one of the 60 Buffalo locations included in the film. This is a photo of the band in the movie, with actor James Caan and Buffalo music booking agent Fred Saia.

From 1963 to 1967 there was a music show called *Music Hop*, which was the Canadian version of *American Bandstand*. Being a Toronto show, Buffalo residents would receive the program on CBC, which was Channel 5 on the antenna station reception at that time. The host of the first season was Alex Trebek, better known as the host of *Jeopardy*.

The oldest bar in Buffalo Is Ulrich's Tavern at 674 Ellicott Street. It was founded in 1868 as a grocery on one side and tavern on the other. The grocery side of the business closed in the late 1880s and originally there was a hotel upstairs, with a barber shop included in the building. Michael Ulrich took over the saloon in 1905 and renamed it Ulrich's in 1910.

The second oldest Buffalo bar is the Swannie House at 170 Ohio Street which was founded in the 1880s. The upstairs area of the tavern was a rooming house with the second floor being rented to ship captains and their officers, while the attic was rented to seaman of lower ranks.

Outside of the city of Buffalo, The Eagle House Tavern in Williamsville dates back to 1827, when it was owned by Oziel Smith and operated as a stage coach stop. When you took the stage coach from Buffalo to Batavia, Williamsville was the overnight stop. It boasts the longest continuously held liquor license in Erie County and New York State.

The M&T Bank Plaza Event Series is the longest running free concert series in WNY. The noontime concerts at 1 M&T Plaza began in 1970 and present a diverse selection of area entertainment every weekday from mid-June to the end of August.

The Taste of Buffalo is the largest two-day food festival in the United States. It began in 1984 and has annually featured a variety of WNY bands.

The Juneteenth Festival was started in 1976 by B.U.I.L.D. to preserve and promote the broad spectrum of African American heritage. It was originally held on Jefferson Avenue but moved to Martin Luther King Park, where the festival features a variety of musical and dance groups. Juneteenth is the oldest known celebration of the ending of slavery in the United States and the Buffalo festival is the third largest Juneteenth celebration in the world.

In 1958 the Allentown Village Society held an outdoor art show in September to stimulate business to the neighborhood. The date of the festival was moved to the second weekend of June in 1959 and in 1966 it adopted the formal name of The Allentown Art Festival. It is now one of the largest art festivals in the Great Lakes Area. Music was part of the early Allentown Art Festival was it was not permitted after a riot in during the 1970 festival. However, the festival now allows licensed buskers and several businesses in the Allentown area feature live bands in their premises.

APPENDIX B - HORN SECTIONS

Following is the listing of the Buffalo bands with horn sections, many of which were touring bands. The horn players are listed, but not the other instrumentalists. In some cases, the lead vocalist of the group is mentioned because groups were often known by their vocalist. The efforts of Bob Meier, for his assistance in compiling this listed, are appreciated.

The list is by the year formed and does not include groups that just had a single horn player or bands where a musician who played another instrument periodically doubled on horn. It also is a listing of rock and commercial rock bands. Jazz groups are not included because they were primarily horn groups. Polka and German bands are not listed for the same reason. Many of the musicians listed here were often members of various jazz or ethnic groups when not playing with area rock bands.

1964 The Coincidentals: Nick Salamone sax and Sebastian (Buster) Russo (RIP) trumpet.

1964 Otis Tolliver & the New Sounds: Maurice Jones trumpet, Stanley Lee sax

1966 Milton's Salsa and the All-Night Workers: Ansel Cureton trumpet, Arthur McBride trombone

1967 SOS (Shades of Soul): Flick Williams sax, Larry Fletcher trumpet

1968 The Underwood Exchange: Nick Gentile Trombone later replaced by Freddy Marshall, John Scathard sax later replaced by Dave Shiavone. Dennis Tribuzzi trumpet, Ken Cosentino (RIP) trumpet, and Steve Martino joined later on trumpet. Lead Vocalist Tom Blenker.

1968 Parkside Zoo: Sam Guarino sax, Malcom Lee trumpet and Ken Kaufmann trumpet. Lead vocalist Mondo Galla.

1969 Penny Farthing's: Lenny Makowski sax & flute, Bob Scocchera trumpet. Lead singers Reggie Roland and Mike Costley.

1969 The Rubber Band: Dick Griffo (RIP) sax, Charlie Fardella trumpet & valve trombone, Mark Josephsberg trumpet.

1969 National Trust: Sam Guarino sax & lead vocals, Lenny Makowski sax & flute, Bob Scocchera trumpet.

1969 Side Winding Express: Broderick Perkins trombone, Daniel Lewis trumpet, Ronny Robinson sax

1970 Glass Menagerie: Bill Long trombone, Bruce Trojan trumpet, Jeff DePaolo trumpet and later Jeff Tysek trumpet.

1971 United Funk: Daniel Lewis trumpet, David Humphrey trombone, Brad Perkins sax

1971 Jennifers Family: Bob Meier trombone, Ron Mendola trumpet and Dick Fron sax. Lead vocalists Mike Piccolo and Jenifer Miller.

1971 Stone Bridge: Bob Meier trombone, Al Schmidt trumpet, Gary Kajewski sax & flute. Lead singer Ray (Soapy) Sobkowiak (RIP).

1971 Hernandez: Tim Gerwitz trumpet, Jeff Hackworth sax, Bob Meier trombone.

1971 Perfect Circle: Jim Tudini sax, Dennis Tribuzzi trumpet. Lead Singers Reggie Roland and Mike Costley.

1971 Opus 1: Ron Mendola trumpet, Dick Fron sax, Mike Migliori sax, Jim Board trombone.

1971 Carnival: John Campanella trombone, Mike Tribuzzi sax, Ken Cosentino (RIP) trumpet, Dennis Tribuzzi trumpet.

1972 Junction West: Jimmy Witherspoon sax, Tom Adcock sax. later John Hill (RIP) sax, Mike Tribuzzi sax, Chuck Gorino trumpet. Lead Singers Harry Stewart (RIP) and Joey James.

1972 Full House: John Hill sax & flute, Dennis Tribuzzi trumpet, Freddy Marshall trombone.

1972 Chenago: Jeff Carr trombone, Nelson Starr trumpet. Walter Lakota sax. Lead Singer Mark Dupen.

1972 New Breed: Ansel Cureton trumpet, Art Mc Bride trombone, later Robert Tatum sax

1973 Hank Soulman Mullins: Jerry Livingston trombone, Vernon Bunch trumpet, Andrew King sax

1973 Seven Miles Per Hour: Stan Lee sax, Maurice (Mo) Jones trumpet.

1973 Funkafize Filth: Jerry Livingston trombone, Hartwell trumpet, Stan Lee sax

1973 Just n Time: Dennis Tribuzzi trumpet, Freddy Marshall trombone, Lenny Makowski sax & flute, later Jake Smith trumpet. Lead Singer Reggie Rowland.

1973 Freedom's Fare: Joe LaPaglia trombone, Ted Kerchner trumpet, Ron Paladino sax.

1973 United Sound: Bob Scocchera trumpet, Dale Pawlowski (RIP) sax, later Bill Pendziawtr sax, Bob White trumpet Bob Meier trombone, Bill Walkowiak trumpet. Lead Singers Dotti Hooks, Bill Miller (RIP) Larry Gilbert, Ike Smith later Johnny Martin.

1974 Lance Diamond Band: Bob Meier trombone, Glen Lista trumpet. Ted Ebert trumpet. Lead Singer Lance Diamond.

1974 Free State of Mind: Brian Freeman trumpet, Robert Tatum sax.

1974 Breckenridge: Glenn Lista trumpet, Russ D'Alba sax, Phil Sims trombone. The horn section changed to Ted Kerchner trumpet, Joe LaPaglia trombone, later Bob Meier trombone, Bill Walkowiak trumpet. Lead Singer Carl Barone.

1975 Isaac: Glenn Lista trumpet, John Campanella trombone. Lead singers Mary Jane Monaco and Lance Diamond.

1975 Mirror's Image: Bob Meier trombone, Gary Kajewski sax & flute, Bill Walkowiak trumpet. Lead singers Jenifer Miller and Ike Smith

1975 Transatlantic: Glenn Lista trumpet, Bob (Jake) Smith trumpet, Mick Molley (sax), Phil Sims trombone.

1977 Emerald City: Phil Simms trombone, Frank Casino sax & flute.

1978 Voyage: Nick Molley sax. Sebastian (Buster) Russo (RIP) trumpet, Bob Meier on trombone. Lead Singer Jackie Gerald and Kihm Watson (RIP).

1979 Topaz: Brian Freeman trumpet, Robert Tatum sax

1980 Buffalo Blues Band: Nick Salamone sax, Pete Pecora sax. Lead Vocalists Billy McEwen and John Rose.

1982 QHR Band: Bob Meier trombone, Mike Tribuzzi sax. Glenn Lista trumpet. Lead singers Charlie Lagattuta and Chick Oletto,

1983 Unity Band: Tommy Sims trumpet, Brian Freeman trumpet, Larry Cheelely sax, Rick McCrea trombone

APPENDIX C – 1970s & 1980s CLUBS

Adam's Como Lounge
After Dark
Anchor Bar
Attica Lanes (Attica)
Bayview
Beachview Inn
Beau Geste
Bedells Candlelight
Bellevue Como Hotel
Big Apple
Big Tree (Jamestown)
Big Willies (Grand Island)
Bonnet
Barrelhead, The
Bixby's
Bruce Jarvis's Lake Casino
Buxton Inn
Caboose (Fredonia)
Candlelight Room
Casey's
Canterbury's
Casablanca
Central Park Grill
Ciro's
City Lights
Cloister, The
Connection, The
Continental, The
Cosmic Casino
Cougar's
Crawdaddy's
Dad's Cafe
Daddy's (Niagara Falls)
Del Mar
Den-Nels
Desiderio's
Depot, The
D.J's Stillery
Dollinger's (Albion)
Dr. Feelgoods
Eagle's Roost (Olcott)

Eggertsville Inn
Engine House (Batavia)
Executive, The
Fast Annie's
Finnlocks
Fireside Inn (Olean)
Four Fathoms
IV Stallions
Foxfire
Frank's Casa Nova
G. Willikers
Gable's
Galaxy of the Stars
Gentlemen Jim's
Gilligans
Godfather's (Olean)
Goldies Apartment
Graffiti's
Groucho's (Niagara Falls)
Ground Round
Harlen Inn, The
Hayloft (Batavia)
Hideaway, The (Darien Center)
Holiday Inn (NF Blvd.)
Hollywood Lounge (Batavia)
Holland Willows (Holland)
Hotel California
Imperial Garage (Niagara Falls)
Inferno, The
Jacobi's
Jimminie's
Jolly Roger
J.P. Morgan's
Knickerbocker's
Korabs
Lamp Post
Lance & Shield (Holland)
Landmark
Laurel & Hardy's
LeClub
Library, The (Niagara Falls)

Lone Star
Longbranch Saloon (Elma)
Longhouse (Holland)
Lou's Inn (Westfield)
Manzell's
Masthead, The
McBean's
McGillicuddy's
Maguire's Arches
McVan's
Mean Alice's
Mean Guys East
Melanie's
Melody Inn (Jamestown)
Mickey Rats (City Bar)
Mickey Rats (Lake)
Molly Hatchet's
Mr. Goodbar
Mulligan's
Nero's
New York Lounge
Nicholsbrook
Niagara Hilton
Nietzche's
Old Beach Inn
Old Harmony
Omni
One Eyed Jack's (Salamanca)
Partner's
Passport Europe
Patrick's Pub
Point Breeze Hotel
Plant 6 – Delaware
Plant 6 - Niagara
Playboy Club, The
Poets Lounge (Holiday Inn)
Pomeroy House
Port Shark
Prince of Wales (Wales)
Pyramid, The
Purple Moose Saloon
Ramada Inn
RC Annas
Red Lantern (Salamanca)
Rhino's

Riverside Tavern (Olean)
Rockers
Rogues II
Rooftops
Ryan's New Federal Pub
Rusty Nail
Salty Dog
September's
Shadrack's
Shangri-la (Wellsville)
Schoney's
Schuper House
Shelby's
Sheraton
Shutters & Boards
Sloan Lanes
Southshore Inn
Southtowner
Stage I
Starting Gate, The
Sestak & Maguires
Subway
Sundown Saloon (Chaffee)
Surf Club (Jamestown)
T-Birds
Tack Room
Three Coins
Thruway Lanes
Tom Jones Club
Town and Country
Trader Jack's (Jamestown)
Tralfamadore Cafe
2001
Uncle Sam's
Union Casino
Union Gap (Batavia)
Urban Inn
Viking Inn
Wayside Manor
Wooden Nickle (Olean)
Woodshed
Whistle Stop

APPENDIX D – BMHOF INDUCTEES
1983-2017

10,000 Maniacs - 1994
Al Hury - 2012
Al Tinney - 1996
Alan Thompson - 1989
Alison Pipitone - 2017
Alyn Syms - 2016
Anatara - 1998
Andy Anselmo - 2013
Andy Kulberg - 2007
Angelo Callea - 2003
Ani DiFranco - 1996
Anne Fadale - 2014
Anthony Marchese - 2008
Anthony Violanti - 2001
Aretha Franklin - 2016
Arlester "Dyke"
   Christian - 2012
Armand John Petri - 2012
Armondo Galla - 2001
Art Kubera - 2002
Barbara St. Clair - 1991
Bernard Kugel - 2012
Big Steve Krzeminski - 2003
Big Wheelie - 1985
Billy McEwen - 1989
Billy Nunn - 2015
Billy Sheehan - 1983
Bob & Gene - 2011
Bob Andalora - 1988
Bob Falk - 2012
Bob James - 2008
Bob Meier - 2014
Bob Mussell - 2011
Bobby Jones - 2004
Bobby Lebel - 2011
Bobby Militello - 1995

Bobby Previte - 2013
Boyd Lee Dunlop - 2012
Brian McKnight - 1998
Bruce Brucato - 1988
Bruce Morgan - 1994
Bruce Moser - 2006
Buffalo Philharmonic
   Orchestra - 1999
Calato Mfg. –
   Regal Tip - 2001
Cameron Baird - 2012
Cannibal Corpse - 2013
Carol Jean Swist - 2001
Carol Wincenc - 1998
Castellani-Andriaccio
   Duo - 2002
Charles "Cholly"
   Atkins - 1999
Charlie O'Neill - 2011
Cheryl Littlejohn - 1996
Chuancey Olcott - 2017
Chuck Madden - 2003
Clint Holmes - 2000
Cory Wells - 1997
Count Rabbit - 1996
Curtis Lee Black - 2004
Dale Anderson - 2003
Danny Cannon & the Vibraharps -
2016
Danny Neaverth - 2000
Dave Berryman - 2003
Dave Constantino - 1983
Dave Elder - 1991
Dave Fridmann - 2013
Dave Schiavone - 2003
Dave Schmeidler - 2017

David Allen - 2003
David Helfman Lucas - 2011
David Kane - 1988
David Lee Shire - 2006
David Meinzer - 2016
David Musial - 2014
Denton Cottier &
  Daniels - 2014
Dick Bauerle - 1988
Dodo Green - 1997
Dolly Durante - 2015
Don Menza - 2005
Donna Palmer - 1991
Doug Morgano - 1996
Doug Ruffin - 2004
Doug Yeomans - 2004
Dr. Joe Baudo - 2014
Dr. Lonnie Smith - 2009
Ed Bentley - 2008
Ed Supple - 2013
Eddie Tice - 2010
Eli Konikoff - 2015
Elizabeth Swados - 2007
Ella Robinson - 1999
Elvin Shepherd - 1997
Emile Latimer - 2000
Eric Andersen - 1999
Ernie Corallo - 1989
Flash - 2015
Fran Scharett - 2003
Frank Brunson - 2002
Frank Grizanti - 2007
Frank Pusateri - 1991
Frankie and - 2012
Fred Caserta - 2013
Fred Raiser - 2015
Fred Rapillo - 2000
Gamalon - 2002
Gary Keller - 2014
Gary Mallaber - 1997

Geno McManus - 2014
Geoffrey Fitzhugh
  Perry - 2004
George "Hound Dog"
  Lorenz - 1996
George Doran - 1988
George Puleo - 1987
Glenn Colton - 2009
Goo Goo Dolls - 1995
Greg Gizzi - 1992
Grover Washington,
  Jr. - 1999
Gurf Morlix - 2005
Guy Nichols - 1992
Harold Arlen - 1997
Hit N Run - 2009
Howard Fleetwood
  Wilson II - 2013
Howie Simon - 2017
J.C. Thompson - 1995
Jack Blanchard &
  Misty Morgan - 2010
Jack Civiletto - 2009
Jack Prybylski - 2014
Jack Yellen - 1996
Jackie Jocko - 1997
Jackson C. Frank - 2015
Jan Williams - 2000
Janice Mitchell - 2000
Jeff Jarvis - 2003
Jeff Miers - 2014
Jeff Schaller - 2016
Jerry Livingston - 2008
Jerry Meyers - 2003
Jerry Nathan - 2002
Jerry Raven - 2009
Jessie Galante - 2010
Jim Brucato - 2015
Jim Calire - 1999
Jim Ehinger - 2007

Jim Linsner - 2017
Jim Runfola - 2016
Jim Santella - 2013
Jim Whitford - 2006
Jim Wozniak - 2007
Jim Wynne - 2015
Jimmy Ralston - 2002
Jimmy Sacca - 2008
Jo Jo McDuffie - 1999
Joanie Marshall - 2016
Joanie Summers - 2008
JoAnn Falletta - 2010
Joe Bompczyk - 2014
Joe Ford - 2004
Joe Guercio - 2001
Joe Head - 1992
Joe Madison - 1997
Joe Parisi - 2014
Joe Pendolino Jr. - 2002
Joe Public - 2013
Joe Romanowski - 2004
Joe Rozler - 2008
Joel DiBartolo - 2001
Joey Diggs - 2016
Joey Reynolds - 2009
John Boylan - 2004
John Brady - 2003
John Connelly - 2015
John Hey - 2005
John Hunt - 2006
John Mahoney - 1997
John Sansone - 2001
John Valby - 1987
John Weitz - 1999
Joie Anes - 1991
Jony James - 2013
Joseph Wincenc - 2006
JoyRyde - 2004
Junction West - 1998
Justin Dicioccio - 2004

Kathy Lynn and the
   Playboys - 2010
Ken Kaufman - 1984
Ken Wilczak - 1984
Kenny Hawkins - 2000
Kenny Thomasula - 2014
Kent Weber - 1994
Kristen Pfaff - 1994
Lance Diamond - 1992
Larry Swist - 2002
Lejaren Hiller - 2006
Lenny Silver - 2000
Leonard Pennario - 2007
Linda Lou Schriver - 2013
Linda Rose Lombardo Appleby -
   2015
Louie Marino - 2001
Lucky Peterson - 1996
M&T Bank - 2015
Mack Luchey - 2008
Macy Favor - 2002
Marc Hunt - 2012
Mark Dixon - 1990
Mark Freeland - 1987
Mark Kohan - 2003
Mark Winsick - 2010
Marlene Ricci - 2004
Marty Peters - 2014
Marylouise Nanna - 2012
Matt Young - 1993
McCarthyizm - 2009
Mel Lewis - 2005
Michael Campagna - 2014
Michael Hund - 1992
Michael Spriggs - 2004
Mike Caputy - 2002
Mike Cox - 1991
Mike Meldrum - 2006
Mike Nowakowski - 2005
Mike Phelps - 2017

moe. - 2009
Morton Feldman - 2011
Natalie Merchant - 2013
Nelson M. Starr - 2006
New Buffalo Shirt
   Factory - 2013
Nick Molfese - 1999
Nick Salamone - 2003
Nick Veltri - 1994
Nino Tempo &
   April Stevens - 1999
Only Humen - 1995
Party Squad - 1993
Patrick Wilson - 2012
Patti Parks - 2016
Paul Varga - 1983
Peter Case - 2000
Phil Dillon - 2000
Phil DiRe - 2004
Pneu Breed - 1998
Process & the
   Doo Rags - 2015
Ralph Parker - 2012
Ramblin' Lou - 1996
Raven - 2009
Ray Chamberlain - 2016
Ray Evans - 2010
Ray Henderson - 2001
Ray Wood - 1993
Rich Pidanick - 2003
Richard Kermode - 2008
Richard Sargent - 2008
Richie Calandra - 2002
Rick James - 1996
Rick McGirr - 1992
Rob Lynch - 2011
Robbie Konikoff - 2004
Robert "Freightrain"
   Parker - 2015
Robert Hughes - 2004

Robert Kinkel - 2007
Robert Moog - 2001
Robin Adair - 2014
Rodney Appleby - 1995
Rockin Rebels a/k/a The Rebels &
   Buffalo Rebels - 2002
Ron Davis - 2000
Ron Rocco - 1986
Ron Urbanczyk - 2011
Ronnie Foster - 2001
Sam Guarino - 2011
Sam Noto - 2003
Sam Scamacca - 2001
Sandy Konikoff - 1997
Schulz Family - 2008
Scott Freilich - 2004
Shakin' Smith - 1985
Shawn McQuiller - 2012
Spoon & The House
   Rockers - 2014
Spyro Gyra - 2000
Stan Szelest - 1986
Stephen Sadoff - 2012
Steve Jordan - 1998
Steve Nathan - 2001
Stone Country - 1997
Stuart Ziff - 2003
Tadj Szymczak - 2012
Take 6 - 2006
Ted Reinhardt - 1985
Terry Buchwald - 2017
Terry Sullivan - 1992
The Barroom
   Buzzards - 2002
The Boys of
   Summer - 2015
The Buffalo Bills Barbershop
   Quartet - 2009
The Colored Musicians
   Club - 2005

The Exoutics - 2011
The Gordon
  Highlanders - 2004
The Hernandez
  Brothers - 1999
The Jumpers - 2017
The Panfil Brothers - 2016
The Road - 1997
The Scintas - 1999
The Soul Invaders - 2006
The Trolls - 1993
The Tweeds - 1990
The Weber Family - 1999
Theresa Quinn - 2014
Tom Calderone - 2014
Tom Hambridge - 2001
Tom Lorentz - 2012
Tom Reinhardt - 2008
Tom Shannon - 2004
Tom Stahl and the
  Dangerfields - 2017
Tom Walsh - 2001
Tommie Rizzo - 2002
Tommy Calandra - 1998
Tommy Tedesco - 1996

Tommy Z - 2007
Tony Canavale - 1999
Tony Galla - 1998
Tony Romano - 2016
Tony Scozarro - 1995
Tune Rockers - 2012
U-Crest Music - 2007
United Sound - 2003
Unity Band - 2003
Valerian Ruminski - 2011
Van Taylor - 1998
Venetta Fields - 2005
Vince Blasio - 2015
Vincent Michaels - 1987
Wanda and
  Stephanie - 1999
Wayne Sharpe - 2017
Weekend - 2000
Wendell Rivera - 2000
William Christie - 2001
Willie Haddath - 1993
Willie Nile - 2005
Willie Schoellkopf - 2011
Yayo Rodriguez - 2004

SOURCE-NOTES

Chapter 1 – Early theaters, Canal Street, Christy's Minstrel's & Jenny Lind

Research material reference section Buffalo & Erie County Public Library Central (downtown), Ranjit Sandhu's Buffalo Theater reference index. Richmond Hill's "A Thespian Temple". Theater in Early Buffalo by Ardis & Kathryn Smith. History of the Germans in Buffalo & Erie County, NY at archivaria.com. Early Theaters in the City of Buffalo 1832-1868 and Assembly Halls & Lecture Halls 1846-1929 at rjbuffalo.com. Chuck LaChiusa's Buffaloah.com website and "WNY Theater: A Timeline" by Ron Ehmke in *Buffalo Spree*. Rathbun info from Buffalohistory.net by Raymond Massey. Christy's Minstrel's and Jenny Lind info from "America's Crossroads" by Vogal, Patton and Redding.

Chapter 2 – Pan-American Exposition

Info on Pan-American music from conversations with Raya Lee. Info on cleaning up Canal Street and vice in the city of Buffalo from "America's Crossroads" by Vogel, Patton and Redding. Info on The Raines Law and English and American brass bands from Wikipedia info for these styles of bands.

Chapter 3 - Theaters

Vaudeville information from Charles Stein's "American Vaudeville." General info on theaters and film distribution through 1962 from conversations with Nicholas Cintorino who assisted John Basil in preparing information for his unpublished "True Theatre History During the 20th Century." General theater information also obtained from cimenatreasuter.org and forgottenbuffalo.com. Information on Mark Brothers from Bill Zimmerman article in Buffalo Rising on "Buffalo Premiers World's first movie theater." Steve Brodie info from notes by Renjit Sandhu. Information on Michal Shea from buffaloah.com and internet sites by, on or about his theaters. Dipson, Basil and Lafayette Theater from John Basil's book and reglenna.com. Information regarding drive-ins from newyorkdriveins.com, drive-ins.com and buffaloah.com. Legitimate theater information from internet sites of the mentioned organizations and Ron Ehmke's "WNY Theater: A Timeline in Buffalo Spree."

Chapter 4 - Amusement Parks

Information about Crystal Beach from conversations with Bill Kae and from his book "Crystal Beach Live." Additional info from Erno Rossi's book "Crystal Beach – The Good Old Days." Additional info on ballroom from conversation with Tommie Rizzo. Info on *Canadiana* from sscanadiana.com. Info about Crystal Beach Boat riots from *Buffalo Evening News* articles in May 1956. Info on amusement parks in WNY from Rose Ann Hirsh book "Western New York Amusement Parks", Steve Cichon's "Buffalo Stories", BN Chronicles article on "WNY Amusement Parks through the ages" and "Abandoned Amusement Parks of New York" from ancestry.com.

Chapter 5 – Nightclubs & 1940s jazz

General information from conversations with Joe Giambra, Dick Riederer and Craig Steger and internet pages on musicians and buisnesses. Additional info on Dellwood Ballroom from Tommie Rizzo, Town Casino from Marjorie Wallens, Chez Ami from Anthony Amigone, Colored Musicians Club from George Scott and Little Harlem from Alison Fraser's manuscript in the Buffalo & Erie County Public Library's Little Harlem Club Collection. Songwriter information on Adolph Deutsh from Oscars.org, the Academy Awards Database, Harold Arlen from his Biography on haroldarlen.com and David Shire from davidshiremusic.com. Club info from Philip Nyhuis articles in *Buffalo Spree* and Joe Giambra articles in *Periente Magazine*. George Steinbrenner and Royal Arms info from Steve Cichon June 17, 2016 article in *The Buffalo News*.

Chapter 6 – Early Radio & Television

Information from radio and television station web pages. Addition information from Forgotten Buffalo media information, postings at Steve Cichon's buffalostories.com and The Buffalo Broadcasters Association archives.

Chapter 7 – Classical Music

Conversations with Raya Lee and information from her book "The BPO Celebrates the First 75 Years." Information on UB from Rene Levine Packer's book "The Life of Sounds: Evenings for New Music in Buffalo" and Sharon Griggs Almquist Master Thesis on "History of the State University of New York at Buffalo Music Department to 1968." Information on music organizations from their respective internet pages.

Chapter 8 – 1950s & Folk

Conversations with Bob & Terri Skurzewski and info in their book "No Stoppin This Boppin." Info from Bob Paxon reviews at WNY.FM. Conversations with Ed Bentley, Michael Gioeli, Jim Kipler and Frank Lorenz. Radio station websites. Ersel Hickey info from rockabillyhall.com bio by Johnny Vallis. Hi-Teen Club info from The Old Time Radio Club publication, *The Illustrated Press*, June 2007 issue.60

Folk information from conversations with Jerry Raven, Tom Naples and Bob Stalder. Info from organization web sites and verification of John Boylan's career from his website.

Chapter 9 – 1960s Buffalo Sound

All information from discussions with band members and from their internet pages.

Chapter 10 – 1960s Teen Club Bands

All information from discussions with band members and from their internet pages. Addition references from Buffalo, NY Garage Bands Facebook page.

Chapter 11- Music Businesses and Education

Information from talking to the businesses and from their internet pages. Info on Wurlitzer and related businesses from "North Tonawanda: The Lumber City" by the North Tonawanda History Museum. Special assistance from Vincent Michaels with Moog Music and related electronic businesses. George A. Prince company info from "New World

Encyclopedia". Musicians Union info from conversations with Dick Riederer, Local 92 AFM. Info on college magazines from Elmer Ploetz 1991 *Buffalo News* article "When Writing Rocked Buffalo".

Chapter 12 – 1960s and 1970s clubs

Information gathered from conversations with various musicians, club patrons and club owners, the associated internet pages, Buffalo/WNY Bands from the 70s Facebook site and World's Disco webpage. Info on Allman Brothers at Alliotta's from David J. Krajicek May 11, 2013 article in *New York Daily News*. Information on Norm Wullen from Jan Schmitt "Composing a Life" article in October 2000 *Business First*.

Chapter 13 – The 1970s

All information from discussions with band members and from their internet pages. Additional data from Buffalo/WNY Bands From the '70s Facebook page and conversations with Don Eckel.

Chapter 14 – Original Music

All information from discussions with band members and from their internet pages. Additional information from the video "BFLO PNK 1.0 – The Buffalo Punk Documentary Project" produced by Elmer Ploetz and articles from *Buffalo Backstage Magazine*.

Chapter 15 – 1970s & 1980s Jazz, Blues and R&B

Buffalo Jazz Ensemble info from Phil DiRe. Info on band and clubs from conversation with band members, from their internet pages and *Buffalo Backstage* music awards programs or magazines. Information on blues groups from conversations with various musicians, specifically Joe "Dr Z" Zappo and from being involved with the formation of the Blues Society of WNY. The overview of the area R&B scene was gathered from conversation with Larry Salter, Tommy Flucker and Van Taylor, along with information from the *Buffalo News* December 3, 1992 article on "Buffalo R&B Musicians," reviews by Bob Paxon at WNY.FM and various band internet sites. Skateland and New Skateland info from Trunnis Goggins obituary in *Buffalo News* on November 8, 2013. Carl

LaRue and Dyke Christian info, including Rick James quote regarding Dyke & the Blazers from Elmer Ploetz *Buffalo News* article on "Buffalo Soul Men" August 11, 1991. Johnny Young Wings 'n' Things info from Calvin Trillin article in the *New Yorker* on August 25, 1980. Hank "Soul Man" Mullen info from Bob "The Record Guy" Paxon review posted on WNY.FM on January 3, 2014. Darrell Banks info from allmusic.com bio by Andrew Hamilton. Frank Brunson info from Elmer Ploetz article "From Funk to Choir" in *Buffalo News* on June 27, 2001. Process and the Doo Rags info from BMHOF web page bio by Melissa Kate and Elmer Ploetz.

Chapter 16 – Ethnic Music

Info on ethnic groups from census data and "History of the Germans in Buffalo & Erie County, NY" at archivaria.com. German Singing Societies info from Chapter V "Germans of Buffalo in History of the City of Buffalo and Erie County" by H. Perry Smith from Niagara University library. Info on German band and club info from articles by Dick Batzer on the German American Musicians Association website. German beer info from "The Brewed: Two centuries of beer in Buffalo" by Ron Ehmke in *Buffalo Spree* March 2011, Irish Music information from conversations with Mary Heneghan at the Buffalo Irish Center and Kevin Townsell from The Shannon Pub. Polish Music information from conversations with Ken Machelski, Stephanie Pietrzak, Mike Kubera, information from band or business internet sites, poloniamusic.com and Charles Keil, Angeliki Keil and Dick Blau's book "Polka Happiness."

Chapter 17 – Country Music

Information from discussions with various bands and their internet pages. Additional info from conversations with Dwane Hall, Ed Bentley and *Buffalo Backstage* articles. Ramblin' Lou information from Mary Kunz Goldman article in the Buffalo News on August 12, 2014. Bluegrass information from conversations with Mark Panfil and from various band internet pages.

Chapter 18 – The 1980s

All information from conversations with various band members, info from their internet pages and *Buffalo Backstage* magazine articles.

Appendix

Information from researching sites for other information or conversations with people referenced in the notes. Info on Vince Gallo from his official website wincentgallo.com. Info on gay scene from *Buffalo Spree* article "Gay in Buffalo" by Anthony Chase, July/August 2000. Info on the Variety Club, festivals and oldest bars from their respective internet pages.

GENERAL INFORMATION. Where specific or general sources are not documented, information included this book was from the accumulated knowledge of conversations and exposure to being involved with Buffalo music for over 50 years. Some information on items from the 1930s to early 1960s was from growing up in a household where I was exposed to conversations between my father, who was a drummer at area nightclubs, and his musician and other entertainment industry friends, who performed in WNY dating back to the 1930s.

PHOTO CREDITS. Every effort has been made to correctly acknowledge and contact the source and/or copyright holder of each photo and the author apologizes for any unintentional errors or omissions, which will be corrected in future editions of this book.

MISSING INFO: If you have information on bands, musicians, clubs, businesses or events from prior to the early 1980s that was not included in this book, please contact me or send it to:
Rick Falkowski
P.O. Box 96
Williamsville NY 14231
buffalomusichistory.com
info@buffalomusichistory.com
Facebook: History of Buffalo Music & Entertainment

BIBLIOGRAPHY

Almquist, Sharon Griggs. History of the State University of New York at Buffalo Music Department to 1968. Masters Thesis SUNY at Buffalo 1986.

Anderson, Dale. Various band articles. Buffalo News, Weekend Pause in TV Topics and Gusto, 1970s.

Baker, Vic. WBEN (WIVB) TV History. Western New York Heritage Magazine, Spring 1998.

Basil, John. True Theatre History During the 20th Century. Unpublished, 2007.

Bohen, Timothy. Against the Grain: The History of Buffalo's First Ward. Buffalo: Western New York Wares Inc., 2012

Ehmke, Ron. WNY Theater: A Timeline. Buffalo Spree, September 2010

Ehmke, Ron. The Brewed: Two Centuries of beer in Buffalo. Buffalo Spree, March 2011

Falkowski, Rick & Marsha. Buffalo Backstage: An Anthology of 1982 Music. February 1983

Falkowski, Rick & Marsha. 1986 Buffalo Area Music Awards Program. November 24, 1986.

Falkowski, Rick & Marsha. Various monthly issues of Buffalo Backstage 1981–1984.

Fink, James. Enraptured by Rhapsody. Buffalo Business First, September 1, 2003.

Fraser, Alison. Little Harlem Club Collection. Buffalo/Erie County Public Library, Rare Books Room. Unpublished, 2013.

Giambra, Joe. The Rise and Fall of Local Jazz. Perniente Magazine. 2016.

Goldman, Mary Kunz. Western New York's soul of country music. Buffalo News, August 12, 2014

Hill, Richmond. A Thespian Temple: A Brief History of the Academy of Music. Buffalo: The Courier Company Printers, 1893

Hirsh, Rose Ann. Western New York Amusement Parks. Charleston: Arcadia Publishing, 2011

Kae, William E. Crystal Beach Live: Buffalo and Toronto Entertainers and More. Cyclone Books, 2009

Keil, Charles & Keil, Angeliki V., Blau, Dick. Polka Happiness. Philadelphia: Temple University Press, 1992

Lee, Gary & Patti Meyer. Don't Bother Knockin' – This Town's A Rockin': A History of Traditional Rhythm and Blues & Early Rock 'n' Roll in Buffalo, New York. Buffalo Sounds Press, 2000

Lee, Raya & Yadzinski, Edward. Buffalo Philharmonic Orchestra: The BPO Celebrates the First 75 Years, Buffalo Heritage Unlimited, 2010

Merriweather, Frank F. editor. It Slipped Away. Buffalo Criterion, Sep 24-30, 1967

Neal, Donna Zellner edited. North Tonawanda: The Lumber City. North Tonawanda History Museum, 2007

Nyhuis, Philip. Jazz: It's Never Too Late. Buffalo Spree, May/June 2005

Packer, Renee Levine. *This Life of Sounds: Evenings for New Music in Buffalo.* Oxford University Press, 2010.

Rossi, Erno. Crystal Beach: The Good Old Days. Port Colborne, Ontario, Canada: Seventy Seven Publishing, 2005

Sandhu, Ranjit. Buffalo Theatres prior to 1930: An ever-growing Index of references. Buffalo & Erie County Public Library, unpublished.

Schmitt, Jane. Composing a Life. Buffalo Business First, October 9, 2000.

Skurzewski, Bob & Terri. "No Stoppin' This Boppin": Let the Good Times Roll. Buffalo: Visible Imagination Press, 2015

Smith, Ardis & Kathryn. Theater in Early Buffalo. Buffalo & Erie County Historical Society, 1975

Smith, H. Perry (edited). History of the City of Buffalo and Erie County. Syracuse: D. Mason & Co. 1884. This digitized monograph is available on the Niagara University Library webpage library.niagara.edu

Stein, Charles W. edited by: American Vaudeville: As Seen by Its Contemporaries. New York: Da Capo Press, 1984

Violanti, Anthony. Imagne: Step inside our dream Rock Hall of Fame. Buffalo News. Buffalo Magazine. March 24, 1996.

Zimmerman, Bill. On this Day, October 19, 1886: Buffalo Premiers World's First Movie Theater. Buffalo Rising, October 19, 2007.

SELECTED INTERNET SOURCES

ALL MUSIC
On line database with discography and bio of musical artists
www.allmusic.com

ANCESTORY.COM
Abandoned Amusements Parks of New York

BN CHRONICLES
A look at WNY history through the pages of the Buffalo News.
Includes many articles by Steve Cichon
buffalonews.com

BUFFALO ARCHICTURE AND HISTORY
www.buffaloah.com

BUFFALO BROADCASTERS
Information on history of various radio/TV stations
www.buffalohistoryworks.com/broadcasters/

BUFFALO NY GARAGE BANDS
www.facebook.com/Buffalo-NY-Garage-Bands-185888771439480/

BUFFALO HISTORY MUSEUM
Research Library
www.buffalohistory.org

BUFFALO STORIES
Stories, blogs and images of things about Buffalo by Steve Cichon
www.buffalostories.com

BUFFALO THEATER RESEARCH
Selected Sources in the Grosvenor Room
www.buffalolib.org

BUFFALO/WESTERN NY BANDS FROM THE 70'S
www.facebook.com/groups/Bandsfromthe.70s/

BUFFALO/WESTERN NY BANDS FROM THE 80'S
www.facebook.com/groups/133386863362880/

CINEMA TREASURES
The ultimate web site about movie theaters.
Information on movie theaters from the past
cinematreasures.org

EARLY THEATRES IN THE CITY OF BUFFALO 1832-1868
ASSEMBLY HALLS & CONCERT HALLS 1846-1929
ARTICLES I DONE WRIT (AND OTHER NICE THINGS TOO]
rjbuffalo.com

FORGOTTEN BUFFALO
Various articles on Buffalo's past
www.forgottenbuffalo.com

JESTERS/ROCK-ITTS
www.facebook.com/groups/Jesters.RockItts/

NOTO-RIETY: THE JAZZ ODYSSEY OF SAM NOTO
Sam Noto bio by Phil Nyhuis
samnoto.jazzgiants.net/biography/

TALAS
www.limelitemusic.com/DCB/project/the-talas-years/

TWEEDS
www.limelitemusic.com/DCB/project/the-early-days/

WESTERN NEW YORK MUSIC
Various Record Reviews by Bob "The Record Guy" Paxon and other writers
https://wny.fm.wordpress.com

WIKIPEDIA
Free online encyclopedia
www.wikipedia.org

Various business and band internet pages.

INDEX